THE LEGACIES OF

BERNARD SMITH

//

ESSAYS ON
AUSTRALIAN ART, HISTORY
AND CULTURAL POLITICS

THE LEGACIES OF

BERNARD SMITH

//

ESSAYS ON AUSTRALIAN ART, HISTORY AND CULTURAL POLITICS

Edited by Jaynie Anderson, Christopher R. Marshall and Andrew Yip

POWER PUBLICATIONS in association with ART GALLERY NSW

The Legacies of Bernard Smith: Essays on Australian Art, History and Cultural Politics
Edited by
Jaynie Anderson, Christopher R. Marshall, Andrew Yip

First published in Australia in 2016 by Power Publications, in association with the Art Gallery of New South Wales

Power Publications
Power Institute Foundation for Art and Visual Culture
University of Sydney
NSW 2006 Australia
www.powerpublications.com.au

Managing editors Marni Williams and Julie Donaldson
Design Analiese Cairis
Production Cara Hickman
Copyeditor Belinda Nemec
Proofreader Amber Cameron

Title: The legacies of Bernard Smith:
essays on Australian art, history and cultural politics
editors: Jaynie Anderson, Christopher R. Marshall, Andrew Yip

ISBN: 9780994306432 (paperback)

Subjects: Smith, Bernard, 1916–2011–Criticism and interpretation.
Art appreciation–Australia.
Art and society–Australia.
Art--Political aspects–Australia.
Art critics–Australia.
Art historians–Australia.
Festschriften–Australia.

Other Creators/Contributors:
Anderson, Jaynie, editor.
Marshall, Christopher R., editor.
Yip, Andrew, editor.

Dewey Number: 709.2

Cover image:
Christopher Pease, *Target*, 2005
Courtesy the artist and the Nelson Family Collection

Back cover:
Bernard Smith in his study, Fitzroy, 1987 (detail)
Photograph by Alex Bolton.
Bernard Smith Private Collection

opposite:
Francis Reiss, Portrait of Bernard Smith,
15 December 1993

POWER PUBLICATIONS in association with ART GALLERY NSW

Editorial Partner THE UNIVERSITY OF MELBOURNE | FACULTY OF ARTS

Project sponsor ART GALLERY SOCIETY NSW

Supported by AUSTRALIAN INSTITUTE OF ART HISTORY, AUSTRALIAN ACADEMY OF THE HUMANITIES

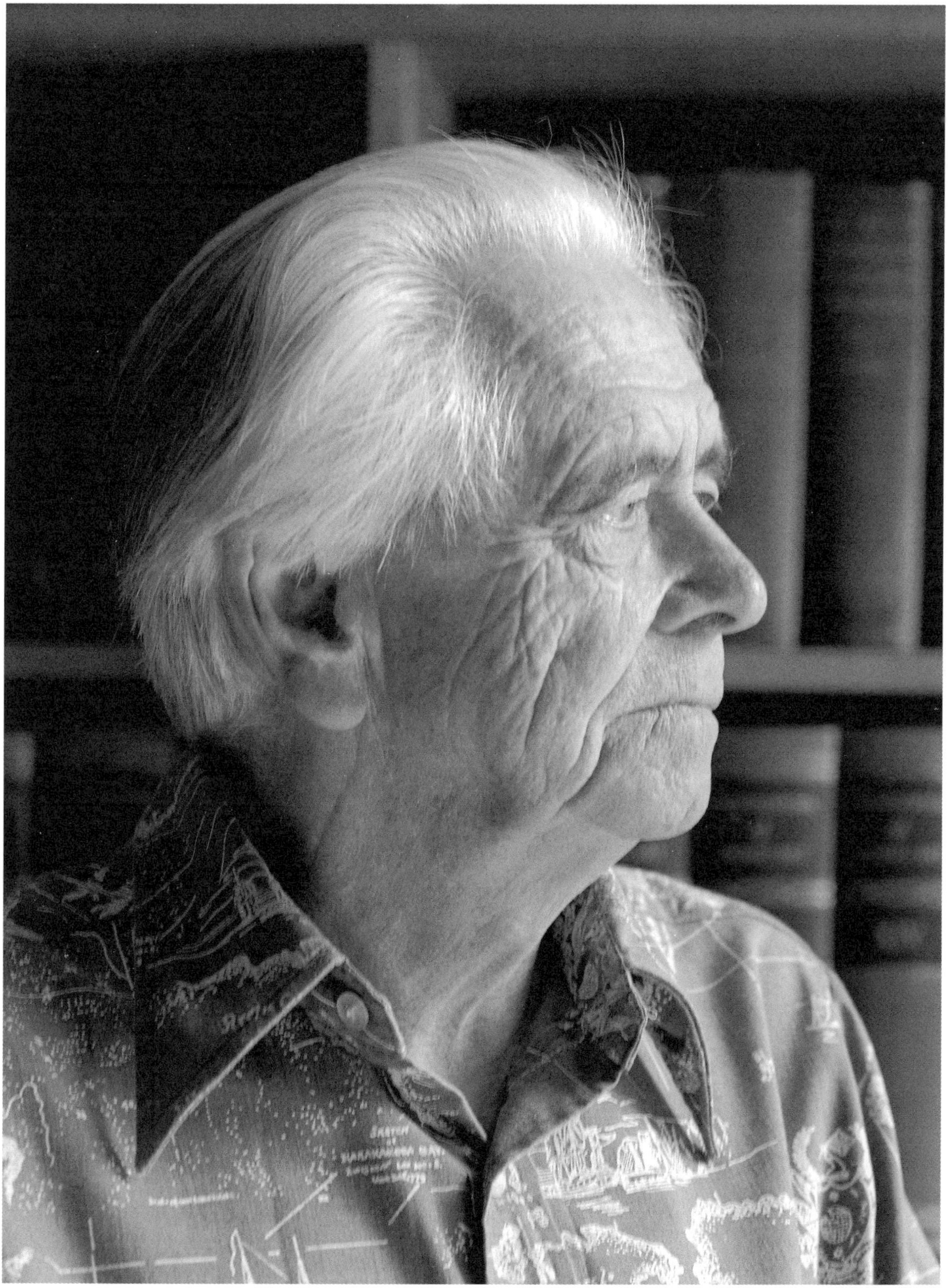

CONTENTS

2 / DEFINING AUSTRALIAN ART

3 / BERNARD SMITH AND THE ART MUSEUM

ILLUSTRATIONS

Section 1: Port Jackson Painter, *A partial view of Sydney Cove taken from the sea side before the Surgeon General's house*, 1790–95 (detail)
Pencil, ink and wash on paper, 32 x 45.4 cm.
Watling Collection, National History Museum, London

Section 2: Rupert Bunny, *Self-portrait*, c. 1920 (detail)
Oil on canvas, 65.1 x 50.4 cm.
National Gallery of Victoria, Melbourne. Felton Bequest, 1927

Section 3: Grace Cossington Smith, *The sock knitter*, 1915 (detail)
Oil on canvas, 61.8 x 51.2 cm.
Art Gallery of New South Wales, Sydney

Section 4: Professor Bernard Smith (with megaphone) leading the more than 200-strong ratepayers and citizens' protest march against Leichhardt Council along Glebe Point Road, *The Glebe*, 10 March 1971 (detail)

Page 191:
Bernard Smith in his study, Fitzroy, 1987
Photograph by Alec Bolton.
Courtesy National Library of Australia, Canberra.

1. Bernard Smith, *The advance of Lot and his brethren*, 1940
Oil on canvas, 71 x 86 cm.
National Gallery of Australia, Canberra

2. Christopher Pease, *Target*, 2005
Oil on canvas, 100 x 180 cm.
Courtesy of the Nelson Family Collection

3. Lin Onus, *They took the children away*, 1992
Fibreglass and pigment, 4 figures, dimensions variable.
Private collection

4. Bernard Smith with his daughter Elizabeth Heathcote, and in the background Gail Feigenbaum (Getty Research Centre, Los Angeles) and Rüdiger Joppien (Hamburg), at the Comité International d'Histoire de l'Art congress 'Crossing Cultures: Conflict, Migration and Convergence', Government House, Melbourne, January 2008
Courtesy of the Australian Institute of Art History, University of Melbourne

5. Bernard Smith in his study in the Abbey Art Centre, 1950
Courtesy of Bienchen Ohly

6. E.H. Gombrich in London in the 1950s
Courtesy of the Literary Estate of E. H. Gombrich

7. William Hodges, *Landing at Mallicollo [Malakula], one of the New Hebrides*, c. 1776
Oil on panel, 24.1 x 47 cm.
National Maritime Museum, London

8. George Baxter, *The massacre of the lamented missionary the Rev. J. Williams and Mr Harris*, 1841
Baxter print, 214 x 320 mm.
National Library of Australia, Canberra

9. *Labour recruit from Malaita, Solomon Islands, wearing ceremonial dress with bead belt featuring the Union Jack, photographed in Fiji*, c. 1880s
Albumen print, 198 x 146 mm.
British Museum, London

10. *Sculpture known as the 'Blue man', Malo, Vanuatu,* collected during the voyage of the *Korrigane* in 1935
Wood with blue, white and green pigment, 300 cm.
Musée du Quai Branly, Paris

11. Tene Waitere, *Pouhaki*, c. 1922,
Carved tree trunk, 800 cm.
Museum of Archaeology and Anthropology, Cambridge

12. Rüdiger Joppien and Bernard Smith in Hamburg, after the publication of the third volume of *The Art of Captain Cook's Voyages*, 1988
Courtesy of Rüdiger Joppien

13. Leveillé (after Bisson Brothers), *Kaour & Kaour-Iga natives of Torres Strait*, 1846
Lithograph after daguerreotype, 28.4 x 35.8 cm.
Art Gallery of New South Wales, Sydney. Tony Gilbert Bequest Fund 2013

14. Henry Barnes, *Echidna skeleton* and *Natural history specimens sent from the British Museum to the Australian Museum*, c. 1864
Albumen silver photographs enclosed in a letter from Gerard Krefft to Richard Owen, 21 October 1864, Richard Owen Correspondence, vol. 27, ff.3–5.
Natural History Museum, London

15. John McGregor, *James Hector*, c. 1863
Carte-de-visite, 9 x 5.7 cm (print).
Alexander Turnbull Library, Wellington, The Webster Collection

16. Rupert Bunny, *Self-portrait*, c. 1920
Oil on canvas, 65.1 x 50.4 cm.
National Gallery of Victoria, Melbourne. Felton Bequest, 1927

17. Peter Purves Smith, *Drought*, 1939/40
Gouache on paper, 48.8 x 40.2 cm.
National Gallery of Australia, Canberra. Gift of anonymous donor, 1986

18. Ola Cohn, *Head of a virgin*, 1926
Bronze, 44.6 x 15.8 x 23.1 cm.
National Gallery of Victoria, Melbourne. Courtesy of the Centre for Adult Education & Box Hill Institute

19. Ida Kar, *Bryan Charles Francis Robertson*, 1958
Vintage bromide print, 230 x 198 mm.
National Portrait Gallery, London

20. The British art critic Peter Fuller (1947–1990), photographed in 1988 by Jane Bown
Courtesy of Jane Bown/*The Observer*

21. Sidney Nolan, *Carcass*, 1953
Enamel on board, 90.8 x 121.3 cm.
Nolan Collection, managed by Canberra Museum and Gallery on behalf of the Australian Government

22. Eric Wilson, *Hospital theme—the sterilizer*, 1942
Oil on hardboard, 81.3 x 47 cm.
Art Gallery of New South Wales, Sydney

23. Grace Cossington Smith, *The sock knitter*, 1915
Oil on canvas, 61.8 x 51.2 cm.
Art Gallery of New South Wales, Sydney

24. Grace Cossington Smith, *The school cape*, 1916
Private collection. Courtesy of The Estate of Grace Cossington Smith

25. Paul Wallace (illustrator), *Typical display gallery, from The National Art Gallery and Cultural Centre of Victoria*, Melbourne, 1960

26. 'Museum madness', *City Alternative News*, October–November, 1996

27. View towards the Melbourne Museum across the Carlton Gardens from Canning Street, Carlton. Photograph by Christopher R. Marshall

28. Jean Tingueley, *Bascule no. 1 Sisyphus*, 1965, in Power Bequest Exhibition, Australia Square, Sydney, *The Australian Women's Weekly*, February 1968

29. Geoge Molnar, Caricature of newly appointed Professor Bernard Smith delivering a lecture, *The Sydney Morning Herald*, 1 July 1967

30. German Consul-General W. C. Brückmann, Elwyn Lynn, newly appointed Power Curator, and Professor Bruce Williams, University of Sydney Vice-Chancellor, at Power Collection exhibition opening, at Farmer's Blaxland Gallery, July 1969

31. Professor Bernard Smith (with megaphone) leading the more than 200-strong ratepayers and citizens' protest march against Leichhardt Council along Glebe Point Road, *The Glebe*, 10 March 1971

32. Bernard Smith with Gerard Dillon's *Boys catching crabs in Connemara*, 1949–50.
Courtesy of Bienchen Ohly

33. Vic O'Connor, *The refugees*, 1942
Oil on board, 42 x 54 cm.
Collection of National Gallery of Australia, Canberra. Courtesy of Bridget McDonnell Gallery

34. John Perceval, *Angel learning to walk*, c. 1958
Glazed ceramic
Whereabouts unknown
Courtesy of John Perceval/Viscopy

35. Eugene von Guérard, *Forest scene near Kiama*, 1863
Oil on canvas, 35.8 x 56 cm.
National Gallery of Australia, Canberra. Purchased 1978

36. Richard Larter, *Well all right, so how*, 1970
Private collection. Courtesy of Richard Larter/Viscopy

37. Donald Friend, *John Bell's party*, c. 1964
Private collection. Courtesy of Donald Friend/Viscopy

38. Colin McCahon, *Waterfall*, 1964
Oil on board.
Private collection. Courtesy of The Colin McCahon Research and Publication Trust

39. Juno Gemes, *Land rights march, NADOC Day Sydney*, 1981
Courtesy of Juno Gemes

40. Myall Creek Massacre Memorial (near Bingara, NSW), 2000. Photograph by Catherine de Lorenzo

41. Installation view of Ace Bourke's exhibition *Lines in the sand*, 2008, Hazelhurst Regional Gallery and Arts Centre, Sydney.
Courtesy of Ace Bourke

Foreword

//

CHRISTOPHER R. MARSHALL
AND MARK LEDBURY

This volume arose out of a series of symposia in honour of Bernard Smith (1916–2011) that were jointly convened in 2012 by the Australian Institute of Art History at the University of Melbourne, the Power Institute at the University of Sydney, and the Art Gallery of New South Wales. In soliciting first papers and then follow-up chapters for this book, the editors sought to do justice to the depth and breadth of Bernard Smith's extraordinary involvement in Australian art, history and cultural politics in all their interlinked complexity. Bernard's simultaneous commitment to the broadest principles of public education and the highest standards of art-historical scholarship, and his passionate participation in the political issues of the day, made him a force to be reckoned with and a major figure on the Australian cultural landscape more generally. It is a status that is, in many respects, hard to conceive of in today's environment of multiple authorities operating in divergent niche specialisations.

While it may not be accurate to credit Bernard Smith with creating the discipline of Australian art history as we know it today, it is certainly appropriate to acknowledge his signal contribution to the development of the discipline, in a manner, moreover, that can truly be termed multidisciplinary in all its aspirations. As a Marxist/Warburgian in the fullest and richest sense in which those traditions can be said to have come together in his own intellectual formation, Bernard

Smith would have taken for granted the need for art history to operate in a fully interconnected and multidisciplinary framework. His writing was continuously informed by the insights deriving from the linked disciplines of history, cultural anthropology and political science, to name only the most obviously related fields of Bernard's ongoing interests. To this he added a prodigious work ethic and a sustained communication of ideas that resulted in one of the most impressive bodies of work produced in the field. His list of publications comprises a sustained run of key texts stretching from 1945 to 2007, which includes such volumes as *Place, Taste and Tradition: A Study of Australian Art Since 1788* (1945), *European Vision and the South Pacific* (1960), *Australian Painting, 1788–1960* (1960), *The Architectural Character of Glebe* (1973), *Documents on Art and Taste in Australia* (1975), *The Antipodean Manifesto: Essays in Art and History* (1975), *The Spectre of Truganini* (1980), *The Boy Adeodatus* (1984), *The Art of Captain Cook's Voyages* (1985–87), *The Art of the First Fleet* (1988), *The Death of the Artist as Hero* (1988), *The Critic as Advocate* (1989), *Imagining the Pacific in the Wake of the Cook Voyages* (1992), *Noel Counihan: Artist and Revolutionary* (1993), *Modernism's History: A Study in Twentieth-Century Art and Ideas* (1998), *A Pavane for Another Time* (2002) and *The Formalesque: A Guide to Modern Art and its History* (2007).

All of this would be remarkable enough, were it not for Smith's ability to combine this intense intellectual activity with an equally vigorous involvement in the public dimensions of the work of producing a distinctly Australian art history. He had a particularly strong influence on contemporary art debates via his involvement with the 'Antipodean manifesto', and shortly thereafter as art critic for *The Age* (1963–66). His energetic participation in contemporary political debates centred above all on his desire to bring public attention to the fight to preserve Glebe, among other aspects of Australian cultural heritage. He also made a vital contribution to public awareness of contemporary Indigenous art and culture, by founding the Kate Challis RAKA (ongoing since 1988). But it was in the field of public education more generally that Smith arguably made the most sustained contribution to the development of Australian art history. This was achieved first through his work for the National Art Gallery of New South Wales (1944–48, 1951–53) and subsequently as a lecturer in the Department of Fine Arts at the University of Melbourne (1955–67), then as the inaugural Power Professor of Contemporary Art and Director of the Power Institute at the University of Sydney (1967–77), and finally as president of the Australian Academy of the Humanities (1977–80).

If there is any one principle that underpinned all Bernard Smith's efforts in these interlinked fields, it would be his insistence that Australia possesses a rich artistic tradition that is every bit as noteworthy, varied and complex as that of anywhere else in the world—including all the other so-called centres of art history. This constitutes, in fact, one of the most powerful and contemporary concepts deriving from Smith's legacy. Bernard Smith's vision of art history confidently recognises its place in the world while seeking to understand its complex interrelationship with a multitude of other traditions and influences from beyond its shores. In so doing, it eloquently communicates what Terry Smith has emphasised elsewhere in this volume as Bernard's efforts in demonstrating 'the agency of the peripheries in precipitating change'. Perhaps we have moved beyond the problem of having to constantly identify with the 'periphery/centrist' divide, given that so much contemporary art practice and theory operates in the expanded field of global art history, world art studies, or whatever other term we choose to designate this paradigm shift in the discipline. But if we have achieved that end, there can be no doubting the particular and long-lasting importance of Bernard Smith's contribution in spearheading the development of Australian art history to the rich and potential-filled point at which we find ourselves today.

BIOGRAPHICAL OVERVIEW

//

The multiple legacies of Bernard Smith

JAYNIE ANDERSON

Bernard William Smith is remembered as the first truly Australian art historian, who consistently and tenaciously saw the need to develop and describe a social aesthetic suited to a contemporary democratic Australian society. What may seem like a narrow agenda opened up many different pathways for future research and resulted in multiple legacies.[1] Bernard Smith espoused this agenda from his earliest publications and consistently maintained it until his death. As the contributions in this volume reveal, Smith had considerable influence over the formation of art history in Australia, over the development of anthropology, and on the creation of Australian collections (especially in Sydney), on Indigenous philanthropy and on the politics of contemporary art.[2] He was not a personality to favour institutions, or become their prisoner, but he did believe in the Australian Academy of the Humanities and its purpose—to promote scholarship in the humanities in Australia—in which he played a leading role.

Before World War II, few people were interested in Australian art. Smith's first book, *Place, Taste and Tradition: A Study of Australian Art Since 1788* (1945),[3] was the earliest account of Australian art to be taken seriously.[4] He took as his method Marx's historical materialism, an act that both encouraged and irritated others to provide alternative accounts of the same tradition, but always building on Smith's groundwork.[5] Smith's book was written as a series of lectures during the war, and later found a publisher, which gave it an understandably nationalist edge. It was written in a raw, young and brilliant style. This first book ended with a vigorous polemic in favour of contemporary social realist artists Noel Counihan, Victor O'Connor and Yosl Bergner, with whom he engaged as a young socialist and who always remained his favourites and best friends among Australian artists. The publication fuelled a healthy debate among artists and critics about nationalism and realism and the search for an Australian subject matter. In global art history it was the first Marxist interpretation of a national artistic culture,[6] and predated Friedrich Antal's *Florentine Painting and its Social Background* (1948) and Arnold Hauser's *The Social History of Art* (1951). Whether Smith knew of Clement Greenberg's Marxist-inspired short essay 'Avant-garde and Kitsch' (1939) is unclear. Later Smith invited Greenberg to Sydney as the first John Power Lecturer in Contemporary Art in 1968, to speak on 'Avant-garde Attitudes: New Art in the Sixties', a sure sign of the high value Smith placed on Greenberg as a critic and fellow Marxist.

Smith loved finding a new nomenclature for art-historical periods and movements. In this first book, he coined the word 'Postmodernism' in relation to art, and later 'Federation Style', and much later the far less popular 'Formalesque'. In his teaching, Smith encouraged his students to redefine art by inventing innovative conceptual terminology. His year-long seminar on the art and writings of William Blake in the print room of the National Gallery of Victoria in 1964 required students to find an original nomenclature to describe the imagery of Blake's *Illustrations to Dante*. It was unforgettable for all of the honours students who participated, including this author and Patrick McCaughey. It was the kind of teaching that inspired original theoretical thinking.

Bernard Smith was born in the inner-Sydney suburb of Balmain in 1916, the illegitimate son of an immigrant Irish woman, Rose Anne Tierney, and Charles Smith of York. Bernard's formation was an unconventional one, when compared with other pioneering art historians in Australia, who all came from privileged European backgrounds and were displaced by World War II, such as Joseph Burke, one of the earliest graduates of the Courtauld Institute in London, and Franz Philipp, a pupil of Julius von Schlosser. Smith was always an outstanding student, graduating dux of Enmore High School in 1933. He was a scholarship boy, whose first career was as a schoolteacher. He was subsequently appointed education officer at the National Art

Gallery of New South Wales (NAGNSW) in 1944, the year before *Place, Taste and Tradition* was published. In 1945 Smith embarked on a study of classical archaeology in evening classes at the University of Sydney with Dale Trendall, an experience that he always proudly remembered as fundamental to his formative development. This is evident in his 1975 essay 'Notes on Elitism and the Arts',[7] in which he analysed the Greek notion of elitism to its disadvantage, compared Australian elitism to fascism, and argued passionately in favour of a broadly based democratic theory of excellence in educational practice, inspired by a reconsideration of French and British utopian socialists. Smith's early career at the NAGNSW (1944 to 1948)[8] is in this volume analysed by Steven Miller and others in the surprising section on Bernard Smith as a creator of collections. At the gallery, Smith's role as an education officer involved staging several exhibitions a year, some of the paintings entering the collection permanently, and in the process he became an adroit politician in the world of artists, difficult trustees, and museum professionals. On occasion he briefly acted as director of the gallery.

In these early years Smith experimented with becoming an artist, and took classes at distinguished Sydney institutions, including the Sydney Teachers' College and the Julian Ashton Art School. Those few paintings by Smith now held in public collections in Australia, *The advance of Lot and his brethren* (1940) and *Pompeii* (1940), both at the National Gallery of Australia, are seemingly conservative in subject matter, but proclaim two themes with which Smith was at times preoccupied: incest and classicism (Fig. 1). Bernard Smith later described the *The advance of Lot* as a political painting, made under severe stress, and which was both surrealist and expressionist. He had joined the Communist Party in May 1939, remaining an active member until 1947, but became disillusioned after a visit to Czechoslovakia in 1949. He resigned in 1951 upon his return from England.[9] Although Smith may have ceased his involvement with the party earlier, in 1949, his papers at the National Library of Australia in Canberra show that he would be continually preoccupied with Marxism in art history for many decades to come.

Always precocious, Smith interrupted his undergraduate studies and his work at the NAGNSW to begin postgraduate research for his doctorate—on the origins of European art in Australia—at the Warburg Institute, London, from 1948 to 1951. He had won a British Council scholarship and postponed completion of his undergraduate degree.[10] The initial English reaction to his choice of subject was disbelief, for, as he always remembered, the reigning sovereigns in art history considered that all the Europeans had brought to the Pacific was the Bible and syphilis. With spirited advice from Charles Mitchell, his supervisor, and in the genial company of Rudolph Wittkower, he began to develop those ideas, which saw fruition in his book *European Vision and the South Pacific* (1960),[11] generally acknowledged as the most influential work of scholarship produced by an Australian art historian, even in 2016. When the book was published it was greeted with enthusiastic reviews, led by the anonymous review in the *Times Literary Supplement* on Friday 1 September 1962, entitled: 'Discovery of the Noble Antipodean'.[12] The reviewer immediately recognised that the book was an extension of Smith's earlier research interests as shown in the early chapters of *Place, Taste and Tradition*, but was also much more.

European Vision shifted the dynamics for considering cross-cultural exchange in the Pacific and antipodes, a shift that animates the cover image of this volume, Christopher Pease's *Target* (2005) (Fig. 2). In a scene appropriated from Louis Auguste de Sainsons' hand-coloured lithograph *Vue du Port du Roi Georges* (1833), we witness the crew of the French corvette *Astrolabe* landing at King George's Sound in Western Australia, a mission led by Dumont D'Urville, the great French explorer of the Pacific and Antarctic. The superimposed target references European territorial desires, but its meaning also changes in relation to the viewer's cultural position. It simultaneously refers to the mark-making practices of the Nyungar people of Western Australia and gestures towards Jasper Johns' alleviation of the icon from its context. The anthropology of images demonstrable in Pease's work speaks to one of *European Vision*'s persistent ideas: that visual images produced initially for information might be transformed in new contexts after their initial use is spent.

In this volume, Robert Gaston analyses the influence of those who taught Bernard at the Warburg Institute, especially his supervisor, Charles Mitchell, a 'teacher of genius', who was of enduring importance.[13] Mitchell had the ability to begin supervisions from first principles, ignoring what had been agreed upon before, and usually arriving at different conclusions via a rigorous analysis of the same texts and images. He was unfailingly curious about new continents. After returning to Australia Bernard sent generations of Australian students from the University of

Melbourne (beginning with Virginia Spate) to study at Bryn Mawr College, where Mitchell developed a highly successful postgraduate school.

Smith was the first art historian to study how the earliest European artists to reach the Pacific represented the very different kinds of flora and fauna they encountered there, and to pose such questions as to how these artists' styles and concepts were affected by genuinely novel and non-European experiences. Smith returned to these subjects, with a series of magnificently illustrated, well-researched volumes, *The Art of the First Fleet and Other Early Australian Drawings* (1988 with Alwyne Wheeler)[14] and three volumes on *The Art of Captain Cook's Voyages* (1985–87, with Rüdiger Joppien).[15]

After his few years in Europe, where he not only worked at the Warburg Institute but travelled widely, Smith returned to Australia on 1 January 1951 to take up his position at the NAGNSW as assistant to the director, Hal Missingham, and to resume his undergraduate degree, which he completed in 1952. Among his voluminous papers at the National Library of Australia are numerous lectures that convey a dramatic intensity, confirming that Smith was a remarkable lecturer, not only in his charismatic style, but also in the ambitious range of his subjects, many conveying European experiences from his London years and the experience of European travel. At the NAGNSW Smith prepared catalogues of everything Australian—paintings, watercolours and works on paper—one of which he published in 1953.[16] While there he arranged enormously successful exhibitions of Australian paintings to tour regional areas of New South Wales, which attracted large numbers of visitors.[17] He later held a senior research fellowship at the Australian National University in Canberra, where he worked with Jim Davidson, who suggested he compile a catalogue of paintings by Captain James Cook's artists. He was already in touch with Joseph Burke, Herald Chair of Fine Arts at the University of Melbourne, who was keen to appoint him to his department in order to develop the study of Australian art history for the first time.

In 1955 Smith was appointed as a lecturer in the Fine Arts Department at the University of Melbourne where, with Burke and Viennese art historian Franz Philipp (lecturer in Renaissance art history), he completed a triad of formidable scholars. Together they gave a generation of students an enviable understanding of art history. All those who were students in the 1960s—Patrick McCaughey, Margaret

Manion, Margaret Plant, Virginia Spate, Robert Gaston, Terry Smith, this author, and many others—remember this period as a life-enhancing and unforgettable experience. The graduates went on to have distinguished careers, including four female professors, surely a record for any department in the world at that time, and perhaps even now.

In 1957 Smith convened the group of artists who would write the 'Antipodean Manifesto', first expressed in a 1959 catalogue essay as a declaration of the value of figurative painting.[18] In some ways it was Bernard's least attractive act. All his life, like his mentor Ernst Gombrich, Bernard disliked abstract painting, as well as hating (but more understandably) the predictability of fashion in art and its history. In alliance with Charles Blackman, Arthur Boyd, David Boyd, John Brack, Robert Dickerson, John Perceval and Clifton Pugh, Bernard signed the manifesto. The Sydney 9, a group that was formed in reaction to the Melbourne push, enabled the brilliant young critic Robert Hughes to defend, as its spokesperson, the values of contemporary abstraction and American collections. From 1963 to 1966 Bernard Smith took the role of art critic on *The Age* newspaper in Melbourne, believing that the constant act of reviewing was the only means of understanding contemporary art.

In 1962 Smith published his authoritative account, *Australian Painting, 1788–1960*,[19] which has been continuously in print for more than half a century. The radical Marxism of *Place, Taste and Tradition* had all but disappeared, to make the book more acceptable to a wider audience. Of all his books, it reached the widest audience and established the study of Australian art in universities and museums. Everyone read it and it became a bestseller over many decades. Terry Smith updated it in 1991;[20] and Christopher Heathcote in 2001.[21] Smith never wished to refine or edit his own text, so it remains very much a voice of the 1960s, with addenda.

At the same time, Smith was contemplating writing a monograph on Sidney Nolan, whom he interviewed extensively. In September 1962 he published a vibrant and perceptive article on Nolan, based on the interviews in September 1962, 'Nolan's Image', in *The London Magazine*.[22] Here he argued that Nolan was essentially a surrealist artist (like himself), whose pictorial processes of ambiguity, conflation, transformation, accident, and the like, was were defined by his use of iconomorphic form. Smith could not understand how Elwyn Lynn, in his 1967 monograph, *Sidney Nolan: Myth and Imagery*', Macmillan, 1967,[23] could stress the early abstract phase of

Nolan to such a degree.[24] In his critical review Bernard wrote:

> To stress an early abstract phase in Nolan's development may lead to confusion, unless that phase is carefully defined. This, surely, is what has happened in Lynn's analysis of the first plate in his book, a free drawing of 1937, which is compared to drawings by New York abstract expressionists of the 1940s.[25]

Smith much preferred Ian Burn's August 1984 analysis in *The Age Monthly Review*, 'Landscape and Life: Nolan and the Australian Tradition',[26] which Smith had heavily annotated in his collection of press cuttings on Nolan.[27] Burn's nuanced review analysed Nolan's relation to modernism in a way of which Smith approved, as when he wrote: 'Nolan's approach to European modernism embraced a dependent relation but also exposed, resisted and even derided that relationship'.[28] Smith decided not to proceed with his book on Nolan.

At a national level, Bernard Smith cared passionately about the humanities, and about the place of art history in them, as is shown by his dedication to the establishment of the Australian Academy of the Humanities (AAH). Smith was one of the fifty-one foundation fellows of the AAH, which was established by royal charter in 1969 to advance the knowledge of, and the pursuit of excellence in, the humanities. Smith had been a member of the academy's predecessor, the Australian Humanities Research Council (AHRC), on which he served as secretary (1963–65), and as a member of the AHRC Australian UNESCO Committee (1965–68) and on the David Nichol Smith Memorial Seminar Committee (1964–70).

The highest distinction in scholarship in the humanities was (and is) required of candidates for election to fellowship of the AAH, and Smith's appointment as a foundation fellow of this important institution is a testament to his standing, not only among his peers in art history and criticism, but also among those in the broader humanities. Bernard Smith was a dedicated servant of the AAH, serving on council from 1976 to 1983, and as president from 1977 to 1980. During his presidency, the AAH expanded its networks and membership by instituting two new categories of fellows, namely 'senior fellow' and 'overseas fellow'. During this time Smith worked hard to promote a stronger relationship with both the Chinese and Japanese humanities academies through several joint projects, such as the *Languages Atlas of the Pacific Area*,[29] and exchange programs such as the successful Australia–

China Exchange Agreement, as mentioned in his friend Stuart Macintyre's *The Poor Relation: A History of Social Sciences in Australia* (2010).[30]

Smith continued to be preoccupied with the affairs of the AAH until his death. During his term as president, he chaired its tenth annual general meeting. As well as serving ex officio on various AAH committees, he served on the Bicentenary Committee, formed in March 1977, which studied special projects and held conferences in connection with the celebrations for 1988. The *Dictionary of Australian English on Historical Principles* project was, unfortunately, abandoned due to lack of financial support, but the History of Culture in Australia project, of which Smith was a member of the steering committee (the first annual seminar being held in September 1979 at the Australian National University), was endorsed by the Bicentenary Committee and went ahead successfully.

Bernard Smith was also an adviser to the *Australian Dictionary of Biography*, and commissioning editor for an important series of monographs published by Georgian House, devoted to individual Australian artists, with scholarly essays and gorgeous illustrations, exemplified by Daniel Thomas on Sali Herman (1962), Viriginia Spate on John Olsen (1963), and Ray Mathew on Charles Blackman (1965), to name just a few of the many successful titles.

The project that Bernard embraced after his retirement was the publication of the art created on the voyages of Captain Cook, which he began in 1973.[31] The germ of the project was a 1949 request from the Hakluyt Society to make a list of the objects obtained by Cook on his three voyages. After years of work, the Hakluyt Society abandoned the project but Bernard continued after his 'retirement' as Power Professor. His friendship with a younger German scholar, Rüdiger Joppien (movingly described by Rüdiger in this volume), resulted in an extraordinarily important set of four volumes, for which Smith was indefatigable in finding financial resources, as shown in the archives of the AAH in Canberra. The publication, after nearly forty years of work, coincided with the celebrations of the bicentenary of European settlement in Australia (1988), and received funding from the Utah Foundation, the governments of New Zealand and Australia, the Hakluyt Society and the AAH. The project was a lengthy one, to which Smith could devote much of his time, while Joppien was given increasingly demanding positions in museums in Germany, where he curated exhibitions and wrote accompanying catalogues. Their correspondence reveals that this was a real collaboration, each scholar contributing to the project, and Joppien's knowledge of European languages became an essential component of the research, for Smith was monolingual.

On 10 April 1979, after the project had been peer-reviewed, John Nicoll, Bernard Smith's editor at Yale University Press, wrote to the AAH, which had assisted Bernard in the enterprise:

> The general editor is to be one of Australia's greatest humanistic scholars, major Australian Scientists will be involved in various of the volumes, and one of the leading Pacific Anthropologists (Professor Douglas Oliver, lately at Harvard and Hawaii) has described it as a scheme 'which cannot fail to be one of the most important historical and artistic publications of our time'.[32]

When the first two volumes were published, Joppien wrote to Smith with relief and joy:

> Yes, the two volumes have arrived, and I am very, very happy with them. They look very good, and it gives me infinite pleasure to browse through them, reading a bit—here and there ... Who would have believed two years ago, that this was still possible. There were times of sleepless nights, when your letters arrived, which can now be forgotten. Though I have written quite a bit, I think I am not a book type of person, and had it not been for your sheer stamina and admonitions, it would have never been completed.[33]

In 1978 Professor Smith delivered the ninth AAH Annual Lecture, entitled *Art as Information: Captain Cook's Voyages*, which was published in the following year's *Proceedings*.[34] An excerpt from Smith's presidential address at the 1980 AAH annual general meeting reads:

> This is my last Annual General Meeting as your President. It has been a very great honour indeed, and I shall treasure it until such a time as the Secretary finds it necessary to move me up to Item II [Obituaries].[35]

On 9 January 1967 Smith was appointed founding Power Professor of Contemporary Art and Director of the Power Institute at the University of Sydney, where he remained until his retirement in 1977. In his inaugural lecture, 'The Role of an Institute of Fine Arts in the University of Sydney',[36] delivered on 11 June 1969, Smith explored the personality and biography of the donor, Dr John Joseph Wardell Power (1881–1943), grandson of one of Australia's most significant architects of the nineteenth century in Australia, William Wilkinson Wardell, who designed—among other things—the Cathedrals of St Patrick in Melbourne and of St Mary in Sydney. Bernard outlined his ambitious plans for the new institute for teaching European art history from the seventeenth to the twentieth century. Although this was the first department in Australia to be resolutely contemporary, Smith's intentions were much broader, and mirrored the remarkable library on art that Power had assembled. Smith believed that:

> The implementation of the Power Bequest, especially through the work of the Power Gallery of Contemporary Art, will help to open up Australia increasingly to the full traffic of international art.[37]

As in Melbourne, a formidable number of students, including Rex Butler, Joanna Mendelssohn and Andrew McNamara, went on to have highly successful careers. Among Smith's most notable achievements was to devise the Power Lectures in Contemporary Art, which began with Clement Greenberg's 'Avant-garde Attitudes' on 17 May 1968, although Smith found Sydney critics' uncritical attitudes to Greenberg most irritating.[38] On his retirement Smith returned to live and write in Melbourne, where his former department made him professor emeritus until his death.

In 1984 Smith published his autobiography, *The Boy Adeodatus: The Portrait of a Lucky Young Bastard*.[39] Among art historians' autobiographies it is unique in that it is a moving literary masterpiece. Comparing the circumstances of his own illegitimate birth with those of St Augustine's son, Smith wrote an account of his early childhood in homage to the two mothers who reared him. Were it not for the fact that his birth mother, Rose Anne Tierney, was a Catholic, he would have been aborted, hence the name 'gift of God' or Adeodatus. The autobiography opens with an evocative description of a lush, enclosed paradise garden where he was reared by his foster mother, Mum Keen, but which is gradually disturbed by knowledge and maturity. The fruitful Australian garden is a microcosm of the South Pacific, a paradise that is gradually disturbed and charted by European voyagers. Bernard Smith created a different literary style for the book, which contrasts with his art-historical writings.

As an adopted child, Bernard had two mothers, neither of whom he rejected. These two mother figures represented both European and Australian cultures.

As a young man Smith had wished to become an artist, but later realised that he was more gifted as a writer than as a painter. It was a wise decision to follow his talents; his autobiography was awarded three Australian literary prizes. Smith's wife, Kate Beatrice Hartley Challis, whom he married in 1942, had also been a foundling, and this mutual experience was a tremendous bond between them. Kate was an honours graduate of the University of London and, like Bernard, she taught in schools. The couple had two children: Elizabeth and John. After Kate's death, Bernard wrote an autobiographical book about their lives together, *A Pavane for Another Time*,[40] which she had forbade him to undertake in her lifetime.

In Kate's memory Smith established the Ruth Adeney Koori Award (Ruth Adeney being the name by which Kate was known during her childhood and adolescence). It was to be awarded to Aboriginal Australian artists in a five-year cycle beginning in 1991, privileging in turn Indigenous artists, poets, novelists, musicians and playwrights. Visionary in scope, it was conceived as a five-year song cycle in a cultural landscape that, at that time, offered few awards of any kind. With sensitivity and thoughtfulness, Bernard came up with an Aboriginal title for the award, known familiarly as RAKA. In the Pintupi language *raka* means five, while in the Warlpiri language *radka* means hand. Both meanings are apt for a prize awarded in a cycle of five years to individual artists whose hands are tools of creativity. The generous award, administered by the University of Melbourne, has been of great significance. Smith omitted almost any reference to Indigenous art in his *Australian Painting*, and later regretted this. Yet his legacy to his wife whom he loved was to make her the muse of Indigenous art in its many forms, making good after the omission of his early books. In the early years of the prize Smith took a particular interest in the recipients, helping them develop their careers. The challenges to Smith represented by Aboriginal art, and his changing attitude towards it, are the subject of Ian McLean's essay in this volume.

In order to endow the award, Bernard sold his art collection, an account of which is given here for the first time by his granddaughter, the second Kate Challis. A conventional assumption might be that Marxists were neither collectors nor philanthropists, but Bernard in his individual way was eccentrically generous and original in both interconnected roles. He often helped his artist friends by buying their works and, like all art historians' collections, it mirrored the art-historical views of its owner, with a pronounced emphasis on those artists who were socialists in their subject matter. When the Smith collection was sold it was to foster further creativity, by creating the RAKA endowment, to which students and colleagues also contributed.

Most of the recipients of the RAKA made bold statements in their works, questioning the provision for human rights for Indigenous people in Australia, as indeed did Bernard in *The Spectre of Truganini*, the Boyer Lectures of 1980.[41] The list of beneficiaries of the RAKA is almost a who's who of Indigenous culture in Australia. Winners were selected by judging panels that included Indigenous selectors, and most of the winners received the award before they became celebrated. The first winner, in 1991, was Bill Rosser for his book *Up Rode the Troopers: The Black Police in Queensland* (1990), an account of the exploitation of Indigenous Queenslanders. A decade later, in 2002, Rosser was awarded the Australian Human Rights Medal. The second RAKA went to playwright Jack Davis for *No Sugar*, a plea against racism. In 1993 Lin Onus was given the award for his sculpture *They took the children away*, a political statement about the separation of Aboriginal children from their parents (Fig. 3).[42] All those who received the award, such as the then very young Tracey Moffatt, beneficiary in 1994 for her script *beDevil*, or the young Brook Andrew for *Sexy and dangerous* in 1998, were recognised at the beginnings of their careers, as was Warwick Thornton for his script for *Samson and Delilah* in 2009, which may prove to be one of the most innovative Australian films of any director in the twenty-first century. How it would have delighted Bernard, always at heart a political activist, whether in his life or writings, that the RAKA has endorsed a series of powerful political statements, so much in Bernard's mould, as Max Solling outlines in his account of Bernard as activist in local politics in Glebe, Sydney.

The group of essays in the first section of this book, 'Encountering Australia: *European Vision and the South Pacific*', defines Bernard Smith's formative interests as an art historian. Andrew Sayers' account of the understanding of *European Vision* among art historians and anthropologists in Australia includes a revealing account of Smith's own dissatisfactions with the critical reception of his best-known work. Smith always longed for it be recognised that Coleridge's poem *The Rime of the Ancient Mariner* (1798) was triggered by reports of Cook's voyages, and that European discovery of the Pacific had put untold pressure on biblical Creation beliefs; much later he was disappointed that his formulation was unappreciated. Although Smith could be his own most severe critic, he believed that everything he had done was of significance.

Robert Gaston gives an account of Smith's years at the Warburg Institute and how its legendary teachers influenced the development of Smith's ideas about how the earliest European artists interpreted the Australian landscape, how they represented different forms of flora and fauna enountered in the Pacific, and how their modes of representation were affected by non-European experience. Once found, this initial theme became a lifelong concern. Smith brought the legacy of Warburg to Australia, where it has continued to attract many followers.

Nicholas Thomas, an anthropologist, reveals how absolutely foundational *European Vision* was to the analysis of travel and colonial history across the Pacific. In his methodology Smith did not limit himself to the conventional study of major paintings, but to visual material of all kinds, such as seemingly crude engravings from missionary periodicals. In this Smith was like Warburg, who would illuminate Florentine social history and major works of art by reference to a popular woodcut. All visual material might be of interest in these two scholars' analyses of a culture, whether Pacific or Florentine. Thomas proposes that Pacific objects may not only express meanings that are local to their own culture, but have hybridity and represent negotiations of meaning across cultures. Thomas was responsible for the first conference about Smith's work, 'Double Vision: Art Histories and Colonial Histories in the Pacific' (1999), convened with Diane Losche and Jennifer Newell. The conference took as its theme Indigenous views of colonial encounters and European perceptions of Pacific cultures.

Rüdiger Joppien continues the story of Smith's preoccupation with the voyage art of Captain Cook which, as mentioned previously, was eventually published in three volumes after forty years of research to coincide with Australia's Bicentennial in 1988. Their collaboration was extraordinary in the historiography of art history, comparable perhaps to that between Joseph Archer Crowe and Giovanni Battista Cavalcaselle. They became friends forever.

Kathleen Davidson examines the role of photography in Smith's writings, beginning with the second edition of *European Vision* (1985), which acknowledges the importance of the emerging power of photography in relation to scientific discovery in the natural sciences. Though photography was not a primary concern for Smith, he made a nod to its significance, which is further discussed by Davidson.

Terry Smith opens the second section of this book, on Australian painting, with an overview of Bernard Smith's achievements, which he rightly claims are unmatched by any other writer on the visual arts in Australia. Bernard Smith assumed the title of foundation Power Professor of Contemporary Art and Director of the Power Institute in 1967 and this section places Smith in a global discourse about art history. Among the many virtues of Terry Smith's essay are his understanding of how Bernard changed his position on Marxism, how he interpreted the role of Power Professor, and the close connections between the Smiths as art historians across generations. Peter Beilharz, who wrote the first monograph on Smith, provides an overview of Bernard as a writer, whose prose is considered according to the task at hand. John Clark examines the role of autobiography in Smith's writings, especially his biography of Noel Counihan (1994) and his own autobiographies in the framework of Australian art biography. Usually biographies are written about artists, while an autobiography from an art historian is unusual, except in the case of museum directors.

Catherine Speck re-reads the classic Smith texts, interrogating them on how to include the narratives of expatriate artists, who spent much of their lives in Paris and London, in Australian art history. While Smith discussed offshore practice as part of a national narrative, his approach has been succeeded by contemporary curatorship, where borderless and inclusive histories are presented in exhibitions such as Anne Gray's *The Edwardians: Secrets and Desires* (2004). Taking as a departure point the 'Antipodean Manifesto' (1959), Paul Giles argues that Smith's most enduring legacy may be as a cultural theorist who moves to reposition the antipodes in world culture. Both Speck and Giles see Smith as an international figure. Simon Pierse contributes to our understanding of why Bernard Smith and Peter Fuller became soul mates, despite the different cultures that surrounded them.

The third section of the book is about Bernard Smith's surprising curatorial contributions to Sydney art museums. Here Joanna Mendelssohn and Jim Berryman reveal how much Smith contributed to the development of the Art Gallery of New South Wales (AGNSW). As Steven Miller shows, there were many tensions between the gallery's trustees and Smith, whom they considered to be too cocksure, intolerant of different opinions and sometimes vain. In his youthful role of scholar-educator in the gallery Smith created travelling exhibitions that were taken to regional venues. For a curator this was a hybrid enterprise, somewhere between a museum show and a commercial opportunity, the works usually being sold either to the gallery itself or to private collectors. Ann Stephen reveals that when Smith returned to Sydney he was also the creator-curator of the Power Collection, acquiring the latest examples of contemporary art from *documenta 4* and the Venice Biennale in 1968. Only some of these 2000 works have ever been exhibited, most of the collection having been always in storage. In the 1980s Smith became the curator's greatest critic, suggesting that curatorial practice neglected scholarly values. In a way Smith was always of this persuasion, as Christopher R. Marshall demonstrates in charting the developing complexities and contradictions of a Marxist approach to the role of museums, beginning with Smith's concerns about Roy Grounds' plans for the National Gallery of Victoria, which Smith and other intellectuals successfully challenged. Several decades later, when he was living in retirement in Melbourne, Smith's concerns about the design of the new Museum of Victoria failed to have any effect.

Smith's politics are present throughout every section of the book, but in the fourth part, 'Bernard Smith's Cultural Politics', certain issues are more fully defined, beginning with Max Solling's vivid account of Smith as a local activist in the Sydney suburb of Glebe. Initially it was difficult for Smith to become involved, but then he became the life and soul of the movement. Smith always longed to write a book about European art that would be taken as seriously as his Australian art history. The younger Kate Challis reveals Smith as the 'Marxist collector', and Sheridan Palmer writes about Bernard's cherished ambition to write on Noel Counihan in relation to Courbet, but the Courbet part of the project never eventuated. Ian McLean and Catherine de Lorenzo both demonstrate with great subtlety the changing positions in Smith's writings about Aboriginal art. With the strength of multiple voices Bernard Smith emerges in this volume as a generous art historian, who tried to create the very best circumstances for scholarship in Australia (Fig. 4).

NOTES

1 Parts of this article are taken from earlier statements by the author about Bernard Smith, such as Jaynie Anderson, 'Smith of the Antipodes', *Modern Painters*, vol. 1, no. 3, September 1988, pp. 91–2; a review of 'A Pavane for Another Time: Bernard Smith', *Australian and New Zealand Journal of Art*, vol. 3, no. 2, 2002, pp. 117–20; and Jaynie Anderson, 'Bernard Smith 1916–2011' [obituary], in Australian Academy of the Humanities, *2012 Annual Report: The Australian Academy of the Humanities*, pp. 39–42, www.humanities.org.au/Fellowship/Obituaries.aspx.

2 Bernard Smith's papers (1938–1999, MS 8680; MS Acc10.088; MS Acc13.037) are in the National Library of Australia in Canberra. Smith's library is in the State Library Victoria, and further papers are at the Mitchell Library, Sydney, and the University of Melbourne Archives.

3 Bernard Smith, *Place, Taste and Tradition: A Study of Australian Art since 1788*, Ure Smith, Sydney 1945; 2nd edition: Oxford University Press, Melbourne, 1979. Reviewed in *Sydney Morning Herald*, 4 August 1945.

4 William Moore's *Story of Australian Art*, published by Angus & Robertson, Sydney, in 1934, sold badly in a small edition, whereas Smith's book was widely discussed and influential.

5 See Smith's reflective introduction to the second edition of *Place, Taste and Tradition*, pp. 15–20. Reviewed in the *Burlington Magazine*, 1981, p. 332.

6 John O'Brian, 'Bernard Smith's Early Marxist Art History', *Thesis Eleven*, vol. 87, August 2005, pp. 29–37.

7 Bernard Smith, 'Notes on Elitism and the Arts', *Meanjin Quarterly*, vol. 34, no. 2, June 1975, pp. 117–20.

8 The gallery dropped 'National' from its name in 1958.

9 There are lengthy descriptions of the sources for the two paintings, in Smith's papers in Canberra, (National Library of Australia, Canberra, Bernard Smith Papers (hereafter NLA, BSP), MS8680, 31).

10 Smith's BA Honours thesis, for the University of Sydney, The Interpretation of Australian Nature During the Nineteenth Century, was submitted soon after his return to Australia in 1952. A copy is in NLA, BSP, MS 8680, Box 3, Item 1. The themes of his Warburg years were developed as an undergraduate thesis before his books were published.

11 Bernard Smith, *European Vision and the South Pacific, 1768–1850: A Study in the History of Art and Ideas*, Clarendon Press, Oxford, 1960; 2nd edition: Yale University Press, New Haven, 1985.

12 *Times Literary Supplement*, 'Discovery of the Noble Antipodean', 1 September 1962, p. 730.

13 Jaynie Anderson, 'Obituary: Professor Charles Mitchell', *The Independent*, 31 October 1995, www.independent.co.uk/news/people/obituary-professor-charles-mitchell-1580287.html, viewed 6 September 2013.

14 Bernard Smith and Alwyne Wheeler (eds), *The Art of the First Fleet and Other Early Australian Drawings*, Oxford University Press in association with the Australian Academy of the Humanities and the British Museum (Natural History), Melbourne; Yale University Press, New Haven, 1988.

15 Rüdiger Joppien and Bernard Smith, *The Art of Captain Cook's Voyages*, 3 vols in 4 parts, Oxford University Press, Melbourne, 1985–87.

16 Bernard Smith, *A Catalogue of Australian Oil Paintings in the National Art Gallery of New South Wales, 1875–1952: With Annotations, Biographies and Index*, National Art Gallery of New South Wales, Sydney, 1953.

17 See Steven Miller's contribution to this volume.

18 Bernard Smith, 'The Antipodean Manifesto', foreword to *The Antipodeans 4th–15th Aug 1959*, exhibition catalogue, Victorian Artists' Society, Melbourne, 1959 (republished in 1975 in *The Antipodean Manifesto*, and in 1988 in *The Death of the Artist as Hero*).

19 Bernard Smith, *Australian Painting, 1788–1960*, Oxford University Press, Melbourne, 1962.

20 Bernard Smith and Terry Smith, *Australian Painting, 1788–1990*, 3rd edn, Oxford University Press, Melbourne, 1991.

21 Bernard Smith, with Terry Smith and Christopher Heathcote, *Australian Painting, 1788–2000*, 4th edn, Oxford University Press, Melbourne, 2001.

22 Bernard Smith, 'Nolan's Image', *The London Magazine*, vol. 2, no. 6, September 1962, pp. 69–74.

23 Elwyn Lynn, *Sidney Nolan: Myth and Imagery*, Macmillan, London, 1967.

24 See Smith's review of Lynn's monograph in *The Bulletin*, 7 October 1967, pp. 77–9.

25 Smith, 'Nolan's Image'.

26 Ian Burn, 'Landscape and Life: Nolan and the Australian Tradition', *The Age Monthly Review*, 1 August 1984, p. 82.

27 NLA, BSP, MS Acc10.088, Box 30.

28 Burn, 'Landscape and Life', p. 82.

29 *Languages Atlas of the Pacific Area*, series eds S.A. Wurm and Shiro Hattori, cartography by Theo Bauman, Australian Academy of the Humanities, Canberra, in collaboration with the Japan Academy, 1981–83.

30 Stuart Macintyre, *The Poor Relation: A History of Social Sciences in Australia*, Melbourne University Press, Melbourne, 2010.

31 See NLA, BSP, MS Acc10.088, Box 24, which contains the beginning of Joppien and Smith's exchange of letters.

32 Archives of the Australian Academy of the Humanities, Canberra.

33 This letter, dated 25 October 1987, is in Smith's correspondence with Joppien, in NLA, BSP, MS Acc10.088, Box 23. It is of such interest that it might be published as an example of transnational collaboration.

34 Bernard Smith, *Art as Information: Reflections on the Art from Captain Cook's Voyages*, Sydney University Press for the Australian Academy of the Humanities, Sydney, 1979.

35 Australian Academy of the Humanities, 1980 Annual General Meeting Papers, 120/12, Minutes of the Eleventh Annual General Meeting, Archives of the Australian Academy of the Humanities, Canberra.

36 Bernard Smith, 'The Role of an Institute of Fine Arts in the University of Sydney', *Arts: The Journal of the Sydney University Arts Association*, vol. 6, 1969, pp. 5–17.

37 ibid., p. 12.

38 ibid., p. 10.

39 Bernard Smith, *The Boy Adeodatus: The Portrait of a Lucky Young Bastard*, Penguin Books Australia, Melbourne, 1984.

40 Bernard Smith, *A Pavane for Another Time*, Macmillan, Melbourne, 2002.

41 Bernard Smith, *The Spectre of Truganini*, The 1980 Boyer Lectures, Australian Broadcasting Commission, Sydney, 1980.

42 For further discussion, see Margo Neale (ed.), *Urban Dingo: The Art and Life of Lin Onus 1948–1996*, exhibition catalogue, Museum of Contemporary Art, Sydney, 2000, pp. 125–6.

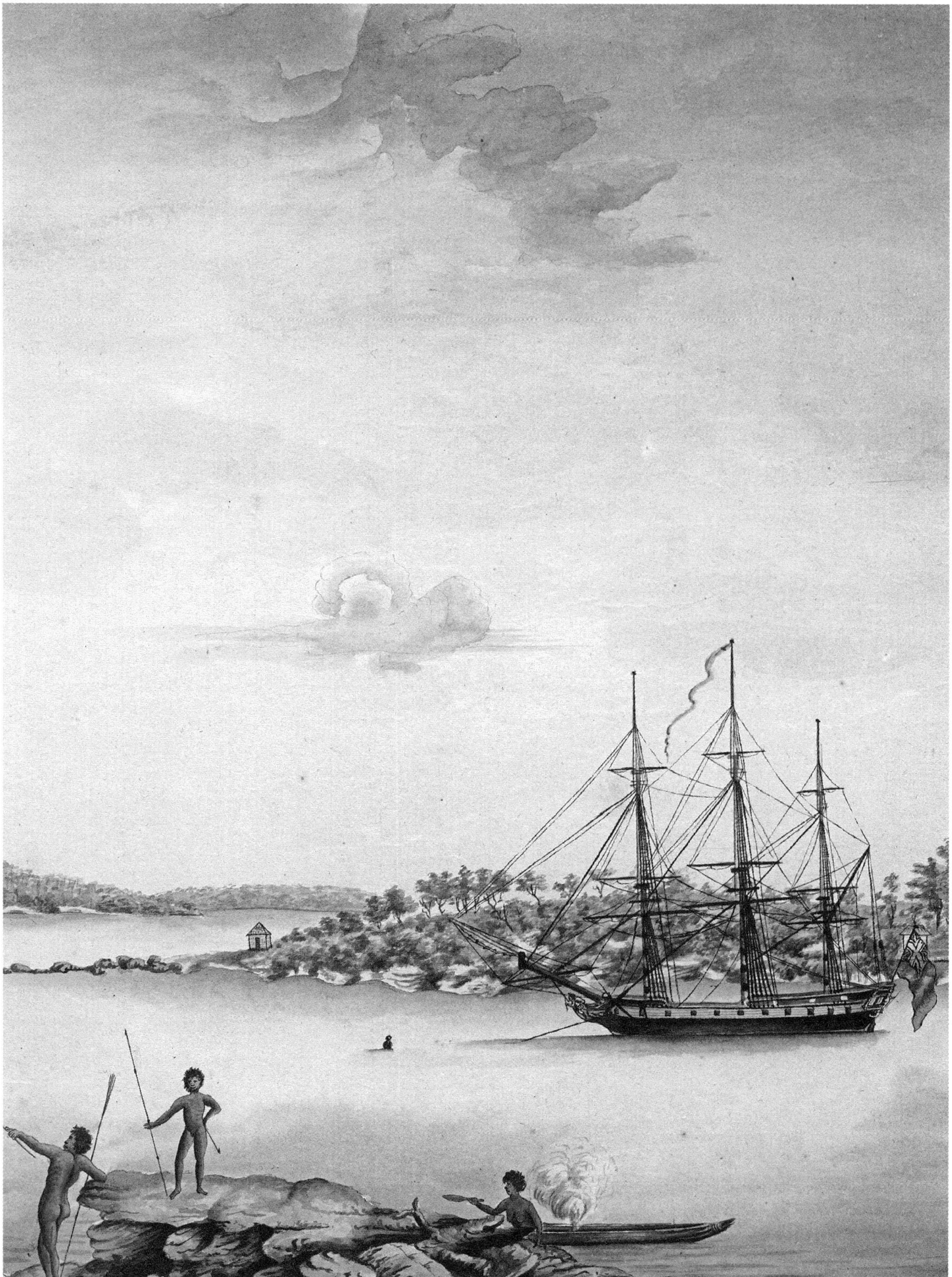

1

ENCOUNTERING AUSTRALIA: *EUROPEAN VISION AND THE SOUTH PACIFIC*

A half-century on: the legacy of *European Vision and the South Pacific*

ANDREW SAYERS

I always beheld Bernard Smith with a certain awe, and from an early age: as a teenager, I wanted to be an art historian when I grew up. In the early 1970s, when I was looking ahead at tertiary study, I somehow got my hands on the careers edition of the University of Sydney's student magazine *Honi Soit* and read an article on the Power Institute of Fine Arts. The article suggested that prospective students seek an interview with the institute head, but when I rang him, Professor Smith said that really wouldn't be necessary—if I wanted to come and study art history at Sydney University, I was welcome.

My career compass was set.

By the time I enrolled, Bernard was in his last year at the Power Institute, so he was a remote figure in my undergraduate days. I encountered him amiably throughout subsequent years and he reviewed a couple of my books—kindly, I remember, despite minor disagreements.

When I was working at the National Portrait Gallery in Canberra, I acquired for the collection Albert Tucker's portrait of Bernard, painted in 1978 from a photograph and from memory; one of Tucker's portraits from the 'Faces I Have Met' series. I think Tucker meant to show Bernard's intellectual toughness—yet there is a hint that he thought Smith's worldview was as enclosing as the doorless and windowless space in which he has placed him. Artist and subject had been very close in their opinions in the early 1940s but, in the ensuing decades, their opinions diverged.

Every time I spoke to Albert Tucker, it felt like an engagement with a mind forged in the ideological furnace of Australia in the 1930s and 1940s, the same crucible that created Bernard Smith's mettle. Tucker had a full-blown anxiety about his legacy. I sensed his determination and his moral certainty, yet also a disappointment that the world had misunderstood him and his art.

In his later years, there were disappointments for Bernard Smith. There was the disappointment that his term 'Formalesque' had failed to kill off the imprecise but resistant term 'modernist' as a descriptor of art produced between 1890 and 1960. That was a last let-down. Yet there were others.

Smith was disappointed that art historians failed to recognise that *plein air* painter William Hodges was a man—one might say a Manet—before his time; he regretted that art made in the Pacific, one-third of the Earth's surface, featured only as a tiny fraction of the broader picture of art history, centred as it was on the northern hemisphere.[1]

He lamented the fact that his discovery of the link between Cook's voyages and Coleridge's imagery in *The Rime of the Ancient Mariner* was still ignored by scholars, thirty-five years after he had brought it to the attention of the world. To this particular slight he devotes the majority of his introduction to the 1992 collection *Imagining the Pacific*.[2] He recounts how, when his essay first appeared in 1956, he sent the offprint to the three eminent Coleridge scholars of the day: Edmund Blunden, Kathleen Coburn and E. L. Griggs. Blunden responded that Smith's thesis was 'sound and good'; Coburn that it was 'right in general' and Griggs replied that he 'had something'. In Smith's recounting of this episode, we infer his sense that he had been dismissed, rather patronisingly, by scholars in whose specialisation he had no business to intervene. These dons' responses implied a disregard that seems to have tainted Smith's assessment of the significance of his broader scholarly endeavour.

I don't know if there is any evidence to suggest that Smith got beyond such disappointments to see with any clarity the possible lines of his legacy. Putting aside Smith's personal perspective, I think it is possible for us, with the passage of time, to discern elements of his legacy. I think we are in a position to look beyond Smith's retrospective grumpiness and his disappointments; in the greater arc of his scholarly achievement they will prove, in the end, to be unjustified.

European Vision in the South Pacific is Bernard Smith's most enduring book, and the author himself acknowledged that it had been 'hailed as a classic'.[3] Yet even in the face of this recognition, he harboured disappointments. In 1984, twenty-five years after the publication of *European Vision*, he wrote that 'the two major themes around which it was written have never become the subject of serious discussion'.[4] The first of these themes concerned the history of science—the idea that observations in the Pacific, in particular, placed unprecedented pressure on biblical Creation belief and provided the evidence on which the theory of evolution was founded. The second was to do with the history of art: 'the contention that the predominant mode of landscape painting in the nineteenth century arose from the need to discover and to evoke what was typical'.[5]

We must remember that Smith wrote this in 1984, and pause to ask whether these two areas have, indeed, been overlooked in the three decades since. On the history of science question, I think we can say that Pacific exploration during the eighteenth century has been more widely acknowledged as creating a precondition for the development of Darwinism. It is clear that the 2009 sesquicentenary of the publication of *On the Origin of Species* provided many opportunities to revisit the maturation of Darwin's ideas and the part played by his antipodean expeditions.

On the art history question, we can give a more confident assessment. Landscape, arranged typologically, may have been an under-appreciated cause of change in landscape painting when Smith wrote *European Vision*, but we now witness a greater awareness of 'typical' landscape in our understanding of nineteenth-century painting. For example, the National Gallery of Victoria's 2012 exhibition of Eugene von Guérard, entitled *Nature Revealed*, gave prominence to the role of Alexander von Humboldt—the central theorist of landscape types—in shaping the worldview, not only of von Guérard himself, but also of his band of Düsseldorf peers. Curator Ruth Pullin's presentation in *Nature Revealed* builds on a great deal of work on von Guérard undertaken in the last thirty years by scholars such as Candice Bruce, Daniel Thomas and Tim Bonyhady.[6] Had Bernard Smith extended the compass of *European Vision* beyond 1850, he doubtless would have found in von Guérard—a thoroughly Humboldtian artist—the most complete antipodean manifestation of 'typical' landscape.

To return to 1984: in his preface to the second edition of *European Vision*, Smith goes on to ask why the themes of the book had not been given the scholarly attention they deserved. The first answer, he surmises, was that from the standpoint of Europe, the Pacific was considered either 'too primitive' or 'too provincial' to matter much. But more profoundly, the fact that his book concerned itself not with art masterpieces, but with visual images produced primarily for information, had made it 'something of an anomaly'.[7]

The phrase 'visual images produced primarily for information' points us to Smith's principal interest in *European Vision*. It was not only the underlying theme of *European Vision*; it spawned many of the most fruitful lines of later enquiry in his work on the art of Pacific exploration. Smith gave his 1978 lecture on the art of Cook's voyages the title 'Art as Information'. In the lecture Smith argued that the 'history of the visual arts in Europe between 1750 and 1890 … can best be understood … as the steady, relentless and continuing triumph of empirical naturalism over classical naturalism'. He went further, suggesting that 'Cook's voyages were not only fact-gathering phenomena: they directly affected conceptual thought; and their influence … penetrated deeply into the aesthetic realm'.[8]

Other writers in the present volume discuss the intellectual voyage that linked the different stages of Smith's early work in art history and led him to the fruitful territory of empirical naturalism. A crucial moment in that journey, highlighted in Smith's autobiography *A Pavane for Another Time*, came during one of the lectures he attended at the Courtauld Institute in 1948–49, in which Ernst Gombrich casually threw out the idea that '… all art is conceptual'.[9] That phrase sailed serenely, yet influentially, into Smith's imaginative ocean at the moment when he was beginning his detailed musing on the drawings of Cook's artists.

From the standpoint of today we can observe with confidence that the idea that 'all art is conceptual' has triumphed. It may have been a novel idea in 1949, but the practice of art itself over the last six decades has changed the practice of art history. It is not possible to draw tidy distinctions between art produced primarily for information and art whose primary purpose is something else. The phrase 'all art is conceptual' must inform our approach to the art of our time, whether we are analysing, say, a painting by Anatjari Tjakamarra, or a work by Ian Burn, in whose practice we recognise the lineaments of 'conceptual art' as an art-historical label. And much (though not all) contemporary art can only be understood in a context that has thoroughly ingested the idea of 'art as information'.

Today it is possible to see that Smith's principal interest in *European Vision* is now a central preoccupation not only of contemporary artists but also of contemporary art historians. Smith's project is, in short, cross-cultural.

The discipline of art history can no longer be characterised fairly as concerned only with explicating the role of artists as individuals in their societies—which Smith described as 'the central myth of art history'—nor is it principally concerned with acknowledged masterpieces.[10] The discipline has changed. Art history admits a much broader range of visual material, approached from diverse perspectives, than it was possible to imagine fifty years ago.

There are two ways in which the discipline has moved towards, not away from, the positioning of *European Vision*. First, as was attested in the International Committee of Art History conference held in Melbourne in 2008, art history has concerned itself in recent years with a global picture.[11] Doubts linger over whether art history is an essentially and irredeemably Western construct, but Smith's work is consciously underpinned by an emphasis on European ways of looking at, and constructing, the world. His subject matter, moreover, deals with a part of the globe that, as he reminded us, constitutes one-third of the Earth's surface. His work, then, opened up the possibility of exchange and conceptual challenge upon which cross-cultural art histories inevitably rest.

The second and related way in which art history has moved is in the increasing merging of art history with the anthropology of images. Hans Belting, in his book *An Anthropology of Images*, proposes:

> If we take an anthropological approach to the subject, it soon becomes clear that the images of the past are constantly being replaced by new and different images. Today's image can be but a temporary answer; it will not satisfy the next generation. Thus, every image, once it has fulfilled its current mission, generates a new image.[12]

The way in which images, having fulfilled their current mission, are transformed is one of Smith's principal preoccupations. He devotes pages of *European Vision* to discussing the distortions and re-interpretations of the visual record of Cook's artists, and searches for the reasons behind them.[13] He carefully charts, for example, the changes to Alexander Buchan's sketches of the inhabitants of Tierra del Fuego. The first falsification comes at the point where Buchan's work is redrawn for engraving by Cipriani and is made to conform to the conventions of neoclassicism demanded in the metropolis. New figures are added and the whole is rendered more comely and graceful, to use the appropriate eighteenth-century words. Thus miserable wretchedness—to borrow another phrase of the day—becomes primitive elegance. Smith follows the image through a further transformation from the middle of the nineteenth century. The connection to the original circumstance of Buchan's drawing degrades yet further. Yet there is still information in the image, information about evangelical imperatives (it becomes, literally, an image to fulfil a mission). In that context, a complete disregard for geographic or climatic precision was of no consequence for the work the image had to do.

The anthropology of images must have at its core an idea of 'art as information'. Yet we should be careful to point out that, although Smith's approach prefigured an anthropology of images, it remained strongly iconological and carried within it the inheritance of Warburg, the self-described 'picture historian'. Smith pointed out that he was not an apologist for extreme relativism; nor did he abandon the category of 'art' in his analysis.[14]

I have always been intrigued by the structure of *European Vision* and have felt that something about its meaning is embodied in the way its narrative unfolds. In the preface to the first edition, Smith sets out the schema in broad terms:

> In its mature forms, the typical landscape provides an artistic counterpart to the biological explanation of life upon the planet provided by the theory of organic evolution. The main outline of this argument is developed in Chapters 1 to 5, 7 and

12. Chapters 6, 8, 9 and 10 are concerned with a cognate theme: the beginnings of European art in Australia.[15]

If we read *European Vision* closely, it is possible to see that much of its material does not fit neatly into this overarching design. Indeed, some of those parts that sit most uneasily with the author's concern with the history of scientific ideas are those that have given rise to the book's enduring legacy. Chapter 5 of *European Vision* is a case in point. It is among the best chapters in the book in terms of the subtlety with which Smith unravels and interweaves his themes. It is a narrative of the changing attitudes of Europeans to the Indigenous peoples of the Pacific. He draws an arc that stretches from George Keate's attempt to cast the inhabitants of Palau as mankind seen 'in a variety of lights' to Chateaubriand's musings on Tahiti, where, even amid great beauty, death is the only reality. Yet this discussion, which tracks back and forth between these ideas and older, yet resilient, ideals of the noble savage, is not directly concerned with science, or landscape, except in the sense that Chateaubriand's ideas contain the classical idea of the presence of death in paradise: *Et in Arcadia Ego*. Smith returns to this theme frequently and, in the penultimate chapter, introduces it as the idea upon which visions of the future ascendancy of the Pacific rested. He appends the phrase to Macaulay's vision of the future in which:

> 'some traveller from New Zealand shall, in the midst of a vast solitude, take his stand upon a broken arch of London Bridge to sketch the ruins of St. Paul's'. *Et in Arcadia Ego*.[16]

Given his understanding of the complexity of contact histories, even in the European imagination, it is hardly surprising that Smith drew a distinction between his project in *European Vision* and Alan Moorehead's approach in his popular history of Pacific exploration, *The Fatal Impact*, published in 1966.[17] As Smith pointed out, any 'fatal impact' was no concern of his text—rather it was an inversion of the very idea—it was the impact of the South Pacific on Europe that interested him.[18]

Such a two-way exchange of ideas is one of the basic tenets of global art history. There is no doubt that, in the past two decades, the history of interactions between settler societies and Indigenous cultures has been a preoccupation of art history, the foundation of cross-cultural studies and the source of some of the most rewarding art-historical scholarship in this country and beyond.

The 2012 conference honouring Bernard Smith's legacy had a predecessor in the conference held to honour his work held in Canberra in 1996.[19] Unlike the 2012 conference, which encompassed the whole career of Bernard Smith, the 1996 conference had *European Vision* as its departure point. In 1996, *European Vision* could be described, still, as 'a *largely unrecognised work* that pioneered … visually astute cultural history'.[20] It was only a departure point in that the conference at large 'struggled to engage' (in the words of Nicholas Thomas, one of the conference organisers) both sides of the colonial encounter that is *European Vision*'s principal subject. It was a cross-cultural and interdisciplinary project in which Bernard Smith was an enthusiastic participant. With two exceptions, the speakers there did not concern themselves with questions of landscape representation or with the history of science, but with the complexities of cross-cultural representation. And they were concerned with 'visual culture' rather than with 'art history'.

Nicholas Thomas was at pains to point out in 1996 that Smith's lack of attention to the Indigenous dimensions of cross-cultural perception in *European Vision* was not a matter of intellectual limitation but was attributable to disciplinary boundaries. Exciting harbinger of change though it would, in hindsight, be, *European Vision* was a work of art history written in an era when art history was not only Eurocentric, but was conceptually separated from anthropology.[21] The downside of that separation was that we had to wait until that demarcation broke down, as it most surely has been breaking down in the intervening decades, before the full import of Smith's book could be appreciated. In his 1984 assessment of the impact or otherwise of *European Vision*, Smith said that the book had given support to a new generation of 'anthropologists, ethnohistorians and others who had come to realise and take an interest in the inescapable relativity of their own perceptions'.[22]

There are indications that Smith recognised that anthropology was going to offer insights into the complexities of colonialism at least as rewarding as those of art history. In his 1980 Boyer Lectures, *The Spectre of Truganini*, he reframed the subject of the colonial enterprise. Discussing the implications of Cook's actions in taking possession of the east coast of Australia in the name of George III, Smith says:

> It was not in the centre, not in London, but in Australia, that the principles of universal justice championed by … the Enlightenment began their long process of degeneration … it was … *upon the frontier* that the Enlightenment ethic began to crumble [my italics].

And he goes on to offer this insight:

> Frontiers are not places … where men meet nature but where they confront other cultures, and systems of law conflict. Malinowski has called such frontiers a 'third cultural reality' and they produce in Professor Stanner's words 'a queer set of shapes'.[23]

'Upon the frontier': Malinowski and W. E. H. Stanner have replaced Lovejoy and Wind as Smith's guides.

The 'third cultural reality' of the frontier is now one of the central preoccupations of the art historian in Australia. Witness the new prevalence of figures in Australian art history who worked in that 'third cultural reality'. We could cite as examples the Aboriginal artists of the nineteenth century, such as Tommy McRae, who have become key figures in the stories of Australian art. One of McRae's drawings of the story of William Buckley graced the cover of *Double Vision*, the publication of the 1996 conference, and another was chosen as the lead image for the CIHA conference in 2008. Both works depict the memory of a meeting at the frontier, the moment when William Buckley escaped from the convict ship *Calcutta* and entered into Aboriginal society. It is intriguing to see how Tommy McRae has become emblematic of that 'other side' of the colonial encounter.[24] Indeed, McRae's drawings include the principal ingredients of many of the images in *European Vision*: the sailing ship sitting off the coast, the ceremonies of Indigenous people, and the Europeans who have come among them. Yet the story is a very different one. As we saw in the case of von Guérard, McRae post-dates the time-compass of *European Vision*, his earliest drawings being dated to the 1860s. Yet McRae's drawings of Buckley stand out as examples of an Indigenous artist looking at the impact of Aboriginal society on the life of the coloniser, at the very moment of settler and Indigenous contact in Victoria.

We are now more deeply engaged with cultural frontiers than ever. Artists such as Albert Namatjira, Tony Tuckson and Mawalan are the ones who engage a new generation of art historians. The foundation myths of Australian art history have come to encompass Corranderrk and Hermannsburg, Yirrkala and Papunya, as much as Encounter Bay and Patterdale, Sydney Cove and Box Hill.

In *The Spectre of Truganini* Smith describes the only drawings of Aboriginal people to survive from Cook's *Endeavour* voyage—Sydney Parkinson's two sketches made at Botany Bay.[25] Parkinson seems to have seen a cross in the subject's body decoration and Smith asks whether the artist perceived that, with Cook's coming, Australian Indigenous people would 'be subjected by his own race to a prolonged humiliation and degradation best symbolised by the tortured body of the Man of Sorrows'. He closes this rhetorical speculation with a suggestion that the drawing is evidence of a troubled conscience at the first moment of European–Indigenous contact on our eastern coast.

There is fragility in the moment when Parkinson glimpsed and sketched an Indigenous Australian. Smith readily concedes that we don't really know what Parkinson had in mind, or if his drawing was meant to have any Christian connotation at all. That lack of definite intention is part of the tentativeness of the encounter. Smith is acutely sensitive to the authenticity of the first attempts to create visual records. They are the most delicate fruits of empirical naturalism; they are easily bruised. For the art historian they are most revealing and the story of the subsequent transformations of images is deeply interesting to the historian who is committed to understanding the dynamism, not the fixity, of cultures.

A final point on a third reality. One might make the point that it is not only frontiers that constitute a third reality. Voyages do, too. The various voyages of exploration in the Pacific that Smith analyses in *European Vision* were each constituted as self-sufficient and self-referential worlds. Of course, these worlds were set in frameworks of institutional expectations and were underpinned by assumptions and allegiances, both personal and intellectual. Yet the anthropology of the voyage, with its peculiar dependencies and spheres of ideological influence—so brilliantly expressed in a book such as Greg Dening's *Mr Bligh's Bad Language* (1992)—is already present in Smith's account.[26] Such was the richness of possibility in these separate worlds that much of Smith's most enduring work arose from even more detailed examination of the voyages of Cook, Baudin and Phillip.

As we saw earlier, Smith described the second part of *European Vision* as an exploration of the beginnings of European art in Australia. I now want to turn to that part of the book and look at its legacy.

Of the 171 illustrations in the first edition of *European Vision*, only two illustrated works were to be found in Australian art galleries. It is little wonder, then, that Smith felt he had to explain that this study of art and ideas was based on images made primarily for information. The distinction between art as information and art as aesthetic artifact held as firmly before the 1960s as the distinction between art and ethnography; it meant that works of art in which there was a strong documentary element were to be found in libraries, ethnographic or historical museums, archives and, in some cases, private collections, but not usually in art galleries. Some institutions that escaped the twentieth century's splitting of art galleries and history museums, such as the Tasmanian Museum and Art Gallery, benefited from the distinction that was drawn with ever-increasing severity elsewhere.

The divisions that grew up over the course of the twentieth century—institutional and disciplinary—are everywhere being erased. We can see this reflected in institutional terms by simply observing that a great deal of the material that Smith investigated in *European Vision* would now be acquired, happily, for art gallery collections in Australia if that were possible. Smith uncovered a wealth of otherwise largely invisible visual material and applied a rigour of connoisseurship that was unique in the writing about Australian art of the 1950s.

To re-read *European Vision* is to be struck by its quality. Not only did the author take on an 82-year time span, he married broader ideas to empirical research of extraordinary depth and detail. With the possible exception of Benjamin Duterrau—whom Smith did not discuss at length in *European Vision* (though he made up for this in *Australian Painting*)—Smith was able to discern the lineaments of colonial art. He was the first to see profound interest in artists who are now the familiar and much-studied names: Augustus Earle, John Skinner Prout, Louisa Anne Meredith and John Glover. He amassed the material necessary to document their careers and essential ideas and made generalisations about their place in Australian art that have been remarkably enduring.

Take, for example, Smith's treatment of J. W. Lewin, Australia's first professional artist. In *European Vision* he analyses Lewin's record of Macquarie's journey across the

Blue Mountains in 1815. The first watercolour painted on the journey was, he writes:

> probably the earliest illustration of those bivouacking, boiling-the-billy scenes that were to achieve almost iconic status in the later years of the century as they came to symbolise the free and adventurous life of the colonies and play a part, eventually, in the *mystique* of colonial nationalism.[27]

The 2012 exhibition devoted to Lewin's work (organised and toured by the State Library of New South Wales) acknowledged *European Vision* in two ways. The exhibition explicitly confirmed Smith's assessment of the way in which Lewin dispensed with various conventions of composition and observed the Australian landscape with a novel accuracy. The accompanying book, while taking issue with Smith's characterisation of Lewin's work as the 'rude yet distinct beginnings of an Australian school of landscape painting', nonetheless acknowledges that *European Vision* remains one of the few pieces of substantial writing about the artist.[28]

So we are reminded, yet again, of the way in which Smith shaped our contemporary picture of the beginnings of European art in Australia. He created an orthodoxy against which all subsequent attempts to make sense of these beginnings have been set. Even some of Smith's provisional place markers have entered the art-historical lexicon—his phantom 'Port Jackson Painter' still walks among us.

Over the last half-century much of the visual record of the voyages sketched in *European Vision* has been catalogued and published; many of the artists introduced there have been the subject of monographic exhibitions; the art of the First Fleet has been closely studied. And there are a great many artists and ideas in the book that would reward detailed study. The story, too, could be carried forward into the period after 1850, when the close relationship between science, art and empirical naturalism continued to be important. I have tried to suggest that the *frontier*—one of the ideas implicit in *European Vision*—continued to move well beyond 1850 and will throw up species of the same questions that engaged Bernard Smith.

One definition of 'a classic' is a work that not only stands up over time, but that suggests new lines of enquiry in new contexts. That was to be one legacy of *European Vision* for Bernard Smith's own scholarly enterprise. It has continued to be its legacy for other workers and there is little doubt that future generations of scholars will find it an exemplar and a stimulus.

Finally I think we can now see, with some clarity, the important place *European Vision* occupies in Smith's journey as a thinker. The book is avowedly an investigation of images and the history of ideas—a work of art history. Yet it is also about *people*. As such, all of its parts embody a moral concern in Smith's wider intellectual position, a dimension that finds its most complete expression in *The Spectre of Truganini*. Smith says there that 'a culture cannot live on other people's universals. It requires moral values born of its own historical experience'.[29] That, surely, is an idea we continue to wrestle with in Australia.

I would suggest that the format of the Boyer Lectures—with their widely ranging cultural and public-intellectual heritage—allowed Smith to expand on the broad import of his enquiry. In *The Spectre of Truganini* he mused that all cultures:

> are challenged by the ethical values of external cultures, values which may be largely foreign to their own experience but ones which have also been evolved in the continuous struggle to be, and to remain, human.[30]

And this is the legacy of Bernard Smith: to help us to understand—in the context of art history and beyond—what it is to be, and to remain, human.

NOTES

1 Bernard Smith, *European Vision and the South Pacific, 1768–1850: A Study in the History of Art and Ideas* (first published by Clarendon Press, Oxford, 1960). In this chapter all references to *European Vision* are from the second edition (Yale University Press, New Haven, 1985). The reference here is to the preface to the second edition, p. ix. The reference to Manet comes from Smith's 1978 lecture *Art as Information: Reflections on the Art from Captain Cook's Voyages*, Sydney University Press for the Australian Academy of the Humanities, Sydney, 1979, p. 22.

2 Bernard Smith, *Imagining the Pacific: In the Wake of the Cook Voyages*, Miegunyah Press, Melbourne University Press, Melbourne, 1992, p. x.

3 Bernard Smith, *A Pavane for Another Time*, Macmillan, Melbourne, 2002, p. 371.

4 Smith, *European Vision and the South Pacific*, p. viii.

5 ibid., p. ix.

6 Ruth Pullin, *Eugene von Guérard: Nature Revealed*, exhibition catalogue, National Gallery of Victoria, Melbourne, 2011; Candice Bruce and Daniel Thomas, *Eugen von Guérard*, exhibition catalogue, Australian Gallery Directors' Council and Australian National Gallery, Canberra, 1980; Tim Bonyhady, *Images in Opposition: Australian Landscape Painting, 1801–1890*, Oxford University Press, Melbourne, 1985.

7 Smith, *European Vision and the South Pacific*, p. ix.

8 Smith, *Art as Information*, p. 4

9 Smith, *A Pavane for Another Time*, p. 240.

10 Smith, *European Vision and the South Pacific*, p. ix.

11 'CIHA 2008: Crossing Cultures: Conflict, Migration, Convergence', University of Melbourne, 2008.

12 Hans Belting, *An Anthropology of Images: Picture, Medium, Body*, Thomas Dunlap (transl.), Princeton University Press, Princeton, 2011, p. xx.

13 Smith, *European Vision and the South Pacific*, pp. 39–40.

14 ibid., p. vii.

15 ibid., p. xi.

16 ibid., p. 332.

17 Alan Moorehead, *The Fatal Impact*, Hamish Hamilton, London, 1966.

18 ibid., p. vii.

19 The conference was held in August 1996 and was organised by the Humanities Research Centre, Australian National University, Canberra. It led to the publication of Nicholas Thomas and Diane Losche (eds), *Double Vision: Art Histories and Colonial Histories in the Pacific*, Cambridge University Press, Cambridge, 1999.

20 ibid., p. 2.

21 ibid., p. 4.

22 Smith, *European Vision and the South Pacific*, p. vii.

23 Bernard Smith, *The Spectre of Truganini*, The 1980 Boyer Lectures, Australian Broadcasting Commission, Sydney, p. 18.

24 Andrew Sayers, 'Jump up Whitefellow: The Iconography of William Buckley', *Voices* (National Library of Australia, Canberra), vol. 6, no. 4, Summer 1996–97, pp. 14–21.

25 Smith, *Spectre of Truganini*, p. 26.

26 Greg Dening, *Mr Bligh's Bad Language: Passion, Power and Theatre on the Bounty*, Cambridge University Press, Cambridge, 1992.

27 Smith, *European Vision and the South Pacific*, p. 251.

28 Richard Neville, *Mr J. W. Lewin: Painter & Naturalist*, exhibition catalogue, University of New South Wales Press, Sydney, 2012, p. 211.

29 Smith, *Spectre of Truganini*, p. 11.

30 ibid., p. 11.

'My greatest debt':
Bernard Smith, the Warburg Institute, and the evolution of *European Vision and the South Pacific*

ROBERT W. GASTON

During the 1940s and 1950s, art history as a discipline at the University of Melbourne was created by several overseas-trained scholars and one Australian: Bernard Smith. The foundation Herald Professor of Fine Arts, the Anglo-Irish Joseph Burke (1913–1992), was an eighteenth-century specialist who held master's degrees from the University of London's King's College and the Courtauld Institute, and took another at Yale University.[1] Franz Philipp (1914–1970) was an Austrian Jewish refugee to England, forcibly transported to Australia on the *Dunera* in 1940. He had been close to completing his doctorate in art history in Vienna when he fled in 1939 to avoid death in the Nazi concentration camps. After the war Philipp recommenced undergraduate studies in history at Melbourne, graduating brilliantly in 1946.[2] In 1947 he and Burke began teaching fine arts, and were joined part-time by Ursula Hoff, who had taken her doctorate in art history from the University of Hamburg in 1935 under Erwin Panofsky's supervision.[3]

This group of European-born scholars was completed in 1955 by Bernard Smith, then a curator at the National Art Gallery of New South Wales (NAGNSW), who had finished his arts degree at the University of Sydney in 1952.[4] Smith, like Philipp, held a mere Bachelor's degree in 1955, but was the most able historian of Australian art and culture in the land, having already published extensively as a critic and curator.[5] Yet despite Smith's undeniable self-generation as critic and art historian, he was not entirely self-made, a fact he willingly acknowledged in his publications.

Acknowledgements appeared in prefaces to art books from the nineteenth century onwards, relics of the early modern author's dedicatory letter to a patron, a rhetorical exercise seeking financial patronage and publishing costs. In a 1987 study of anthropologists' publications, Eyal Ben-Ari concludes that:

> The *expressions of debts and gratitude* found in acknowledgements well bring out how anthropologists are enmeshed in webs of relations … and are subject to a range of duties and obligations … A number of special social and literary constraints guide the writing of acknowledgements.[6]

Ken Hyland, writing in 2004 on dissertation acknowledgements, notes how they 'provide writers with a unique rhetorical opportunity … to promote … their observance of the valued academic ideals of modesty, gratitude and appropriate self-effacement'. The decorum of acknowledgements is thus at once professionally assertive and obsequious.[7] A perfect example is in Robert Hobart Cust's preface to his 1906 book on the Renaissance artist Sodoma: 'The list of persons to whom I owe direct thanks for assistance is a long one, and contains many names distinguished in the world of Art and History'.[8] Contrast the sheer English arrogance of Ruskin in the *The Stones of Venice*: 'I do not care to point out the deficiencies of other works on this subject', however, 'my taking the pains so to examine what I had to describe, was a subject of grave surprise to my Italian friends'.[9]

Smith's first version of *European Vision*, published in the *Journal of the Warburg and Courtauld Institutes* (hereafter *JWCI*) in 1950,[10] certainly had its conceptual roots in his own thinking about art, imperialism and culture from 1940 onwards, as demonstrated by Peter Beilharz.[11] In the present essay I explore whether and how Smith's visits to the Warburg and Courtauld Institutes in London during 1948 and 1949 may have contributed to the formation of his ideas in the 1950 article, the 1960 book and certain later publications (Fig. 5).

The acknowledgements in Smith's 1950 article thank the British Council for funding, and 'Mr. Charles Mitchell for his interest and invaluable advice'.[12] Smith's reading of Mitchell in the *JWCI* on Zoffany's *Death of Cook*, of Edgar Wind's 'The Revolution in History Painting' and of essays by Erwin Panofsky and Rudolf Wittkower is amply documented in the article's footnotes. The 1960 book's acknowledgements record more extensive scholarly debts, but pride of place is again given to the Warburg group:

> It is a pleasant duty to mention that Dr K. Badt's *John Constable's Clouds*, Dr O. Pächt's 'Early Italian Nature Studies,' and Professor Wind's 'The Revolution in History Painting' have been most suggestive and are, in a sense, germinal to the central argument of the study ... My greatest debt is to the members of the staff of the Warburg Institute for their helpful interest in my work and their stimulating criticism—above all to the invaluable discussions and spendid advice of Mr Charles Mitchell.[13]

Smith's two versions of *European Vision* differ in scale and content. The 1950 article bears the hallmarks of the *JWCI*'s editorial policy. In Anthony Grafton's perceptive words:

> Many of the great Warburg scholars began their careers as writers in its [the *JWCI*'s] pages. And most of them adopted something like a house style. Their articles varied widely in subject and method, but all of them were terse and precise in style and largely devoid of sweeping theoretical statements. All of them rested on magnificent footnotes hewn from the original sources, dark and solid as Piranesi dungeons.[14]

In 1950 the *JWCI*'s editors were E. H. Gombrich, Rudolf Wittkower, Frances Yates, Anthony Blunt and T. S. R. Boase, the latter two from the Courtauld. Of these, Wittkower is cited in the article, and Boase is thanked in the 1960 acknowledgements for reading a partial draft of the book. Smith notes there that he followed the 'illuminating anticipations in early Italian art of processes studied in this book' offered by Otto Pächt in his 1950 *JWCI* article on 'Early Italian Nature Studies'.[15] Beilharz rightly includes Gombrich in his select group of Smith's 'elective affinities', although Smith is silent about Gombrich in both works I am considering.[16]

And we might well ponder the complexity of reconstructing how far Smith was influenced by the Warburg group, whom he so warmly thanks. I note the relevance of Edward Said's comment that:

> intellectual descent entails more than a linear (or vulgar) idea of influence. It also involves a basic tension—between continuity and discontinuity, amplification

> and refinement, or repetition and rebuttal—which the stress on innovation and development infuses into the relations between intellectuals, particularly between teachers and pupils.[17]

Let us begin our consideration of these Warburg-based scholars with Otto Pächt, a refugee from the Nazis who during the 1940s worked on fifteenth-century northern Italian and Netherlandish panel painting and manuscript illumination.[18] In his article 'Early Italian Nature Studies', Pächt argues that only in the fourteenth century did '*nature observation*, the study of the individual appearance of the external world, [become] of topical interest to Italian artists'.[19] Such representations, Pächt suggests:

> are not drawn from memory or in conformity with a more or less abstract mental image, but aim at real portrait *likeness*, i.e. . . . they have been produced by immediate transfer into pictorial form of the visual experience of an external object, as a direct recording of an optical impression, a kind of pictorial off-set from nature.[20]

Pächt's notion of 'real portrait likeness' is of small assistance to scholars working on eighteenth-century ideas. It begs the question of the representational ontology of a portrait, a topic that had seemed weirdly theoretical when I raised it with some portrait scholars in Washington as late as 1989. Smith wisely did not adopt Pächt's terminology, although he was influenced by what Pächt said about the novel accuracy of early Renaissance botanical drawing.

In both the 1950 and 1960 versions Smith used the appraisive terms 'faithful' or 'accurate' to denote the empirical nature of Joseph Banks' intentions in his visual cataloguing of flora, fauna and topography.[21] In 1960 Smith introduced the concept of 'typical' landscape, developing from Linnaeus's work on types.[22] Smith was concerned in 1950 with 'the picturesque or heroic landscape formulae' present in Cook's artists' work.[23] In 1960 he positioned this visual work between the Linnaean 'typical landscape' and Alexander von Humboldt's later research on the 'portrayal of characteristic types of scenery'.[24] He moved further away from Pächt's rudimentary understanding of 'nature studies'.

Smith was seeking to account for diverse artists' and travellers' visual perspectives, as conditioned by artistic styles, visual traditions and cultural receptions: an ambitious project that predated the theories of 'visual anthropology' and the 'period eye' that Michael Baxandall developed at the Warburg Institute between 1972 and 1980, extrapolating the latter from Gombrich's notion in *Art and Illusion* of the 'beholder's share'.[25] The touch of genius in Smith's argument was that Europe's envisioning of the South Pacific changed Europe's understanding of its own visual history and lived visuality. He did not acquire this insight from Gombrich.

In 1950 Smith had found illuminating research on representations of human 'marvels' in Rudolf Wittkower's publications, but Charles Mitchell is again given pride of place as adviser.[26] In his 2002 memoir Smith stated that Mitchell's questioning of his research presuppositions was the most significant event in the crystallisation of his ideas in London. Mitchell (1912–1995), a middle-class Oxford graduate in history and in philosophy, politics and ethics, was appointed to the Warburg in 1946, having previously worked at the National Maritime Museum, Greenwich.[27] He was drawn to the Warburg refugees, partly by his shared hatred of the Nazis and partly by his fascination with Warburgian scholarship. Mitchell, along with D. J. Gordon and Frances Yates, helped Oxbridge scholars to enter the intellectual world of the Warburg by facilitating their contact with its inspiring director, Fritz Saxl (1890–1948).[28] Fluent in German, Mitchell had completed his BLitt thesis at Oxford on Grünewald with the partial assistance of Saxl.[29] Mitchell had a daunting scholarly range, covering fifteenth-century Italian humanism, eighteenth-century English art, and modernism. He owned a folio of Picasso's *Vollard suite*. On occasion he poked fun at the lack of commitment to twentieth-century art among some of his Warburg colleagues.[30] Mitchell was notably encouraging to young Australian scholars during the 1960s and 1970s (including Virginia Spate, Jaynie Anderson, Margaret Manion and the writer, whom he appointed to teach art history at Bryn Mawr in 1970), and visited Australia in 1970, attending a memorable lunch arranged by Ann Galbally at John Olsen's studio at Cottlesbridge. Mitchell marvelled at the particularity of the Australian landscape, having visualised it partly through the lens provided by Smith.

Smith recorded in 2002 that Wittkower, then deputy director of the Warburg, had put him in touch with Mitchell, who 'began to redeem my view of Englishmen'. He was a 'teacher of genius':

> The first thing he said to me was, 'So you want to study the Europeans in the Pacific. Tell me what the Europeans gave to the Pacific apart from the Bible and

> syphilis.' He kept that sort of thing up all the time, constantly challenging my critical judgment.[31]

Mitchell directed Smith to R. W. Frantz's scholarly work of 1934 on English travellers and to Panofsky's article on Poussin's Arcadian landscape.[32] But Mitchell's own work on the fifteenth-century antiquarian traveller Cyriacus of Ancona, who sketched foreign topography and artifacts, made him especially relevant to Smith, as did Mitchell's publications on eighteenth-century history painting.[33] And Mitchell's terse, gently argumentative English prose style deeply influenced Smith.

Kurt Badt was another Warburg-based scholar, whose work ranged from Renaissance to seventeenth-century Dutch painting and modernism. Smith used Badt's brilliant 1950 book on Constable's cloud studies. Here he learnt about Luke Howard's research of 1802–03 on cloud formations, and compared Augustus Earle's pictures to those of Constable. Constable's idea that 'By a *close* observation of nature, the artist discovers qualities existing in her which have never been portrayed before' had a bearing on Smith's work on Australian images.[34] And Badt's conviction that 'the scientific insight of the Renaissance was concerned with space' may have hardened a similar conviction in Smith, who remained oblivious to recent research that questioned such an exclusive emphasis.[35] Smith doubtless absorbed Badt's 1959 *JWCI* essay on Raphael's Vatican fresco *Fire in the Borgo*, where he constructed a fresh iconographic analysis on the foundation of the 'exact description' and 'careful observation' of the fresco offered by several early modern art critics.[36] Here Badt retrospectively applied modern scientific theory to Renaissance art by correlating two critical modes that were incommensurate: early modern rhetorical ekphrasis was not really like modern scientific observation.[37] Smith did not follow Badt into this analytical cul-de-sac.

Both Rudolf Wittkower and Charles Mitchell had directed Smith to Panofsky's classic essay on Poussin's landscape. Today, Panofsky's pioneering 1920s work on perspective has been historicised, and diverse accounts of the discovery and influence of single-point Renaissance perspective have lately emerged.[38] In Smith's comprehension of perspective's history, the 'scientific' Renaissance phase remains frozen as a historical fact. We may now compare Paul Carter's summary in 1996 of Francastel's view that 'Brunelleschi's perspectival rationalisation of the third dimension was not only a new method of representing space: it transformed the social space itself'.[39] In 1987 Carter had also criticised Smith's reading of Sir Francis Bacon's thoughts on sea voyages and diaries of them.[40] Ian McLean's 1999 essay 'Under Saturn: Melancholy and the Colonial Imagination' has some Panofskian insights to offer, but, broadly speaking, the early modern territory in Smith's historical imagination remains unexplored.[41] Recent work on early modern 'social space' and its genesis in visualising habits, as in Marvin Trachtenberg's publications, has not been used by scholars of Australian visual culture.[42] Thus Enlightenment thought is allowed to stand as a roadblock, a false and late starting point. Smith knew that the roots of what he was studying in *European Vision* lay deep in Renaissance Europe's soil, but his persistent faith in Marx and Jack Lindsay left him with an immutable impression of what Renaissance thinkers and artists had achieved.

When Smith encountered the Warburg group they were using their knowledge of Renaissance visual culture to identify, by contrast, the new and 'revolutionary' visual culture emerging in eighteenth-century Europe. Smith acknowledged their contributions, but did not proceed further into Renaissance scholarship. He had the half of the equation that he needed, or so he initially thought.

The most fascinating episode in Smith's interaction with the Warburg group arose later, from E. H. Gombrich's complimentary reaction to Smith's 1998 book, *Modernism's History*, which in 2002 Smith characterised as 'the book I regard as my most important contribution to the history of art' (Fig. 6).[43] Gombrich had published his fundamental essay 'Renaissance Artistic Theory and the Development of Landscape Painting' in 1953, but it was not cited by Smith in 1960.[44] Gombrich's theoretical book *Art and Illusion*, with its text completed in 1959, appeared in 1960, just too late for *European Vision*. I have to disagree with Rex Butler's idea that 'Smith wrote *European Vision* under the guidance of Ernst Gombrich, whose *Art and Illusion* addresses similar kinds of questions'.[45] This is certainly not true of Smith's 1960 edition. The second edition, of 1984, would tell a different story.

In 1998, in *Modernism's History*, Smith praises aspects of Gombrich's *Story of Art* (first edition 1950, and some 200 editions to 2000) and *Art and Illusion*, and admires Gombrich's humanist, internationalist viewpoint. But he trumps this with his own Australian, Polynesian and Melanesian perspective on modern European art.[46] Smith lives dangerously in criticising Gombrich's account of modernism while praising Blunt's work on Picasso, a fatal mistake to make with Gombrich, who had scant respect for Blunt's scholarship, an opinion not shared by all of the Warburg group.[47] Gombrich had served during the war as an intelligence monitor of Axis broadcasts, however his personal political views and his reaction to learning of Blunt's spying for the Russians, something known in intelligence circles from the early 1960s and made public in 1979, remain unclear. Margot Wittkower recorded that, in the 1930s, 'many of the Warburg scholars were very sympathetic to the Left, though none of them was a Communist'.[48]

Smith records in 2002 that a lecture on Renaissance sculpture by Gombrich at the Courtauld in 1948 included:

> a throw away comment, 'but then all art is conceptual'. It acted as a revelation. I shall never forget it ... Gombrich unwittingly provided me with a paradigm that seems to have guided my work for the next two years, *though I was quite unaware of it at the time*.[49]

In 1948 Gombrich had not yet emerged as the dominant scholar in the field. He shared some of the theory interests that activated Wind and Panofsky. Wind was concerned with art and philosophy, science, and history.[50] Panofsky offered a history of art theory combined with a new formal method of analysing images.[51] In the 1930s and 1940s, Gombrich seemed on a similar path, but diverged into visual psychology, establishing himself as a major theorist, widely read by scientists. Gombrich opposed Panofsky's interpretations of images, regarding them as overstating the presumed relations between artists and humanists. Gombrich trained a generation of art historians to be sceptical, in a rather empirical English way, about the historical meanings of images, and about Panofsky's 'disguised symbolism' in particular.[52]

In J. B. Trapp's phrase, Gombrich possessed a 'lambent' intelligence, one that subtly radiated through disciplines after 1960, elevating the study of the visual from being an hermetically closed discipline based on connoisseurship and iconography, into one that became a focal point for the study of visual experience in human life.[53] Gombrich became the most widely read art historian in disciplines outside art history, a position Smith certainly enjoyed in Australia.

A full study of the Smith–Gombrich correspondence would be necessary to afford a deeper account of the relations between these two scholars over time. But as I see it, in 1998 Smith was deeply affected by Gombrich's private response to *Modernism's History*, which was being ostentatiously ignored by international scholars, though published by Yale University Press. Sixty-three review copies drew but a single response in the United States and little attention in Britain.[54] Smith was outraged, certain that scholars were suppressing the book because he was an Australian, a colonial daring to re-conceptualise art history's stylistic terminology, substituting 'the Formalesque' for 'modernism'. Smith should surely have realised that style names are virtually immoveable, regardless of the merits of the case. Too many senior art historians have too much published work invested to contemplate rendering any one of these style names obsolete. Smith's revisionist study of modernism was bound to run into a brick wall. As he wrote to the present writer in 2004: 'As you say, I do not expect my case for the Formalesque to be accepted by the art establishment. But I do hope that it will not be met by the silence of contempt. I long for a discourse'.[55] Gombrich's letter gave Smith hope that powerful intellects like his own would open that discourse.

Yet Gombrich's response was more complex than Smith could readily admit. Gombrich praised Smith privately and also in his own posthumously published book *The Preference for the Primitive* of 2002, but there offered a critical account that substantially undermined Smith's. This was a characteristic response from Gombrich. He would encourage one's research in a genuinely collegial manner, but would always have in reserve his own theory, leading to a distinctly Gombrichian reading. Smith's *Modernism's History* offered not only 'the Formalesque', but a bold description of Aby Warburg's work and its relation with modernism. Smith was challenging Gombrich on his own turf, and Gombrich responded by inferring that he had anticipated Smith's argument, and that Smith did not understand either modernism or Warburg.[56] It is touching to see Smith dedicate his 2002 memoir to Gombrich and to identify him as an important teacher. Smith struck back, though, in reviewing Gombrich's *Preference for the Primitive* in 2004, protesting that he too had taken on board Gombrich's friend Karl Popper's concept of the 'logic of situations'. He sided with Clifford Geertz's critical review of Gombrich's book, thus having the last word.[57] Yet Smith reiterated his debt to Gombrich in his introduction to *The Formalesque* of 2007.[58]

But Smith never really grasped that Gombrich was not an enthusiastic follower of Warburg. Gombrich recoiled, as he stated in 1999, from some of

Warburg's notions, especially his 'faith in the historical psychology of human expression', which had led to 'national, racial or cultural' stereotyping under the Nazis.[59] And the only sense in which Smith had an idea in common with Warburg was in their mutual attention to art's 'social context'. But Smith's Marxism held no attraction for either Warburg or Gombrich.[60] Gombrich's Viennese training gave him a perspective on the Hamburg group: Warburg, Panofsky and Wind. Gombrich was, like Smith himself, a critical outsider with an alternative, and inimitable, methodology. As Perloff has noted, Gombrich stated in 1999: 'Ich bin kein Engländer', declaring his 'sense of being a citizen nowhere but rather a member of an intellectual community that knew no national borders'.[61] The Warburg refugees respected a colonial scholar like Smith, but reserved the right to contest his ideas. Smith was correct in detecting cold colonialist superiority in Blunt, and a warm generosity among the Warburg group.[62] But I think he was wrong in suspecting that the international abreaction to his *Modernism's History* in 1998 was a manifestation of colonialism. And like all great scholars Gombrich saw in Smith's idea an opportunity to develop an idea of his own. Both men were of the *auteur* variety of scholar: men who claimed, with some justification, to be self-generating thinkers, like those great artists who, art history claimed, had not merely surpassed their masters, but eclipsed their very existence. One could view this self-perception as a kind of romanticist obsession with originality. Yet it is true that each man in his own way acknowledged his indebtedness to others, Smith being perhaps more forthcoming than Gombrich.[63]

The Warburg Institute was, as Gombrich tirelessly explained, not essentially a place for studying art history: it was dedicated to research in the 'classical tradition' and the 'civilisation' of the Renaissance. In 1967, when I began my doctorate there, it still had the intimidating atmosphere of Germanic scholarship that Smith encountered. Gombrich's staff and PhD work-in-progress seminar was a nerve-wracking experience, matched in its critical intensity by Arnaldo Momigliano's ancient history seminar. Both seminar chairs invited some scholars, whose work would be publicly demolished as object lessons to one's students. Grafton comments on how Gombrich and Otto Kurz, my supervisor, had viewed British and American scholarship in the 1950s:

> As students, my contemporaries and I looked up in awe and bafflement at these great figures. And we were not wrong to find them scary. The critic Marjorie Perloff ... recalled what ... Ernst Gombrich ... [and] Otto Kurz used to say about England in the fifties, in their own circle: 'One made fun of almost all British art historians—especially Kenneth Clark and Anthony Blunt—who were said to *know nothing*. One despised Bernard Berenson ... But the greatest contempt in this almost exclusively émigré circle was for American graduate students, who obviously lacked the languages and historical knowledge to do the work required at the Warburg Institute or at Oxford.[64]

At the Vienna School of Art History, where Kurz, Gombrich and Franz Philipp had studied, classical and modern European languages were assumed in art history training; teaching began with reading original medieval and Renaissance documents, and then moved to object-based study in art museums. As Gombrich has commented, the Vienna department was founded on 'a manifesto against amateurism', namely belle-lettristic art writing.[65] Yet the Viennese art historians were passionate scholars of art theory and, like Smith, skilled historians of culture. With the exception of Friedrich Antal, they were not drawn to Marxism. Escaping to London they practised a discipline initially inaccessible to most British art writers.[66] To some Oxbridge scholars addicted to 'straightforward historical narrative' the Warburg approach was tainted with theory. Grafton describes the great ancient historian Arnaldo Momigliano being puzzled when he arrived at Oxford in 1939: 'It was enough to mention the word "idea" to be given the address of the Warburg Institute'.[67] The Oxbridge training of my history lecturers at Melbourne (1961–64) dictated a similar hostile attitude to 'German theory'. I was warned in my honours year to stay away from ideas and to concentrate on narrative.

The Warburg émigrés quickly spotted the British aversion to theory, and devoted their journal to 'historical' contributions. Thus they could draw Oxbridge scholars into their embrace, while subtly teaching them how to do German-Austrian-style iconography.[68] They learnt to lecture in elegant English, but in their homes they were back in old Vienna, Berlin or Hamburg. Gombrich received a knighthood in 1972, yet the gulf between the lofty social world of the British-founded Courtauld Institute and that of the Warburg was painfully obvious. Gombrich was a middle-class Viennese of Jewish extraction. His family were Lutheran converts, his mother close to Freud and Mahler.[69] But in England he was initially just another intellectually gifted refugee. Many of the early Courtauld students radiated British class privilege; there were, as Miranda Carter says, many 'nice young ladies' studying there in the 1940s and 1950s. By the 1960s, however, the Courtauld had become a powerhouse of art-historical scholarship, using European refugee scholars and their newly trained British students, shedding forever its 'amateur' status.[70] However, when Anthony Blunt enrolled me at the Courtauld in 1967, descending the Adam staircase in dressing-gown, slippers and silk cravat, he behaved like an elegant duke disturbed at his breakfast. We doctoral students at the Warburg in the 1960s were, with a couple of sleek exceptions, a variegated bunch of regional Brits and colonials, ill-equipped for cocktail parties and gossipy small talk.

Expats like Smith and, I might say, myself strove to maintain our personal dignity at the Courtauld in those early days. But the Warburg was always an intellectual haven: a comforting and rewarding destination for the alterity that British colonialism had shaped in us. And so it remains today. And this was where Smith conceived his first, wonderful version of *European Vision*.

I should like to thank Jaynie Anderson, Kate Challis, Leonie Gombrich, John Mitchell and Claudia Wedepohl for help with obtaining photographs, and permission to use them.

NOTES

1 Bernard Smith, 'The Teaching of Fine Arts in Australian Universities: The Present Situation', *The Australian University*, vol. 13, no. 1, May 1975, p. 8; Sheridan Palmer, 'Intersecting Cultures: European Influences in the Fine Arts: Melbourne 1940–1960', PhD thesis, University of Melbourne, 2004, pp. 82–93; Jaynie Anderson, 'Interrogating Joe Burke and His Legacy', *Melbourne Art Journal*, no. 8, 2005, pp. 88–101; Sheridan Palmer, *Centre of the Periphery: Three European Art Historians in Melbourne*, Australian Scholarly Publishing, North Melbourne, 2008.

2 Jaynie Anderson, 'Art History's History in Melbourne: Franz Philipp in Correspondence with Arthur Boyd', *Australian and New Zealand Journal of Art*, vol. 1, no. 2, 2000, pp. 111–29; Monica Lausch, 'Franz Philipp and the Vienna School of Art History in Australia', *Melbourne Art Journal*, no. 8, 2005, pp. 116–27; Palmer, *Centre of the Periphery*.

3 Jaynie Anderson, 'In Homage to Ursula Hoff, on her Ninetieth Birthday', *Art in Australia*, vol. 38, no. 2, 1999, pp. 250–7; Palmer, Intersecting Cultures; Palmer, *Centre of the Periphery*.

4 For an earlier bibliography, see Peter Beilharz, *Imagining the Antipodes: Culture, Theory and the Visual in the Work of Bernard Smith*, Cambridge University Press, Cambridge, 1997, p. 194, n. 2; Sheridan Palmer, 'The Importance of being Bernard Smith', *Art and Australia*, vol. 46, no. 4, Winter 2009, pp. 576–9; Sheridan Palmer, 'The Importance of *Leitmotifs* and Distance in the Biography of Bernard Smith', *Australian Historical Studies*, no. 43, no. 1, March 2012, p. 38.

5 The art history doctorate had been a nineteenth-century German professional qualification, taken up by the Americans. But even in the United States in the 1930s the PhD was 'not the goal of graduate studies at Princeton', where 'an M.F.A. had the job-getting power of a doctorate'. See Craig H. Smyth and Peter M. Lukehart (eds), *The Early Years of Art History in the United States*, Department of Art and Archaeology, Princeton University, Princeton, 1993, p. 41. In Australia the Master's degree was, through the 1960s, tied to a weighty thesis that brought professional respect.

6 Eyal Ben-Ari, 'On Acknowledgements in Ethnographies', *Journal of Anthropological Research*, vol. 43, no. 1, Spring 1987, pp. 63–84.

7 Ken Hyland, 'Graduates' Gratitude: The Generic Structure of Dissertation Acknowledgements', *English for Specific Purposes*, vol. 23, no. 3, 2004, pp. 303–24.

8 Robert Henry Hobart Cust, *Giovanni Antonio Bazzi, Hitherto Usually Styled 'Sodoma': The Man and the Painter, 1477–1549: A Study*, John Murray, London, 1906, p. ix.

9 John Ruskin, *The Stones of Venice*, 3 vols, new edn, George Allen, London, 1898, vol. 1, pp. v–vi.

10 Bernard Smith, 'European Vision and the South Pacific', *Journal of the Warburg and Courtauld Institutes*, vol. 13, nos 1–2, 1950, pp. 65–100.

11 Beilharz, *Imagining the Antipodes*, pp. 64–70.

12 Smith, 'European Vision and the South Pacific', p. 65.

13 Bernard Smith, *European Vision and the South Pacific, 1768–1850: A Study in the History of Art and Ideas*, Clarendon Press, Oxford, 1960, p. vi.

14 Anthony Grafton, 'Momigliano at the Warburg: The Origins of a Style', *The American Scholar*, vol. 73, no. 4, Autumn 2004, p. 130.

15 Smith, *European Vision and the South Pacific*, p. 20, n. 3.

16 Beilharz, *Imagining the Antipodes*, pp. 186–7.

17 Edward Said, *Beginnings: Intention and Method*, Johns Hopkins University Press, Baltimore, 1975, p. 15, quoted in Ben-Ari, 'On Acknowledgements in Ethnographies', p. 73.

18 See Lee Sorensen, 'Pächt, Otto', in *Dictionary of Art Historians*, www.dictionaryofarthistorians.org/pachto.htm, viewed 3 September 2013.

19 Otto Pächt, 'Early Italian Nature Studies and the Early Calendar Landscape', *Journal of the Warburg and Courtauld Institutes*, vol. 13, nos 1–2, 1950, pp. 16–17.

20 ibid.

21 Smith, 'European Vision and the South Pacific', pp. 67–70; Smith, *European Vision and the South Pacific*, p. 4.

22 Smith, 'European Vision and the South Pacific', p. 70, n. 1. Linnaeus is mentioned in relation to his pupil Daniel Solander, who contracted Joseph Banks as his botanist for the voyage.

23 Smith, 'European Vision and the South Pacific', p. 73.

24 Smith, *European Vision and the South Pacific*, especially pp. 151–7.

25 Michael Baxandall, *Painting and Experience in Fifteenth-Century Italy: A Primer in the Social History of Pictorial Style*, Clarendon Press, Oxford, 1972; Michael Baxandall, *The Limewood Sculptors of Renaissance Germany*, Yale University Press, New Haven, 1980; on Gombrich's 'beholder's share', see his *Art and Illusion: A Study in the Psychology of*

Pictorial Representation, Phaidon, London, 1959, pp. 154–69, 185, 246, 329.

26 Rudolf Wittkower, 'Marvels of the East: A Study in the History of Monsters', *Journal of the Warburg and Courtauld Institutes*, no. 5, 1942, pp. 159–97, cited by Smith in 'European Vision and the South Pacific', p. 87, n. 1.

27 See Jaynie Anderson, 'Obituary: Professor Charles Mitchell', *The Independent*, 31 October 1995, www.independent.co.uk/news/people/obituary-professor-charles-mitchell-1580287.html, viewed 6 September 2013.

28 See D. J. Gordon (ed.), *Fritz Saxl, 1890–1948: A Volume of Memorial Essays from his Friends in England*, Nelson, London, 1957.

29 A fact I learnt from Anderson, 'Obituary: Professor Charles Mitchell'.

30 For more detail, see Robert W. Gaston, 'Leonard Barkan, *Unearthing the Past: Archaeology and Aesthetics in the Making of Renaissance Culture*' [book review], *Art Bulletin*, vol. 82, no. 4, December 2000, p. 770. At Bryn Mawr, Mitchell required me to teach a graduate seminar on modern art (I chose Paul Klee) in addition to normal duties in early Christian and Byzantine art.

31 Bernard Smith, *A Pavane for Another Time*, Macmillan, Sydney, 2002, pp. 247–8. Smith also praised Wittkower because, apart from his polyglot learning, 'He did not appear to appreciate the fact that I was merely a colonial—a modern Antipodean'.

32 ibid., pp. 248–9.

33 Smith cited Charles Mitchell's 'Zoffany's *Death of Captain Cook*', *Burlington Magazine*, vol. 84, no. 492, March 1944, pp. 56–63, twice in his 1950 article (pp. 79, 92) and Charles Mitchell, 'Benjamin West's "Death of General Wolfe" and the Popular History Piece', *Journal of the Warburg and Courtauld Institutes*, vol. 7, 1944, pp. 20–33, and additionally in Smith, *European Vision and the South Pacific*, pp. 33, 83–4; on Cyriacus, see Edward G. Bodnar and Charles Mitchell (eds), *Cyriacus of Ancona's Journeys in the Propontis and Northern Aegean, 1444–1445*, American Philosophical Society, Philadelphia, 1972; Francesco Scalamonti, *Vita viri clarissimi et famosissimi Kyriaci Anconitani*, Charles Mitchell and Edward G. Bodnar (eds and transl.), American Philosophical Society, Philadelphia, 1996.

34 Kurt Badt, *John Constable's Clouds*, Routledge & Kegan Paul, London, 1950, p. 73. Badt's discussion of Ruskin's account in *Modern Painters* of Turner's landscapes (ibid., pp. 6–7), relating to the 'faithful representation' of 'the appearance of objects' was of interest to Smith, as was his observing that Turner's 'pictures were not subject to the principles of objectivity, normality and the typical'.

35 Badt, *John Constable's Clouds*, p. 21: '... A man like Leonardo or Piero della Francesca was intent on raising painting to the status of a science, whilst Goethe was intent on delivering art and science from their exclusive isolation ...' Compare this, on place seen in relation to space, with Edward S. Casey, *The Fate of Place: A Philosophical Inquiry*, University of California Press, Berkeley, 1997; Robert W. Gaston, 'Sacred Place and Liturgical Space: Florence's Renaissance Churches', in J. Paoletti and Roger Crum (eds), *Renaissance Florence: A Social History*, Cambridge University Press, New York, 2006, pp. 331–52, 566–82; Robert W. Gaston, 'Some Meditations on Place and Space', in David R. Marshall (ed.), *Art, Site and Spectacle: Studies in Early Modern Visual Culture*, The Fine Arts Network, Melbourne, 2007, pp. 9–13.

36 Kurt Badt, 'Raphael's *Incendio del Borgo*', *Journal of the Warburg and Courtauld Institutes*, no. 22, 1959, pp. 35–59.

37 See Peter Wagner (ed.), *Icons, Texts, Iconotexts: Essays on Ekphrasis and Intermediality*, Walter de Gruyter, Berlin, 1996.

38 Erwin Panofsky, *Perspective as Symbolic Form*, Christopher S. Wood (transl. and ed., with introduction), Zone Books, New York, 1991; among recent revisionist studies are Leonhard Schmeiser, *Die Erfindung der Zentralperspektive und die Entstehung der neuzeitlichen Wissenschaft*, W. Fink, Munich, 2002; Samuel Y. Edgerton, *The Mirror, the Window, and the Telescope: How Renaissance Linear Perspective Changed our Vision of the Universe*, Cornell University Press, Ithaca, NY, 2009; Monique Dubois, *Zentralperspektive in der florentinischen Kunstpraxis des 15. Jahrhunderts*, M. Imhof, Petersberg, 2010; John Shannon Hendrix and Charles H. Carman (eds), *Renaissance Theories of Vision*, Ashgate, Farnham, UK, 2010.

39 Paul Carter, 'Second Sight: Looking Back as Colonial Vision', Franz Philipp Memorial Lecture 1995, *Australian Journal of Art*, no. 13, 1996, p. 12, n. 11.

40 Paul Carter, *The Road to Botany Bay: An Exploration of Landscape and History*, University of Minnesota Press, Minneapolis, 1987, p. 142; cf. p. 43.

41 Ian McLean, 'Under Saturn: Melancholy and the Colonial Imagination', in Nicholas Thomas and Diane Losche (eds), *Double Vision: Art Histories and Colonial Histories in the Pacific*, Cambridge University Press, Cambridge, 1998, pp. 131–62. The first edition of Smith's *Place, Taste, and Tradition* (Ure Smith, Sydney, 1945) proves his early acquisition of some German-Austrian art theory on

Renaissance and Baroque art. This Renaissance material expanded in his essays from 1962 to 1986 in *The Death of the Artist as Hero: Essays in History and Culture*, Oxford University Press, Melbourne, 1988; on this collection see Beilharz, *Imagining the Antipodes*, pp. 127–54.

42 Marvin Trachtenberg, *Dominion of the Eye: Urbanism, Art, and Power in Early Modern Florence*, Cambridge University Press, Cambridge, 1997.

43 Smith, *A Pavane for Another Time*, p. v.

44 Ernst H. Gombrich, 'The Renaissance Theory of Art and the Rise of Landscape', *Gazette des Beaux-Arts*, series 6, no. 41, 1953, pp. 335–60: see J. B. Trapp, *E. H. Gombrich: A Bibliography*, Phaidon, London, 2000, p. 24. Gombrich had completed the study by 1950, but evidently did not show it to Smith.

45 Rex Butler, 'Australian Art History and Revisionism', in *A Secret History of Australian Art*, Craftsman House, Sydney, 2002, p. 107.

46 Bernard Smith, *Modernism's History: A Study in Twentieth-Century Art and Ideas*, Yale University Press, New Haven, 1998, p. 3. See p. 6, on Smith's claim to a 'synthetic view', a 'broader viewpoint', of European modernism than that possessed by Gombrich. On Gombrich's resistance to being defined as a Jew, see below.

47 Miranda Carter, *Anthony Blunt: His Lives*, Pan Books, London, 2001, pp. 142–3, citing Richard Krautheimer's praise.

48 ibid., p. 143; for the unsubstantiated allegation that Blunt's student Enriqueta Harris, who was employed at the Ministry of Information during the war and in the photographic collection at the Warburg after the war, had been, from the 1930s onward, a Russian spy, see Jimmy Burns, *Papa Spy: Love, Faith, and Betrayal in Wartime Spain*, Walker & Company, New York, 2009, pp. 243, 333, 378. Her brother, the art dealer and MI5 agent Tomás Harris, widely suspected of being a Soviet agent, was a close friend of Blunt. Harris died in a car accident in 1964, just prior to Blunt's confession, and was never interrogated.

49 Smith, *A Pavane for Another Time*, p. 240.

50 On Wind, see Edgar Wind, *The Eloquence of Symbols: Studies in Humanist Art*, ed. Jaynie Anderson, Clarendon Press, Oxford, 1983; Edgar Wind, *Hume and the Heroic Portrait: Studies in Eighteenth-century Imagery*, ed. Jaynie Anderson, Clarendon Press, Oxford, 1986; Consolato Latella, 'Wind and Riegl: The Meaning of a "Problematical" Grammar', *Journal of Art Historiography*, no. 1, December 2009, www.arthistoriography.wordpress.com, viewed 11 September 2013.

51 See Irving Lavin (ed.), *Meaning in the Visual Arts: Views from the Outside: A Centennial Commemoration of Erwin Panofsky (1892–1968)*, Institute for Advanced Study, Princeton, 1995; Robert W. Gaston, 'Erwin Panofsky and the Classical Tradition', *International Journal of the Classical Tradition*, vol. 4, no. 4, Spring 1998, pp. 613–23.

52 On Panofsky and Gombrich, see Gaston, 'Erwin Panofsky and the Classical Tradition'.

53 Trapp, *E. H. Gombrich: A Bibliography*, p. 7.

54 These details given by Smith in '*The Preference for the Primitive* and on Writing Art History in Australia', *Third Text*, vol. 18, no. 5, 2004, pp. 515. Cf. Bernard Smith, *The Formalesque: A Guide to Modern Art and its History*, Macmillan, Melbourne, 2007, p. 14.

55 Bernard Smith to Robert W. Gaston, 25 August 2004.

56 Ernst H. Gombrich, *The Preference for the Primitive: Episodes in the History of Western Taste and Art*, Phaidon, London, 2002, p. 177: '... when that book [Smith's] came out this present chapter had long been written. I have read *Modernism's History* with much profit and admiration, but I wonder whether this theory offers a sufficient explanation for the momentous change in orientation the very notion of art underwent in the period concerned. I should like to argue that the philosophical speculations to which Bernard Smith refers did not arise in a void, as it were. They were connected with what Karl Popper calls the "logic of situations", the situation in which artists find themselves.' At p. 217 Gombrich attacks Smith's idea that Picasso's *Demoiselles d'Avignon* 'borrowed' from African 'artefacts' for 'formal reasons', preferring Picasso's account, with his own Freudian 'taboo' reading, of the African works appearing 'to embody a mysterious menace or magic power which made all traditional works seem irrelevant'. Gombrich adds: 'Conceivably Smith even underrated the support this movement [Modernism] received from examples of other styles and traditions. The genre of devotional art might also be considered a testing ground for this hypothesis ...'

57 Smith, '*The Preference for the Primitive* and on Writing Art History in Australia', p. 515: '... like Gombrich himself, I have read Popper "with much profit and admiration", particularly on his concept of the "logic of the situation", for it is central to his account of historical explanation formulating my concept of the Formalesque as a period style. Many examples from *Modernism's History* might be cited. I shall cite but one ... "The emergence of the Formalesque as a period style is basically the story of the reduction of the concept of style to that of form under the overarching conditions of cultural

imperialism" ... I agree reluctantly with Clifford Geertz's criticism, in the *New York Review of Books* (26 September 2002), of the "psychological law of gravity" by means of which Gombrich seeks to clinch his case at the end of the book. But I do not agree with the weight that Geertz gives to it to berate the book's value.'

58 Smith, *The Formalesque*, p. 14: 'Sir Ernst Gombrich, unquestionably the greatest art historian of the second half of the 20th century, read a copy sent to him by the publisher and wrote a letter to me shortly after he had read it in which he said: "I was very pleased to receive your wonderful book on *Modernism's History*, which I very much admire. I am sure that it will remain the focus of discussion for many years to come."' Smith goes on to note Gombrich's *The Preference for the Primitive* of 2002, its criticism of one of Smith's arguments, and his acceptance of that as valid. He adds: 'It was Gombrich's interest in my book that encouraged me to write the present one, in which I give the Formalesque a much more up-front role, whereas in *Modernism's History* it is embedded deeply in empirical history'. In 2007 Smith clearly sought to minimise Gombrich's critical disagreement with *Modernism's History*, in order to gain traction from Gombrich's (albeit private) support for his exploration of the Formalesque.

59 Ernst H. Gombrich, 'Aby Warburg: His Aims and Methods: An Anniversary Lecture', *Journal of the Warburg and Courtauld Institutes*, no. 26, 1999, p. 275.

60 See Ernst H. Gombrich, 'Arnold Hauser, *The Social History of Art*' [book review], *Art Bulletin*, no. 35, 1953, pp. 79–84; also his defence of Johan Huizinga's rejection of Marx, in 'The High Seriousness of Play: Reflections on *Homo ludens* by J. Huizinga (1872–1945)', in Ernst H. Gombrich, *Tributes: Interpreters of our Cultural Tradition*, Cornell University Press, Ithaca, NY, 1984, pp. 151–2.

61 See Marjorie Perloff, *The Vienna Paradox: A Memoir*, New Directions Books, New York, 2004, p. 139, cited in Grafton, 'Momigliano at the Warburg', p. 129. Perloff (on pp. 77–8) discusses the complexity of Gombrich's saying, in an interview with Deutschland Radio in 1999, 'I am what Hitler called a Jew. That's what I am'. Perloff comments (p. 82): '... Gombrich's disclaimer ... should more accurately read, 'I am what most "native" German writers and intellectuals called a Jew'.

62 Smith, in *A Pavane for Another Time* (p. 246), comments on showing Blunt *Place, Taste, and Tradition*: '"Oh", he said, in a most supercilious manner, "I see you have neo-Surrealist developments in Australia", referring to one of the chapter sections of the book. It was the way he said it. I riled in silent fury. In England, class differences, I soon came to realise, were more powerful than political affinities. A colonial was a colonial whatever his politics'. Cf. Palmer, *Centre of the Periphery*, p. 211, and Carter, *Anthony Blunt*, pp. 406–7. Carter (pp. 366, 369) also gives evidence of Blunt not exercising class snobbery with students. Colonialist prejudice, though, may then either have been a subset of class prejudice (as Smith implies) or a distinct category of prejudice, not exclusive to the English upper class.

63 On Gombrich's 'reticence' about his owing key ideas to Curt Bühler and Heinrich Gomperz, see Richard Woodfield, 'Ernst Gombrich: Iconology and the "Linguistics of the Image"', *Journal of Art Historiography*, vol. 5, December 2011, http://arthistoriography.wordpress.com/, viewed 11 September 2013 .

64 Perloff, *The Vienna Paradox*, p. 219; Grafton, 'Momigliano at the Warburg', p. 129.

65 Ernst H. Gombrich and Didier Eribon, *Looking for Answers: Conversations on Art and Science*, Harry N. Abrams, New York, 1993, p. 39.

66 Carter quotes John Summerson on encountering the Warburg scholars in the 1930s: 'We found ourselves faced with a range and quality of scholarship we had never met before' (Carter, *Anthony Blunt*, p. 142). See Ian Verstegen, 'John White's and John Shearman's Viennese Art Historical Method', *Journal of Art Historiography*, no. 1, December 2009, arthistoriography.wordpress.com/, viewed 11 September 2013, on the postwar influence of Johannes Wilde at the Courtauld, and his English students' aversion to 'theoretical methodology'.

67 Anthony Grafton, 'The History of Ideas: Precept and Practice, 1950–2000 and Beyond', *Journal of the History of Ideas*, vol. 67, no. 1, January 2006, p. 12.

68 Carter, *Anthony Blunt*, p. 143: Gombrich said that Saxl hoped to cure his 'self-taught' English 'fans' of their 'insularity' and 'amateurishness'.

69 Gombrich and Eribon, *Looking for Answers*, pp. 14–33; cf. Perloff, *The Vienna Paradox*, p. 77.

70 Carter, *Anthony Blunt*, pp. 360, 368, adding that 'a good proportion of' the female students 'were quite as bright and motivated as their male counterparts'.

History, art history and museology in the Pacific

NICHOLAS THOMAS

Bernard Smith's *European Vision and the South Pacific* (1960)[1] was a study of foundational importance for its innovative, ambitious and sophisticated consideration of the arts of travel and colonial settlement across a major region of the world. The book was, moreover, notable for its discovery of a complex and widely dispersed visual archive: that of the Cook voyages and of Cook's various naval, missionary, colonial, and scientific successors in the Pacific. Smith's interest was neither limited to the voyage sketches that amount to the 'primary' visual evidence from observation and cross-cultural encounter, nor did it privilege the grander oil paintings that artists such as William Hodges and John Webber produced for patrons on their return to the metropolis. He was surely ahead of the game, interested in both field observation and finished compositions, in the spectrum of work between, and in derivative and popular iconography—crude engravings of heathen idols in missionary periodicals, for example. Much of this material had never been considered by scholars: *European Vision* brought it into view.

Among the works we know through *European Vision* are a series of post-voyage paintings by William Hodges, which dramatise the mariners' landings at several islands that today are part of the nation of Vanuatu, as well as Eua in the Tongan archipelago (Fig. 7). Each was engraved for the official narrative, Cook's *Voyage* of 1777,[2] which at the time was probably the most fully and extensively illustrated travel narrative ever published. The paintings are the same size as the published engravings. They were not works that Hodges happened to paint and were then adapted for the book; rather, they were called for, prompted by a sense that the book ought to include representations of this kind. As Smith pointed out, the images were history paintings, as they conveyed the historic nature of the meetings they represented, in some cases the first contact between Islanders and Europeans. They reflect a sense that, even in their immediate aftermath, interest in the voyages was centred upon questions of the nature and morality of cross-cultural encounters. That interest has waxed and waned since, but has received particular attention over the last thirty or so years, with the emergence of broadly post-colonial debates—debates about culture, travel and empire—that *European Vision* anticipated.

It is notable, too, that *European Vision* considered in passing a genre that might previously have been dismissed as almost nondescript: that of the illustration of ethnographic artifacts. The conventions of showing objects—often not all at the same scale, typically in a neutral manner, lacking even shadow—drew upon natural history prints and on engraved images of other specimens, antiquities and technical devices found in various eighteenth-century illustrated works. The Cook voyage publications inaugurated a mode of illustration that came to be typical of succeeding publications, but comment on the artifacts in the text was frequently sparse or non-existent. The images signalled that the pieces collected were of interest and significance, but the texts mostly refrained from interpreting them or adjudicating their quality or sophistication. These prints exemplified, in other words, the tentative beginnings of a European recognition of the art traditions of Oceania, an interest in engaging with the details of their forms and styles, which anticipated a coherent discourse.

Smith's *European Vision* and associated publications, notably *The Art of Captain Cook's Voyages*, prepared in collaboration with Rüdiger Joppien,[3] and *Imagining the Pacific*,[4] offered superb maps of the European understanding of Pacific history and culture as it emerged from the late eighteenth century onwards. This chapter responds to the question of what understandings may be adequate now. It asks whether the foundational image of encounter between native and stranger exemplified in Hodges' *Landings* remains salient as a paradigm, and what the implications of a different paradigm of that history might be for the arts of Oceania.

On Wednesday 26 January 1791, snow and sludge along the banks of the river Thames melted into the brown tide that surged up past Deptford, Southwark and the City. Among the many vessels on the river, a rowboat plied back and forth, two tars pulling the oars, two other men at times conversing, at times simply taking in the spectacle and squalor. The younger of the two gestured towards St Paul's Cathedral and observed, 'Hare nui etua'. Kualelo was a young Hawaiian, aged around fifteen. On this occasion, he was said to be not himself. He wanted to return home, and to that end was about to embark on a ship headed for the Pacific Ocean. But he had been in England for the better part of two years, and the prospect of departure made him melancholy, his companion thought. Archibald Menzies, botanist and surgeon, had encountered Kualelo in China. The Hawaiian had arrived there on an English trading sloop, the *Princess Royal*, which he had joined in January 1788 when it stopped for food and water at Molokai, in the Hawaiian archipelago, en route to the north-west coast of America. Having obtained a cargo of fur, the *Princess Royal* called at the island again, but Kualelo—out of what Menzies took to be 'instinctive curiosity'—begged the captain, Charles Duncan, to let him be taken to Britain rather than deposited at home. In China he was transferred to another trader, the *Prince of Wales*, in which one James Johnstone was commander and Menzies both surgeon and naturalist. Menzies was collecting privately for Sir Joseph Banks, the greatest scientific entrepreneur of the epoch, and he shared Banks' eager curiosity about exotic peoples as well as unfamiliar plants.[5]

On the *Prince of Wales* Kualelo travelled to England, residing largely in Plymouth with Johnstone, where he was inoculated against smallpox and sent to school. He sailed with Duncan again, commissioned by the Hudson's Bay Company to make an exploratory voyage across the Atlantic into far northern waters, which seems to have accomplished little. Kualelo returned to London and was now joining, with Johnstone and Menzies, what would be considered one of the great expeditions of the epoch. George Vancouver, one of Cook's former lieutenants, was the commander; his ship was the *Discovery*, and discovery was its business, from the European point of view. Yet it would take Kualelo, not into the unknown, but back to his place of birth, to the port where his own voyage had begun.

In Vancouver's opinion, Kualelo had not 'in the least ... benefitted by his residence in this country'.[6] Efforts to teach him to read had failed, but he had proven to be good at drawing, and particularly enjoyed dashing off caricatures of friends and acquaintances. He had equipped himself with a number of prints of great London buildings—Westminster Abbey, Greenwich Hospital and St Paul's Cathedral—that he wanted to show to his people. The last was the building he had called 'the great house of god', 'harre noui eatua', and it was one he was said to have 'often gazed on with admiration and astonishment'.[7]

A narrative about the Pacific should surely begin in the Pacific itself. But the occasion in London draws attention to the diverse, and maybe unexpected, voyages that have made up the lives of Islanders over the last two hundred or so years. In general, it is assumed that dealings between Europeans and Indigenous peoples—whether in the Pacific, the Americas or Africa—have amounted, essentially, to a series of depredations perpetrated by the former upon the latter: the incursions of explorers are followed by those of traders, missionaries, settlers, colonial powers, and latterly multinational companies and credit-rating agencies. These are histories, in other words, of 'impact'. Pacific Islanders were those 'impacted on'; they are presumed not to have been mobile, not visitors, not making impacts themselves.

Over the epoch of decolonisation, historians came to emphasise that Islanders, among other native peoples, were not merely victims but actors, who resisted colonisers' impositions or creatively accommodated them. This rethinking was associated with a broader effort to understand colonial histories in a two-sided way, complementing the old emphasis on European policy and practice with an account of the perspectives of the colonised. If the necessity of this step was obvious, it also raised, or begged, a host of questions, both practical and philosophical. The issue most relevant here is that the 'both sides' rhetoric preserved the idea that on one side we found Indigenous communities, communities that were bounded, firmly situated in place, and culturally coherent. Islanders still seem in situ, the 'local' opponents, translators, or recipients of 'global' forces, meanings and commodities that emanate largely from the West.

Kualelo's story suggests a Pacific history written on different assumptions. There is a cultural condition that we rarely attribute to native people at all, and never at this early stage of their interactions with the colonial world—that of cosmopolitanism.

As Menzies wrote, barely a decade after contacts between Hawaiians and Europeans had been inaugurated by Cook's visits, Kualelo was prompted to visit not only England but 'several other parts of the globe'. He encountered a range of Pacific Islanders, the Indigenous peoples of north-west America and the Arctic, the ports of China and Europe, the multicultural decks of naval and merchant ships, and London, a place of starkly unequal social classes and, already in the late eighteenth century, one of diverse immigrants and refugees.

If Kualelo did not lose his engravings on the way home, printed pictures of British temples were being shown to Hawaiians at the same time as images of Hawaiian temples were being shown to Britons. Certainly, the European discovery of the Pacific was accompanied by a Pacific discovery of Europe. Here I make a different point, though a simple one, about Pacific history. If we think of 'natives' as locals, Islanders were never natives. In the encounters dramatised in Hodges' *Landings*, right and left did not correspond to global and local. I have a simple point, too, about art, about the great Pacific artifacts that grace the ethnographic museums of Europe and their antipodean counterparts. Works have been celebrated in part because they are representative of ancient cultures. A good many of them might, to the contrary, be celebrated because they represent those cultures' transformations; their modernity. I will conclude with a third, perhaps less simple, point about what, given all this, we now take the collections held by such museums to represent and reveal.

In no part of the world is the stereotype of the closed customary society more profoundly misleading than in the Pacific. It did not require the stimulus of Western contact to make Islanders' lives inter-social. In Vanuatu, in northern New Guinea, even in the more widely separated archipelagos of eastern Oceania, communities were linked by exchange systems and trade routes that saw raw materials and specialised products, but also intangibles such as songs and spells, regularly gifted or trafficked. Maps of such networks are mind-boggling,[8] but there are no diagrams for the imaginations that such wide-ranging and manifold relationships engendered. Consciousness everywhere was regional and relational as well as culturally particular. This knowledge of a wider world that Islanders, to varying degrees, already possessed, was rapidly enlarged during the earliest decades of sustained contact, particularly in Polynesia.

In the wake of Cook's voyages, traders such as Kualelo's captains began seeking furs from the American north-west, which they sold on in China. The establishment of the British colony in Sydney stimulated further commercial ventures, and ships were soon calling frequently for refreshment in Tahiti and Hawaii and at many other islands they knew of or happened upon. Almost anywhere ships stopped, one or two mariners tended to desert and one or two eager Islanders were recruited to replace them. A good many of these Pacific maritime workers eventually made their way home, but many instead, or on the way, left ships at islands other than their own. Before contact intensified, a few Tahitians might for example have been found in the Cook Islands, blown there in the course of a storm, while Tongans, Fijians and Samoans had long made regular and reciprocal visits. But by as early as 1800, there were also Hawaiians in the Marquesas, Tahiti and Fiji; Māori in Tahiti; and Tahitians in Tonga and Palau. A decade or so later, there were very likely hundreds of temporary or permanent Islander migrants in the region. So, not only had individuals such as Kualelo visited Asian ports and European cities, they had called at a good many Pacific islands, discovering peoples with whom they had ancestral links, but who lived beyond the ambit of regular canoe voyages. Those who travelled, those who received travellers, and those who heard stories when travellers returned, all gained a new sense of a plethora of communities sharing certain Oceanic affinities, and of other more distant and profoundly different societies. They made comparisons, they noticed differences, and they acted upon them.

We know that these interactions took place, but Europeans were often mere bystanders to them, hence their nature and ramifications are at best obliquely recorded in the European documentary record. But for Tahiti, which together with Hawaii was the crucible for the transformation of the Pacific over the first decades of the nineteenth century, we have a clearer sense. Captain Cook's reports had made the reality of practices such as human sacrifice vivid and immediate; evangelicals were powerfully affected, and the 1790s witnessed new excitement about the prospects for missionary work. The founding venture of the London Missionary Society entailed what they called 'a plan of great extent and importance': the establishment of a Tahitian mission that would provide a staging point for the conversion of the Pacific.

On 16 March 1797 this venture appeared to get off to an auspicious start. The high chief, Pomare I, ceded, through his priest, the entire district of Matavai to the mission—or so the new arrivals thought.[9] In fact the offer was of a place to stay, and since Pomare enjoyed no sovereignty over the island as a whole, but was involved in ongoing conflict with rivals, it was conditional upon military assistance: earlier European visitors such as the *Bounty* mutineers had helped their friends and hosts by fighting alongside them, so it was naturally assumed that the missionaries might do the same. This mismatch of expectations meant that the deal would come unstuck even before a celebratory historical painting and engraving were produced back in London. But if the missionaries' 'plan of great extent' was almost immediately diminished and compromised, it nevertheless progressed by fits and starts. The man who would become known as Pomare II would spend the succeeding twenty years doing his best to turn the missionaries' error—that he was king—into a truth. But in so doing, he was inspired and closely guided by a third party, an irritant to the missionaries' efforts to introduce and broker Western civilisation.

Just twelve months after the evangelists' landing, the trading ship *Nautilus* arrived seeking supplies. The missionaries angered Pomare the elder by obstructing a trade in muskets and gunpowder, but also by trying to round up five Hawaiian deserters. These men stayed on and made themselves useful to the high chief in ways the missionaries could not, and they were soon prominent members of his entourage. The missionaries grudgingly acknowledged them to be a 'daring and hardened race', but lamented their influence. Their wickedness involved setting up stills and trafficking in alcohol, but had broader dimensions to it. One of the Hawaiians had been to England, and was 'constantly telling him [Pomare], something of what he saw there; so that his ideas of things are much enlarged'. In the early years of the nineteenth century, Pomare II became increasingly aware of Kamehameha's conquest of the whole of the Hawaiian archipelago and his establishment of a true kingdom; he was made aware of Hawaiian techniques and strategies of sovereignty and warfare, of ways of dealing with Europeans, and what Europeans elsewhere had offered and perpetrated.

In 1808, during a crisis, the chief hoped he would recover his authority, but remarked in an offhand way to one of the missionaries that 'perhaps the people would cut off his head as the people of France had done with their king'. A similar understanding of what was going on in a wider world lay behind opposition to the few petty commercial ventures attempted by the mission. In 1818 a scheme to establish a sugar plantation had to be hastily abandoned, 'in consequence of the king's jealousy, excited by false alarms insinuated into his mind, that slavery and the culture of the cane were necessarily associated'. Pomare II never travelled beyond the archipelagos that in due course became subject to him, but for the remainder of his life he had these Hawaiians, or other Hawaiians, around him, and he would remain a cosmopolitan in his mind. Not long before he died he asked William Crook, a missionary he had known for over twenty years:

> to point out ... Lima in the map that hung up [in his house], and he pointed out Cape Horn as a place he knew well, and the River Amazonia under the Line. He amused himself by looking over the West India Islands, and Jamaica, in particular, from whence Mr. Gyles [a fellow missionary] came. He said he was going to send some Sandwich Islanders [that is, some Hawaiians] to Teturoa [a neighbouring atoll] to make salt, as they had learned to make it in their own country.[10]

As Pomare had been inspired by Hawaiian history, Māori and Marquesans were in turn inspired by Tahitian events. One Whetoi, a North Island Māori chief, went as far as to rename himself Pomare, his settlement Matauwhi, after Tahiti's Matavai Bay, and ally himself with missionaries as he understood Pomare had done. On Tahuatu, in the southern Marquesas in the 1830s, a chief gave David Darling an account of why he was unable to convert, which the missionary found convoluted. The chief, Iotete, was heavily tattooed. He knew that Pomare I had been tattooed, and that it was under Pomare II that Christianity had been embraced, therefore it should be under his son, who was not tattooed, that Marquesans would turn to the Church and, Iotete hoped, create a kingdom of their own. In short, the radical changes associated with conversion to Christianity—which were marked by differences in dress, work, the organisation of time, architecture, and sexuality, among other domains—were embraced, not because a European project was acquiesced in or locally appropriated, but to an important degree via a kind of re-enactment, an interest in re-staging a transformation that had been splendidly accomplished by Islanders elsewhere.

The first great stimulant to Pacific cosmopolitan imaginations in the colonial age was commerce: the growing mutual awareness among Islanders, achieved via the decks of the increasing numbers of traders and whalers from the 1790s onward.

The second great force would be the evangelical project itself, since Pomare's conversion and ascendancy in Tahiti—accomplished by 1815—would be succeeded by a sustained effort to spread the Gospel westwards, through the Cook Islands, Samoa, Tonga and Fiji into southern Melanesia and, by the end of the nineteenth century, to the Pacific's continent: the great, populous and multilingual island of New Guinea.[11] Islanders were not always receptive to the Word of God—George Baxter's print of the death of John Williams is another image known to a wider public and scholarly community, through *European Vision*—but in many instances those typically referred to as 'native teachers' were in the vanguard and were better able to excite prospective converts than white missionaries were (Fig. 8). Tahitians played crucial roles in securing Christian conversion in much of the Cook Islands and Samoa, for example. Samoans and Fijians went on to work extensively in Melanesia, the New England missionaries despatched Hawaiians to many parts of Micronesia, and so on.

One of Christianity's great attractions, for Islanders, was literacy. Early on Pomare, among others, was intrigued by script, print and books. By late 1803 he had learnt 'to make the letters of the English alphabet, to know their names, and to put them together so as to form sundry words and short sentences'. Around this time, the missionaries standardised a Tahitian orthography and, only six months later, Pomare was said to be in the habit of writing short letters to the missionaries. He asked them to build a small house that might be set aside for him to write in, and in due course regularly kept a private journal. It would be easy to impute a naive fetishism to the chief, to suggest that he and other Polynesians thought writing to be in some way magical. They did indeed consider it a practice charged with power—as in fact it was. Pomare may well have known that in Hawaii Kamehameha had written to King George III, soliciting the gift of a ship—a request eagerly supported by naval men wanting to sustain British influence in the archipelago, and which therefore did result in the presentation of a small vessel. Writing was, for these Islanders, a technology of modernity. It made their action at a distance more efficient, also enabling them to seek out alliances, and gifts of great and potent things.

Commerce had enlarged the inter-island imaginations that Islanders already possessed. Conversion entailed new passages from island to island, and new imaginations again. A third great source of cross-cultural and cosmopolitan imagining in the Pacific was the process of labour migration. This had got underway in a piecemeal sense before 1850, as groups of men from one island were persuaded to travel to others for periods of plantation work. As colonial settlements in Fiji, Samoa and New Caledonia expanded, and the sugar economy in Queensland developed, the demand for workers escalated and what would become a violent and controversial business got under way. It was widely understood that unscrupulous recruiters routinely kidnapped men and women from various parts of Vanuatu and the Solomon Islands, and there were indeed proven cases of abduction.[12]

Islanders who considered themselves wronged attacked boats and killed traders, while traders were frequently guilty of pre-emptive violence or unauthorised punitive raids. Yet recruitment and migration came to involve tens of thousands of Melanesians, the great majority of whom were more-or-less willing recruits—younger men who had much to gain from travel and the status that their experience, and the goods that they brought back, in due course would earn them. The upshot was not only the experience of an onerous plantation regime and the ports and towns of Queensland among other colonies; it was the formation of new communities among workers from many islands, the formation of a pidgin language and much else that they shared.

Whatever else it was, empire gave people lives both here and there, foisting new imaginations upon those who travelled and also those who stayed at home. Labour recruitment engendered new art forms, such as the shell-inlaid guns and bead belts worn by Solomon Islander recruits photographed in studios in Queensland and Fiji (Fig. 9). The artifacts do not tell us their own story, but they do indicate that some sort of relationship with the Union Jack and the power behind it was important to these men.

More surprisingly, sculptures that appear entirely 'traditional', such as the figure of a man from the village Sakavas on the island of Malo in north Vanuatu, are in fact also products of this moment of colonial engagement (Fig. 10). The figure is among a small number of objects representing what are called 'les arts premiers' in the Louvre. It is good that this sculpture is shown there and affirmed as a masterpiece, but, as Michael Baxandall famously argued with respect to Fra Angelico and his contemporaries, it pays to pay attention to the blue paint, which in this case was produced not from ground-down lapis lazuli, but what was, in nineteenth-century

Melanesia, a similarly scarce and prestigious import. Reckitts Blue was regularly mentioned by labour traders among the goods such as mirrors and scissors that had to be distributed among the kin of prospective recruits during often tense and hurried exchanges, before a young man or woman would be allowed away, to enter a boat. In the islands it was employed not as a laundry product but as a paint, on the man in the Louvre and similar sculptures such as a pair also from north Vanuatu and now in Berlin, and for that matter a fish in Cambridge, collected by John Layard. For all the upheaval and violence of the time, these works do not just represent a local culture, one we take to have been threatened by change. They are expressions rather of a knowing engagement, a capacity, against all the odds, to balance the rapacious demands of an international economy against a group's interest in celebrating ancestors, indeed a capacity to celebrate them in a fresh and splendid way.[13]

The trend in a range of museums in Britain, Europe and elsewhere has been to re-brand anthropological as 'world cultures' collections. However desirable, indeed essential, it may be to acknowledge and affirm human variety, the rubric may do no more than the patently awkward category of 'les arts premiers' to recognise that many of these great works speak of the start of relationships across cultures. To be sure, they express local meanings and beliefs and art styles, but they also express a negotiation—they are artifacts of encounter and engagement. To view them, from Europe, as exemplifications of the cultures of elsewhere, is to overlook the sense that their creation was an act that engaged Europe, that reached over both sides of this image.

I do not mean that objects of this kind should be valued, not for the authenticity that the Louvre suggests they bear, but for a hybridity that marks the mixed-up world we all inhabit. That caption would only obscure the work of Pacific art in a different way. We would still lose any particular sense of Islanders' creations and Islanders' projects, indeed of the global salience of a form of sociality that was made up, from the start, of relationships rather than groups or identities. We would miss any sense that the creation or the presentation of such a work of art might be a form of action, a way of dealing with Europeans, a technique of engaging with them.

A Māori object that recently entered the collections of the Museum of Archaeology and Anthropology in Cambridge suggests possibilities of this kind (Fig. 11). Its maker was Tene Waitere (1854–1931), one of the greatest Māori artists of the colonial period, and the carver of the *Ta Moko panel*, an icon of Oceanic art in the collections of the Museum of New Zealand Te Papa Tongarewa.[14] Waitere was trained in a customary context and had a profound understanding of customary techniques and forms, but is renowned for departing from them, both in works created for non-Māori—such as the panel, essentially an illustration of male and female tattoos, commissioned by an ethnologist and colonial museum director—and for Māori clients, for whom, for example, he created this monument in a European form. Waitere was also involved in carving houses for kin and for other tribes, such as *Hinemihi*, famously acquired by Lord Onslow, a colonial governor, and brought back by him to the family estate, Clandon Park in Surrey.

Though other expatriate Waitere carvings, such as a model canoe in the British Museum, given to the Duke and Duchess of York and Cornwall in 1903, were well known among interested Māori, researchers and curators, a major work located on a naval base in Portsmouth came to light only a few years ago. Māori had a long history of interest in European expressions of power and sovereignty and began to create flags and flagpoles in the second half of the nineteenth century. Fully carved posts were square in section and typically incorporated a cross-piece; the hanging of flags from angled ropes suggests an intention to mimic the array of pennants that might be displayed on a sailing ship. By the early twentieth century, at any rate, poles known as *pouhaki* were commonly erected beside meeting houses. A pole of this kind was presented, together with a host of other gifts, to Edward, Prince of Wales, when he visited Rotorua in April 1920 on a tour of the dominions to convey the King's thanks for their support during World War I—which had been yet another process that brought Islanders, as well as other peoples, into contact with each other, in an imperial theatre.

The prince presented the pole in turn to the commander of HMS *Excellent*, a shore base in Portsmouth Harbour, where it was erected in a rose garden, and remained for some eighty-five years. Though it was in good condition, given its extended exposure to coastal weather, at the time it was examined in 2007 by the carver's descendant James Schuster, and me, it was clear that it needed to be moved somewhere indoors. The family welcomed the suggestion that the pouhaki might be placed in the context of Pacific and Native American works in Cambridge, and displayed for a wider public there; in due course the Ministry of Defence agreed that it could be placed on deposit at the Museum of Archaeology and Anthropology at Cambridge, and we proceeded to make arrangements for its physical move and for conservation work.

A question that was not much discussed was whether the flagpole could or should be returned to New Zealand. The community felt that as a gift to the Crown it could appropriately stay in Britain. But there was a good deal more debate about its conservation. The standard approach in museums today would be to preserve the object in its state at the time it entered the institution, but Jim Schuster pointed out that, were the pouhaki at home, it would be given a good coat of paint, and that not renewing it in some way implied a lack of care. Options such as the emulation of traditional stains were considered, but in the end Schuster's proposal was that a coat of linseed oil would reinvigorate the wood, and create an appearance consistent with those of other historic carvings in the museum. A year later a ceremony took place, blessing and marking the flagpole's arrival, possibly unprecedented, as an instance of a major historic artifact entering a European museum with the active support of the family and community concerned. A report in the *New Zealand Herald* was headlined 'Historic Flagpole Recovers its Mana'.

At the very time the pouhaki was making its way from the South Pacific to the North Atlantic, Emile Durkheim's pupil and nephew Marcel Mauss was at work in Paris, composing what would be considered one of the foundational works of twentieth-century anthropology, his *Essai sur le don*, published in English as *The Gift*. One of the essay's key sources of inspiration, indeed of the entire book's paradigm, was a quotation from Māori elder Tamati Ranaipiri, outlining the spirit of the gift in terms that have been much debated ever since:

> Now this taonga I received from him is the spirit—the hau—of the taonga I received from you and which I passed on to him. The taonga which I receive on account of the taonga that came from you, I must return to you … I must give them to you since they are the hau of the taonga which you gave me.[15]

Both the pouhaki and Mauss's text were products of World War I. Mauss served in the armed forces and survived, but many of his peers, a whole cohort of French sociologists and ethnologists, died on the Western Front. *The Gift* ended with a set of what Mauss called 'ethical' conclusions:

> It is by opposing reason to emotion and setting up the will to peace against rash follies ... that peoples succeed in substituting alliance, gift and commerce, for war, isolation and stagnation ... There is no other course feasible.[16]

The Māori, for their part, had gifted their service and in some cases their lives to the cause of the Crown and the Empire. In return they were honoured by a visit from the prince and they recognised that honour through gifts including the pouhaki. Their participation—their presentations—was in no sense an expression of colonial servility. Their gifts were assertive, seeking to remind the Crown of longstanding obligations to Māori, dating back to the 1840 Treaty of Waitangi, that had been neglected; they implied some form of tribal sovereignty within the British Empire.

When we exhibit the pouhaki we exhibit many things: a work of art by an individual master, an artifact of a hybrid history, the heritage of a particular people. But also, and above all, a gift.

> The thing given is not inert. It is animated, often personified; it tends to return to what Hertz called its place of origin, or to produce, for the clan and the land from which it originated, an equivalent to replace it.[17]

The gift in general, like Mauss's book, is concerned with the future; it is an expression of hope, a question. The thing having been given, one asks: what will come of that? What will become of us now? The challenge for us, as curators in Cambridge, is to exhibit not only the object but the gift, not only the gift but the question. What could Britain, the Crown, or the Museum of Archaeology and Anthropology, offer the clan, Ngati Tarawhai, Māori in general—what tangible or intangible thing might we give, that would in some sense replace this remarkable thing?

CODA

In November 2015, at the start of a conference associated with the Tate Gallery's landmark *Artist and Empire* exhibition—the first large-scale, wide-ranging exhibition the gallery had undertaken that addressed the history of the British Empire, comparatively and globally—the work of Bernard Smith, and *European Vision* in particular, were cited as key precursors for the consideration of art in the colonial and imperial context. Smith's studies were indeed not only foundational, in opening up the question of the role art played in colonial history, but also methodologically exemplary in bringing into view an extraordinary variety of representations, ranging from natural history sketches in field notebooks and navigators' coastal profiles, through draughtsmen's images of Indigenous artifacts, to cheap engravings in evangelical magazines. Smith gave dedicated attention to oil paintings, such as those of William Hodges and John Webber, but did so with unprecedented attention to this much wider range of imagery, and in the context of an archive of published and unpublished texts that were similarly varied.

Such were the 'European visions' of the Pacific. Inspired by the imaginations and narratives of Islanders, and also by Smith's work, scholars, curators and artists have since explored and documented Indigenous visions of the Pacific. Understanding the cultures of Europeans and Islanders, and the exchanges that connected them, is a project that raises many challenges yet is of much more than local interest: it demands a cross-disciplinary imagination, informed by art history, anthropology and history, and it exemplifies the effort to give the academic humanities genuinely global, cross-cultural and comparative range.

Many thanks to Jaynie Anderson for her invitations, to the Melbourne conference on 'The legacies of Bernard Smith', and to contribute to this book. The research reported upon has received funding from the European Research Council under the European Union's Seventh Framework Programme (FP7/2007–2013) / ERC grant agreement n° [324146]11.

NOTES

1 Bernard Smith, *European Vision and the South Pacific, 1768–1850: A Study in the History of Art and Ideas*, Clarendon Press, Oxford, 1960; 2nd edition: Yale University Press, New Haven, 1985.

2 James Cook, *A Voyage Toward the South Pole, and Around the World*, 2 vols, Strahan and Cadell, London, 1777.

3 Rüdiger Joppien and Bernard Smith, *The Art of Captain Cook's Voyages*, 3 vols in 4 parts, Oxford University Press, Melbourne, 1985–87.

4 Bernard Smith, *Imagining the Pacific: In the Wake of the Cook Voyages*, Yale University Press, New Haven, 1992.

5 Archibald Menzies, 'Journal 1791–1794', British Library, London, Add. Ms. 32641, pp. 4–5. This discussion, and the bulk of this chapter, draw on Nicholas Thomas, *Islanders: The Pacific in the Age of Empire*, Yale University Press, New Haven, 2010, which may be referred to for fuller discussion and citation.

6 W. Kaye Lamb (ed.), *The Voyage of George Vancouver, 1791–1795*, Hakluyt Society, London, 1984, vol. 1, p. 307.

7 ibid.

8 See, for example, Kirk Huffman, 'Exchange, Community and Value', in Lissant Bolton *et al.* (eds), *Melanesia: Art and Encounter*, British Museum Press, London, 2013, pp. 287–93.

9 The key sources on the foundation of the mission are William Wilson, *A Missionary Voyage to the Southern Pacific Ocean*, T. Chapman, London, 1799; and John Davies, *The History of the Tahitian Mission*, C. W. Newbury (ed.), Hakluyt Society, London, 1961.

10 Thomas, *Islanders*, pp. 94–9.

11 The best overview of missionary history in the Pacific for the early period remains W. N. Gunson, *Messengers of Grace: Evangelical Missionaries in the South Seas*, Oxford University Press, Melbourne, 1978. There have been a number of monographic studies of particular missions and missionary biographies for various parts of Melanesia.

12 The labour trade has been a major theme in studies of Pacific history since the 1960s. An early and a more recent work are Peter Corris, *Passage, Port and Plantation: A History of the Solomon Islands Labour Trade 1870–1914*, Melbourne University Press, Melbourne, 1973; and Tracy Banivanua-Mar, *Violence and Colonial Dialogue*, University of Hawaii Press, Honolulu, 2007.

13 For fuller discussion of Island Melanesian art in the context of the labour trade and nineteenth-century change in Melanesia, see Peter Brunt *et al.*, *Art in Oceania: A New History*, Thames & Hudson, London, 2012, especially pp. 187–217.

14 For fuller discussion of Waitere and the pouhaki, see Nicholas Thomas *et al.*, *Rauru: Tene Waitere, Māori Carving, Colonial History*, Otago University Press, Dunedin, 2009.

15 Marcel Mauss, *The Gift: Forms and Functions of Exchange in Archaic Societies*, transl. Ian Cunnison, Cohen and West, London, 1954, p. 9.

16 ibid., p. 80.

17 ibid., p. 10.

Cooperation and friendship:
in tribute to Bernard Smith

RÜDIGER JOPPIEN

Bernard Smith and I worked together for thirty-eight years. Our correspondence spanned the years 1972 to 2010, and provides the basis for my essay.[1] In 1973 I organised an exhibition for Kenwood House, London,[2] on the French-British painter Philippe Jacques de Loutherbourg, the artist on whom I had written my doctoral dissertation.[3] In 1785 Loutherbourg had designed the pantomime *Omai, or a Trip Around the World*, performed at Covent Garden in London,[4] which was a travelogue of Captain Cook's third voyage. Included in the exhibition were some costume designs on paper, which belonged to the National Library of Australia; three of them had been illustrated in Bernard Smith's outstanding study *European Vision and the South Pacific*,[5] which I had read for my thesis. In mid-1972 I had sent a copy of my thesis to Bernard at the Power Institute, for which he very kindly thanked me. Only in late 1973, when Bernard and his wife, Kate, stayed in London, did we actually meet, through a mutual acquaintance, Geoffrey Philipps.

After I had finished my thesis, my professor of art history at the University of Cologne, Heinz Ladendorf, suggested that on the basis of my research on Omai I should do a more thorough study of artists accompanying expeditions, to be called 'Images of Voyages and Travels of the Eighteenth and Nineteenth Centuries'. For this I received a grant from the Deutsche Forschungsgemeinschaft (German Research Society). When Bernard and I first met, in December 1973, I had already begun work on the subject. Bernard was most interested in my project and suggested that I should come to Australia in order to look at the material in the National Library of Australia in Canberra, and other places. The newly founded Humanities Research Centre might provide a platform for this. So I spent my first sojourn in Australia—from August to December 1975—attached to the centre, of which Professor Ian Donaldson was director.

In the print room of the National Library I was particularly lucky, for during my time there many parcels arrived from London, containing drawings of historical expeditions collected over the years by Sir Rex Nan Kivell. It was said at the time that Nan Kivell had received a knighthood in exchange for his extremely valuable collection. Many of the drawings, sketches and gouaches that arrived had not yet been identified. Here I could help. For the previous two years I had been researching in the British Library, looking through practically all illustrated travelogues and folio volumes of expeditions. Having a reasonably good memory for pictures, I could identify quite a few of those arriving in Canberra and attribute them to various artists. It soon became obvious to me that the drawings which derived from Cook's voyages were among the most interesting.

Australia made me feel welcome. The Smiths, then still living in Sydney, as Bernard was professor at the Power Institute, invited me into their home in Glebe. I learnt about the struggle to protect the buildings of Glebe and got to know *Place, Taste and Tradition*, Bernard's first book, of 1945.[6] I began to understand the dimension of his subject, increasingly so when on my flight home I read Bernard's *Documents of Art and Taste in Australia*, which had just been published.[7] It was an anthology of manifestos of the formation of art in Australia during the colonial period, with a commentary. The anthology demonstrated how art in the nineteenth century developed from modest beginnings, with no preconditions, into a broad movement of taste and education. I reviewed the book, of course most favourably, for *The Times Literary Supplement* and *The Burlington Magazine*.[8]

Two-and-a-half years later Bernard and I took part in a conference in Vancouver on Captain Cook. The head of our section was Professor Douglas Cole, a historian of British Columbia who wrote the biography of Franz Boas.[9] He told Bernard that *Place, Taste and Tradition* had had a great influence on him and his wife, Maria Tippett, for their book *From Desolation to Splendour: Changing Perceptions of the British*

Columbia Landscape.[10] Douglas was interested not so much in regional art history but in the idea of identity—in other words, how artists, most of them of European stock, accustomed themselves to a new environment, a different kind of landscape and climate, and how they perceived the unknown. These questions Bernard had also addressed in *European Vision and the South Pacific*. As I got to know Bernard better over the years, I increasingly realised that these studies had developed out of his love for his country. I also understood the importance he placed upon the education of young students of art history. By focusing on Australian and Pacific subject matter, he wished to make them aware of the artistic origins of their own country—which up to that time had attracted little attention.

When I was in Australia in 1975 I became interested in Australian art and toyed with the idea of bringing an exhibition of nineteenth-century Australian art to Germany. Bernard arranged a lunch with Leon Paroissien from the Visual Arts Board (the Australian Government's funding body) to discuss such a possibility. I went back to Germany with the best of intentions, but for various reasons the idea did not materialise: I had to continue my research on images of French voyages of the late eighteenth and early nineteenth centuries,[11] my attempts to interest German museums in such a show did not receive much enthusiasm, and visits to the Australian Embassy in Bonn did not help.

While I was still in Australia, Bernard suggested that I might come to the University of Exeter in the spring of 1976 for a conference on Australian art, being organised by Peter Quartermaine. My lecture was called 'The Iconography of the Burke and Wills Expedition in Australian Art' and the research kindled my love and admiration for the work of Sidney Nolan.[12]

In the summer of 1976 my stipend from the German Research Society ran out and I was back in Cologne. I had hoped for a position in the Wallraf-Richartz Museum, but instead I was given the option of joining the Kunstgewerbemuseum (Museum of Decorative Arts) as a trainee. At that stage I knew absolutely nothing about the decorative arts. Out of necessity, I began to work there, starting on 1 March 1977. At that time I was still working with my colleague Peter Whitehead from the Natural History Museum, London, on Dutch artists in Brazil in the seventeenth century; this research became part of an exhibition on Count Johan Moritz of Nassau, held at the Mauritshuis in The Hague in 1979.[13]

At about that time Bernard asked me to join him in preparing a complete catalogue of all works of art from Captain Cook's three voyages. He had started a checklist back in 1948 at the suggestion of the late John C. Beaglehole, who was planning a fourth volume to accompany his three-volume edition of Cook's journals.[14] Bernard began to work on this but, when he received a British Council scholarship that took him to London to study at the Warburg Institute, he had to abandon the project, and after his return to Sydney he became involved in curatorial duties at the National Art Gallery of New South Wales (NAGNSW). From those beginnings, however, he eventually developed the ideas for his seminal study *European Vision and the South Pacific*.

In 1977 Bernard retired from the Power Institute. Resuming his Cook project, he may have decided it would be useful to work with a young collaborator who had, by that time, gained some experience in the field. We agreed to work together. I liked Bernard and I had benefited from my earlier stay in Australia. Moreover, I had been looking for some professional training before I finished my own book on artists accompanying voyages and travels. At that moment I did not anticipate that our project would entail ten agonising years, for it took us much longer than we expected. By the time *Cook* was finished in 1987 I had missed all deadlines for my own book on voyages and travels, thus damaging my reputation with the German Research Society, but I consoled myself with the thought that, instead of the broader survey that I had originally intended, I had confined myself to one topic. At least one major chapter in the art of voyages was completed.

After three years of friendly exchange, from late 1973 to 1976, a new period in Bernard's and my relationship began in 1977. Living so far apart meant our relationship was conducted at a great distance, for better or worse. Our dealings had to be done by mail, except for the rare occasions when we met, in Honolulu, Vancouver, London, Cologne, Canberra, or for some length of time in Melbourne at the very end of 1981, when I returned to the Humanities Research Centre for a second time. After his retirement in 1977 Bernard had moved to Melbourne and there pursued his scholarly work, while I had just begun my first professional post in a museum. There I soon despaired at my lack of knowledge, for I had to learn the history of the applied arts, from Byzantine ivories to twentieth-century design.

Bernard and I were beginning our catalogue from scratch, as except for Bernard's checklist, begun in 1948, no preliminary work had been done. The artists whom we dealt with, such as Parkinson, Hodges and Webber, were minor masters and, on the whole, had not yet received much attention in the art-historical world.[15] We knew only about the material in the obvious collections in London (such as the British Library, British Museum, Natural History Museum and National Maritime Museum), in Sydney (Dixson and Mitchell Libraries), Canberra (National Library of Australia) and Wellington (Alexander Turnbull Library).[16] We had no idea of other collections, whether public or private, or what the art market might reveal. Our first task therefore was to compile a body of works. We confined ourselves to the so-called human drawings, for we did not feel knowledgeable enough to deal with the scientific images of animals, plants and ethnographica.

Through my previous research on voyages and travels I knew quite a number of sources that could be explored. We went to the Royal College of Surgeons in London, and enquired at the Historical Museum in Bern, Switzerland. I drew Bernard's attention to a photograph that I had found in the Frick Collection in New York of a painting by Giovanni Battista Cipriani, representing dancing girls from Raiatea, previously owned by the Duke of Richmond and then still unpublished.[17] We contacted Lord Brabourne, a descendant of Sir Joseph Banks, and discovered drawings his ancestor had commissioned.[18] In the La Trobe Library in Melbourne I had found a drawing by Hodges that tied in with a figure study contained in an album of sketches by de Loutherbourg, held in the Department of Prints and Drawings at the British Museum.[19] Or to mention another example, in 1975 London art gallery Hartnoll & Eyre offered a collection of drawings relating to the second and third voyages, which I could identify as works by Georg Forster, Hodges, and Webber.[20] Originally from an eighteenth-century library in Germany, they had been sold in England before World War II. Thus we realised that the material from Cook's voyages was scattered all over the world, from England to Australia and New Zealand, Canada and the United States, Germany and Switzerland.

Identifying the material and its subject matter was another concern. Many works had been erroneously attributed to Cook's artists. Who were the artists? Who drew what on the voyages? Who, for example, was Charles Praval, a seaman of the first voyage?[21] Was he an original draughtsman or merely a copyist? Who was the artist of *The chief mourner* (since identified as the Tahitian Tupaia)?[22] Was the drawing among the Forster collection really by Georg Forster, rather than by Hodges? Was the gouache portrait of Magnus von Behm, governor of Kamchatka, which had once belonged to the naturalist Thomas Pennant and was later tipped into the official travel account of Cook's third voyage, a work by John Webber?[23] Dozens of questions like these had to be addressed.

Our intention was to establish a chronology of all known drawings and paintings in relation to the three voyages, solving questions such as dates of images when places like New Zealand or Tahiti were visited more than once. Interesting too was the chronology of individual works, such as when an artist had developed a sketch into a preparatory drawing, further into a watercolour, or a presentation copy for the Admiralty into a painting. And which drawings were the ones that had served as models for the engravings in the published accounts of the voyage? How truthful was the final engraving—had the copyist understood the original drawing? These were some of the intriguing questions we had to pursue. Our aim was a catalogue raisonée, in which all original works were identified: their artists, sitters, geographical locations and dates of execution.

For the third voyage some progress was brought about by the discovery of a checklist in the National Library of Australia, which contained up to 200 titles of presentation drawings, as well as paintings, that John Webber had finished for the British Admiralty on the homeward voyage. All titles had been numbered, and suddenly it became clear why so many drawings in various collections bore faint pencil numbers. By understanding their concordance, it became possible to reconstruct the main body of Webber's works and correlate their titles with entries in Cook's journals. I published the list in 1978 in the *Journal of the British Library*.[24] All this was a slow process of discovery, constructing an overview, describing the groundwork, and as yet we had no idea how much more work was still ahead of us.

When Bernard and I started, we were optimistic that we could finish the project in about two years. So we soon began looking for a publisher. Our first approach was to the University of British Columbia Press, who expressed interest. In 1978

Simon Fraser University at Vancouver organised a major conference to mark the bicentenary of Cook's arrival on the north-west coast of America in 1778, to which Bernard and I were invited. This gave us the opportunity to speak to the people from the publishing house, who, when they realised the vast scope of the material, decided that the project was too expensive to take on. But Bernard was not deterred. He then approached Yale University Press, which had established itself as a publisher with a great interest in British art. Yale, under editor John Nicoll, showed interest in the project and even considered—in 1979—publishing *all* drawings from Cook's voyages, including the 'scientific' ones. The cost for seven volumes was estimated at £120,000. Bernard sent them some sections of the manuscript and illustrations, and at the same time asked me to continue writing. On 4 June 1980 I had to confess that I would not make it in time, for my new job in the museum was too time-consuming. With some irritation Bernard answered on 16 July 1980: 'I am sorry about the tone of this letter but if we are to keep our agreement with Yale, you will have to try to give your work on the Cook catalogue a higher priority than it has been given during the last twelve months'.

I was in trouble, but relief came, at least for me. Yale decided not to proceed with the publication. Yale had accepted the Cook project on the understanding that the British Museum of Natural History would participate, providing all its drawings from Cook's voyages. But in the end the museum decided to publish its material independently.[25] Yale had taken the view, all or nothing, and consequently gave up the project.

At the beginning of 1981 Bernard was looking for a new publisher. He contacted Oxford University Press (OUP) in Melbourne and sent a draft text about the first voyage and a good deal of photographic material. OUP gave us the impression that it was interested but did not wish to commit itself, as the project required outside funding. We approached the Visual Arts Board of Australia, who responded that 'such a project should need no financial assistance'.[26]

To my mind our catalogue was still far from perfect. Bernard suggested I come to Australia again to do more research. From October 1981 to early February 1982 I was, for the second time, a guest of the Humanities Research Centre in Canberra. As a fellow one was expected to give talks within and outside the centre on a variety of subjects. Among the talks I offered was one on the history of the Nazi action of 'Degenerate Art', which was received with great interest. Bernard asked for my manuscript and sent it to the Melbourne *Age* newspaper. To my surprise they published it.[27] More important for the Cook project was my talk 'Cataloguing the Drawings from Captain Cook's Voyages: A Task Completed', later published in the *Australian Journal of Art*.[28] In Canberra I had an interested audience which included Alec Bolton, Dennis Carr, Neil Gunson, Bob Langdon, Oskar Spate, Daniel Thomas and many others. Bernard heard about the favourable reception of my lecture and congratulated me.

My second stay in Australia proved successful in several ways. Just before I arrived in mid-October, our eldest daughter, Charlotte, had been born, two weeks after Bernard and Kate's granddaughter Emily. In December my wife, Kathrin, came out to Australia with the baby, and from mid-December over Christmas the three Joppiens stayed with the Smiths in Fitzroy. The hospitality that Bernard and Kate extended was absolutely charming. They were fond of the baby, and my Kathrin got on extremely well with Kate. From that moment we were not only partners but friends, bound together by our families. This was to prove a great asset for our future collaboration.

A few weeks after my family and I had returned to Germany, a new sign of hope occurred. On 26 March 1982 Bernard wrote that Ian Donaldson of the Australian Humanities Research Council had 'agreed to a proposal I made that the assistance required be included in the general costing for the 1988 Conference on "Australia and the European Imagination" which the Humanities Academy is planning'. Now the Cook project was connected with the Australian Bicentenary of 1988. At last, we had solid ground for our research. A month later Bernard drew up a synopsis of the project, its genesis and complexities, the need for further research and for funding the publication. This he sent to the acting secretary of the Australian Academy of the Humanities (AAH), John Hardy. In July 1982 I received the news from Bernard that:

> the Australian Academy of Humanities has accepted the whole project, i.e. the Art (3 vols.) and the Charts and Views (3 vols.) as an Academy project. This means that they take the responsibility of finding the subsidies needed for publication—a very important step.

An important step indeed! Progress followed almost immediately: in October 1982 the AAH reported that it had received a cheque for $25,000 (Australian) from the

Utah Foundation. Due to this happy turn of affairs, in December Bernard and I received contracts for the first two volumes from Oxford University Press. From this moment editing commenced, followed by printing. A month later, Bernard and John Hardy met the New Zealand high commissioner for Australia to ask for a further subsidy. As a footnote, I might add that in May 1983 the Australian millionaire Alan Bond had bought a portrait of James Cook by John Webber for the then astronomical hammer price of $500,000 (Australian) plus charges.[29] The purchase was widely publicised and may have thrown some favourable light on the importance of our project. We only needed a fraction of that amount, but we were sailing all the same. Bernard was pressing hard to get the 'old man off the sea', as he put it.

From now on Bernard and the publisher were imposing constant deadlines. In January 1984 Bernard advised me to continue writing, 'otherwise the Academy and the publisher will begin to get restive'. In October 1984 the venture took a new twist: at the Frankfurt Book Fair, Oxford University Press and Yale University Press agreed to cooperate on the project. In other words, Yale was back with us: Oxford would be responsible for production and would supply the Australian market, while Yale would look after the United Kingdom, United States and Europe under its imprint. In spring of 1984 Yale had already decided to publish a second edition of Bernard's *European Vision*.

On 3 January 1985 Bernard wrote to me: 'What I must impress upon you now is that time is seriously running out. Would it be possible to get a fortnight from your work towards finishing? We are really in a state of crisis now'. My temporary incapacity to deliver more material was indeed unfortunate. In the meanwhile Bernard had finished the introductions to Volumes 1 and 2, and on 7 March 1985 the books were launched at University House, Canberra. But when subscribers asked when Volume 3 would appear, neither the publisher nor the co-author was yet able to say.

There were times when Bernard feared that we would never make it. Once he wrote: 'Above all, don't get depressed, but for God's sake press on' (3 January 1985). But in the next letter, of 16 January 1985, he softened the pressure by saying: 'Be sensible and don't let the Cook catalogue or anything place too great a strain on your family'. When, on 28 April 1986, he sent me some serious queries, he said that these were 'minor irritations … all in all it's a magnificent achievement'. On 4 July 1986 he encouraged me again: 'Don't be depressed, it's going to be an outstanding book'. Thus I had mixed feelings; Bernard cared for my health and family but expected me to accelerate my pace. His letters sounded at one time impatient, at other moments full of understanding, and there was always room for private matters, discussions about children or grandchildren, sending cordial greetings and the like. But our relationship never became sour. I knew he was right, and I had no right to complain.

But why did my work take so long? To answer this, I have to return to the late 1970s. When I returned from Vancouver in spring 1978, my superior in the museum, Carl-Wolfgang Schümann, left to become director of the Textile Museum in Krefeld, and his post was offered to me. However, I feared that after only a year of apprenticeship I was not ready for it. But the museum had faith in me, and the new post meant life tenure. I gave in. The museum had lost its building during the war and was operating in a provisional building. Exhibitions were organised in other distant locations, requiring careful transporting of objects. The director, Brigitte Klesse, tried to keep the museum on the map through exhibitions and catalogues of the collection. There were three staff members and one trainee. In other words, we worked under very tight conditions. When I had joined the museum in 1977 my director had asked me to re-edit a catalogue of Italian and Spanish majolica, which had gone out of print. My new job as curator, however, required different duties. I had to look after the so-called unbreakables, which comprised all objects except glass, ceramics and textiles, from the eleventh to the twentieth centuries. My first big exhibition, in May 1980, was on Renaissance and Baroque silver plate, for which I had to finish the catalogue that my predecessor had left me.[30] My next exhibition, in 1981, was on Victorian designer Christopher Dresser—the first show of this artist in Germany.[31] There were innumerable obligations that kept me away from Cook. Though Bernard knew about my museum work and sympathised with my situation, he had no idea of the internal drama. I worked for the museum at daytime and for Cook at night, on weekends and in my holidays. From Cologne it was easy to nip over to London, where I had lots of support from friends and colleagues like Peter Whitehead, Jonathan King, Peter Gathercole, occasionally Adrienne Kaeppler (when she flew in from the United States), and Emma Hicks.[32]

Between 1983 and 1985 I was heavily involved in a jewellery catalogue for the museum, on which I collaborated with a colleague, Anna Beatriz Chadour, now a well-known authority on international jewellery. Anna Beatriz had the bigger part in the project, but when in spring 1985 her contract expired it was my job to finish the manuscript and see it through the press. On top of that I prepared the exhibition 5000 *Years of Jewellery*, which opened at the museum in October. The two-volume catalogue appeared an hour before the start of the press conference.[33] Finally I confessed to Bernard what had kept me away from Cook studies for so long.

Now, at last, my desk was clear for Cook. Most of 1986 was spent on Volume 3, first on the catalogue raisonée, then on the introduction. In early April 1986 I was finally able to send Bernard the manuscript for the catalogue; on 22 July I wrote: 'The last lot of the introduction went off yesterday'. For Bernard then began the hard slog of checking and correcting my English.

Postponements, corrections, urgent orders for photographs, and many other factors contributed to the race against time. That my text had become much longer than had been expected did not help. Oxford University Press told us about increased editing costs and that they would only go on with the production if we gave them a guarantee of an extra $1800. As I felt responsible for the delay I offered my royalties instead. At this point the royalties became an issue, as the Australian Academy of the Humanities told us that—if I understand its arguments—the authors were not entitled to royalties to begin with, as the AAH had supported the publication. The financial security that I had wished to offer OUP thus seemed meaningless and made us fearful that OUP would stop production. Bernard would not accept this, and, fighting for our royalties, took legal advice from Professor James Lahore. Then on 27 September 1986 he wrote: 'we have resolved all the problems of financing the third voyage and in a simpler and better way than I had expected'. How he resolved this, he never told me.

In November 1986 I received the first galley proofs of Volume 3, but it took me another half-year of checking and counter-checking, involving travelling to London again, writing and asking for copyright permissions and the like. All this was necessary and slowed down the process of editing. And there was yet another hold-up.

In May 1986 I had received a call from the Museum für Kunst und Gewerbe (Museum of Art and Industry) in Hamburg, offering me the position of keeper of the department of art nouveau and twentieth-century arts, crafts and design. This eventually led to my leaving Cologne for Hamburg on 1 January 1987. My last half-year in Cologne had been devoted to finishing Cook, before I could pack up and move to Hamburg. There, however, I found myself with other obligations. The museum owned a fabulous collection of nineteenth- and twentieth-century photographs, but had no proper gallery in which to display them. Friends of the museum had collected 600,000 Deutschmarks to refurbish a new wing to be opened in February 1987. The museum did not have a keeper for this section, and, since I was the only one in the museum who had some knowledge of the twentieth century, the choice fell on me to become interim keeper of that department too. I had to rapidly learn the history of photography, and deal with temporary exhibitions. All this happened in the last months of the Cook project, but finally, in the early summer of 1987, all editorial work on Cook's artists was finished. In October 1987 the two parts of Volume 3 were launched by Oxford University Press in a gallery in Sydney. But I was not present.

I am happy to say we got very good reviews and, thanks to the successful marketing of the volumes through Oxford University Press and Yale University Press, the books soon sold out. The most prestigious review had already appeared in 1985 in the *New York Times Book Review*, following the publication of Volumes 1 and 2.[34] In 1988 another Cook edition of high importance appeared: *The Charts and Coastal Views* by Commander Andrew David, published by the Hakluyt Society in London.[35] Andrew was a former officer at the Hydrographic Department of the Admiralty in Taunton, Somerset. Through all those years Bernard and I had collaborated with him most amiably on points of geographical identification and the matter of coastal profiles. And he was so very generous as to include our names on the title page, as assistant editors.

After 1987 Bernard and I opened up a new chapter in our relationship. Bernard stuck to Cook and Pacific studies for a while and published a number of essays on diverse subjects in the area of the history of ideas.[36] He also co-edited three catalogues for the Australian Bicentenary in 1988: one on the artists of the First Fleet,[37] a second on Terra Australis,[38] and a third on drawings from Nicolas Baudin's voyage, held in the museum of Le Havre, France.[39] We kept on corresponding and told each other about our families. On two occasions, in 1988 and 1992, Bernard came to visit us in Hamburg (Fig. 12). But when his interests turned to more theoretical issues, our correspondence slowed down.

In January 1989 Kate died of leukemia, which was a great grief to all who knew her. She had been Bernard's heart and soul. By January 1993 Bernard had regained some strength and he wrote to me that he was thinking about a book on art of the twentieth century. Almost twelve months later, on 30 December 1993, he became more specific, saying the book should be written from a non-European point of view: something like what Edward Said had done in *Culture and Imperialism*, 'but I do not expect that I shall be quite as polemical as he'. On 1 August 1994 Bernard sent me a manuscript which he called 'Modernism, Postmodernism and the Formalesque'. This was the first time he used the term 'Formalesque' in our correspondence. The book was eventually published in 1998 by Yale University Press under the title *Modernism's History: A Study in Twentieth-Century Art and Ideas*.

Our correspondence had become a bit of a one-way traffic, with Bernard telling me about his academic successes while I wrote about my job situation, the family and general affairs. In August 1996 an international congress, 'Re-imagining the Pacific', was held in Canberra to honour Bernard's eightieth birthday; it was attended by illustrious scholars such as Marshall Sahlins and Nicholas Thomas. Bernard spoke to an audience of 450 people in the Manning Clark Lecture Theatre, later writing to me: 'I received a great deal of adulation which was flattering but made me rather embarrassed as I am more used to defending myself against criticism'. One year later, on 31 August 1997, he proudly told me that Jaynie Anderson, one of his 'brightest students', had accepted the Herald Chair of Fine Arts at the University of Melbourne. In 1997 Peter Beilharz, who had written a biography of Trotsky, published a book on Bernard Smith.[40] In an earlier letter, from December 1994, Bernard had written to me that he no longer wanted to travel but only to write a book, but in January 2000 he told me about a trip to New Zealand in order to give a lecture: 'In Defence of Art History'. He was flattered that he had been invited to the International Congress of Art History in London in the spring of 2001. He contemplated a lecture tour through the United States, on the invitation of his good friend Ihab Hassan. Bernard seemed rejuvenated and was full of ideas. This may have been due to his partnership with Maggi Forster, a relationship with 'ups and downs', as he once put it. In January 2000 Bernard had finished the first three chapters of his memoir of the 1940s, which was to become *A Pavane for Another Time*, published at the end of 2002.[41] In a much later letter (January 2004) he would say that the book was really 'a tribute to my own Kate that you knew so well'. In it he remembered their getting to know each other and their love.

It was perhaps typical of Bernard's working method that he often worked like Picasso, with several projects at a time. When we were in the midst of Cook's voyages, for example, he began his research on *The Boy Adeodatus*.[42] Now that he was back into art-historical and theoretical thinking, he worked on his memoirs of the 1940s. For Bernard, double-tasking was a way of keeping fresh. While he actively pursued the *Pavane*, he was thinking about the 'Formalesque'. At the same time, he planned an anthology of his lectures of the 1950s and 1960s, arguing that Australia's history of art deserved to be much better known. He seemed concerned about the forgetfulness of the younger generation. In a later letter, of 5 February 2004, he even spoke of art history as being under threat as a discipline in Australia, 'because of the pressure of cultural studies and other new disciplines'. Did he fear his contribution might be forgotten? He still wished to be heard. He was planning a book that, in his words, 'brings together some lectures of mine written during the past ten years' (3 July 2003), while at another moment he reported to me about favourable reviews and radio interviews. On 9 April 2005 he told me that the journal *Thesis Eleven* 'is publishing a special issue on my work shortly'. For the last dozen years, however, Bernard's main thinking was devoted to the 'Formalesque'. He lamented the fact that after abstract expressionism there was no nomination of a style; it seemed that he needed the security of a stylistic period, and he wished to give it a name. On 15 May 2003 he wrote:

> If archaeologists and art historians have been able to divide the past into series of periods, styles back to time immemorial, surely there is no reason why they cannot adopt a period style name to the art that dominated the first half of the twentieth century. So being 'bloody-minded', I shall persist.

Summing up, it seems to me that Bernard's main preoccupations during the last two decades of his working life were, firstly, twentieth-century Western art in countries outside Europe, such as Australia; secondly, the loss of, or changes to, Australian art history as he had known and helped to shape it; and thirdly, the classification of modern art and the 'Formalesque'. Repeatedly he would state that he had completely disentangled himself from Cook. It was obvious that he had revived his lifelong interest in the twentieth century. And he felt that he still had much to say.

In our correspondence a number of personal matters were raised, which may shed some light on Bernard's personality. These concern political news such as the 'Terra Nullius Act' and the question of whether Australia would become a republic, his steadfast admiration for the art historian and polymath Jack Lindsay (in whom he admired the Marxist), or his congratulations on my work on Irish arts and crafts. Ireland was always in the back of his mind—he cherished his roots. He talked about Maggi, with whom he travelled to Japan in 1994, and his new habit of drinking Jameson's Irish whiskey with her. That Maggi was of Irish stock 'on both sides' certainly contributed to his admiration for her. With her he had the ambition to keep fit; in December 1996 he told me of his plans to climb Mount Kosciusko and Mount Townsend. Sport or extreme bodily endurance was not quite Bernard's favourite pastime, making such attempts all the more surprising. Bernard and Maggi differed in temperament; at Christmas in 2002 Bernard reported that they had separated but would remain good friends. In 2003 an Italian housekeeper, Daniella, was mentioned, but Bernard said he was not going for 'a romantic affair'. He increasingly became a recluse, who struggled with new technology. 'One way to find space for oneself', he wrote on 15 May 2003:

> is not to use email, mobile phones or the internet. At my age this gives me space for my own thinking. But Daniella and her son Alex [then aged thirteen] help me to keep up with the new things in modern life.

Were they eventually responsible for Bernard buying a computer? When I visited him in 2008 he did own one. A young friend from next door helped him with his correspondence, because Bernard had partially lost his eyesight to the point where he could no longer write, only dictate letters and read with a magnifying glass. Bernard first mentioned to me the deterioration of his eyesight in August 2003, and wrote: 'I don't think I'll be plodding on much longer'. Several months later, in January 2004, he confessed that he was now living alone: 'I try to be as active as I can be to avoid loneliness or nostalgia. But ageing of course is not a happy affair'.

During his last years Bernard expressed several times the wish to see me again and also Kathrin. Thus on 9 April 2005 he suggested we come out to Melbourne for the Comité International d'Histoire de l'Art (CIHA) in 2008, the world's biggest congress of the history of art. He underpinned his suggestion by saying:

> It would be great if you could come and give a paper. You are one of the few art historians of the northern hemisphere who has made an original contribution to art history of the southern hemisphere.

In the following year Bernard reminded me several times about the CIHA congress, and in March 2007 he reported that Jaynie Anderson had told him I had been invited. When I wrote that it had been my original plan to come with Kathrin but that this was not possible for financial reasons, Bernard offered to pay her airfare, but we did not let that happen.

For a fortnight in January–February 2008 I was in Melbourne to attend the conference, and I stayed in Bernard's house. In the mornings we would take a taxi to the University of Melbourne. A lot of people still knew Bernard, and he was received with great warmth. It did him good. At the end of the last day of the conference we went to a party at Government House. Bernard had just received a letter from the publishers of the Oxford English Dictionary, informing him that the word 'Formalesque' had been accepted into the English language. Bernard was beside himself with joy and broke the happy news to a good many friends and former students.

In the evenings after the conference, Bernard and I would sit at home or go out for a meal. Afterwards, on four or five nights, I would recite poems to him, which he could no longer read, mainly by W. H. Auden and T. S. Eliot. I read the whole of the *The Waste Land* to him and, to my surprise, as soon as I started a line Bernard would continue—he knew it all by heart. He explained that as a young man he had been addicted to English poetry. That was at a time when he also did painting, and he showed me some of his works from the 1940s. One got the impression that life-art, practising art, had been as important to him as the theoretical part of it. I remember him once saying, when I told him of my expected job in Hamburg and the art of the twentieth century that awaited me there: 'The only way to enjoy 20th century art is to get to know the artists and try to grasp what they are up to'. This active understanding of modern, even contemporary, art must have formed his own eye as an art critic, first in Sydney and later for the Melbourne *Age*. But how did this passion for modern art fit in with his academic views about the history of art as a discipline? In Bernard's mind there was no contradiction. He could enjoy the work of art in the state of its making and still adopt a broader view on historical theory.

When I returned home after my sojourn in Melbourne, I told Kathrin that I had slept in the front room of Bernard's house. She remembered the room's name: 'bear room'. This I quoted to Bernard and he replied:

> It was called that because Kate always kept Bruno, the family bear, and other animal toys, etc. in the front room to keep children happy when they came with their parents to see us. It seemed to work wonderfully.

I found this explanation, going back to the time of his happy marriage with Kate, to be very touching.

During those days in Bernard's house in Fitzroy in January 2008 I sensed for the first time the forebodings of his decline, asking myself how long he could sustain life, and what treasures of thought, experience and academic virtues would go with him. One night I took a note of what he had told me. I knew that as a student at the Warburg Institute he had been impressed by Rudolf Wittkower and Edgar Wind, but now he told me that the greatest influence on him were two Austrian refugees to Australia: George Berger and Hedi Spiegel. There is more about them in *A Pavane for Another Time*. Bernard also thought very highly of Ursula Hoff, when she was working as a curator at the National Gallery of Victoria and became a Felton adviser. Bernard greatly admired German and German-Jewish scholarship. He had a great liking for German art and letters, particularly for philosophy, being an admirer of Hegel and, of course, Marx. During our long friendship he asked me to write letters on his behalf to Heinrich Böll and to Jürgen Habermas. He set himself the task of reading Theodor Adorno and wanted to know what I knew about the Frankfurt Socio-Cultural School. My own knowledge was inadequate, but I profited from Bernard's admiration for German thought. Even when we went through difficult patches over Cook in the mid-1980s, he was always kindly disposed towards me and, even when I fell behind schedule, continued to encourage me.

In 2010 the School of Art at RMIT University in Melbourne invited me to speak about my work on jewellery and the decorative arts in general. My good friend Professor Robert Baines, who that year had become a National Treasure and been honoured with a solo exhibition in Sydney, brought me out for this. During my week in Melbourne I enquired about Bernard and learnt that he was now living in an old people's home not far from his old house. There I visited him one afternoon, where he lived in one room. Some of his books were piled up on a shelf on the wall. It reflected the hopeless situation of old age whereby, after endless years of academic work, after triumphs and failures, hundreds of PhD students, thousands of miles travelling in the pursuit of scholarship, dozens of books, hundreds of articles, the last refuge is a room with a bed, a table and a chair. Our conversation did not last long, as Bernard's deafness had worsened. I told him that I had been made an adjunct professor at RMIT. He, in his generous way, replied: 'Quite rightly so, they should have done that years ago'. Certainly a favourable remark for me, but there may have been more underneath. Bernard had been an academic all his life, and he had held the duties of academic life in high esteem. How often have I heard him mention names like Virginia Spate, Terry Smith, Jaynie Anderson and many others, all of whom had been his students, and of whom he was so proud, because they had gone on and shaped their own careers. Bernard stuck to the idea that one must not squander time, one had to do things, work purposefully, get things done. He felt a great responsibility for his students and all those with whom he worked. And he believed in academic progress. He was devoted to books and scholarship. In that way he had an enormous influence on me and, needless to say, on many others.

Throughout my correspondence with Bernard runs a sense of gratitude on my part. On 14 July 2006 I told him about a talk I had given in Hamburg on 'Images of the South Seas, from Captain Cook to Gauguin', and of my plans for an exhibition of the ceramics of Gauguin, and continued mentioning a forthcoming exhibition at the British Museum, *Power and Taboo*, previously shown at the

Sainsbury Centre in Norwich. I concluded, certainly a bit over-emphatically, but true to my heart:

> When we worked together, Bernard, perhaps we did not see the future clear enough, at least I did not, I was not aware that in a more and more globalised world our studies could become so important … You were the pioneer of all this, and there will be a time when scholars remember 'European Vision' as a lighthouse in an otherwise dark world. When I retire, in just over four years, I shall retrieve all my correspondence, all your letters (which) I kept, and then I shall write a piece of how much you meant to me, and how much we all owe to you.

Bernard did not reply to this, but I hoped that my foresight into years to come would give him pleasure.

NOTES

1 Throughout this chapter I quote from this correspondence. For the present time all letters are in my possession, but I intend to donate them to the University of Melbourne Archives.

2 Rüdiger Joppien, *Philippe Jacques de Loutherbourg, R.A.*, exhibition catalogue (The Iveagh Bequest, Kenwood House), Greater London Council, London, 1973.

3 Rüdiger Joppien, *Die Szenenbilder Philippe Jacques de Loutherbourgs: Eine Untersuchung zu ihrer Stellung zwischen Malerei und Theater*, dissertation print, Cologne, 1972.

4 Rüdiger Joppien, 'P. J. de Loutherbourg's pantomime *Omai, or a Trip Around the World* and the Artists of Captain Cook's Voyages', *British Museum Yearbook*, no. 3, British Museum, London, 1979, pp. 81–136.

5 Bernard Smith, *European Vision and the South Pacific, 1768–1850: A Study in the History of Art and Ideas*, Clarendon Press, Oxford, 1960; 2nd edn: Yale University Press, New Haven, 1985.

6 Bernard Smith, *Place, Taste and Tradition: A Study of Australian Art Since 1788*, Ure Smith, Sydney, 1945; 2nd edn: Oxford University Press, Melbourne, 1979.

7 Bernard Smith, *Documents on Art and Taste in Australia: The Colonial Period, 1770–1914*, Oxford University Press, Melbourne, 1975.

8 Rüdiger Joppien, 'Home and Country' [book review], *The Times Literary Supplement*, 9 April 1976; Rüdiger Joppien, 'Documents on Art and Taste in Australia. The Colonial Period 1770–1914' [book review], *Burlington Magazine*, no. 886, January 1977, pp. 46–7.

9 Douglas Cole, *Franz Boas: The Early Years, 1858–1906*, University of Washington Press, Seattle, 1999. Cole's premature death in 1997 prevented the continuation of the Boas project, into which he had invested years of research.

10 Maria Tippett and Douglas Cole, *From Desolation to Splendour: Changing Perceptions of the British Columbia Landscape*, Clarke, Irwin, Toronto, 1977.

11 One result of my research in this field was Rüdiger Joppien, 'Die Bildillustrationen zum Atlas der Voyage de la Pérouse: Zur Dokumentation ihrer Entstehung', in *Die Bildillustration im 18. Jahrhundert*, Gesamthochschule Wuppertal and Universität Münster, Heidelberg, 1980, pp. 234–45.

12 Rüdiger Joppien, 'The Iconography of the Burke and Wills Expedition in Australian Art', in Peter Quartermaine (ed.), *Readings in Australian Art: Papers from the 1976 Exeter Symposium*, University of Exeter, Exeter, 1978, pp. 49–61.

13 Rüdiger Joppien, 'The Dutch Vision of Brazil: Johan Maurits and his Artists', in Ernst van den Boogaart (ed.), *Johann Maurits van Nassau-Siegen, 1604–1679: A Humanist Prince in Europe and Brazil: Essays on the Occasion of the Tercentenary of his Death*, Johan Maurits Van Nassau Stichting, The Hague, 1979, pp. 297–376.

14 John C. Beaglehole (ed.), *The Journals of Captain James Cook on his Voyages of Discovery*, 3 vols, Hakluyt Society, Cambridge, 1955–67.

15 An exception was Isabel Stuebe, who wrote her dissertation on William Hodges: *The Life and Works of William Hodges*, Garland Outstanding Dissertations in the Fine Arts, New York, 1979. Bernard was often in correspondence with Ms Stuebe.

16 In the print room of the National Library of Australia I received much help from the keeper, Ms Bernice Murphy, and in the Alexander Turnbull Library I enjoyed the assistance of the director, Mr Jim Traue.

17 Rüdiger Joppien and Bernard Smith, *The Art of Captain Cook's Voyages*, 3 vols in 4 parts, Oxford University Press, Melbourne, 1985–87; on the Cipriani picture, see vol. 1, pp. 151, 152.

18 ibid., vol. 1, p. 65, under 'Kent, England, Knatchbull Collection'.

19 Joppien and Smith, *The Art of Captain Cook's Voyages*, vol. 2, p. 153, 154. I had published the La Trobe Library drawing in 'Three Drawings by William Hodges (1744–1797)', *La Trobe Library Journal*, no. 18, October 1976, pp. 25–33.

20 Rüdiger Joppien, *Drawings from Captain Cook's Voyages: An Unrecorded Collection of Fourteen Ethnographical and Natural History Drawings Relating to the Second and Third Voyage*, exhibition catalogue, Hartnoll & Eyre Art Gallery, London, 1976.

21 Bernard Smith established Praval's identity; see Joppien and Smith, *The Art of Captain Cook's Voyages*, vol. 1, pp. 56–9.

22 ibid., pp. 60–3. Based on a note by Banks, Harold B. Carter suggested that the Tahitian native Tupaia was the draughtsman; see Anne Salmond, *Between Worlds: Early Exchanges between Māori and Europeans, 1773–1815*, Viking, Auckland, 1997 (for this I am grateful to Nicholas Thomas).

23 The portrait of Magnus von Behm is preserved in James Cook and James King, *A Voyage to the Pacific Ocean …*, 2nd edn, London, 1785, vol. 3, following p. 226, held in the Dixson Library, State Library of

New South Wales, Sydney; see Joppien and Smith, *The Art of Captain Cook's Voyages*, vol. 3, catalogue, p. 569.

24 Rüdiger Joppien, 'John Webber's South Sea Drawings for the Admiralty: A Newly Discovered Catalogue among the Papers of Sir Joseph Banks', *British Library Journal*, vol. 4, no. 1, Spring 1978, pp. 49–77.

25 The most valuable collection of natural history drawings was commissioned by Joseph Banks on Cook's first voyage; see *Catalogue of the Natural History Drawings Commissioned by Joseph Banks on the Endeavour Voyage 1768–1771 Held in the British Museum (Natural History)*, 3 vols, London, 1984–87: vol. 1: *Botany: Australia*, by Judith A. Diment *et al.*, 1984; vol. 2: *Botany: Brazil, Java. Madeira, New Zealand, Society Islands and Tierra del Fuego*, by Judith A. Diment *et al.*, 1987; vol. 3: *Zoology*, by Alwyne Wheeler, 1986 (by kind information of Paul Cooper, British Museum, Natural History).

26 Bernard Smith to John Hardy, 28 April 1982.

27 Rüdiger Joppien, 'Art Beyond the Reich', *The Age Monthly Review* (Melbourne), vol. 2, no. 1, 3 May 1982, p. 7.

28 Rüdiger Joppien, 'Cataloguing the Drawings from Captain Cook's Voyages: A Task Completed', *Australian Journal of Art*, no. 3, 1983, pp. 59–78.

29 Joppien and Smith, *The Art of Captain Cook's Voyages*, vol. 3, catalogue, p. 647.

30 *Ein rheinischer Silberschatz: Schmuck und Gerät aus Privatbesitz*, exhibition catalogue, Kunstgewerbe-museum, Cologne, 1980.

31 Rüdiger Joppien (ed.), *Christopher Dresser: ein Viktorianischer Designer, 1834–1904*, exhibition catalogue, Kunstgewerbemusuem, Cologne, 1981.

32 Peter Whitehead, British Museum (Natural History), London; Jonathan King, Museum of Mankind, London; Peter Gathercole, Museum of Archaeology and Anthropology, Cambridge; Adrienne Kaeppler, Bernice Bishop Museum, Honolulu (later at the Smithsonian Institution, Washington); and Emma Hicks, Australian independent researcher in London, who was of eminent value, both to Bernard and me.

33 Anna Beatriz Chadour and Rüdiger Joppien, *Schmuck*, Kataloge des Kunstgewerbemuseums Köln, Bd. 10, 2 vols, Kunstgewerbemuseum der Stadt Köln, Cologne, 1985.

34 Greg Dening, 'Discoveries from the Great Cabin', *The New York Times Book Review*, 11 August 1985, p. 1.

35 Andrew David (chief ed.), *The Charts and Coastal Views of Captain Cook's Voyages: The Voyage of the Endeavour, 1768–1771*, assistant eds Rüdiger Joppien and Bernard Smith, Hakluyt Society, London, 1988.

36 Bernard Smith, *Imagining the Pacific: In the Wake of the Cook Voyages*, Yale University Press, New Haven, 1992.

37 Bernard Smith and Alwyne Wheeler, *The Art of the First Fleet and Other Early Australian Drawings*, Yale University Press, New Haven, 1988.

38 William Eisler and Bernard Smith, *Terra Australis: The Furthest Shore*, exhibition catalogue, Art Gallery of New South Wales, Sydney, 1988.

39 Jacqueline Bonnemains, E. C. Forsyth and Bernard Smith (eds), *Baudin in Australian Waters: The Artwork of the French Voyage of Discovery to the Southern Lands, 1800–1804*, Oxford University Press, Melbourne, 1988.

40 Peter Beilharz, *Imagining the Antipodes: Culture, Theory and the Visual in the Work of Bernard Smith*, Cambridge University Press, Cambridge, 1997.

41 Bernard Smith, *A Pavane for Another Time*, Macmillan, South Melbourne, 2002.

42 Bernard Smith, *The Boy Adeodatus: The Portrait of a Lucky Young Bastard*, Penguin Books Australia, Melbourne, 1984.

Photography and the triumph of science
in *European Vision and the South Pacific*

KATHLEEN DAVIDSON

When Bernard Smith wrote the preface to the revised edition of *Place, Taste and Tradition*, he candidly advised that on re-reading his book: 'I have found themes and issues mentioned that have dogged me for most of my life'.[1] This ongoing analysis of certain themes was similarly evident in the second edition of his best-known work, *European Vision and the South Pacific*, in which Smith used his new preface to re-state and clarify several underlying ideas in his argument. This chapter addresses the latter publication. It examines a subject introduced by Smith in the final pages of that most influential study, which he never really resolved: the emergent role of photography in making and communicating new knowledge, and its significance for natural history as part of the work of empire.

In any investigation of the representation and dissemination of natural history in the imperial context, the approach developed in *European Vision* must surely represent a major starting point. Smith's book has become a model for exploring the Western visual imagination in non-European settings.[2] While similar in its premise to other studies in visual perception, Smith's book takes a very precise perspective by addressing the subject of vision and pictorial representation through the prism of European expansionism. In other words, Ernst Gombrich's question in *Art and Illusion*—'Why is it that different ages and different nations have represented the visible world in such different ways?'[3]—is framed in Smith's contemporaneous enquiry as 'How did [Europeans] see [the] new world of the Pacific? Did their entry into it stimulate thought and affect in any way traditional forms of expression?'[4] Central to Smith's study is the interconnection of art and science—the role of art as information and the principal part it plays in the natural sciences.

Crucially, *European Vision* addresses the relativity of European perception in relation to the demands of Enlightenment science and art, giving much consideration to the promotion of the biological sciences by the Royal Society through voyages of exploration to the Pacific, as well as to British reactions to antipodean nature, and the convergence of art and science as complementary pursuits in the Australian colonies. Yet, in his preface to the book's second edition, Smith comments on the dearth of serious discussion on one of his principal themes, declaring:

> that in the century preceding the publication of *The Origin of Species* (1859) the Pacific region provided a challenging new field of experience for Europeans … [and] new evidence out of which was fashioned eventually the first scientifically credible theory of evolution. That theory was not simply an ideology but an attempt to account accurately for what had been observed.[5]

Smith invokes Thomas Kuhn's *Structure of Scientific Revolutions*, which was published soon after *European Vision*, and claims a complementary role for his own materialist account of historical change by including the 'external social, economic and intellectual conditions' that Kuhn's theoretical work did not encompass.[6] Smith describes the South Pacific as presenting many anomalies to existing paradigms of nature, evidenced in the images and specimens brought back from European voyages, which finally created the impetus for Darwin's theory of natural selection. In seeking to reconcile the imperatives of science with the art of the period, he contends that the material evidence from South Pacific expeditions was mediated in various ways —primarily in the way artists' and scientists' perceptions were informed by their European sensibilities, but also through new practices and visual technologies.

Although the period addressed in Smith's account predates the widespread use of photography, the emerging presence of that medium is given some consideration. In a similar vein to more conventional histories of scientific illustration, Smith emphasises the continuing dominance of established illustrative techniques in natural history throughout the nineteenth century. However, in a manner that is quite uncritical and with almost no attention paid to the circumstances of its transformation, he then declares that this illustrative task was eventually passed on to photography as the genre's inevitable successor.

In the last chapter of *European Vision*, Smith describes the parallels between photographic vision in nineteenth-century image-making and the detail and precision with which biological and anthropological subjects came to be depicted with the 'near-photographic accuracy' of landscapes produced using the *camera obscura*.[7] 'Scientific photography, as it perfected its techniques', Smith argues, 'was to follow a similar path'.[8] Mentioning Louis-Jacques-Mandé Daguerre and William Henry Fox Talbot in that same section, he thus invokes a well-rehearsed—but more recently contested—lineage of photographic image-making whereby the *camera obscura* led directly and inexorably to the 1839 public announcements of photography's invention and then to subsequent technological developments, with each stage facilitating an enhanced application for science.[9] To illustrate his argument about photography's antecedents and early trajectory, Smith cites Dumont D'Urville's second voyage to the southern hemisphere, 1837–38, which he claims marked the end of a chapter in the history of the depiction of native peoples and views (Fig. 13). He states that at this time photography, measuring instruments and modelling—as well as drawing—were 'brought into service to render the illustrations accurate' for the anthropological studies in D'Urville's published report of the voyage.[10] The accuracy of the landscapes thus produced, Smith points out, was consistent with the same desire for objectivity applied to the depiction of native peoples. Accordingly, landscape views produced by Ernest Goupil, D'Urville's artist on the *Zélée*, such as *Site dans l'Île Mangareva* (1846), indicate the use of a *camera lucida*: they are a faithful transcript from nature, indicating '[n]o attempt at composition'.[11] A *camera lucida* was similarly present on the United States Exploring Expedition of 1838–42 led by Charles Wilkes and was used to precisely document the landscape with the aim of recording changes to the topography over time.[12] But, as Smith points out:

> before [these] voyages were officially published ... Daguerre, who had long interested himself in the production of naturalistic effects, invented photography. The invention brought the close alliance between art and science which had characterised the exploring expeditions of the preceding seventy years to a close.[13]

Leading up to this departure, he suggests, there was an increasing emphasis in scientific illustration on geological structures in preference to botanical detail in landscape studies and, correspondingly, any feeling of compassion in representations of native peoples was diminishing.[14] In making this observation, Smith effectively ties up some major thematic strands: the visual stereotypes of the ignoble and the romantic savage, and the development of the idea of 'typical' landscape as a new form of landscape art based on Alexander von Humboldt's analyses of distinct climatic zones.

While Smith's discussion of photography and its precursors in relation to his thesis on vision and the European imagination is brief and inconclusive, it represents more than just a convenient point at which to end *European Vision*. His final section underscores the epistemological context of photography and tacitly indicates how science was also being transformed. His account of the growing propensity for more reliable and detailed comparative studies directly links back to an earlier chapter, in which he describes the investigations by Charles Darwin and his supporters Joseph Hooker and Thomas Huxley into prehistoric life forms and the distinctive living plants and animals of Australia and the South Pacific, these scientists' attentiveness to the organisms' structural affinities, and the ramifications for evolutionary theory.[15] As Smith remarks:

> Science adopted photographic methods for making its graphic records ... Yet, even before the appearance of photography, scientific draughtsmanship was revealing a tendency to move away from a preoccupation with the graphic delineation of surfaces towards an analytical interpretation of the structure of things.[16]

Likewise, in the introduction to his companion volume, *Imagining the Pacific*, Smith speculates on the role of photography in testing the validity of scientific theories, and returns to virtually the same point at which he concluded *European Vision* by reasserting that the development and introduction of photography represented a significant juncture in the use of images as records and for interpreting visible phenomena.

As his opening gambit in *Imagining the Pacific*, Smith refers to William Ivins' example in his book *Prints and Visual Communication*, whereby Albert Einstein's theory of general relativity was verified by photographs taken in Brazil and the

Gulf of Guinea in 1919 under the direction of British astrophysicist Arthur Eddington.[17] Smith illustrates this point with a single photograph indicating how Einstein's hypothesis concerning the action of gravity upon light was confirmed. More accurately, though, this image of a solar eclipse tells only part of this historical episode. In focusing on this one image, Smith discounts the greater scope of photography's application in science. While the evidentiary value of Eddington's iconic photograph is still commonly assumed, that status is not entirely deserved. Proof for Einstein's theory, instead, came from an expedition to Wallal, near Broome in Western Australia, in 1922 to film and photograph another eclipse.[18] This later expedition involved four parties: the United States Lick Observatory party; a group from the University of Toronto; an Indian expedition; and a group from the Perth Observatory. The suite of photographs taken by this transnational expedition privileges the collaborative nature and practical processes of scientific endeavour over the actual eclipse, of which the latter represents just a brief moment in the expedition. In referring only to the evidentiary purpose of Eddington's photograph, Smith overlooks the larger, more complex role of photography in science, as demonstrated by the Wallal photographs. Moreover, this aspect of his argument remains unresolved and is an elusive and problematic element of his overall thesis. To a large degree, this lack of resolution is due to his reliance on the standard master narrative of photographic history as a linear progression wherein certain exceptional images have come to epitomise technological or aesthetic triumphs at each stage of the medium's development. Unfortunately, as evidenced across a range of historical studies of Western knowledge, such canonical accounts usually fall short in representing the complexity of the situation. Instead, they merely create an impression of historical analysis in their chronological ordering of innovations that, when linked retrospectively and with perfect hindsight, create a narrow, 'linear-progress story'.[19] Elsewhere Smith demonstrates that technological innovation tends to follow or coincide with changes in values, ideas and perceptions, rather than propelling them.[20] Consequently his rather programmatic treatment of the effect of photographic technology in the sciences, while a recurrent issue that concerned him over a number of years, is something of an anachronism within his own writings and his otherwise pioneering approach.

In other respects, however, Smith's interdisciplinary study provides a model, both methodologically and thematically, for examining the complex role of visual media in the work of empire and, thus, also for considering the different ways photography would be taken up for imperial science as part of that process. In *European Vision*, Smith describes a dual approach, which was directed, as needed, towards fulfilling an official agenda or satisfying the appetite of a European public eager for curiosities suitably composed to current tastes.[21] Hence, images of natural history subjects were produced not only as scientific documents or as artistic conceits but also to validate and promote Britain's expanding empire. That is, they did not exist solely as original works in the Royal Society or as engravings in the drawing rooms of armchair travellers, but as more capricious images that moved unpredictably between different spheres, sometimes fulfilling several functions simultaneously. This pluralistic attitude to natural history illustration foreshadowed changes throughout the natural sciences—which were becoming increasingly specialised but more heterogeneous as a profession and attracting new audiences—and indicates the potential of photography, with its 'multiple conditions and contexts of production', to perform even more diverse roles across the arts and sciences.[22]

As with many cultural advances, the increasing popularity and gradual overhaul of natural history owed less to technological developments or individual genius than to the collective enterprise of an immense network of practitioners, enthusiasts and consumers. Pivotal in this transformation were the role of the periphery—through discoveries by colonists and others—and the expansion of scientific networks that contributed new knowledge exponentially. Smith's latter chapters in *European Vision*, which address art, science and taste in the Australian colonies, describe the early stages of this process.[23] In most other studies, the inclination had been to follow the accepted paradigm of the spread of Western science, wherein naturalists on the ground are cast as mere scribes for European science, with the study of natural history in the colonies thought to involve little more than being a gatherer for metropolitan elites.[24] Undeniably, there is some truth in this model. But Smith brings more nuance to the premise. He takes into account both the centre and periphery in his characterisation of empire in the post-settlement period by considering neither colonial nor metropolitan interests in the sciences and arts in isolation. Thus scientific circles in London, stimulated by Robert

Brown's and Joseph Hooker's botanical discoveries, found a counterpart in Sydney and the growing circle of resident naturalists and visiting luminaries that orbited the Macleay family. Similarly, in Hobart, Sir John and Lady Franklin formed the Tasmanian Natural History Society, which became the Royal Society of Tasmania, the first branch of the Royal Society to be established outside Britain.[25] Smith's portrayal of colonial science is not idealistic, though. He makes sure to outline the limitations of practising in the colonies with scarce technical resources. But he also shows the beginnings of a dynamic, productive colonial culture which, from the 1830s, was capable of contributing intellectually as well as materially to imperial and global science. Both the Sydney and Hobart circles and the associations they engendered included figures who were among the first in Britain's colonies to promote photography for this purpose.[26]

As photography was introduced into imperial and colonial science, it became more strategically integrated into natural history practice than Smith's analysis of its potential indicates. Photography was not just a new form of illustration or authentication, as Smith posits, but, rather, was part of a broader cultural process that was transforming the natural sciences—structurally as well as philosophically That is to say, its function was certainly observational but it was also relational in the way it created and reinforced connections between individuals and like-minded groups at home and across the globe. Photography was generally taken up for this purpose more actively in the colonial context than in the metropolis, prompted by the rise of modern museums, the professionalisation of natural history and the gradual recognition of colonial achievements. As a result, natural history photography in the age of empire rapidly surpassed the limitations of the genre to become a viable means of exchange. The movement of traditional natural history illustrations—often prized aesthetic objects—unquestionably remained much more visible than that of photographs, which tended to be treated ephemerally.[27] Yet, the fact that it is not unusual to find photographs being repeatedly referred to and circulated among naturalists from the 1850s indicates a turning point in how observations and speculations were shared.

Of the nineteenth century's new visual technologies, the social and cultural consequences of photography were unrivalled—due not only to the way it generated accurate, seemingly objective, records of visual phenomena but also in the way it both markedly increased the number of reproduced images and progressively 'enabled most individuals to produce and reproduce their own visual imagery'.[28] This allowed images to be circulated more widely by an unprecedented range of participants and contributors to imperial science. In official realms, photography was promoted for this purpose by figures such as Governor William Denison. While not specifically mentioned in Smith's account, the influence of Denison's active interest in natural history is very evident in London and the colonies of New South Wales and Tasmania from the 1840s. Denison's activities and connections in the natural sciences facilitated a steady flow of museum-quality specimens and, in the later years of his governorship, were instrumental in expanding the range of natural history illustrations circulated between the centre and periphery. This included photographs and stereographs of significant fossil discoveries, which were innovative and fascinating not only to the metropolitan savants—at the Geological Society and the British Museum, for example, where they were studied and publicised—but would also captivate general audiences and fuel the growing popular interest in palaeontology stimulated by the many new discoveries of prehistoric life in Britain's colonies and the debates swirling around differing theories of evolution.[29] Even when occurring under the imprimatur of a governor, the procurement and passage of these and many other specimens and images from the colonies necessitated the cooperation and input of reliable colonial naturalists and collectors, influential contacts in the peak scientific societies in London, as well as collaboration with Royal Navy personnel, and, increasingly, dedicated and well-connected museum officials. This elaborate series of transactions explicitly demonstrated the way in which Britain's formal empire advanced and influenced the arts and sciences, and was itself continually shaped by them.

However, the majority of photographs taken by or for naturalists were disseminated through more casual or private exchanges. In contrast to the orderly movement of official documents between the centre and periphery of empire, informal exchanges reveal a more nuanced situation comprising alternative and complex flows of information, debate and speculation between individuals, and the multifarious uses of photography that these prompted.[30] During this period, the medium assumed a significant role in the day-to-day routines and behind-the-scenes procedures of naturalists. The exchange of photographs between naturalists located in the centre and on the periphery of empire introduced a personal element into their professional dealings that was also frequently quite strategic. For instance in 1864 Gerard Krefft, curator at the Australian Museum in Sydney, sent three tiny photographs to Richard Owen, superintendent of natural history at the British Museum (Fig. 14). This initiated a vigorous, productive exchange of observations in correspondence between the young German naturalist and the professor, which continued over the next decade or so. Most remarkable about these communications is the variety of photographs exchanged and the different ways the photographs were used to supplement, or even entirely replace, other types of communication. In two of the first photographs sent by Krefft, an articulated echidna skeleton has been placed against a neutral background to delineate its complex structure. This adherence to scientific and aesthetic conventions faithfully follows the protocols of natural history illustration and was surely intended to demonstrate not only the expertise of the museum articulator but the efficacy of photography for making this kind of scientific record. The third photograph from that group, however, is more indicative of the difficulties of practising natural history on a global scale. As Krefft points out in his accompanying letter, a shipment of specimens selected by Owen for the Australian Museum had arrived in 'a wretched condition'.[31] Presenting a direct view into the chaotic interior of the shipping case, the image is clearly intended to corroborate Krefft's claims. A shattered jumble of fragile bones betrays the careless work of the British Museum's taxidermist who packed the specimens for transport. Krefft's use of photography, therefore, clearly had a dual purpose. While he took the trouble to arrange a photograph showing the poor condition of the skeletons sent from London, he was just as careful to ensure that he also enclosed for the professor's 'inspection photographs of specimens prepared at the Australian Museum' demonstrating his professional expertise and the high standards of his own institution.[32] Whereas the subject of these two photographs would probably have seemed unremarkable to Owen, the image conjured by the third photograph would previously have been conveyed only through written exchanges.

This practice of sending photographs of specimens instead of the actual objects, detailed written descriptions or conventional illustrations was always a delicate affair. Metropolitan scientists noted the difficulties in discerning from photographs all the particulars they required. For example, in response to a photograph sent by Krefft, purportedly of the jaw bone of a new species of the prehistoric marsupial *Nototherium*, Owen declared how 'puzzled' he was by what the image actually showed.[33] As he had argued on an earlier occasion:

> a photograph does not always give the precise testimony required by him who uses it: it may tell more than is wanted; it may represent an object in a position which conveys an erroneous idea of the facts at issue; it may show a manipulation and not a natural structure.[34]

Yet, in his key position at the British Museum—a cynosure of imperial science—Owen found himself increasingly on the receiving end of photographs intended as substitutes for actual specimens or presented as an alternative mode of natural history illustration. Sometimes photographs that were sent were inadvertently or conveniently overlooked and simply not acknowledged.[35] On other occasions, the exchange of photographs prompted expansive and thoughtful responses, and thus for colonial naturalists remained an expedient, if not always dependable, way of extracting information from correspondents and adding to their knowledge without forfeiting their own collections. Krefft used the medium intentionally in this way as he corresponded with Owen. Using photographs to test and corroborate his hypotheses about recently discovered fossil remains—of species including the *Diprotodon* and *Thylacoleo*—and query Owen's published descriptions of the extinct mammals of Australia, Krefft became an early, enthusiastic supporter of Darwin's theory of natural selection and openly challenged Owen's views and investigations into the process of evolution. By sending photographs along with, or instead of, written queries or views, Krefft and other colonial naturalists showed themselves unwilling to be cast as invisible apparatchiks deferentially sending specimens to London and were increasingly inclined to more assertively incorporate their own expertise into the process of knowledge formation.

In addition to the documentation of exotic specimens, views and native peoples, photography had the capability to advance the work of naturalists across the globe in other crucial but less obvious ways. Photographic portraiture, for example, became an important vehicle for demonstrating professional authority and integrity in an era when the trustworthiness of new knowledge very often centred on the figure of the individual naturalist. With science's growing profile and status depending heavily on the kinds of people it attracted, there seemed to be a genuine awareness of the temperament, motivations and virtues of those involved in formulating new knowledge.[36] *Cartes-de-visite*, especially, were mobilised to cultivate and acknowledge relationships between naturalists at home and abroad. In this respect, these extremely popular, mass-produced photographs performed a similar function as for others across society and, for the most part, amateur and professional scientists were portrayed in the same manner as every other sitter: posed against domestic-style backdrops in commercial photographic studios. For the sitter, and ultimately the viewer, these relatively informal and somewhat familiar portraits visually united these sitters and implied a social connection between them. Many *cartes-de-visite* were available for purchase by the general public, who were active in collecting and circulating them as well. Thus, photographic portraits of men of science were used to convey scientific authority to others in their field and also to the broader public. Specific information about naturalists' discoveries and their emerging roles in museum-building were similarly promoted though photographic portraiture. In this way, the scientific enterprise was socially sanctified. Across the empire, colonial naturalists were very much involved in the same self-fashioning as their metropolitan counterparts. If anything, naturalists working at the periphery had to work even harder to prove their credentials in the imperial realm of science. As James Hector, geologist and future director of New Zealand's Geological Survey and Colonial Museum, exemplified in his own *carte-de-visite*, the naturalist's powers of observation and attention to detail were essential skills and characteristics that typically distinguished the most accomplished individuals from others in their field (Fig. 15). In a portrait taken in a photographer's studio but nevertheless portraying the geologist at work with a loupe and a sample from his collection of rocks, fossils and minerals, Hector presents himself as a consummate observer of nature and, concomitantly, reinforces his reputation for carrying out pioneering work in the natural sciences. Rather than being a faceless contributor to the empire's expanding body of scientific knowledge, Hector used this portrait as a calling card that could be distributed widely and which would enable him to be recognised by other scientists of empire as a colleague, rather than dismissed as an anonymous colonial collector.

In *European Vision*, Bernard Smith identifies the invention of photography and its technological forerunners as a key development for the natural sciences that contributed to fundamental changes in the ways artists and scientists represented their encounters with nature in the South Pacific. Yet his exploration of this idea is relatively brief and, even though broached again in a subsequent study, is never satisfactorily worked through. An examination of this overlooked aspect of his thesis on the interrelationship of art and science in British expansionism entails some consideration about the ways natural history itself was being transformed and a broader investigation of the principal uses of photography by nineteenth-century naturalists. In this chapter, I have highlighted the proliferation of different types of photographic images and their circulation between metropolitan and colonial scientists, of whom the latter were contributing materially to evolutionary theory and actively redefining the very structure of imperial science. The role of photography in this process, and its longer-term potential, were far more complex than simply offering more naturalistic or objective images. Besides the recording of exotic life forms and views, other realms and genres of photography, such as commercial studio portraits, were just as essential to scientists' day-to-day activities and the advancement of imperial natural history. Consequently, photography was enlisted in any number of ways: towards fulfilling an official agenda but also in response to contemporary fashion and professional etiquette by incorporating more popular photographic genres. In Britain's expanding empire, photography was enlisted to document not only external nature but also the changing institutions and social realm of natural history itself. Furthermore, photographs, even more than other media, were accessible to a wide range of viewers.[37] Taking on a variety of distinct but often complementary roles, they could be construed quite differently or assume a new status as they moved between the centre and periphery. Addressing these other, equally significant applications—which encompassed or supported a widening range of activities and audiences, from the popular dissemination of scientific discovery to the expansion of scientific networks—reveals the rather more multifarious relationship between photography and natural history, and their corresponding roles in the context of empire.

NOTES

1 Bernard Smith, *Place, Taste and Tradition: A Study of Australian Art Since 1788*, 2nd edn, Oxford University Press, Melbourne, 1979 (1945), p. 20.

2 See W. J. T. Mitchell (ed.), *Landscape and Power*, Chicago University Press, Chicago, 1994; also Hugh Honour, *The European Vision of America*, exhibition catalogue, Cleveland Museum of Art, Cleveland, 1975.

3 Ernst H. Gombrich, *Art and Illusion: A Study in the Psychology of Pictorial Representation*, Phaidon Press, Oxford, 1980 (1960), p. 3.

4 Bernard Smith, *European Vision and the South Pacific*, 2nd edn (reprint), Yale University Press, New Haven, 1988, p. xi.

5 Smith, *European Vision and the South Pacific*, p. viii.

6 Thomas Kuhn, *The Structure of Scientific Revolutions*, 2nd edn, University of Chicago Press, Chicago, 1970, p. x, quoted in Smith, *European Vision and the South Pacific*, p. viii.

7 Smith, *European Vision and the South Pacific*, p. 335.

8 ibid., pp. 337–9.

9 ibid., p. 339; see Geoff Batchen, *Burning with Desire: The Conception of Photography*, MIT Press, Cambridge, Mass., 1997.

10 ibid., p. 335.

11 ibid.

12 Smith, *European Vision and the South Pacific*, p. 337; Charles Wilkes, *Narrative of the United States Exploring Expedition during the Years 1838, 1839, 1840, 1841, 1842*, vol. 4, G. P. Putnam, New York, 1859, p. 125.

13 Smith, *European Vision and the South Pacific*, p. 337.

14 ibid., pp. 335–7.

15 ibid., pp. 314–5.

16 ibid., p. 337.

17 Bernard Smith, *Imagining the Pacific: In the Wake of the Cook Voyages*, Miegunyah Press, Melbourne University Press, Melbourne, 1992, p. 1; William Ivins, *Prints and Visual Communication*, MIT Press, Cambridge, Mass., 1969.

18 I am indebted to Simon Schaffer for bringing this to my attention, in his lecture 'In Transit: European Cosmologies in the Pacific', delivered at the University of Sydney on 5 August 2010. The film produced was *The Sun Worshippers*, directed by Ernest 'Bud' Brandon-Cremer, 1922; alternative titles: *Solar Eclipse Expedition at Wallal* and *Astronomers and Aborigines*.

19 Frank Jovanovik, 'The Construction of the Canonical History of Financial Economics', *History of Political Economy*, vol. 40, no. 2, 2008, p. 230.

20 Smith, *Imagining the Pacific*, pp. 236–7.

21 Smith, *European Vision and the South Pacific*, pp. 13–14, 27–9.

22 Anne-Marie Willis, *Picturing Australia: A History of Photography*, Angus & Robertson, Sydney, 1988, p. 2; see also Helen Ennis, 'Other Histories: Photography and Australia', *Journal of Art Historiography*, no. 4, 2011, pp. 1–15.

23 Smith, *European Vision and the South Pacific*, pp. 274, 314–15.

24 George Basalla, 'The Spread of Western Science', in William K. Storey (ed.), *Scientific Aspects of European Expansion*, Variorum, Brookfield, Vt, 1996, pp. 1–21.

25 Smith, *European Vision and the South Pacific*, pp. 274–5.

26 Gael Newton, *et al.*, *Shades of Light: Photography and Australia 1839–1988*, exhibition catalogue, Australian National Gallery and Collins Australia with assistance from Kodak, Canberra, 1988, pp. 1–4.

27 See Richard Neville, *A Rage for Curiosity: Visualising Australia 1788–1830*, exhibition catalogue, State Library of New South Wales, Sydney, 1997; Caroline Jordan, *Picturesque Pursuits: Colonial Women Artists and the Amateur Tradition*, Melbourne University Press, Melbourne, 2005.

28 Ruth Pelzer, 'Technical Reproduction and its Significance', in Matthew Rampley (ed.), *Exploring Visual Culture: Definitions, Concepts, Contexts*, Edinburgh University Press, Edinburgh, 2005, p. 197.

29 Richard Owen, 'On some Outline-Drawings and Photographs of the Skull of the Zygomaturus Trilobus, *Macleay* (Nototherium, *Owen?*)', *Quarterly Journal of the Geological Society of London*, vol. 15, nos 1–2, February 1859, pp. 168–76.

30 Alan Atkinson, *The Europeans in Australia: A History*, vol. 1, Oxford University Press, Melbourne, 1997–2004, p. x.

31 Gerard Krefft to Richard Owen, 21 October 1864, Natural History Museum, London, General and Zoology Library, the Owen Collection: Correspondence, 27, ff. 3–5.

32 ibid.

33 Richard Owen to Gerard Krefft, 26 February 1870 and 22 April 1870, Owen Collection: Correspondence, 27, ff. 30–2 and 39–41 respectively.

34 Richard Owen, 'The Gorilla', *The Athenaeum*, 5 October 1861, pp. 445–6.

35 Julius von Haast to Richard Owen, 26 July 1872, Owen Collection: Correspondence, 14, ff. 163–9.

36 Michael Shortland and Richard Yeo (eds), *Telling Lives in Science: Essays on Scientific Biography*, Cambridge University Press, Cambridge, 1996, p. 37.

37 Eleanor Hight and Gary Sampson (eds), *Colonialist Photography: Imag(in)ing Race and Place*, Routledge, London, 2002, pp. 1–2.

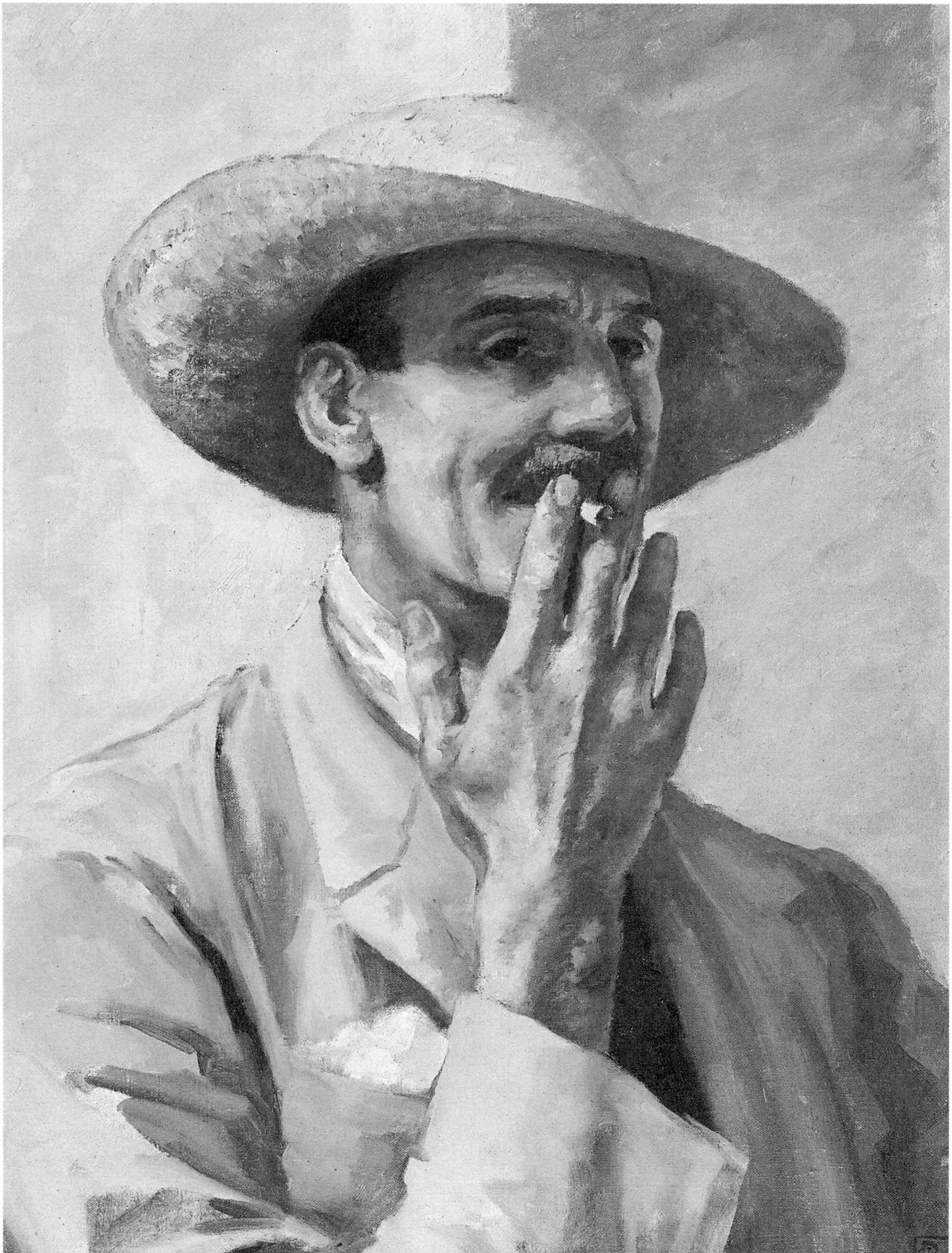

2

DEFINING AUSTRALIAN ART

Bernard Smith: the art historian as hero

TERRY SMITH

In the course of his long and immensely productive working life, Bernard Smith took on most of the roles afforded by the visual arts in the period of their expansive development in Western societies during the second half of the twentieth century: art teacher, artist, art historian, cultural historian, art critic, museum official, curator, university administrator, academician, collector, patron, and art theorist. To this daunting list, unmatched in its range by any other Australian writer on the visual arts, we must add his contributions in areas not confined to those arts: as a memoirist, of his own life and that of artist Noel Counihan; as a cultural commentator, notably in the Boyer Lectures of 1980, *The Spectre of Truganini*, and as a community activist on heritage matters. For an individual to pursue a variety of vocations is not, however, exceptional in places where the main task is building an arts infrastructure sufficiently strong, critically alert and diverse enough to encourage specialisation on the part of those to come. This was how it was in the Australian capital cities during Bernard's formative and mature years. As the essays in this volume amply demonstrate, he was a leader in many of these fields, and made pivotal, often controversial, contributions to all of them. Yet he believed that his most original and sustained achievements were as an art historian and a thinker about the histories of cultures, especially the roles of visual images and visual imagining within them. Certainly, it was in these two fields that he tackled the biggest challenges and the largest questions.

Bernard's contributions to the latter field are the subject of sociologist Peter Beilharz's invaluable book *Imagining the Antipodes: Culture, Theory and the Visual in the Work of Bernard Smith*, in which he explores the operative nature of Bernard's 'social theory' of 'peripheral vision'.[1] He argues that 'Bernard Smith's work adds up to the most sophisticated social theory which has yet been developed in Australia'.[2] A complementary task suggests itself. How might we assess the character and the quality of Bernard Smith's contributions as a historian of art, one who, throughout his career, saw himself as studying art in the broader field of the history of cultures?

COMPARATIVE GREATNESS

If we were asking this question in the middle of the last century, or during the second half of the century before then (that is, within the scope of the modern history of art history as a discipline), we would most likely answer it in terms of degree and kind of greatness. We would compare Bernard's achievement with those of his predecessors and contemporaries whose pre-eminence is widely acknowledged, and make a considered judgement based on its originality, its comprehensiveness, and its influence relative to theirs. Bernard himself did not hesitate to make such judgements; for example, he regarded Sir Ernst Gombrich as 'the greatest art historian of the twentieth century'.[3] He regularly returned to the writings of other deep transformers of the discipline, notably Jacob Burckhardt, Aby Warburg and Erwin Panofsky. Bernard drew his strongest sense of what art history was as a discipline from men such as these. He also rated Rudolf Wittkower, Edgar Wind, Gertrud Bing, Dame Frances Yates, and others at the Warburg and Courtauld Institutes, University of London, including Anthony Blunt, very highly for their erudition and technical brilliance. Others, notably Sir Nikolaus Pevsner, doyen of architectural historians, and the lexicographer Julius Meier-Graefe, he respected for their persistence in sustaining essential research projects over long periods of time. Some of us value Bernard's lifetime achievement as at least equivalent to that of these men and women.

When, however, we compare Bernard's work to that of his leading contemporaries, the exercise becomes less of a rating game, and more instructive as to the nature of his achievement. At this point, it is appropriate to become more specific about tendencies in twentieth-century art-historical thought. *Place, Taste and Tradition* (1945) was the first complete history of the art of a nation written from a Marxist perspective. It remains one of the few such histories, although there are some parallels in Barry Lord's *The History of Painting in Canada: Towards a People's Art* (1974), a Trotskyite text. In the first and second editions of *Australian Painting* (1962 and 1970), Bernard modified his radical critique, perhaps (as Humphrey McQueen suggests) due to pervasive Cold War pressures, or, as Bernard himself often observed, in repulsion from the doctrinaire rigidities of social realist orthodoxy.[4] A more immediate cause might well have been the exigencies of writing a textbook intended for a wide and relatively uninformed audience. When it comes to art historians of his own generation, however, the relevant comparison is not to narrators of national art histories but to those with a much wider reach and scope, such as Hans Belting in Germany and, in the United States, Meyer Schapiro, Leo Steinberg and Linda Nochlin.

Of these scholars, comparison with Meyer Schapiro offers the most illumination. In the chapter that he devotes to Schapiro in *The Intelligence of Art*, Thomas Crow characterises him not only as a great American art historian but also as 'the quintessential outsider writing art history'.[5] Although Smith was born twelve years later, there are many similar turning points in the life stories of these two men. Born in Lithuania in 1904, Schapiro was brought by his father a few years later to the United States, where he studied in Brooklyn and Manhattan. He forged his career almost entirely at Columbia University, New York. Schapiro travelled regularly to Europe on research trips, but remained tied to his base in New York, rarely teaching elsewhere. Smith, likewise, was based in Melbourne or Sydney for all of his working life. He undertook research trips to Europe, beginning with his years at the Warburg Institute (1948–51), intermittently thereafter, then, soon after his retirement to Melbourne in 1977, intensively to work on the materials in London and Paris related to Cook's and Baudin's voyages. Smith moved on from the Marxist polemics with which he concluded *Place, Taste and Tradition* and the direct engagement with artists evident in 'The Antipodean Manifesto' (1959) to become not only the leading historian of Australian art but also the most prominent art historian working in Australia in any field. Schapiro, likewise, was a Marxist polemicist during the 1930s, who became arguably the world's leading scholar of medieval art, and was doubtless the most prominent academic advocate of contemporary American art during the abstract expressionist era. Eventually, he became an enormously influential writer on modern art in general.[6] By the 1970s and 1980s, as the work of European scholars shaken loose by Hitler (Panofsky above all) established itself as the orthodoxy for the discipline in the United States, Schapiro became widely regarded as the home-schooled 'great' who represented the best of these traditional aspects of the discipline as they may be pursued by an American in America.[7] He was also acknowledged, late in his career, for his pioneering studies of semiotics in relation to art, a result of his openness to scientific developments as constitutive of modern cultures. Although, to my knowledge, the two men did not know each other, the parallels between the Brooklyn Jew who became a University Professor at Columbia University and 'the lucky young bastard' who became Power Professor of Contemporary Art at the University of Sydney hardly need underscoring.

More interesting than these situational similarities, however, are the parallels in the two men's thinking, the consonances between the intellectual edifices—or, more accurately, the collection of working theories—that they both slowly and carefully pieced together in order to tackle the specific challenges that they saw before them in a cluster of fields and on a variety of levels. Pursuing Schapiro's side of the parallel would carry us too far away from the subject, so I will leave that for now. I have already introduced two crucial elements of Bernard's conceptual armature: Karl Marx's acute, thorough and revolutionary critique of modern capitalism, and the acute, thorough but decidedly unrevolutionary narrative of the afterlife of ancient imagery in the modern world, the main subject of Warburgian and Panofskian iconography, especially as it had been institutionalised at the Warburg Institute in London, and in the United States at the Institute of Fine Arts, New York, and at Princeton. When, in 1949, the closet communist Anthony Blunt, director of the exclusivist, connoisseurship-based Courtauld Institute, sent the young antipodean student over to the Warburg Institute, these two systems came into a very productive convergence, one that resulted in *European Vision and the South Pacific*.

THE ENLIGHTENMENT AT ITS LIMITS

In *European Vision and the South Pacific* Bernard tracked, more thoroughly than ever before attempted, the exigencies of image-making during the voyages of exploration and scientific record-making in the South Pacific during the later eighteenth century, and those that attended colonial settlement in the decades that followed. Motivated by a desire to map out the prehistory and early years of professional and semi-professional art practice in the colonies on Terra Australis, Smith also wanted to show how the experiences of artists in this, the last great area of the world unknown to European science, contributed to the development of European art. He argued that, in the South Pacific, the aesthetic limits of neoclassicism were reached, and, while picturesque conventions came in handy when artists such as Thomas Watling and Sir Oswald Brierly dressed up their sketches as paintings intended for viewers in London, the objectivity required by scientific reporting led to the triumph of 'analytical naturalism' in nineteenth-century art, most notably in landscape painting. If his notion of the 'typical landscape' has not been widely adopted, few would doubt the general claim about the important connections between art and science during this period. In Europe itself, of course, industrialisation was a key causal factor, and romanticism had evolved as a more complex response to social change. It was these factors that attracted the attention of European-based historians of the period.

Nevertheless, in taking up such distant, and 'low art' materials, we can see that, art-historiographically, this was a project pursued at the outer edges of institutionalised iconographic art history, although it does fall well within the fascination for exotic visual cultures, and correspondences between elements of exotic imagery and that of European cultures, that inspired the Warburg Institute scholars to seek a broader, more worldly view of what, for modernists, was a form of primitivism. Nevertheless, unlike Warburg's quest in New Mexico, there is little indication in *European Vision and the South Pacific* of an interest in the view from the other side of the encounter. In Bernard's view, unexceptional in its time, these were concerns proper to anthropology. This aside, by taking up European 'vision' as its main subject, *European Vision and the South Pacific* is one of the first sustained studies of what would come to be called the 'visual culture' of a time and place—in this case, a culture at its limits, striving to make sense of what it was seeing on distant and alien shores. Bernard himself would never use an expression such as 'visual culture', especially not if it indicated any sense of an approach that might displace art history as the central discipline for the study of all forms of visual imagination. Indeed, in the preface to the second edition of 1985 he rejected any such suggestion as 'extreme cultural relativism'.[8]

CONSISTENCY AND CHANGE

Throughout his working life, Bernard maintained a deep fealty to both of the frameworks I have identified, despite the very different politics that animated each. On one side, the engaged critic, committed to realism in art, with a Marxist understanding of society and culture, one that owed much more to Australians V. Gordon Childe and Jack Lindsay than it did to the party-line orthodoxies of Andrei Zhdanov, codifier of socialist realism, although it owed most, as Beilharz shows, to historian Arnold Toynbee.[9] It became, by the 1950s, more Marxian than Marxist. The other foundation is the history of art as a modern, university- and museum-based professional discipline, above all as it developed in Germany in the late nineteenth and early twentieth centuries, then spread to universities elsewhere in Europe and the United States, and on to their spheres of influence, including Australia. Within this, as we have noted, it was the wide-ranging iconographic studies of these scholars that attracted Bernard, as much as their ability to show how images meant something in their contexts of use ('iconology', as Panofsky named it, or 'cultural history' à la Burckhardt), and how images change meaning when used differently, or used in different combinations ('iconomorphic', he called it).[10] Bernard seems to have found the pairing of these foundations continuously enabling, however overtly contradictory on the level of ideology they may have been. Yet they have common roots in nineteenth-century Hegelianism, and they share significant affinities with twentieth-century humanism, a combination that, for Bernard, constituted his philosophical ground plan, in so far as he had one.

On this matter, as on most others, Beilharz is closest to the bull's-eye, again:

> Bernard Smith, then, is a civilisational thinker with a difference: there is no system in his work. Sorokin, Spengler, Toynbee and Marx all together laboured in

> massive multi-volume projects of majestic synthesis. Smith read all these tomes, but chose instead to write monographs on aspects as they summoned him.[11]

The word 'civilisational' here might give us pause, but Beilharz has picked up an echo of the dynamic that drove art history as a discipline in Germany in the mid-nineteenth century, and that continues to do so today: the interplay between *Kunstwissenschaft* and *Kulturgeschichte*, or between aesthetics and cultural history. The foundational modern text of 'cultural history' as it relates to the visual arts is Jacob Burckhardt's *The Civilization of the Renaissance in Italy* (1860). In Chapter 2 of *The Formalesque*, Bernard's final summary of the history of the discipline of art history as he understood it, Hegel and Burckhardt are joined as demonstrating that art history was, from the beginning, 'deeply embedded in cultural history'.[12] It is no accident that 'taste' is the central term of *Place, Taste and Tradition*, or that his collection of primary source materials for the study of Australian art is entitled *Documents on Art and Taste in Australia*.[13] Nor is it incidental that he looked for a theory within aesthetics that allowed for ways of valuing the variety of visual cultural forms produced by humans. Never satisfied with the modernist distinction between high and low art, or the older one between fine art and folk art, because both are loaded in favour of the elites, he kept searching for a description of the zone between art and popular imagery, between professional image-making and the people's imagining.

Yet, if Bernard sought no system, he certainly insisted on developing a working framework, a tool kit of concepts and procedures that had a degree of internal consistency as well as a capacity to adapt to changing demands. The framework, always a double dynamic, changed considerably over the years, and may be understood in four phases which, due to delays in publication, cannot be confined to dates, and therefore overlap somewhat: (i) 1940s and 1950s, the principal monuments being *Place, Taste and Tradition* and *European Vision and the South Pacific*; (ii) 1959 through to the late 1970s, marked by *The Antipodean Manifesto*, *Australian Painting*, his practice as an art critic, and the founding decade of the Power Institute; (iii) the post-retirement years, 1977 to the later 1980s, during which *The Spectre of Truganini*, *The Boy Adeodatus*, *The Art of Captain Cook's Voyages* and *Noel Counihan: Artist and Revolutionary* were written; and (iv) the 1990s to 2011, the main outcomes of which were *Modernism's History* and *The Formalesque*.

The overall progression is from the Marxist critic and antipodean cultural historian described above through many transitions until, in the 1990s, another doubled working framework emerges: on the one hand, the conservative art-historical scholar and reactionary aesthetician, and on the other, the revolutionary theorist of comparative visual cultures and the speculative art historiographer. Bernard continued to deploy this framework to deal with the contemporary art that was being made around him, and, while shaping his art-historical narratives, with period style terms such as 'modernism' and 'postmodernism'. Increasingly, concern with such concepts came to preoccupy his cultural-historical thinking as well. Modernism and postmodernism, as the names of art-historical tendencies, artistic practices and art-critical attitudes, were for him largely negative indicators.[14] The claims to aesthetic autonomy inherent in much modernist art, criticism and historical writing challenged his framework, especially during the years of their ascendancy—the 1950s through the 1970s (phases ii and iii above). Postmodernism in all its varieties was his *bête noire* during the last stages of his working life. Committed as he was to his roles—from interventionist, through chronicler, to critic—as a maker and shaper of culture, he did not resile from grappling with both of them.

TWO SPECTRES: MODERNISM AND POSTMODERNISM

In an unpublished essay, 'Adult Aesthetic Education', submitted on 28 June 1944 to the Education Department in Sydney, the would-be graduate student surveys the education of artists and of 'consumers' of art, from the Renaissance academies to the Encouragement of Art Movement then active in Sydney factories. Among models for educating artists, the Bauhaus and the United States' Works Progress Administration are given pride of place, whereas educating public taste has been most successfully done, he argues, by the Metropolitan Museum and the Museum of Modern Art in New York, and by the Council for the Encouragement of Art and Music in London. Bernard's link to MoMA was design curator Edgar Kaufmann Jr, in Sydney as a cultural liaison officer for the US Army. While Alfred H. Barr Jr had committed MoMA to a French modernism, in which formal innovation and finesse were the paramount indicators of quality and modernity, the educational program of the museum, and some of its exhibitions, especially its travelling shows, were more broadly and inclusively conceived.[15]

Bernard understood that European avant-gardism, including modernist abstraction, was an important engine in the development of modern art. Realism, however, was the other, and that was where his commitment lay. When he had the chance to intervene and influence the way art might be going, he fought, in the 1940s, against surrealism as a perversion of realism, and then in the 1950s against American-type abstraction. Both, he believed, pointed art along the wrong pathways, away from the figuring of social being towards, in the case of surrealism, atomised individualism and eventually fascism, or, in the case of abstraction, towards conformist, consumerist cultures. *Place, Taste and Tradition* was forged in the furnace of the first struggle, the first two editions of *Australian Painting* in the latter. In both texts, especially the first, the complex and contradictory demands of each moment are plain to see as part of the subject matter. But they also shape the art-historical methods that Smith deploys in each, concentrating them powerfully in *Place, Taste and Tradition*, while fragmenting them in *Australian Painting*, despite its surface tone as a narrative textbook.[16]

By the later 1960s Bernard could see that, when it came to naming the main line of twentieth-century modernism, formalism had prevailed. It had become the core methodology of modernist art histories of modern art, those that privileged modernism as the definitive tendency in twentieth-century art. This approach was represented especially strongly in the United States, by then the powerhouse of institutionalised art-historical studies, in textbooks such as H. H. Arnason's *A History of Modern Art: Painting, Sculpture, Architecture*, in multiple editions since 1969, and in the influential art criticism of Clement Greenberg and his many followers among art writers, curators, educators and artists. In inviting Greenberg to give the inaugural John Power Memorial Lecture in 1968, Bernard assuaged those who wanted the Power Institute to simply present 'the latest ideas and theories concerning contemporary art to the people of Australia', as Power's will stipulated. In the event, everybody, except some of the local ultra-avant-gardists, got what they wanted: a deeply reactionary linking of the most innovative modernism with the lineage of the Old Masters, along with the assertion that avant-gardism was not the basis of authentic art, but merely an art world 'attitude'.[17]

There is much in *Modernism's History* (1998) that is, in art-historiographical terms, as revolutionary as was *European Vision and the South Pacific* for the history of cultures.[18] The view from the peripheries that inspired the earlier volume returns with a vengeance. Smith again argues for the agency of the peripheries in precipitating change in the centres, and reaffirms that the peripheries have always made choices about which innovations from the centres they will adopt and which they will reject in their ongoing process of adapting traditions to change. But awareness of the continuing concentration of power at the centres prevents him from adding these two together, to write 'Modernism's Histories', a move that would have lead to the multiple-modernities project that was being theorised at the same time by Rasheed Araeen, Kobena Mercer, Okwui Enwezor and others.[19] Perhaps Bernard simply took it for granted, that this was what he had been doing all along. Now, it is the main interest of historians and curators of modern art all over the world.

It is unfortunate that the advent of postmodernism blindsided Bernard into believing that a new style term for the art of the late-nineteenth to later-twentieth centuries was required, despite the universal acceptance of 'modernism' as a contested and limiting but accurate enough general descriptor for the mainstream of art during this period. It was difficult for many of us to reconcile the core meanings of 'modern' ('of today', 'new', 'not the past', 'progressive') with the historical closure of the era in which art made according to these values was significantly definitive of it. Those of us raised in the values of that era did assume that these meanings were complex enough, and sufficiently contestable, to drive all imaginable futures. Otherwise, we would not have deployed a term so universal that it ran the risk of historical supercession. Yet this was a potential from day one, as it has been, since the 1980s, for the use of 'contemporary' as the primary name for contemporary art. The strategy is to complicate and layer the meanings that are in play within these terms, not reduce them to one prescriptive meaning that must always apply, irrespective of the situation. Only someone who wants modernism to come again in a guise yet to be recognised would wish to label the art of the period that has passed with a name other than the one it adopted as its own. It is strange that that someone turned out to be Bernard Smith.

In the 1992 lecture in which he first sets out his response to the challenges of the 1980s, Bernard gives the art-historical period from c. 1910 to c. 1970 the name 'formalism'. Another puzzle: a lifelong opponent of Greenbergian formalism promotes it to titular leadership. In this lecture, Bernard argues that postmodernism, having replaced the earlier phase, is the modernism of the present. It, too, he asserts, will be replaced by modernisms to come. Somehow, artistic modernism, an art-historical and critical term, has become a word in ordinary language and means, simply, 'modern'.[20] In the book *Modernism's History*, Smith recognises that artistic modernism has in fact been a dissimulative and distortive tendency, and thus deserves a name that reflects this quality. Typically, he draws on the art-historical precedent of using reductive, negative style terms, as he knows from the record that these have the best chance of sticking. Thus 'formalism' becomes 'the Formalesque'. In this smart-alecky anti-theory attempt to outsmart a kind of theorisation that he finds contemptible, the least felicitous aspect of his thinking blinks awkwardly in the light. The central chapters of *The Formalesque* (2007) are the unfortunate outcome of the same mistake.

ANACHRONISM REVERSED

In an essay that is as perceptive about Bernard Smith the art historian as Beilharz's book is about Bernard Smith the cultural historian, Ian McLean pinpoints the root cause of what he calls Bernard's 'reverse anachronism'.[21] Bernard's devotion to the originators of modern art history as a discipline, from Winckelmann to the scholars identified above, locked him into what McLean, drawing on Gerard Delanty, identifies as 'the classic idea of Europe', in which the most significant social values were fashioned by class struggle within each country, national rivalry on the continent, and imperial contestation abroad.[22] While it is too simple to say that early modern art history as a discipline served this European ideal consciously and whole-heartedly, it is rare indeed to find an art historian among 'the greats' who thought beyond its ideological parameters. Nevertheless, it should be recalled that these scholars, while devoted to profiling the historical evolution of the arts and crafts in the European region, took the art of the known world as the proper *scope* of the discipline itself.[23] Seen from Sydney in the late 1930s and early 1940s, such an approach seemed far broader in scope, and longer in duration, than those tied to the ultra-nationalist conflagration then consuming Europe and spreading throughout the world.

Yet, as McLean convincingly shows, it was an approach increasingly difficult to sustain in postwar Europe. It would become even more so during the Cold War, as the 'idea of Europe' receded in favour of 'the West', and a set of alliances led by the United States became engaged in pitched ideological battle and proxy wars with the 'Second World', in the shadow of a potentially world-destroying nuclear arms race. The art-historical narratives of modern art, and the art-critical 'theory' of artistic modernism, are products of this change in the world picture. Bernard opposed these in the name of a critically engaged social realism in art practice (*The Antipodean Manifesto*) and in the name of an ideal European art historiography. His antipodeanism—as Beilharz demonstrates throughout his study—is founded on the basic insight that our shared histories mean that all of us, like it or not, are both Australian and European at the same time, all the time, inescapably. This includes the recognition that Europeans are, equally inescapably, always already also Australians, or, more generally, in a reciprocal relationship with their colonised. This 'reverse perspective' holds in theory, at least. In practice of course Eurocentrism meant that many, perhaps most, Europeans remained oblivious to, or refused to recognise, their obligation to this relationship, just as many, perhaps most, Australians might believe naively that they can choose to be nationalists only.[24] These relationships are fundamental, but they are not wholly, mechanically determinative. Marx taught, and Bernard knew, that to some degree we could all act to shape just where we stood in these relationships, that we could decide at least some aspects of what kind of antipodean we aspired to become. Thus the passionate commitment of Bernard's interventions, and the sustained pursuit of his goals as an educator.

However much man might make himself, as Marx put it, the larger force-field within which he does so is, in fundamental respects, beyond his control. Bernard took the fight against North American style cultural imperialism to the abstract painters whom he saw as embodying it and to the institutions spreading it around the world, including to Australia (especially Sydney). Yet, as McLean concludes:

> Smith's reputation as an historian of national art is deserved, but if his histories are written against the grain of Western avant-gardism they are written within the context of a global rather than a Western worldview and one that identifies with the classic idea of Europe and an earlier avant-garde culture … In clinging to the German professors Smith rejected the discipline's Cold War retreat into the Occident but he also missed an opportunity to develop a historiography adequate to the post-imperial world.[25]

Precisely at the point that Bernard found that his operative framework was reaching its limits with regard to the challenge of understanding the art of his time, and how that art was changing perceptions of past art, many others faced the same dilemma. Yet they found ways out of the impasse that were productive, and have remained so until quite recently. Augmenting McLean's insightful analysis, I draw attention to the 'social history of art' project as articulated by T. J. Clark in 1974, and as developed by him and others into a critical art-historical practice. Clark proposed a dynamic alliance of 'the young Marx' (the experimental critic of systematised Hegelianism) and the 'early Marxist art historians', such as Max Raphael, Ernst Bloch and Walter Benjamin, as a recipe for revolutionising art-historical orthodoxy.[26] I know that Bernard greatly admired Clark's books of the early 1970s, and that Clark has the same view of Bernard's early achievement. But the double-sided framework we have discerned could, it seems, no longer be adapted to changing circumstances. The changes in art, thought and human affairs that began during the 1970s became a bridge too far for attitudes formed in crucibles more than a century earlier—in 1848 and the years following.

Bernard would not update his Marxism back towards the Karl Marx of the *Economic and Philosophical Manuscripts of 1844*, which was unknown to him before being translated in the 1960s, but subsequently much discussed by members of the English-speaking New Left.[27] To change would have required an embrace of at least some of the new perspectives, of the kind being advanced by French Marxists such as Louis Althusser among others, which Bernard found repugnant in all respects. As we have seen, he also chose not to update his art-historical methodology, spurning much of the revisionary radicalism that inspired what was called 'the New Art History'.[28] An explicit rejection of these initiatives as 'unlikely to propose any basic alternatives to the enduring concerns of art history: style, image and context' appears in his 1984 review essay for the Australian Academy of the Humanities: 'Art Historical Studies in Australia with Comments on Research and Publication since 1974'.[29]

These rejections meant that Bernard was unprepared to adjust his overall philosophical ground plan when confronted with post-structuralism during the following decade, dismissing it wholesale. Although he incessantly revised many specific elements of his approach, and constantly revisited his earlier achievements as the key books were issued in new editions and as they attracted two, then three, generations of commentary, the result was that, after the 1980s, he found himself in the position of constantly defending the orthodoxies that his own earlier work had already pointed ways past.

CONTEMPORARY CONCERNS

There is no absolute requirement to be absolutely contemporary, not now, not ever. Indeed, as all serious commentators on contemporaneity point out as their first move, updating one's attitudes so as to follow the latest ideas and theories is to become a contemporary in only the most mindless of senses, to be a passive recipient of that which originates elsewhere, to value everything not because it is new or useful or full of potential but because it is now.[30] It is unsurprising that, in his very first piece of art criticism, Bernard excoriated this tendency, by attacking the organisers of the Contemporary Art Society (CAS) for removing all criteria for entry into their annual exhibition in Sydney in 1943. This, he argued, condemned them to a state of 'permanent contemporaneity'.[31] He saw this as a mindless kind of modernism, in contrast to the engaged realism he favoured against the 'purely abstract and constructivist work', which, he noted with grim satisfaction, was 'definitely losing its adherents'.[32] In the local battle over what was the truly modern art of the moment, he was an outsider to the CAS definition, as formulated by the Melbourne branch in 1938:

> By the expression 'contemporary art' is meant all contemporary painting, sculpture, drawing and other visual art forms which is or are original and creative

> or which strive to give expression to contemporary thought and life as opposed to work which is reactionary and retrogressive including work which has no other aim than representation.[33]

Based on distinctions made by the London CAS, founded in 1910 and the model for the Australian branches, this statement of intent was mainly aimed against academic naturalism. Yet, in the case of Herbert Read in England, and John Reed and the Heide cohort in Melbourne, it also provided sufficient grounds to be wary of the local social realists.

Contemporary art became a vital category for Bernard again when, as a practising art critic in Melbourne, he joined in the debate about how best to implement the Power Bequest to the University of Sydney, announced in 1962. He was dismayed by Herbert Read's advice that the sole focus should be on instructing the general public in international contemporary painting and sculpture through exhibitions, demonstrations, and participation with visiting artists, free from the 'dead hands of historians'.[34] Although Power's will stipulated that his core intent was to fund a 'Faculty of Arts' that would 'bring the latest ideas and theories concerning contemporary art to the people of Australia ... by means of lectures, exhibitions, and the like', Bernard was adamant that Power 'did not possess the grotesque and bizarre notion' that this faculty should 'concern itself in the most literal way only with "the latest ideas and theories"', treating them as 'so many sacred cows beyond the reach of criticism'.[35] Because 'ideas and theories enter history as soon as they are uttered, any division into the most recent, the recent and the past must be arbitrary', historians are essential to what he saw as the main challenge:

> to fashion an honest critical style that can approach the present without shedding the values of the past; to bring dispassionate and responsible evaluation grounded in tolerance and the scholarly disciplines of the humanist to the disturbing and complex art of our time.[36]

Only this could fulfil what he saw as Power's core concern:

> for the education of the patron of art, that is to train taste, sensibility and critical understanding so that Australians may be able to approach the most recent manifestations of art with an informed and open mind.[37]

Sounds like the basis of a program for an institute, and so it proved.

During the institute's early years, the question of what might be meant by 'contemporary art' was a constant in debates about the institute and between those of us in it. In 1965 the University Senate settled the main issue concerning orientation by changing the name used during preliminary discussion from Power Institute of Contemporary Art to Power Institute of Fine Arts, within which the teaching arm became the Department of Fine Arts, while the gallery and the library were to focus on contemporary art. Bernard became the Power Professor of Contemporary Art and Director of the Power Institute of Fine Arts. In his 1969 inaugural lecture there is more than a touch of the self-portrait in Bernard's profile of John Power and of the institute itself in these words: 'The Power Institute is a kind of institutionalisation of restlessness, the gift of an alienated man, a gift for the promotion of change'.[38]

Of the many occasions during this period on which Bernard commented on questions of contemporaneity, I will note just one, as it typifies his acuity and prescience. *Concerning Contemporary Art* (1975) is a collection of the first six Power Memorial Lectures, given between 1968 and 1973 by Clement Greenberg, Donald Brook, Charles Mitchell, Patrick Hutchings, Richard Wollheim, and Patrick Heron. Bernard's brief introduction, written in London in 1973, profiles the state of debate regarding 'the contemporary' in terms that we continue to revisit. Noting that half of the lecturers presumed 'contemporary' to cover 'the advanced art of the twentieth century considered as a whole', while the others focused on 'the advanced art of the 1960s', he deemed the coexistence of these two understandings quite satisfactory, as it would be prejudicial—uncontemporary, we might now say—to 'delimit the field of enquiry too firmly'.[39] So far, so sage. Next, out come the historian's talons:

> Contemporary art is, of course, a question-begging term. All art was once contemporary; and all art which still exists even though produced in remote antiquity is, in an important sense contemporary. It is in the present and may be seen and admired in the present.

The talons retract when he notes that the lecturers have not tackled such 'larger issues'. Instead, they work within the 'general present usage: that which denotes the *avant garde* art of the twentieth century'. Out come the talons again:

> Like all substantive definitions of the contemporary it is bound to go out of date one day. There is always a moment in history when the contemporary becomes gothic, and already the usage adopted here is beginning to fade into history.

The talons remain out as he goes on to observe that while many of us remain tied to the 'visual systematising of the genuinely new' (that is, modernism—a word he does not use directly), commitment to such a value 'seems to be less compelling for many—and many who are young—than it once was'. He concludes:

> We appear to be living through a period during which one system of hitherto contemporary art is losing its visual grasp upon an increasingly intractable present, while another slouches towards the second millennium to be born.[40]

The changes that he had in mind were already receiving a bewildering variety of names, from tendency labels such as minimal, conceptual, performance, or land art, to more general ones such as 'post-object art', a term advanced with vigour by our colleague Donald Brook. I have always thought that, by inviting Donald to give the second Power Lecture, Bernard was not only seeking to keep the enemy close, but also to illustrate, by contrast, the divide that was taking place between the two systems: one dying away, the other 'a rough beast', the monstrosity, or perhaps the luminosity, to come.[41]

The true contemporary stands at an angle to her times, sceptical of its most attractive claims about itself, and with an eye on pasts, and on possibilities, seeing the present as a work in historical formation. There is no question that Bernard did this, more sharply, and more broadly, than most of his contemporaries, and that he did so for most of his working life. He battled the millennial monsters born in the 1980s—postmodernism, and official, market-driven, spectacularist Contemporary Art—but, as is being suggested, fought them with weapons from earlier times, weapons too worn, by then, to be effective.

MEASURE FOR MEASURE

The debt to Bernard owed by everyone working on art in Australia is obvious to all who do so: almost everywhere you look, you find that Bernard has been there before you. Indigenous art, much art by women, and increasingly, for more obvious reasons, contemporary art, were the exceptions. Those who also work on art from elsewhere, and on exchanges between cultures, likewise owe him a great debt. His life's work illuminates much of the architecture of the trafficking in images between cultures from the mid-eighteenth century to the later twentieth. It is, therefore, foundational not only to regional studies of such exchanges but also to visual cultural studies as a discipline devoted to the examination of ways of world-picturing. Among the many examples of his influence in this regard, I cite just two major instances: Nicholas Thomas's studies of the entanglement between cultures in Oceania and Nicholas Mirzoeff's exploration of *The Right to Look: A Counterhistory of Visuality*.[42] Both acknowledge Bernard's precedence; neither project would have been possible without his work and example.

Antipodean consciousness was developed to challenge the master–slave dialectic that drove the age of imperialism. Now, it must take on the contractions and dispersions at war in contemporary world-making—including the modernities and other kinds of pasts that shoot through it—from a perspective that is not only global, but also planetary in compass. Contemporary antipodeans are deeply indebted to Bernard's lifelong enterprise, even as we continue to contest it. He was always ready for a contest, and enjoyed every battle. More than the 'greats' he so admired, his life and work, from his beginnings to his end, demonstrate that an art-historian hero is something to be.

NOTES

1 Peter Beilharz, *Imagining the Antipodes: Culture, Theory and the Visual in the Work of Bernard Smith*, Cambridge University Press, Cambridge, 1997, pp. xii, 183ff.

2 ibid., p. 183.

3 Bernard Smith, 'Introduction: A Bibliographical Memoir', in John Spencer and Peter Wright (eds), *The Writings of Bernard Smith: Bibliography 1938–1998*, Power Institute: Foundation for Art and Visual Culture, Power Publications, Sydney, 2000, p. 9.

4 Humphrey McQueen, 'Critic and Community: Some Recent Writings of Bernard Smith' [book review], *Meanjin*, vol. 36, no. 1, May 1977, p. 42–5.

5 Thomas E. Crow, *The Intelligence of Art*, University of North Carolina Press, Chapel Hill, 1999, pp. 6–23.

6 Representative texts are Meyer Schapiro, *Romanesque Art*, Selected Papers, vol. 1, George Braziller, New York, 1977; *Modern Art: 19th and 20th Centuries*, Selected Papers, vol. 2, George Braziller, New York, 1978; *Late Antique, Early Christian and Medieval Art*, Selected Papers, vol. 3, George Braziller, New York, 1979. As to commentary, see, for example, Michael Camille, 'How New York Stole the Idea of Romanesque Art: Medieval, Modern and Postmodern in Meyer Schapiro', *Oxford Art Journal*, vol. 17, no. 1, 1994, pp. 65–75. My personal debt to Schapiro is registered in the introductory remarks to 'Meyer Schapiro on Style in Art and Science: Notes from a Theory and Methods of Art History Graduate Seminar Lecture Course, Columbia University, New York, 1973', *Journal of Art Historiography*, no. 7, December 2012, http://arthistoriography.wordpress.com/2012/12/smith.pdf.

7 See Erwin Panofsky, 'Epilogue: Three Decades of Art History in the United States: Impressions of a Transplanted European' (1955), in *Meaning in the Visual Arts*, University of Chicago Press, Chicago, 1983; for Crow on Schapiro as an American art historian, see Crow, *The Intelligence of Art*, Chapter 1.

8 Bernard Smith, *European Vision and the South Pacific*, 2nd edn, Harper & Row, Sydney, 1985, p. vii.

9 Beilharz, *Imagining the Antipodes*, pp. 10–12, 190–2.

10 Bernard Smith, 'Image and Meaning in Western Painting', *The Listener*, vol. 68, no. 1738, 19 July 1962, pp. 93–6.

11 Beilharz, *Imagining the Antipodes*, pp. 192–3.

12 Bernard Smith, *The Formalesque: A Guide to Modern Art and Its History*, Macmillan, Melbourne, 2007, p. 50.

13 Bernard Smith (ed.), *Documents on Art and Taste in Australia: The Colonial Period, 1770–1914*, Oxford University Press, Melbourne, 1975.

14 Bernard was hardly alone among art historians in this view. Belting identifies the modernist stream in art-historical writing as the major parallel to those based on connoisseurship and iconography/iconology. See Hans Belting, *The End of the History of Art?*, University of Chicago Press, Chicago, 1987.

15 See Richard Myer, *When Was Contemporary Art?*, MIT Press, Cambridge, Mass., 2013.

16 For further analysis of this aspect, see Terry Smith, 'Writing the History of Australian Art: Its Past, Present, and Possible Future', *Australian Journal of Art*, vol. 3, 1983, pp. 14–17, 20–2, http://arthistoriography.files.wordpress.com/2011/05/smith-writing-the-history.pdf.

17 Clement Greenberg, *Avant-garde Attitudes: New Art in the Sixties*, The John Power Lecture in Contemporary Art, Delivered at the University of Sydney on Friday 17 May 1968, Power Institute of Fine Arts, University of Sydney, Sydney, 1969; in Bernard Smith (ed.), *Concerning Contemporary Art*, Clarendon Press, Oxford, 1975, pp. 5–15. For a local commentary, see Terry Smith, 'The "Style of the Sixties"', *Quadrant*, no. 58, March–April 1969, pp. 49–53.

18 Bernard Smith, *Modernism's History: A Study in Twentieth-Century Art and Ideas*, Yale University Press, New Haven, 1998; University of New South Wales Press, Sydney, 1998.

19 See Kobena Mercer, *Cosmopolitan Modernisms*, Institute of International Visual Arts, London, in association with MIT Press, Cambridge, Mass., 2005.

20 Bernard Smith, *Modernism and Post-Modernism: A Neo-Colonial Viewpoint*, Working Papers in Australian Studies, no. 81, Sir Robert Menzies Centre for Australian Studies, University of London, London, 1992, pp. 5–7.

21 See Ian McLean, 'Reverse Perspective: Bernard Smith's Worldview and the Cosmopolitan Imagination', *Journal of Art Historiography*, no. 4, June 2011, pp. 1–18.

22 Gerard Delanty, *The Cosmopolitan Imagination: The Renewal of Critical Social Theory*, Cambridge University Press, Cambridge, 2009.

23 See Thomas DaCosta Kaufmann, *Toward a Geography of Art*, Chicago University Press, Chicago, 2004. On the evolution of the concept 'world art', see my essay 'World Art', in Michael Kelley (ed.), *Oxford Encyclopedia of Aesthetics*, Oxford University Press, New York, 2014, 313–17.

24 This reciprocal logic, and the inequities built into it, is the basis of my understanding of provincialism as a worldwide structural system. It, too, begins from an antipodean position, and owes much to Bernard's work and to discussions with him from the late 1960s to the end of his life. I will not develop this line of thought here, as I intend to write more about it separately, on the fortieth anniversary of my essay 'The Provincialism Problem', *Artforum*, vol. 13, no. 1, September, 1974, pp. 54–59. See Terry Smith, 'The Provincialism Problem Then and Now', *Artmargins*, forthcoming.

25 Ian McLean, 'Reverse Perspective: Bernard Smith's Worldview and the Cosmopolitan Imagination', *Journal of Art Historiography*, no. 4, June 2011, pp. 9, 17.

26 Announced in Timothy J. Clark, 'The Conditions of Artistic Creation', *The Times Literary Supplement*, 24 May 1974, pp. 561–2; and exemplified in his books, including *Image of the People: Gustave Courbet and the 1848 Revolution*, Thames & Hudson, London, 1973.

27 Karl Marx, *Economic and Philosophical Manuscripts of 1844*, Dirk J. Struik (ed.), Lawrence & Wishart, London, 1964.

28 See A. L. Rees and Frances Borzello, *The New Art History*, Camden Press, London, 1986; Jonathan Harris, *The New Art History: A Critical Introduction*, Routledge, London, 2001.

29 Bernard Smith, 'Art Historical Studies in Australia with Comments on Research and Publication Since 1974', in *The Australian Academy of the Humanities: Proceedings*, no. 12, 1982–83, Australian Academy of the Humanities, Sydney, 1984, pp. 43–73.

30 Each of my lectures, books and essays on contemporaneity since 2000 has begun from this premise. See also Giorgio Agamben, 'What is the Contemporary?', in *What is an Apparatus? And Other Essays*, Stanford University Press, Stanford, Calif., 2009.

31 Bernard Smith, 'Some Aspects of Contemporary Art in Australia', *Education: Official Organ of the N.S.W. Public School Teachers' Federation*, vol. 24, no. 4, 22 February 1943, pp. 85–6, reprinted in *The Critic As Advocate: Selected Essays, 1948–1988*, Oxford University Press, Melbourne, 1989, p. 22.

32 ibid., p. 23.

33 Cited in Bernard Smith, with Terry Smith and Christopher Heathcote, *Australian Painting, 1788–2000*, 4th edn, Oxford University Press, Melbourne, 2001, p. 218.

34 Herbert Read, 'Art in an Australian University', *Art and Australia*, vol. 1, no. 3, November 1963, pp. 174–5.

35 Bernard Smith, 'Sir Herbert Read and the Power Bequest', *Meanjin Quarterly*, vol. 23, no. 1, March 1964, pp. 40, 39; republished in Bernard Smith, *The Antipodean Manifesto: Essays in Art and History*, Oxford University Press, Melbourne, 1975.

36 ibid., pp. 50, 44.

37 ibid., p. 44.

38 Bernard Smith, 'The Role of an Institute of Fine Arts in the University of Sydney' (lecture delivered on 11 June 1969), *Arts: The Journal of the Sydney University Arts Association*, no. 6, 1969, p. 17.

39 Bernard Smith, 'Introduction', *Concerning Contemporary Art*, Clarendon Press, Oxford, 1975, p. 1.

40 ibid., p. 2.

41 The allusion is, of course, to W. B. Yeats' post-World War I apocalyptic poem *The Second Coming* (1919).

42 See, for example, Nicholas Thomas, *Entangled Objects: Exchange, Material Culture and Colonialism in the Pacific*, Harvard University Press, Cambridge, Mass., 1991; Nicholas Mirzoeff, *The Right to Look: A Counterhistory of Visuality*, Duke University Press, Durham, NC, 2011; my review, at Terry Smith, 'If Looks Could Kill Empires', *Public Books*, website of *Public Culture*, posted 18 July 2012, www.publicbooks.org/nonfiction/if-looks-could-kill-empires.

Bernard, wordsmith

PETER BEILHARZ

The work of Bernard Smith has substance. Within a strong, but elastic, conceptual structure, it arcs from the 1950 Courtauld paper,[1] right through *European Vision* and *Australian Painting*, to *Modernism's History* and his swansong, *The Formalesque*. Along with others I have dedicated time to seeking to interpret the concepts that hold his work together. That project still demands more work. What I want to discuss here, in contrast, is style. With others, I read out loud to Bernard in his last years, beginning with *European Vision*. This raises questions of voice, and audience. Here I will turn my attention to the styles or genres in Bernard's work, more particularly in *The Boy Adeodatus* and *A Pavane for Another Time*, but also in his public work, from 'The Myth of Isolation' to *The Spectre of Truganini* and 'Lemontey'. It should come as no surprise, but this opens an intriguing field: Bernard was a wordsmith.

European Vision and the South Pacific is a dazzling work—we allow it to overshadow Bernard's other work. Did I do justice to it in my book, *Imagining the Antipodes*? I am sure not; this reminds us of Calvino's man with the map that was the same size as the area it proposed to represent, a scale of 1:1. Representation is never easy, and misunderstanding always comes together with its friend, in the attempt to understand. The strength of *European Vision and the South Pacific* is in its detail, and, as Robert Gaston suggests, it has that Viennese *Kunstgeschichte* cadence of the *Journal of the Warburg and Courtauld Institutes*: every word matters, but there are lots of them, and they lead us through the labyrinth in a way that is both intellectually demanding and also somehow like watching Fred Astaire.

Some of us around Bernard in Melbourne read out aloud to him in those last years. When he suggested that he would like to hear his own voice via mine, I said sure, and on my next visit took along my beaten copy of *European Vision and the South Pacific*. I think Bernard may have enjoyed this experience more than I did. What I had not anticipated, grabbing the book off my shelf and hopping on the tram, was that it is indeed a book to be read, in silence, to be laboured over in isolation. Its prose is crystalline, but writerly, if you like, rather than readerly:

> In the year 1768 the Royal Academy was established and the Royal Society promoted Cook's first voyage to the South Seas. The two events fittingly represent two influential attitudes to nature current in English eighteenth-century thought. The formation of the Academy constituted the official recognition in England of those neo-classical theories of Italian origin which had been transmitted to Britain through French theorists like de Chambray and de Piles. Nature, it was said, was to be rendered by the artist not with her imperfections clinging to her but in her perfect forms; what those perfect forms were the artist could only learn by a close study of the masterpieces of the ancients and their Renaissance disciples. The Royal Society, on the other hand, approached nature in a different way, appealing to travellers, virtuosi, and scientists to observe carefully, record accurately, and to experiment.[2]

This is astonishingly powerful, precise, directive prose: Time, Manner and Place. Smith opens the optic, and anticipates some of its key terms, even though, as I have said, the entire argument as such is ill-given to summary: it is difficult to condense, and Bernard (unlike, say, Robert Hughes at his best) was not given to condensation. Just one observation, in passing: thinking about the *title* of *European Vision and the South Pacific*, and this opening anticipation, it seems to me that there is an implicit or invisible third term between or connecting the two to which Bernard gave presence: *European Vision* and the *South Pacific*. This missing third term might be something like *experience*, because the canvas of the book is really something more like *European Vision and the Experience of the South Pacific*. It is a challenge, perhaps, to explain the empirical temper of Bernard's work, but it is there, as firmly in its substrate as his Marxism.

To return to my own narrative: enchanted by reading *European Vision and the South Pacific* in silence, I was challenged by reading it aloud, especially in Bernard's presence. So when I next travelled overseas I took an old paperback or two—this is a habit of mine, a habit of mind, which I'd recommend: to re-read something like Raymond Williams' *Keywords*, or Hannah Arendt's *Human Condition*, or some such, while stuck on a plane. As you sit in cattle class over a long-haul flight, your mind drifts in and out of focus. You can read and read again, let your mind both focus and stray. So on this trip I took two books: Trotsky's autobiography and *The Boy Adeodatus*. Bernard liked the fact that Trotsky had been my subject before he was.[3] Trotsky toys with the third person, only to reject it. Bernard, of course, relies entirely upon it, as though he is watching himself, or someone else called Bernard Smith. It is as though he is *beside* himself. This serves to remind us of the centrality of *distance* for Bernard Smith.

'He would remember the garden.' Five words: a famous opening line; we are hooked. It suggests distance, the power of memory, the romantic type of Eden combined with the domestic backyard narrative we might associate, say, with George Seddon, hydrangea with rusty nails, chooks, the Reckitt's Blue bags that Nicholas Thomas draws to our attention, here even closer to home than to the artworks of the South Pacific.

> He would remember the garden. In the middle of the yard the Japanese plum, shot through with sunlight in the spring like a bride's veil, its confetti petals covering the smooth lawn swelling with new green; the loquat trees, full of furry blossom in winter. There were two kinds of loquat in the garden: one, a speckled orange, very sweet, and another, green-yellow, that grew tall and was more bitter to the taste. Bert had planted the sweet loquat near the Carradice fence where it got plenty of sun and grew into a nice round tree, but the two green-yellow loquats just shot up by the back door where someone had once spat out the pips. Mum

> Keen said that the twin seedlings were too close to the house but she did not have the heart to pull them out, they looked so healthy. The garden was full of citrus trees too; lemons, mandarins, oranges. Mum Keen sometimes poured her chamber pot, and sometimes her husband's, around their roots. Urine, she said, was good for them.[4]

The prose implies a photographic eye, which Bernard himself suggests explicitly, a boy possessed of a 'clear visual memory'.[5] Even I myself make a marginal ghostly cameo here, as Peter, the kookaburra, the fisherman.

Bernard's narrative works as history, self-consciously. He writes as a scribe, or a witness, more than as an actor—as the historian of his own times. That garden so evocatively described above is gone today—'so that', as he says, 'had I not written this down, no trace of that garden would have survived'.[6]

The logic of Bernard's line-in then—his own fisherman's hook—is dual: there's a double hook, opening line, opening local chapter; then the Celtic step back, to the prehistory of his people.

It's well recognised that Bernard here is paying *femmage* to the women who made his life. Rose Anne Tierney, his birth mother, keeps her baby. Bernard's is a life spared by Catholicism, by his other. The issue of naming becomes important (as Cornelius Castoriadis once said to me on examining the contents of the Botanic Gardens in Melbourne: two-thirds of human activity is naming). Naming is central to Bernard Smith, naming and classification.

Bernard is named by Catholics and Anglicans, the bastard, like Adeodatus for Augustine. Patrick William has Joseph added in by Charlie Smith on behalf of Rose Anne.[7] Finally the boy becomes Bernard William; but he also remains Joseph Tierney, in his 1980s revival as a painter, and in his last months toys with the idea of changing his name back to Joseph Tierney, so that he might be able to deal with his death in terms of the return to his birth. A circle. Joseph Tierney is Bernard's ghost, or alter ego, the other he could have become; though he could also have become nothing, a total absence. So he is finally baptised at St Augustine of Hippo, Balmain, and then becomes little Ben, Bennie, *Bernard*: it fits; but not, later, when Rose Anne tries it out on him, *not* Bennie Kahl, her later married name. You can feel this in Bernard's response: Who is Bennie Kahl? Not me.

What holds all this narrative together? Short sentences, almost incomplete, a kind of staccato. 'He would remember the garden.' The well-chosen *word*, the well-chosen *phrase*: the influence of *poetry* for Bernard, but also of *journalism*: his reviewing.

> Poor Miss Crick (stop). You had to feel for her really (stop). But you just couldn't tell her anything (stop). So English (stop).[8]

Or:

> Never absent, never late.

Salvation was part of his boyhood: the Salvos. (Would anyone apart from us, in the antipodes, call them Salvos?) Some astonishing insights into his own contingency: 'young Bernard could have done well, become a clerk in a big city firm'. Not *our* Bernard Smith![9]

More short sentences, later:

> It was amazing how quickly she could dress herself.
> It was all over in a matter of seconds.
> So hard on the women.
> He would give up painting. Entirely.

And in all this he positions himself, conspicuously, as the outsider; so he writes that:

> Because for those who are born out of family the inner door of the house is closed quietly and locked securely.[10]

As more powerfully, earlier, in his Boyer Lectures,[11] there is the locked cupboard of settler memory. The outsider never feels fully safe, or at home. Though Bernard also plainly became an actor within the system of art, the university and its apparatus.

Then there is the scaffolding, or subtexts: Augustine, in italics. But mainly Augustine, not exclusively: also Dante, and even a surprise appearance by a young Marx, from the 'Reflections of a Young Man on the Choice of a Profession'.

And then there is Murraguldrie, *pinus radiatus*, rural poverty, and siren-like distractions of the flesh to be resisted by the young Bernard Smith. Three long years in which there are three predominant features: plump and alluring young female flesh; his sketchbook—a kind of stationery, stationary chastity belt; and *pinus radiatus*. The first had to be resisted, for there could be no more little bastards here, as far as his own authorship was concerned; the second instead filled in the weekends; the third, something less than or something different from Ruskin's tendrils.[12] And there is the wonderful sex scene, first time with Annie in Sydney, poignant, clumsy and beautiful, and its cheeky tag, 'He had gained his ASICAS (Annie's Short Intensive Course in Adult Sexuality) he told himself.'[13]

What role has Adeodatus to play in this? A parallel line? A play within a play? A *sotto voce* from Augustine? A third referent, after Bernard Smith and Joseph Tierney?

Plainly it is fashionable, nowadays, to talk (or obsess) about identity—and Bernard was never really big on fashion. But the identity issue was a kind of sleeper, since Freud, or since Nietzsche, the death of God. Who am I? Who could I have been? Bernard touches gently on these issues of voice and identity in closing *The Boy Adeodatus*:

> Who then was this Bernard, registered and baptised Patrick? ... They had made him one of them and yet not one of them. A stranger within their gates; a child among them taking notes.[14]

There is some connection here, then, between being the third person, and the voice of third person. Bernard Smith *is* the third person. And the issue of naming still hovers. For he was, to us, unmistakably Bernard Smith. But he could have been Joseph Tierney. Go through the exercise—think of it as a thought experiment: look at the bibliography, and say it out aloud:

> Joseph Tierney, *Place, Time and Tradition*, 1945
> Joseph Tierney, *European Vision and the South Pacific*, 1960
> Joseph Tierney, *Australian Painting*, 1962
> *Imagining the Antipodes: Culture, Theory and the Visual in the Work of Joseph Tierney*

Or this book—*The Legacies of Joseph Tierney*.

We leap forward eighteen years, to 2002, to *A Pavane for Another Time*, by Joseph Tierney. It's a book for his wife, Kate. Its flag is posted on the point of his greatest disappointment, the non-reception of *Modernism's History*. *Pavane* is a kind of backstory, a settling of memory's accounts. It is not a magical story, unlike *Adeodatus*, at least not in terms of its prose or its construction. It is a documentary, a memoir: often first-person. It lacks the craft or finesse of *A Boy Adeodatus*; it represents a different, and sadder, moment in its composition.

It is characterised by data-driven detail; it is a diary, an antipodean scrapbook. Some continuities nevertheless present themselves: the power of the short sentence. 'After two cups of coffee I had fallen desperately in love.' And much more, for Kate Challis is also two, is also Ruth Adeney. '"You're not the only one", she said, and told her story.'[15] And here are some carnal continuities: 'I was thinking about how I could get Kate into bed'. More painfully, situationally: 'England in the 1930s was a frightening place'. More characteristically, in the Soviet embassy:

> 'You are English', he said with slow deliberation. 'No', I said, 'I am Australian'.
>
> And he with even slower deliberation:
>
> 'It is the same thing'.
>
> 'No', I said, 'not quite'.
>
> Slowly, he said, 'Not quite'.[16]

Not quite.

Various other issues open, once we take on this question of voice, or style. What, for example, is the place of *Australian Painting* here? On first appearances, at least, its voice is still under the influence of the boys from Vienna. It makes some gestures towards its readers, but the voice is like that of *European Vision and the South Pacific*:

> When Lieutenant James Cook discovered the east coast of Australia in 1770 in the Endeavour, the ship's company included Joseph Banks, a young gentleman of considerable wealth and social standing, who possessed keen scientific interests and was, especially devoted to the study of botany.[17]

... time, manner, place.

But then there is the matter of his other voice in outer-directed writing. What was Bernard's other voice, his more public voice? (Though the autobiographical writing already shifts significantly in that direction.)

I shall touch on three examples here: the Macrossan Lectures, 1961, the Boyer Lectures, 1980, and the return Boyer Lecture, 1988.

What's most striking about the Macrossan Lectures, *Australian Painting Today*, especially 'The Myth of Isolation', is their combination of academic and more public voice. On this occasion Bernard combines his polemic against the British construction/reception of Australian art with the cultural claim that distance and isolation are not the same. White Australian civilisation cannot be defined by isolation, as it is constituted through maritime traffic, empire, colony, and cultural traffic. This against the exoticisation, or romanticisation, of white Australian painting, viewed by others as somehow miraculously standing outside the Renaissance tradition. The Macrossan Lectures are a theoretical capsule, presented in public form.[18]

The Boyer Lectures are more direct, though no less sophisticated. Already in their introduction there stand two words that frame the horizon of settlement: *forcible dispossession*. The text opens with an academic, though also political, nod to Stanner, and a step back in terms of competence. Smith knows whereof he speaks, and of the limits of his capacity.

Are the Boyer Lectures a manifesto? Not quite. (Is *The Antipodean Manifesto* a manifesto? Discuss. Maybe: a manifest. A ship's manifest.) They open with another spectre, not Marx's, but the spectre of Truganini. The message is plain, plain from the history of forcible dispossession, plain from Marx, plain from Freud: we inhabit a world of ghosts, at least some of them of our own making. Forgetting—the locked cupboard of history—the well-chosen phrase, arrows pointed at the heart of Australian modernity. Again, the short (almost blunt?) sentence:

> Australians have tried to forget.
> A culture cannot live on other people's universals.

Then a long sentence, written as it were with Freud:

> How shall we redeem it from the guilty awareness that these acts of genocide and attempted genocide were being enacted most vigorously at that very time when our own white Australian culture was being conceived and born, and that its very growth pre-supposed the termination of a black culture which for the rest of the world, apart from ourselves, has come to be regarded as more interesting, coherent, and identifiable as a unique human achievement than our own European-derived culture?[19]

This is, it might be observed, a cosmetically similar strategy to Marx's in *The Communist Manifesto*: short, powerful sentences stacked against longer, serial, alliterative sentences, where a change in pace or register, mood or pronunciation, again brings to mind the spoken word, the edict.

This prose is tough, but Bernard also manages to maintain a voice that is avuncular—that of a white elder, Uncle Bernard. He uses habitual, spoken formulations like 'you see'—at once vernacular and Enlightenment.[20]

But of course he also speaks and thinks like an historian, explaining 'how I think' as a preliminary to the lesson. And this *is* a lesson, a lecture or sermon on morals, ethics and foundation values, delivered on the premise that Australian morality represents 'damaged goods'. For the damage of forcible possession is also natural, even though it is clearly asymmetrical. Smith's narrative rolls, though it is also punctuated by sparks of connection to other things. One bastard connects to another, in the case of Charles Perkins; or the horrible image of whites hunting Aboriginal people evokes one of the most awful terms in Nazi German language, *Judenjagd*. Bernard powerfully negotiates the deep ambivalence of the Cook voyages, indicating the Pacific as the site of degeneration of the Enlightenment's principles of universal judgement. Civilisation rests on barbarism, as Walter Benjamin had it. Hughes has published *The Fatal Shore* the year before, but Smith does not here turn to it; for his message is rather per C. D. Rowley: that if the colonies had gulags, or camps, they were for black folk.

Closing the Boyer Lectures, Bernard discusses Aboriginal culture as the foundation of Western social sciences, and anticipates the desirability of a treaty for 1988. In 1988 he returns, among others, as a Boyer Lecturer.[21] Here, in the published version, the printer has dropped the plates, so that Bernard's lecture is accompanied by the image of Nugget Coombs. (Anthropologists, parse that!) In compressed compass, in this lecture, we get one line, one hope, one prospect.

Lemontey, writing in 1792 'at the height of the French Revolution', predicted that New Holland would be the major locus of a multicultural, Eurasian world, stimulated by European science and technology; this just at the moment the First Fleet was sailing to Botany Bay. Australia, here, for Bernard Smith is a kind of third space—'not quite' English, but distinct in its mix, for 'both multiculturalism and industrialism are intrinsic components of modernity'. There's a kind of presentism here which is striking, alongside his usual historicism; as he says against populist nostalgia, 'the past is not a place to live in'—a different tenor from *The Spectre of Truganini*. And he repeats well-coined phrases—'not quite', for example, again indicative of the third space, that which does not always easily fit pre-existing categories.[22]

Who then was Bernard Smith, Joseph Tierney? We know that naming mattered, for Bernard Smith. We know that he named the Port Jackson Painter. We know that at some level he associated with the Port Jackson Painter, or with his swan. We know that Bernard's books wore the Port Jackson Painter and his swan as a bookplate, or a badge, a flag or a mirror. A puzzle. A stubborn presence. A stranger within their gates; a child among them taking notes. An older man, having spoken his piece, looking to outlive other bastards. A presence among us, now. A wordsmith; a swansong.

NOTES

1 Bernard Smith, 'European Vision and the South Pacific', *Journal of the Warburg and Courtauld Institutes*, no. 13, nos 1–2, 1950, pp. 65–100.

2 Bernard Smith, *European Vision and the South Pacific*, Oxford University Press, Melbourne, 1960, p. 1; and see generally Peter Beilharz, *Imagining the Antipodes: Theory, Culture and the Visual in the Work of Bernard Smith*, Cambridge University Press, Cambridge, 1997.

3 Peter Beilharz, *Trotsky, Trotskyism and the Transition to Socialism*, Croom Helm, London, 1987.

4 Bernard Smith, *The Boy Adeodatus: The Portrait of a Lucky Young Bastard*, Penguin Books Australia, Melbourne, 1984, p. 1.

5 ibid., p. 162.

6 ibid., p. 20.

7 ibid., pp. 68–9.

8 ibid., p. 119.

9 ibid., p. 147.

10 ibid., p. 151.

11 Bernard Smith, *The Spectre of Truganini*, The 1980 Boyer Lectures, Australian Broadcasting Commission, Sydney, 1980.

12 Smith, *The Boy Adeodatus*, p. 214.

13 ibid., p. 275.

14 ibid., p. 300.

15 Bernard Smith, *A Pavane for Another Time*, Macmillan, Melbourne, 2002, pp. 10–11.

16 ibid., p. 306.

17 Bernard Smith, *Australian Painting, 1788–1960*, Oxford University Press, Melbourne, 1962, p. 1.

18 Bernard Smith, *Australian Painting Today*, The John Murtagh Macrossan Lectures, 1961, University of Queensland Press, Brisbane, 1962; and see Rex Butler, 'Bernard Smith and the Myth of Isolation—A Symposium', *Eyeline: Contemporary Visual Arts*, nos 78–79, Autumn–Winter 2013, pp. 50–1, and Peter Beilharz, 'Bernard Smith: Taking a Distance', *Eyeline: Contemporary Visual Arts*, nos 78–79, Autumn–Winter 2013, pp. 59–63.

19 Smith, *The Spectre of Truganini*, p. 10.

20 Neville Meaney, *Bernard Smith: Oral History Section, NLA*, National Library of Australia, Canberra, 1986.

21 Bernard Smith, 'Lemontey's Prophecy', in Malcolm Long (ed.), *Post Scripts: 1988 Boyer Lectures*, Australian Broadcasting Commission, Sydney, 1989, pp. 61–72.

22 ibid.

Re-reading Bernard Smith on what constitutes Australian art

CATHERINE SPECK

Expatriate artists working offshore are central to a complete history of Australian art, although the position they have occupied has been one of shifting sands. This chapter examines Bernard Smith's writings about Australian art, with specific reference to expatriate artists based in the metropolitan centres of Paris and London from 1880 to 1940. Much of Smith's writing on Australian art is focused on defining what constitutes a national art, whereas numerous artists included in the canon of Australian art were based in Paris for periods of their working life and engaged with cosmopolitan rather than national subjects. For instance, in his *Self-portrait* painted in Paris in about 1920, Rupert Bunny presents himself with the sophistication, confidence and ease of a successful artist at the cultural centre of the world (Fig. 16). His modern painting, in a reduced palette, and employing a vertically divided backdrop and loose neo-impressionist style, aligns him to French painting styles. As a consequence, Smith situated such work within English or French traditions, reserving the term 'Australian art' in *Place, Taste and Tradition* for a national art as 'reflecting the life of the Australian people', and linking the emergence of that art with the landscape work of Louis Buvelot, then to Tom Roberts and Frederick McCubbin.[1]

Yet the art produced by Australian expatriates is embraced within collections of Australian art, and their work produced offshore is intrinsic to contemporary art-historical writing and exhibitions centred on Australian artists' lives and their oeuvre. This suggests a mismatch between Smith's writing and the praxis of Australian art. This chapter focuses on Bernard Smith's writing on expatriate artists and Australian art, and how, ironically, his own definition of Australian art, when compounded with his description of his practice as that of 'pragmatic Hegelian', provides the conceptual tools to read 'Australian' content more broadly in the work of expatriate artists living offshore from the 1880s to the 1940s.[2]

Initially Bernard Smith discussed expatriate artists under William Moore's umbrella term of an 'exodus', although in his 1962 book *Australian Painting* he had difficulty situating long-term *belle époque* and Edwardian expatriates comfortably in the arena of Australian art. He felt that their respect for the European tradition took them away from the cut and thrust of Australian art practice.[3] Bunny, who spent forty-seven years away, is dismissed as 'barely an Australian painter' because he 'assimilated the French tradition thoroughly'.[4] Arthur Streeton, who was in Britain for twenty years, failed because he attempted to 'emulate' the major English landscape painters like Constable, Sargent and Steer, who, Smith said, 'were not tourists in search of culture, but men with a deep intimacy with the scenes they painted', whereas 'there was little intimacy between Streeton and the English landscape'.[5] Smith appeared not to notice Streeton's *Corfe Castle* (1909), even though it was singled out for its 'mastery of execution' by *The Herald*'s art critic when shown in Melbourne in 1914.[6] The roll call continued in a similar vein for the others, Smith calling them 'exiles caught between two societies', whose Edwardian excursion 'did not bring much of lasting value to Australia'.[7] The expatriates' motives are explained in *Australian Painting* as follows:

> In refusing to be satisfied with the provincial and second-rate standards prevailing in Australia around 1900, their instincts were soundly based, and their years abroad bravely asserted the fact that the world of art, at its best, is always an international community.[8]

Smith's lack of affinity with the subjects portrayed by the expatriates was never entirely resolved. But late in his career, and in a broader contemporary art-historical ethos of writing about modernism as an international movement, he pointed out in *The Formalesque: A Guide to Modern Art and its History* (2007) that modernism was spread unevenly between the centre and the periphery, which is of course why the expatriate artists travelled to work in the cosmopolitan centres.[9]

When *Place, Taste and Tradition* was published, in 1945, Smith set out what constituted Australian art. In the preface to the 1979 edition, he pointed to the main ideas and methods underpinning his book: Australian art was 'in some way a connected skein linked by ties of influence or causation'; it was based on methods of historical materialism so the inter-links between the economic base and the cultural superstructure account for change; and 'it took realism as its base and sought to provide some sense of identity with Australian life and experience'.[10] This third exclusionary aspect overshadowed the first two components, so that the idea of defining a national tradition as reflecting 'the life of the Australian people and their movement in the imbricated structure of Australian society' took hold.[11] But it has been insufficiently appreciated *how much* Smith's idea of geographical 'place' is bound up with his associated theory of how 'ties of influence' of our European cultural heritage affect what constitutes Australian art. For instance, Hans Heysen's *From the apartment window, Paris* (1901), painted from his sixth-floor room at the Grand Hôtel de la Haute-Loire in Montparnasse, looking down on the snow in the cityscape below, was ostensibly a European subject. It didn't fit the mould of a Federation-era Heysen, or even a 1930s Heysen, until his oeuvre was looked at in its entirety in the Art Gallery of South Australia's 2008 *Hans Heysen* exhibition. Heysen's painting of ethereal, sun-hazed views in *St Mark's Basin looking east, Venice* (c. 1902), is now also seen as pivotal to his enduring interest in light, of which his gum trees, like Claude Monet's haystacks, are a subject.[12]

Central, therefore, to repositioning expatriate art is extending Bernard Smith's idea of how 'ties of influence or causation' of a wider European heritage operate in the overriding historical materialist structure he set out in *Place, Taste and Tradition*. Smith's antipodal approach to the formation of culture was doubtless assisted by his own expatriate period in London from 1948 to 1950 on a British Council scholarship, during which time he researched the British foundations of early Australian colonial art. His resulting essay, published in the *Journal of the Warburg and Courtauld Institutes*,[13] became the foundation for his ground-breaking book *European Vision and the South Pacific*.[14] He experienced what it was like to be a 'colonial' student at the Courtauld, and he lived for a while with a group of Australian expatriate artists outside London at The Abbey Arts Centre. More importantly, he understood and experienced how to exercise an antipodean viewpoint.[15]

While Smith pointed out how Edwardian expatriates had 'a continuous influence upon the course of Australian art' due to their training overseas,[16] his comments on their connection to 'place' were insufficiently understood. The issue came abruptly to the fore in 1961 with the Whitechapel Gallery's exhibition *Recent Australian Painting*, which featured the work of a new generation of expatriates, including Arthur Boyd and James Gleeson. It prompted Smith to re-state his views. The exhibition's curator, Bryan Robertson, explained the work on show in terms of cultural difference and 'primitivism', because, he said, Australian art was 'cut off from our European environment, was highly inventive and had one unifying factor: an unremitting sense of the drama of the isolated moment'.[17] While much of the abstract and figurative work on display had been selected by Robertson on a visit to Australia, his views about cultural isolation took little account of the fact that many of the participating artists, like Godfrey Miller, had worked in London, or, like Sidney Nolan and Brett Whiteley, were then based in London.[18] That perception of 'primitivism' was compounded by Robert Hughes' catalogue essay, which echoed Robertson's opinions by speaking of Australian artists as working in a cultural environment devoid of all history, in 'complete isolation from the Renascence [*sic*] tradition', and yet having the advantage of being 'confronted virtually with a *tabula rasa*'.[19]

Smith bristled, not only because he had been angling to stage the very exhibition Robertson had put on, featuring the Melbourne-based, figurative-oriented, Antipodeans group, but also because he could not accept claims of cultural isolation.[20] He mounted a vigorous defence in the Macrossan Lecture *The Myth of Isolation*, which he delivered in Brisbane in 1961. In his reply to Robertson and Hughes he set out how expatriate art was intrinsically linked to ideas of place, while also drawing on a wider European visual language. He argued that a so-called Australian School, as the paintings were being described in London, fuelled by Australia's cultural isolation and primitivism, was a myth.[21] He described colonial art as a branch of English art (a view that is now contested), pointing out that there was a continuous flow of expatriates working in London, Paris, Brussels and Antwerp in the 1880s and 1890s, and so the links with Europe were never broken.[22]

He explained how a perceived cultural conservatism before World War I was not due to a lack of engagement with international modernism, but to a Darwinian process of selection and rejection, 'precisely what one might expect of an art like Australian art closely affiliated with European culture yet displaying distinct qualities of its own'.[23] He also pointed to a generation of women artists in the 1920s and the 1930s, such as Dorrit Black, who had engaged with modern movements in Paris and London.

Thirteen years later, Smith revisited these ideas in another public lecture: 'Is there a Radical Tradition in Australian art?' (1984). Again he turned to the role of expatriates in Australian art. In the course of a subtle argument, he distinguished between radicals and innovators, and he pointed out how some expatriates, as radicals, have forged change in our national art by bringing about radical insertions on 'place'. He singled out three: Tom Roberts, for finding subjects in colonial history; Norman Lindsay, for confronting puritanical social mores with a liberating sexuality; and Margaret Preston, for promoting Aboriginal art. Each, he said, had their roots in Europe. For Roberts it was the *plein air* tradition, for Lindsay it was situating his subjects in Greek mythology, and for Preston it was looking to European modernism and 'primitivism'. He commented:

> There is a firm national component in all these early manifestations of radical art in Australia; but they are not due to an ignorance either of the European tradition or of the modernist art of the time. But all accepted the imperative of place; that art in Australia had to be, was bound to be, different from art in Europe.[24]

About other expatriate artists, Smith was less complimentary, calling them 'messenger boys [*sic*] bringing news to Australia of the innovations of others', adding that 'what they and their successors are still doing, was and is to ensure that innovations that had been accepted into the traditions of European art were and are acclimatised to Australian soil'.[25]

The idea of artists being engaged in some kind of time-delayed messenger service offended many, and it deflected attention from the more complex issue of a European–Australian dynamic. Smith was also critical of some returning expatriates, especially the Edwardians: 'the expatriates became the patriots, became trustees, directors of galleries, art critics, and received official honours; became in short, the establishment in painting'. He was, of course, alluding to George Lambert, Will Ashton, Lionel Lindsay and Hans Heysen, among others, and how this too led to what he called a 'lazy dialectic' between the centre and the periphery.[26] He was fleshing out the thesis that an interconnected dialectical skein of a national art is linked to, and causally involved in, a European tradition. Thus what we now call local inflections of modernism he attributed not to formal qualities, but to 'place', writing that 'art is always a dialogue with life, and that life is where you are'.[27]

Late in his career Smith synthesised all these elements of expatriate artists engaging with Europe and yet retaining one's connections to home, and in doing so he imaginatively invoked ideas of the antipodes. He had been writing about his own practice as an art historian who usually wrote about Australian art and the Pacific, but in *Modernism's History* (1998) he was writing about European art. He said: 'I shall be writing therefore with Europe as my antipodes, seeing it from a distance, and yet seeing it also as part of myself, my cognitive space and my culture'.[28] This statement implied that he was continuing to see Europe in an antipodal relationship to Australia; that each sits opposite the other, and that there is a cultural, spatial and cognitive relationship between the two continents. Europe is his antipodes in that the cultural links between it and Australia are deep and constant. The same could be said of artists working in Australia with Europe as their antipodes. But given how Smith contended, in *A Pavane for Another Time* (2002), that someone working in Europe could have an antipodean view,[29] then it could be argued that artists working offshore may well work in Europe in an antipodal relationship to home.

This in turn means that 'place', which was posited in *Place, Taste and Tradition* as geographical, and within Australia, has the capacity to become an antipodean place, a cognitive place rather than a physical place, occupied by expatriates working offshore. Thus late-career Smith set out an *extended* idea of place in an Australian–European dialogue, and, with shared understandings of culture that more accurately explain the framework of expatriate artists working in Paris and London from 1880 to 1940, he provided the conceptual tools to re-read their art produced offshore. For example, consider Peter Purves Smith's modern painting *Drought* (1939–40), painted in London, and showing a certain death by starvation for the animal depicted (Fig. 17). The image may be a metaphor for the dilemmas facing everyone during another world war,[30] but in its invoking of Australian subject matter it is based in an antipodean imagination.

Other Australian artists in Paris and London, such as Emanuel Phillips Fox and George Lambert, embraced a cosmopolitan imagination and put aside overt ideas of nationality. As Smith was to comment of himself many years later, Europe was their antipodes, but they were not in dialogue with it in an antipodean sense, rather, they immersed themselves in Europe. They had the 'cultural baggage', so to speak, to do so; Australia had been in constant dialogue with Europe through its art and culture generally. Bunny, who was based in Paris, was well versed in music, the theatre and modern dance, and partook of the fashion for the Orient. Those cultural perspectives informed his rendition of *Salome* (c. 1919). Eric Wilson, based in London, embraced abstract design. He took classes from Elmslie Owen, and was introduced to the language of cubism and the work of Braque, which opened up a new world for him, one that he said was not possible in Australia, whereas in London it seemed a logical progression.[31] His *Abstract* (1939) shows these ideas of compressed space and rhythm at work. Ola Cohn spent five years in London, took classes with Henry Moore at the Royal College of Art, and studied the modern sculptures of Jacob Epstein, Eric Gill and Ossip Zadkine. She moved from mimesis to confronting one of the key elements of modernist practice: the autonomous nature of the work of art. On returning to Australia, she exhibited a very modern *Head of a virgin* (1926), with reductive quasi-oriental features and a simplified elongated neck (Fig. 18). It puzzled many Melbourne viewers because her focus was no longer centred on classical beauty.[32]

Expatriate artists' capacity to respond to the liberating stimuli of the cosmopolitan city, to endure dislocation and even alienation induced by working in a metropolis without the familiar networks of 'home', prompted creative leaps of the kind Ola Cohn experienced. Raymond Williams has attributed these changes to the 'complexity' and 'miscellaneity' of this modern environment, which liberates artists and results in changes in form. He writes:

> Thus the key cultural factor of the modernist shift is the character of the metropolis … [and] its direct effect on form … this underlies in an obvious way, the elements of strangeness and distance, indeed alienation, which so regularly form part of the repertory. But the decisive aesthetic effect is at a deeper level. Liberated or breaking from their national or provincial cultures, placed in quite new relations

> to those other native languages or native visual traditions, encountering meanwhile a novel and dynamic common environment from which many of the older forms were obviously distant, the artists and writers and thinkers of this phase found the only commonality available to them: a community of the medium; of their own practices.[33]

However, it is very likely that underpinning that shift in expatriate artists' practice is a *weak* sense of Europe as their antipodes, because each of them could not have engaged with European cosmopolitanism and international modernism without that foundation.

So while theorists like Williams have developed an explanation as to how expatriates' artistic practices change, the fundamental point is that Australian artists working in Paris or London unconsciously invoke an antipodean imagination as their starting point, and from that basis move forward. It operates like an umbilical cord between the polar opposites of the north and south, but not in a simple way, since the antipodean relationship is dialectical and the cultural traffic of expatriates oils the dialectical engine.

This way of viewing offshore practice—as based, in some shape or form, on an antipodean imagination—means Australian artists' offshore work is coterminous with their onshore work, and that a national art need not have borders. This in turn means that any idea of artwork being 'un-Australian' because it is made outside Australia is not correct.[34] Smith, therefore, provided the conceptual framework and a Hegelian methodology for seeing an antipodal relationship in Australian art as 'a process determined by a continuous dialectic, a persistent interrogation of the dominant by the subdominant and the supressed'.[35]

The idea that a national art can include art produced offshore has underpinned much research and writing over the last four decades. As Ruth Zubans commented, since the 1980s a 'more complex and diverse sense of Australian culture' began to unfold, and as the work of women artists was being reassessed, there was 'a new openness to artists who chose to pursue their art abroad in milieus sympathetic to their work'.[36] Authors of recent monographs on E. Phillips Fox (1995), George Lambert (1996), Hilda Rix Nicholas (2000), Peter Purves Smith (2000), Charles Conder (2002), Bessie Davidson (2003), Anne Dangar (2004) and John Peter Russell (2008) among others, and curators of recent exhibitions, freed from the obligations of constructing national art histories with borders, have embraced this approach of including expatriate work in an artist's oeuvre, to present a complete account.[37] But curators too are engaged in shaping narratives. Exhibitions do not sit outside the politics of representation. They too adopt 'strategic systems', including their accompanying catalogues, to present an art-historical viewpoint, with every aspect of an exhibition dovetailing to convey a particular focus.[38] But it is a focus that folds expatriate art into the mainstream.

The National Gallery of Australia's 2004 exhibition *The Edwardians: Secrets and Desires* focused on artists working in the Edwardian worlds in France and England. It presented an account of Australian expatriate artists who, by virtue of their location and contingent social and intellectual mores, operated outside national frameworks. As Ann Galbally astutely observed in the exhibition catalogue, those artists have, to date, only ever attracted 'bipolar critical attention': either lauded for Royal Academy or Salon successes or 'dismissed as merging too closely with artistic mores of their adopted countries'. Thus those writing national accounts have lost 'sight of what it was to be an Australian artist'.[39] The subjects of their paintings have been ill-understood, and glossed over as lacking the nationalism of late nineteenth-century art or that of World War I. But the expatriate artists among this group were responding to shifting cultural practices in London and Paris, changing exhibiting systems, and modern subjects in place of grand historical or Victorian social realist ones. They turned to what Galbally calls 'subjectless' human forms, in which the 'mastery of the draughtsmanship and technique could be admired for its own sake', with paintings praised for 'their surface attributes such as pose, dress, colour and paint application'. This meant that these qualities were valued 'almost as abstract elements'. This resulted in artists like Hugh Ramsay producing numerous self-portraits and portraits of associates, family and friends. Sometimes they were highly theatrical, as in Hilda Rix Nicholas's staged and fashionable orientalist study of her sister Elsie in *La robe chinois* (c. 1913). At other times they were portrayed as 'art for pleasure'.[40] Little wonder this stood outside Smith's working definition of Australian art. Even so, it is not outside his 'ties of influence or causation with the European tradition', if only he had used his own methodology to read the work as Australian.

In her catalogue for the Art Gallery of New South Wales' 2009 exhibition *Rupert Bunny: Artist in Paris*, Deborah Edwards too pointed to the narrow understandings of what it was it was to be an Australian artist in the *belle époque* and Edwardian years. Bunny may well be the most successful long-term expatriate artist in terms of success at the time overseas. But Edwards noted that 'when success and honours from the European establishment did come to expatriates, questions were raised in the artists' own countries about the validity of their art in national terms'.[41] Bunny's cosmopolitan subjects confounded many, including former National Gallery of Victoria director J. S. MacDonald, who commented in 1948:

> Rupert allowed himself to become boulevard-bound and matters outside his self-imposed bounds did not interest him. This limited him technically to excellence only in those subjects which passed muster with the French: who have little interest in what is produced or goes on beyond their boundaries.[42]

This account is far from accurate; the subjects of Bunny's *belle époque* and postwar paintings were aligned with cosmopolitan taste. He paid close attention to all aspects of cultural production, including the critics, and astutely produced work for differing markets, including those in Europe and Australia.[43]

Meanwhile Elena Taylor, in the catalogue accompanying her 2006 National Gallery of Australia exhibition *Grace Crowley: Being Modern*, focused more on how this expatriate, once back home in 1930 and with a well-developed understanding of cubism, maintained the modernist momentum she had built up during her expatriate years in France. Crowley was aided in this by her correspondence with Anne Dangar, who stayed on in Europe. Taylor writes of Crowley:

> Over the next decade she kept her sights firmly on the latest developments in Europe and, in the early 1940s, was one of the first Australians to move into pure abstraction—her work was out of step with trends in Australian art, but part of the international movement of geometric abstraction.[44]

Then, in her 2013 exhibition for the National Gallery of Victoria, *Australian Impressionists in France*, Elena Taylor explored the extent of Australian artists' engagement with French impressionist practice from 1885 to 1915. What she encountered was much cultural traffic between Australia and France of artists, their work and ideas. She concluded:

> The expatriates and their exhibitions thus brought art in Australia into contact with the vital developments in early twentieth century French art, and played an important role in the reception and development of the modern movement in Australia in the decade to follow.[45]

Anne Gray similarly commented that the returning expatriates, through their close attention to style, subject matter and modern methods of painting, 'considerably broadened the local perspective and contributed a more cosmopolitan, cross-cultural approach to art in Australia'.[46]

Therefore Bernard Smith and recent authors, including those of exhibition catalogues, have something in common: an embrace of offshore work as part of the national oeuvre. Smith did so obliquely via his Hegelian methodology of adopting an antipodal perspective and seeing in Australian art links to a deeper European heritage, whereas later art historians and curators are directly constructing borderless and inclusive histories of Australian art. It is Smith's methodology, reflexive and dialectical in nature, that provides the intellectual underpinnings for this strand of contemporary scholarship in Australian art.

NOTES

1 Bernard Smith, *Place, Taste and Tradition: A Study in Australian Art Since 1788*, Oxford University Press, Melbourne, 1979, pp. 30, 117, 125.

2 Bernard Smith, *Modernism's History: A Study in Twentieth-Century Art and Ideas*, University of New South Wales Press, Sydney, 1988, p. 8.

3 Bernard Smith, *Australian Painting, 1788–1970*, Oxford University Press, Melbourne, 1971, p. 129.

4 ibid., p. 148.

5 ibid., p. 151.

6 *The Herald* (Melbourne), 4 June 1914, p. 10, cited in Geoffrey Smith, *Arthur Streeton, 1867–1943*, exhibition catalogue, National Gallery of Victoria, Melbourne, 1995, p. 150.

7 Smith, *Australian Painting, 1788–1970*, pp. 145, 165.

8 ibid., p. 165.

9 See, for instance, Melba Cuddy-Keane, 'Modernism, Geopolitics, Globalisation', *Modernism/Modernity*, vol. 10, no. 3, September 2003, pp. 539–58; Bernard Smith, *The Formalesque: A Guide to Modern Art and its History*, Macmillan, Melbourne, 2007, p. 7.

10 Smith, *Place, Taste and Tradition*, 1988, pp. 15, 18–19.

11 ibid., p. 30. This also became the working method for later histories, such as that by Andrew Sayers, who in his 2001 book *Australian Art* focused on work 'created in Australia', due to there being an 'over-emphasis on work made outside Australia': Andrew Sayers, *Australian Art*, Oxford University Press, Oxford, pp. 5–6.

12 When writing to Nora Heysen on 5 March 1935 about the snow in London, Hans Heysen recalled the snow in Paris: 'the news of the first snow did certainly awaken the imagination and memories of my first snow—seeing it softly falling towards evening from my sixth story window overlooking Boulevard Montparnasse. And then after school was over at 10pm. The snow falling in the streets! It was all great fun—the hurrying down to Charautou on the next day and experiencing my first painting of snow. That wonderful transformation of the whole landscape I can still clearly visualise—all so captivating and enchanting', in Catherine Speck (ed.), *Selected Letters of Hans Heysen and Nora Heysen*, National Library of Australia, Canberra, 2011, p. 32. Hans Heysen, in his early twenties, studied in Paris from 1899 to 1903, at the Académie Julian, Colarossi's Academy, and the École des Beaux-Arts. The Grand Hôtel de la Haute Loire is on the corner of the Boulevard Raspail and Boulevard du Montparnasse: Colin Thiele, *Heysen of Hahndorf*, Rigby, Adelaide, 1968, p. 50.

13 Bernard Smith, 'European Vision and the South Pacific', *Journal of the Warburg and Courtauld Institutes*, vol. 13, nos 1–2, 1950, pp. 65–100.

14 Bernard Smith, *European Vision and the South Pacific, 1768–1850: A Study in the History of Art and Ideas*, Clarendon Press, Oxford, 1960.

15 Bernard Smith, *A Pavane for Another Time*, Macmillan, Melbourne, 2002, p. 451. On an antipodean relationship, see Peter Beilharz, *Imagining the Antipodes: Culture, Theory and the Visual in the Work of Bernard Smith*, Cambridge University Press, Cambridge, 1997.

16 Smith, *Australian Painting, 1788–1970*, p. 128.

17 Bryan Robertson, 'Preface', in *Recent Australian Painting*, exhibition catalogue, foreword by Kenneth Clark, with introduction by Robert Hughes and preface by Bryan Robertson, Whitechapel Gallery, London, 1961, p. 10; Simon Pierse, *Australian Art and Artists in London, 1950–1965: An Antipodean Summer*, Ashgate, Surrey, 2012, p. 119.

18 Eleven of the artists were living in London: Pierse, *Australian Art and Artists in London*, p. 138.

19 Robert Hughes, 'Introduction', in *Recent Australian Painting*, pp. 13, 14. Hughes later admitted he overstated the case and made a virtue of Australia's distance from Europe in *Things I Didn't Know: A Memoir*, Knopf and Random House, Sydney, 2006, p. 267.

20 Pierse, *Australian Art and Artists in London*, pp. 80–7.

21 Bernard Smith, 'The Myth of Isolation', in *The Death of the Artist as Hero: Essays in History and Culture*, Oxford University Press, Melbourne, 1988, p. 218.

22 Terry Smith, 'Land into Landscape: The Setting of Settlement', in *Transformations in Australian Art: The Nineteenth Century: Landscape, Colony, and Nation*, Craftsman House, Sydney, 2002, p. 47; Tim Bonyhady, *Images in Opposition*, Oxford University Press, Melbourne, 1985, p. xii.

23 Smith, 'The Myth of Isolation', p. 222–4. Ian McLean has argued that Bernard Smith is Darwinian as well as Marxist, in 'Hegel or Darwin? The Role of Tendencies in Bernard Smith's Historiography', *Thesis Eleven*, no. 82, 2005, pp. 54–61; Peter Beilharz has argued that Smith is more a Marxist, in Peter Beilharz, 'Bernard Smith: The Quality of Marxism', *Thesis Eleven*, vol. 114, no. 1, February 2013, pp. 94–102.

24 Bernard Smith, 'Is there a Radical Tradition in Australian Art?', in *The Death of the Artist as Hero*, p. 236.

25 ibid., p. 233.

26 ibid., p. 233.

27 ibid., p. 240.

28 Smith, *Modernism's History*, p. 7.

29 Smith, *A Pavane for Another Time*, p. 451.

30 Mary Eagle, *Peter Purves Smith: A Painter in Peace and War*, Beagle Press, Sydney, 2000, p. 45.

31 Eric Wilson, diary, 17 September 1937, cited in Andrew Sayers, *Eric Wilson*, exhibition catalogue, Newcastle Regional Art Gallery, Newcastle, NSW, 1983, p. 8.

32 Graeme Sturgeon, *The Development of Australian Sculpture, 1788–1975*, Thames & Hudson, London, 1978, pp. 111–12; Ola Cohn found Henry Moore's work very different, very new, and wrote in her diary: 'The stuff on show was so different from what we had been used to seeing, that at first it was a shock. Then later after one or two visits, one saw more and more work. All pieces were severely simple in design. They needed no camaflage [*sic*] weakness, for they were strong to the very core'. Cited in Angela Woollacott, *To Try Her Fortune in London: Australian Women, Colonialism, and Modernity*, Oxford University Press, Oxford, 2001, p. 210.

33 Raymond Williams, 'The Metropolis and the Emergence of Modernism', in P. Brooker (ed.), *Modernism/Postmodernism*, Longman, London, 1992, pp. 91–2.

34 See Rex Butler and A. D. S. Donaldson, 'Stay, Go or Come: A History of Australian Art 1920–1940', *Australian and New Zealand Journal of Art*, vol. 9, nos 1–2, 2008–09, pp. 119–20; Rex Butler and A. D. S. Donaldson, 'Bernard Smith's Real Choice: Surrealism or Abstraction 1930–1950', *Eyeline: Contemporary Visual Arts*, nos 78–9, 2013, pp. 64–71.

35 Smith, *Modernism's History*, p. 8.

36 Ruth Zubans, *E. Phillips Fox: His Life and Art*, Miegunyah Press, Melbourne University Press, Melbourne, 1995, p. ix; see also Catherine Speck and Georgina Downey, 'Cosmopolitanism and Modernism: On Writing a New Australian Art History', *Australian and New Zealand Journal of Art*, vol. 9, nos 1–2, 2009, pp. 101–18.

37 See Zubans, *E. Phillips Fox*; Anne Gray, *Art and Artifice: George Lambert, 1873–1930*, Craftsman House, Sydney, 1996; John Pigot, *Hilda Rix Nicholas: Her Life and Art*, Miegunyah Press, Melbourne University Press, Melbourne, 2000; Mary Eagle, *Peter Purves Smith: A Painter in Peace and War*, Beagle Press, Sydney, 2000; Ann Galbally, *Charles Conder: The Last Bohemian*, Melbourne University Press, Melbourne, 2002; Penelope Little, *A Studio in Montparnasse: Bessie Davidson: An Australian Artist in Paris*, Craftsman House, Melbourne, 2003; Bruce Adams, *Rustic Cubism: Anne Dangar and the Art Colony at Moly-Sabata*, University of Chicago Press, Chicago, 2004; Ann Galbally, *A Remarkable Friendship: Vincent van Gogh and John Peter Russell*, Miegunyah Press, Melbourne University Press, Melbourne, 2008. For exhibition catalogues, see in particular Deborah Edwards, *Bertram Mackennal*, The Fifth Balnaves Foundation Sculpture Project, exhibition catalogue, Art Gallery of New South Wales, Sydney, 2007.

38 Bruce Ferguson, 'Exhibition Rhetorics: Material Speech and Utter Sense', in Reesa Greenberg, Bruce W. Ferguson and Sandy Nairne, *Thinking about Exhibitions*, Routledge, London, 1996, p. 178.

39 Ann Galbally, 'Reflective Selves: Australian Expatriates in an Edwardian World', in Anne Gray (ed.), *The Edwardians: Secrets and Desires*, exhibition catalogue, National Gallery of Australia, Canberra, 2004, p. 107.

40 Ann Galbally, 'Reflective Selves', pp. 107–18.

41 Deborah Edwards, *Rupert Bunny: Artist in Paris*, exhibition catalogue, Art Gallery of New South Wales, Sydney, 2009, p. 29.

42 J. S. MacDonald to Tristan Buesst, 28 November 1948, State Library Victoria, Melbourne, Tristan Nigel Marchand Buesst Papers, MS 10620/IV/12.

43 For a Bourdieuian analysis, see Catherine Speck, 'Rupert Bunny in Paris: Playing the Field', *Australian and New Zealand Journal of Art*, vol. 15, no. 1, 2015, pp. 75–93.

44 Elena Taylor, *Grace Crowley: Being Modern*, exhibition catalogue, National Gallery of Australia, Canberra, 2006, p. 6.

45 Elena Taylor, *Australian Impressionists in France*, exhibition catalogue, National Gallery of Victoria, Melbourne, 2013, p. 148.

46 Anne Gray, 'Australian Artists Within a Wider World 1900–1930', in Jaynie Anderson (ed.), *The Cambridge Companion to Australian Art*, Cambridge University Press, Melbourne, 2011, p. 96.

Bernard Smith in space and time: 'The Antipodean Manifesto' fifty years later

PAUL GILES

As with all major cultural figures, the legacy of Bernard Smith is a complex phenomenon, one not necessarily best served by the simpler forms of hagiography. It is, for example, not necessarily the case that because his work engaged with the Pacific, it was therefore prophetic of the more general twenty-first century focus on this region in what Australian Prime Minister Julia Gillard called 'the Asian century' and President Obama, with a significant shift of emphasis, 'America's Pacific century'. If such straightforwardly teleological charts of influence could be plausibly adduced, then almost every Australian anthropologist or cultural historian of the twentieth century might have a claim to be so honoured, but of course this renewed emphasis on the Pacific owes more to the evolving dynamics of globalisation in a more general sense. Moreover, there are always difficulties in properly assessing intellectual legacies so soon after someone's death, since anecdotal reminiscence, with its implicitly proprietorial dimensions, can often cloud rather than clarify any given subject's more enduring contribution. My purpose here, however, is to take a longer view of Smith's achievement by re-examining 'The Antipodean Manifesto' from a retrospective vantage point of more than fifty years, in an attempt to determine where the most important and lasting aspects of his intellectual legacy might lie.

'The Antipodean Manifesto' was originally published as the foreword to the catalogue of the painting exhibition *The Antipodeans* held in Melbourne in August

1959. It was signed by eight people, of whom Smith was one; the others were Charles Blackman, Arthur Boyd, David Boyd, John Brack, Robert Dickerson, John Perceval and Clifton Pugh. When the piece was reprinted in a book of essays under the same name in 1975, Smith explained in the foreword that its title essay:

> was produced as a result of discussion (continued over a period of six months) among the members of that short-lived group. A number of draft statements were prepared by several members of the group during those discussions. My own task was to write a manifesto-style statement which combined the common intent of the group with the rather diverse artistic interests of individual members.[1]

There are several aspects here that speak to the more slippery, chameleonic aspects of Smith's intellectual profile. One is the way in which he attempts to reconcile the individual and the collective: as an avowed Marxist fellow-traveller, Smith liked to give the impression that he was articulating the perspective of a common body, though in fact his highly idiosyncratic voice never sat comfortably in such a collective rubric, and the explanation here of his putting together a 'manifesto-style statement' in response to the 'draft statements' prepared by others suitably reflects this kind of tension. (Raymond Williams, another Marxist cultural historian of this same period, experienced a similar dilemma of attempting at times to suppress his own voice in the interests of representing wider class interests.) Another ambiguity in Smith's work involves the way the title of a jointly written catalogue essay from 1959 morphs into the title of a book of Smith's individual essays in 1975: despite its collective provenance, 'The Antipodean Manifesto' became associated in its afterlife almost exclusively with Smith himself. Over time, this 'Antipodean Manifesto' became synecdochic of Smith's critical method more broadly, rather than speaking merely about the circumstances of one particular art exhibition, and by titling his book in this way Smith was evidently not discouraging such an affiliation. The explicit denomination of this statement as a 'manifesto' also highlighted Smith's own indebtedness to the aesthetic practice of modernism, the period in between the world wars when artistic and political manifestos of all kinds were rife. Smith's own last major book, *Modernism's History* (1998), demonstrates clearly enough his temperamental affinity with the modernist assumption of art as a utopian condition, a source of cultural polemic and quasi-religious redemption, rather than the more typically postmodernist understanding of it as one discursive formation among others, an idea that was already becoming commonplace by the late 1950s. As an antipodean late modernist, someone who regarded art with religious fervour, Smith was displaced during the second half of the twentieth century in relation to time as well as space.

Smith's own investments in modernism betoken another aspect of his constitutional doubleness, since the *Antipodeans* exhibition represented, in part, a protest against the increasing dominance in the art scene of abstract expressionism, which was gaining considerable public attention as a result of an exhibition organised by New York's Museum of Modern Art, *The New American Painting*, which toured Europe in 1958 and 1959. Whereas in their more purist forms the works of the abstract expressionists conveyed the visual language of an apocalyptic new broom designed to sweep away the last vestiges of representational art, Smith's pitch for an antipodean perspective characteristically turned, much less stridently, on a recognition of the continual play between similarity and difference. If abstract expressionism emphasised a principle of regeneration, Smith's antipodean style involved states of transposition. 'Life here in this country has similarities to life elsewhere and also significant differences', he wrote in 'The Antipodean Manifesto'. 'It is natural ... that we should see and experience nature differently in some degree from the artists of the northern hemisphere.'[2] Note that qualifying clause, 'in some degree': the lack of finality in Smith's writing was attributable not to a lack of self-confidence, still less to the infamous 'cultural cringe', but to a sense of irony as something like an ontological condition, where no condition could remain unchallenged by its opposite.[3] Crucially, Smith did not intend simply to abjure the northern hemisphere, any more than he wished to disparage abstract expressionism; instead, he sought to rotate the intellectual axis so that Australian figurative art could be amalgamated into the modernist spectrum. Rather than letting Jackson Pollock's imposing, gargantuan canvases hold unchallenged sway, Smith wished also to draw attention, for example, to Sidney Nolan's paintings of the Australian desert, in which the depersonalised shapes of Pollock's geometric style are given more literal referents. Nolan was one of the painters included by British museum director Kenneth Clark in his 1961 exhibition *Recent Australian Painting*, held at the Whitechapel Gallery in London, and for Smith the antipodean theory did not involve the promulgation of national culture so much as bringing Australian art into dialogue with its European and American counterparts. Rather than promoting any conception of Australian culture as an organic phenomenon, Smith was endorsing it as a relational notion, one organised around questions of alterity and the problematic affinities between local and global, province and centre. As Peter Beilharz has observed, Smith's understanding of antipodes 'as a *relation*, not a place' was commensurate with his 'lifelong interest in unequal cultural exchange', the power dynamics inevitably involved in unequal encounters across space.[4] In this sense, his commitment to an antipodean manifesto was itself another version of Marx's *Communist Manifesto*; Smith joined the Communist Party in 1940, the year he stopped painting to concentrate full-time on critical work, but for him power inequalities were worked out according to an underlying logic of space rather than class.

Smith was always highly self-conscious about his own illegitimate provenance: his autobiography, *The Boy Adeodatus*, chronicles his fortunes as a 'lucky young bastard' born to an unmarried Irish Catholic maidservant who had left Ireland for Australia in 1914. He took from his mother a strong sense of cultural Catholicism, the religion into which he had been baptised, and although he declared that he would 'die an atheist' he nevertheless specified for himself a Catholic funeral service.[5] Perhaps in part because of this personal background, Smith found himself throughout his life almost pathologically at odds not only with traditional cultural elites in Europe and North America, but also with the Protestant establishment in Australia, which in his eyes tended to adhere in sycophantic fashion to the values of king and country. This was one of the reasons Smith argued with Lionel Lindsay in the early 1940s, after Lindsay had extolled Arthur Streeton's idyllic pastoral paintings in the Heidelberg tradition as embodying an authentic Australia. Smith accused Lindsay and art gallery director J. S. Macdonald of being 'racists' and 'anti-Semitic', and, for all of his antipodean commitments, he was always keen to avoid simplistic identifications of the native landscape with a spirit of Australia.[6] In his 1975 essay 'On Perceiving the Australian Suburb', Smith pointed out how suburbs had not until recently featured at all in Australian painting, and how an 'old European romanticism' had instead constructed 'the view of Australia as a wilderness inhabited by wild men of the woods', something that his own focus on the heretofore marginalised space of the Australian suburb was designed to amend. Indeed, Smith's argument about the suburb, given its inherently subordinate position in relation to the city, might be seen as embodying the terms of his antipodean manifesto in another guise, since it took the power plays involved in spatial relations between southern and northern hemisphere and applied them to a more domestic setting. Rather than acquiescing in the superannuated notion of 'a mythical Australia; a creature who lives on the other side of history', Smith's criticism always invoked history to correct what he took to be the illusory atemporal abstractions associated with myth.[7] We see this demythologising impetus as well in 'The Myth of Isolation' (1961), where Smith took issue with what he saw as Robert Hughes' reductive notion that the 'vital resources' of Australian art were connected inextricably to its remoteness from European exemplars. For Smith, this myth of isolation 'smells of exceptionalism: an endeavour to prove that Australian culture for better or worse is in some ways unique'.[8] Eschewing such idealistic and essentialist assumptions, Smith was concerned more with what Beilharz has called 'peripheral vision, and double vision': the ways in which art and culture get institutionalised, the links between representation and power, the ways in which the effective marginalisation of Australian scenarios raises wider questions about how hegemonic formations become embedded in the circulation of narratives about art and society.[9]

In this sense, 'The Antipodean Manifesto' spoke to an antipodean perspective that Smith brought to his cultural criticism more generally, engaged as it was with strategies of inversion, in the prospect of turning things around the other way. While this position was to some extent politically oppositional, it was also, through the kind of ambiguity inherent in the very term *antipodean*, also paradoxically dependent on the very constraints it was fighting against. This is one of the reasons Smith's work remains elusive and difficult to categorise; his aim was not simply to put Australian art and culture on the map, but deliberately to assume an antagonistic posture towards dominant cultures. This oppositional context manifests itself in one of the oddest pieces he wrote, one of his very few forays into literary criticism, the essay 'Coleridge's "Ancient Mariner" and Cook's Second Voyage', which was published in the *Journal of the Warburg and Courtauld Institutes* in 1956. Here Smith made a case for Coleridge's poem having been influenced by landscapes of the South Pacific, on the grounds that the poet was taught at school, at Christ's Hospital in London, by William Wales, who had served as astronomer on Cook's *Resolution*. But the obvious problem here is that Smith's argument, which might be understood in methodological terms as a very early form of New Historicism, relies on a tenuous form of juxtaposition. It uses a peripheral connection and a speculative hypothesis to try to tease out something more integral to Coleridge's poem:

> It is reasonable to suppose, then, that Wales, by talking to Coleridge, by means of stories passed on by other boys, or by means of the library in the Mathematics School, was able to bring to his knowledge the main incidents of Cook's second voyage.[10]

What is more interesting for a reader of Smith today, however, is not so much the pertinacity of his argument, but how much he obviously had invested in it, and how furious he became when the essay was received in a polite but lukewarm fashion: the director of the Warburg Institute commented condescendingly that he had 'got something'. In his preface thirty-six years later to *Imagining the Pacific: In the Wake of the Cook Voyages*, Smith was still fuming at the way his analysis of *The Rime of the Ancient Mariner* had 'been disregarded by a generation of Coleridge scholars', something he attributed to the incapacity of 'the insular British mind' to properly countenance 'the vast ocean spaces of the Pacific'.[11] Yet what this shows above all is how Smith's critical insights drew energy and strength from their fringe position, their deliberate attempts to upend established convention. The director of the Warburg Institute was probably accurate in his assessment of Smith's essay on Coleridge, which is provocative and interesting but by no means definitive; what carries more significance in retrospect is what it says about Smith's constitutionally antipodean mentality, an outlook that in his case took on the status of something like an all-encompassing ideology.

This antipodean ideology, turning as it did on questions of positionality, was not only hostile in principle to the idea of Australian exceptionalism, as we have seen, but to any reified or isolationist definition of culture. Just as Smith sought belligerently to situate European culture in relation to the Pacific, so he sought to situate Australian culture in relation to wider global orbits.

This created particular complications for Smith's treatment of Indigenous cultures in Australia, to which he similarly denied a self-validating status. For Smith, Australian Indigenous cultures were necessarily framed through politics and aesthetics, rather than through phenomenology or anthropology. As a belligerent non-Platonist, Smith refused on principle to entertain a phenomenological view of anything, and his description of Aboriginal culture in his 1980 Boyer Lectures, published as *The Spectre of Truganini*, derived from his recognition of how these peoples had been mistreated and misrepresented by white Australians. As with his essay on the Australian suburb, it is not difficult to find an analogy between Smith's account of how Australian art had been subordinated to European norms in 'The Antipodean Manifesto' and his analysis in *The Spectre of Truganini* of those 'psycho-cultural mechanisms by means of which the new Australian society sought to put the Aborigine out of sight': again, the model here is of a more powerful society suppressing a less powerful one. Smith's concern is thus with how discursive structures reinforce conventional norms, not with the definition or identification of Indigenous culture in its own right; in fact, the artists he cites with approbation here are those who address the idea of 'cultural convergence', as with the 'meeting of two cultures' in the poems of Les Murray or the movement away from 'narrow Europeanism' in the music of Peter Sculthorpe.[12] Unlike social scientists who probe what they take to be the internal drivers of distinct forms of culture, Smith was more interested in their external aspects: their modes of representation, their ways of relating to the world. In this light, his antipodean manifesto implied an understanding of cultural narratives organised through various versions of intertextual transposition, rather than a universe positioned according to the categorically discrete phenomena of local laws or native customs.

In his foreword to Peter Fuller's book *The Antipodean Scapegoat*, published in 1986, Smith praised Fuller for being 'the first person to grasp the trans-national implications of the Antipodean intervention of 1959'.[13] Suggesting in this book that Australians 'need to evolve an aesthetic rooted in the imaginative response to nature', Fuller argued that 'We can be at our most provincial, even parochial … so long, that is, as we are prepared to respect the provincialism of others, as well as our own'. It was in part Fuller's disdain for what he called the 'corporate internationalism' of American mass culture, together with a willingness to understand 'creative and aesthetic work' as involving a play between competing tropes of space and power, that led Smith to conclude: 'As I read Fuller I gain the impression frequently that I am traversing my own past'.[14] In this sense, Smith might be seen as a precursor not so much of Pacific studies but of transnational cultural studies more generally. It is not surprising that Smith (writing in 1986) should have picked up on 'trans-national' methodologies soon after they began to emerge in the 1980s, since his own work has much in common with that of Homi K. Bhabha, Paul Gilroy and others in the way it attempts historically to situate disparate cultures in time and space by reading them in the comparative light of each other.[15] This is commensurate also with Smith's revisionist narrative in the subsequent *Modernism's History*, where his attempts to validate what he called the 'Formalesque' arose out of his efforts to disestablish the canonical version of modernism as an abstract form of aesthetic purity. Again, Smith associated such reified forms of abstraction with what he called the 'imperial dominance' of modernism in institutional terms, and he sought to replace this with a densely contextualised analysis whereby the movement's aesthetic emphasis on form was itself framed within a historical matrix.[16] This was the rationale behind Smith's term 'Formalesque', a neologism that was designed to distinguish the aesthetic idiosyncrasies of modernism from the condition of modernity more generally.

In his introduction to *Modernism's History*, Smith cites literary and cultural critics such as Erich Auerbach, Fredric Jameson, Ihab Hassan and others, and his conceptual range here is much broader than art history in the narrow academic sense.[17] This raises the question of how far Smith's antipodean manifestos might be transferable to other intellectual horizons, and the extent to which his legacy might traverse different fields. The more domestic valorisations of him—as an Australian, or as an art historian—seem signally inappropriate for an intellectual who used art history primarily as his professional base, and who was interested not in sentimental appropriations of native landscapes but in more expansive processes of transaction and exchange. He also preserved a lifelong interest in dadaism and surrealism, not just as art movements but as forms of resistance to the universalising, imperialising gestures of modernism as it institutionalised itself after World War II. In a 1940 paper he characteristically described surrealism as a cyclical, transhistorical phenomenon, rather than merely a twentieth-century art movement: Smith here identified Hieronymous Bosch, for example, as a proto-surrealist.[18] *Modernism's History* comments frequently on the work of Marcel Duchamp, and all of this can be correlated again with Smith's central concern, which was the way in which artistic traditions had accumulated cultural prestige and, conversely, the ways in which other forms had become marginalised. Rather than being organised merely around geographical location or benign forms of open transaction, Smith's version of the antipodean imaginary was both psychological and political, a circuit where contrary impulses were held in tension and where dominant and subordinate impulses were held paradoxically (and sometimes pathologically) within the same spectrum. Indeed, it was the very lopsided nature of this antipodean matrix, and the heft of the forces contributing to its consolidation, that fired Smith's counter-suggestible scholarship.

Since he was committed, as a matter of principle, to the position of underdog, Smith always ran the risk of restraining himself with the manacles of subordination, and indeed this circuit between empowerment and disempowerment might be seen as fundamental to the trajectory of his writing. In *Modernism's History* he described how as an 'Australian art historian' he regarded 'Europe as my antipodes', since 'antipodes is not a place but a relationship'; this idiom of perpetual displacement is also fundamental to the way his work operates.[19] Often his books conjoin opposites, in form as well as content, as in the title *European Vision and the South Pacific*, which brings two opposing areas of the globe into antipodean juxtaposition. This book's subtitle is *A Study in the History of Art and Ideas* and this latter emphasis, 'and Ideas', testifies again to his desire to exceed the institutional parameters of art history. Indeed, Smith's movement across disciplinary boundaries might be seen as analogous to, and commensurate with, his restless movement across the frontiers of national cultures. The conventional binary opposition pitting the values of the autochthonous local against those of an abstract international can thus be seen in his case as a false dichotomy, since Smith's antipodean idiom repositions internationalism in a more political sphere, where the rhetorical language of aesthetics becomes integral to a dynamic exchange of ideas across national territories. As with the work of scholars such as Gilroy or James Clifford, which he in many ways presaged, the transnational methodology developed by Smith involves a more materialistic version of globalisation theory, whose forms of exchange involve not abstract flows of finance capital but unequal exchanges of money, power and prestige, with all of the cultural capital around race, class and indigeneity associated with those asymmetrical interactions.[20] Taking intellectual advantage as he did of his situation in a geographically marginalised part of the world, at a time predating the instantaneous communications of the digital era, Smith developed his particular antipodean stance to adumbrate a planetary perspective based upon relativities of power, one where the uneven distribution of geographic space became a prime constant.

Evidence of the way in which Smith's work has been influential can be found in Sarah Phillips Casteel's *Second Arrivals: Landscape and Belonging in Contemporary Writing of the Americas* (2007), a critical work that deploys Smith's work on the inherent doubleness of pastoral forms to make its point about how diasporic writers in the Americas, from Derek Walcott to Philip Roth to Jamaica Kincaid, renegotiate pastoral landscapes to elucidate ways in which they carry resonances of political complexity and colonial power struggle. Just as Smith writes in *European Vision and the South Pacific* of how the 'emergence of pastoral imagery in colonial Australia made it possible to present a version of Australian nature more amenable to the European imagination', so Casteel describes how the Canadian poet Oliver Goldsmith wrote in 1825 a work called *The Rising Village*, where he specifically responded to a poem *The Deserted Village*, written by his great-uncle of the same name, which was published in England in 1770.[21] According to Casteel:

> The younger Goldsmith's *The Rising Village* inverts the pattern of its English predecessor by arguing that the pastoral landscape can be recreated in the New World, specifically in Acadia (Nova Scotia).[22]

Like Smith, Casteel thus suggests how colonialism and pastoralism are intertwined, and how idyll and its unmasking play constituent roles in the formation and representation of picturesque landscapes. She aligns Smith's enquiry into the spatialised dimensions of narrative with Edouard Glissant's work on the 'rhizomatic' nature of discourse, Arjun Appadurai's influential theories of globalisation, and the interventions of Gilles Deleuze and Félix Guattari on the contours of deterritorialisation, through which disparate geographical zones might be seen to relate to one another in complicated ways.[23]

All of this suggests that Smith's most enduring intellectual legacy may well be as a cultural theorist, rather than as an art historian *per se*. It is almost certainly the case that, as is usual in affairs of this kind, the anecdotal reminiscences of friends and colleagues with whom the subject associated are a mixed blessing in terms of evaluating his more lasting contribution. Though interesting enough in their own gossipy way, such personal recollections tend almost inevitably to trivialise the broader domain in which an intellectual figure of such power and influence operated, and, as with Deleuze or Jacques Derrida, it may well be that the shape of this legacy will not become clearer until one or two generations have passed. But if I were prophetically to risk a guess, I would suggest that Smith may be recognised in a hundred years as a forerunner of the effort to relate Australian landscapes more systematically to the circulation of global art and culture, and also celebrated as a twentieth-century forerunner, working as he was at a time of defensive national chauvinism and benighted provincialism, of the more enlightened move to reposition an antipodean imaginary on the axis of world culture.

NOTES

1 Bernard Smith, *The Antipodean Manifesto: Essays in Art and History*, Oxford University Press, Melbourne, 1975, p. vii.

2 Bernard Smith, 'The Antipodean Manifesto', in *The Antipodean Manifesto*, p. 166.

3 On the 'cultural cringe', see Arthur Phillips, 'The Cultural Cringe', *Meanjin*, vol. 9, no. 4, Summer 1950, pp. 299–302.

4 Peter Beilharz, *Imagining the Antipodes: Culture, Theory and the Visual in the Work of Bernard Smith*, Cambridge University Press, Cambridge, 1997, pp. xiii, 94.

5 Sheridan Palmer, 'Father of Art History Had Far-Reaching Influence', *Sydney Morning Herald*, 8 September 2011, p. 22.

6 John F. Williams, *The Quarantined Culture: Australian Reactions to Modernism 1913–1939*, Cambridge University Press, Cambridge, 1995, p. 226.

7 Bernard Smith, 'On Perceiving the Australian Suburb', in Rosemary Dobson (ed.), *Australian Voices: Poetry and Prose of the 1970s*, Canberra Fellowship of Australian Writers in association with Australian National University Press, Canberra, 1975, pp. 106–19; reprinted in *The Antipodean Manifesto* (here quoting pp. 88–9).

8 Bernard Smith, 'The Myth of Isolation', in *The Antipodean Manifesto*, pp. 60, 62.

9 Beilharz, *Imagining the Antipodes*, p. 99.

10 Bernard Smith, 'Coleridge's "Ancient Mariner" and Cook's Second Voyage', in *The Antipodean Manifesto*, p. 175.

11 Bernard Smith, *Imagining the Pacific: In the Wake of the Cook Voyages*, Miegunyah Press, Melbourne University Press, Melbourne, 1992, p. x.

12 Bernard Smith, *The Spectre of Truganini*, The 1980 Boyer Lectures, Australian Broadcasting Commission, Sydney, 1980, pp. 16, 44, 50–1.

13 Bernard Smith, 'Foreword', in Peter Fuller, *The Australian Scapegoat: Towards an Antipodean Aesthetic*, University of Western Australia Press, Nedlands, WA, 1986, p. xiii.

14 Fuller, *The Australian Scapegoat*, pp. 44, 33, 54; Smith, 'Foreword', p. xiii.

15 See, for example, Homi K. Bhabha, *The Location of Culture*, Routledge, London, 1994; and Paul Gilroy, *The Black Atlantic: Modernity and Double Consciousness*, Harvard University Press, Cambridge, Mass., 1993.

16 Bernard Smith, *Modernism's History: A Study in Twentieth-Century Art and Ideas*, Yale University Press, New Haven, 1998, p. 8.

17 ibid., pp. 3, 7.

18 Beilharz, *Imagining the Antipodes*, p. 66.

19 Smith, *Modernism's History*, p. 7.

20 See, for example, James Clifford, *Routes: Travel and Translation in the Late Twentieth Century*, Harvard University Press, Cambridge, Mass., 1997.

21 Bernard Smith, *European Vision and the South Pacific, 1768–1850: A Study in the History of Art and Ideas*, Clarendon Press, Oxford, 1960, p. 202.

22 Sarah Phillips Casteel, *Second Arrivals: Landscape and Belonging in Contemporary Writing of the Americas*, University of Virginia Press, Charlottesville, 2007, p. 11.

23 ibid., pp. 8, 110–11.

Peter Fuller, the Celtic midwife and some [other] Northern critics of Southern art

SIMON PIERSE

First published as a foreword to Peter Fuller's *The Australian Scapegoat: Towards an Antipodean Aesthetic* (1986), Bernard Smith's essay 'Some Northern Critics of Southern Art' is a personalised account of his encounters with British and American critics who visited Australia in the postwar period.[1] Written retrospectively, the essay is more than an appraisal of how these critics perceived postwar Australian art 'from the outside' and how their appreciation of it (or lack of appreciation in the case of a few) was formulated through a critical or curatorial bias in relation to the antipodes. Smith's long academic career included his appointment as inaugural Power Professor of Contemporary Art and Director of the Power Institute of Fine Arts, a post that he held until 1977. He had previously been involved with the Antipodeans group of artists when, as co-signatory and architect of the 'Antipodean Manifesto' in 1959, he had helped to shape the development of postwar Australian art. In 'Some Northern Critics of Southern Art' Smith projects himself, if not exactly as protagonist, as something more than mere 'uninvolved spectator' to a period recently lived through and events that he saw taking place.[2] His critique of the views of Sir Kenneth Clark and theories of Fuller link directly to his own acquaintance with them as people. Sidney Nolan, an artist revered in equal measure by Clark, Fuller and Bryan Robertson, but viewed rather less favourably by Smith, is central to the artistic sensibilities of all three of these 'Northern critics', who shared a friendship with Nolan and were collectors of his work.

Smith described Clark as a 'genius spotter' who appropriated Nolan and, like St Francis, used him to prop up the 'waning vigour of British art'.[3] Clark first met Nolan at his home in northern Sydney in 1949 and, in Nolan's own words, Clark:

> saw something in me, something I don't understand, not being able to see the back of my neck. He saw something in me that would be attracted by European civilisation and wouldn't let go of it easily.[4]

It would also be true to say that Nolan hung on pretty tightly to Clark's patronage and support in the decades that followed. Shortly after his first encounter with Nolan, Clark gave a lecture at the National Gallery of Victoria, in which he spoke of a young, vital and adventurous school of Australian painting.[5] His new enthusiasm for Australian painting, especially the work of Nolan, can best be understood in relation to his views about the state of British contemporary art in the postwar period. Clark's growing pessimism about abstraction and internationalist trends in modern art was tempered by the belief that contemporary Australian art had evolved nothing less than a new figurative language. Back in England, when Clark told his friends that Australia was about to add something entirely fresh to contemporary painting, they thought he was out of his mind. 'And when they asked me to account for it', he wrote, 'I could only mumble something about the light, and the dead white trees and the feeling of an Australian myth'.[6] Clark's interest in Australian art was, as Smith observes, essentially 'environmental'. Clark argued that Nolan had 'extracted its essences: the red desert, the dead animals, the stranded, ridiculous towns'.[7] Significantly, Clark did not consider the jungle authentically Australian, and throughout the mid-1950s to early 1960s, as Nolan looked to northern Queensland and elsewhere for new subjects, which he painted in dark-green smears of polyvinyl acetate, Clark's enthusiasm slowly began to cool.

Smith's first encounter with Clark was in London in 1949, after Clark's return from Australia. Smith had arrived to take up a research scholarship at the Warburg Institute and was living with his wife Kate in rented rooms at The Abbey Arts Centre.[8] It was there, while on a visit to The Abbey, that Clark walked into Smith's first-floor study. Clark began to sound Smith out as a possible candidate for the directorship of the Art Gallery of South Australia—a post that was about to become vacant. They met subsequently at Clark's Hampstead home but Smith's Marxist politics failed to strike a chord. Clark had read *Place, Taste and Tradition*, Smith recalls, 'but I think it was probably a bit too far to the left for him'.[9] A decade later, when Smith sent Clark a copy of *The Antipodean Manifesto*, it elicited some qualified support: 'I agree with a great deal that the manifesto contains, and I like the vigorous way in which it is worded', Clark wrote. 'Sometimes it seems to go a little bit outside the proper scope of a group of painters.' 'I am in sympathy with their aims', he would later write, 'but it does not follow that I shall like their pictures'.[10] They met again several times over the years, after Smith became director of the Power Institute. On a return visit to England, Smith received an invitation to Clark's home at Saltwood Castle and was amazed to discover that it was a real castle. Clark did his best to slum it, driving to the station dressed in an old sweater to pick up Kate and Bernard, and telling the self-effacing story of how the previous owner of Saltwood had thought him a vagrant when he knocked on the door to enquire about buying it.[11] But Clark's patrician manner and condescending attitude towards the 'colonies' would remain a stumbling block. Smith saw that Clark had co-opted Australian painting for his own ends, using it as a much-needed transfusion into the arm of an anaemic and ailing postwar British art scene. In 1963 Bernard Smith had written of 'London Australiana' as an art form that had 'emerged armed and fully grown from the head of Sir Kenneth Clark, after it had been neatly cleft by the boomerang of Mr Bryan Robertson' whom Smith satirised as the 'Chief Celtic midwife to our London Australiana' (Fig. 19).[12] Such art was an invention—the offspring of one Briton's imagination, given birth or brought into being by a second, while the Whitechapel Gallery was where, with Nolan's one-man exhibition in 1957, it had come of age.

Of all the Northern critics of Australian art, it is perhaps Robertson of whom Smith is most critical, for his stance on postwar Australian art, which he curated in terms of perceived national and geographical characteristics and projected in the 1961 show *Recent Australian Painting*. In declining Smith's exhibition proposal to the Whitechapel Gallery, Robertson had effectively thwarted the Antipodeans' plans for a show in London. To the end, Smith remained of the opinion that the Antipodeans' request had directly led Robertson to initiate plans for the survey show that became *Recent Australian Painting*, even though research has since revealed that Hal Missingham, director of the Art Gallery of New South Wales, had raised the idea of an exhibition with Bryan Robertson in early 1958, well before Bernard Smith and the Antipodeans had come together.[13]

The elusive Robertson eventually crossed Smith's path in Melbourne in 1960 while the Whitechapel director was touring Australia, selecting paintings for the forthcoming Whitechapel exhibition. Robertson was invited to a rather uncomfortable formal dinner at University House, University of Melbourne, where an impromptu exhibition had been arranged around the walls in an attempt to show 'that abstract painting was alive and kicking whatever the manifesto said'. Joseph Burke, the first Herald Chair of Fine Arts at the University of Melbourne, and five or six other guests sat around the dinner table where Robertson gave Smith 'an extremely cool reception'.[14]

Smith's disappointment over the Whitechapel Gallery coloured his opinion of Robertson, whom he criticised as a curator in love with the exotic and primitive: a man whose artistic heroes were the American abstract expressionists, especially Jackson Pollock. Robertson was in fact extremely broad and eclectic (at times even maverick) in his tastes, but it is certainly true that, for the purposes of curating *Recent Australian Painting*, he had joined forces with Hal Missingham to oppose the Commonwealth Art Advisory Board with a selection of contemporary Australian paintings that was fifty per cent abstract. Robertson, briefed by his London-based Australian friends on the rivalry that existed between abstract and figurative painters in late-1950s Australia, was not prepared to accept an exhibition that projected just one side of that debate. Consequently the Whitechapel show was criticised by some for presenting a colonialist and somewhat eclectic overview of postwar Australian painting, its diversity tenuously linked by perceived nationalistic traits of character. Nevertheless, as Elwyn Lynn observed at the time, critical reception of *Recent Australian Painting* in the British press tended to focus on the figurative paintings, finding 'verbal equivalents for what was pictorially obvious in the works of Pugh, Dickerson, Blackman, Drysdale, Tucker and Nolan'.[15] Abstract paintings, insofar as they were mentioned at all, were, with the exception of the works of Whiteley, dismissed as weak, flimsy and derivative of New York. Smith later voiced the opinion that two distinct shows—an Antipodeans exhibition, followed up by another of Australian abstract painting, both held at the Whitechapel Gallery—would have been a better solution, a possibility that in retrospect still has much to recommend it. In Smith's view, Bryan Robertson had 'looked to America for salvation and in doing so, led British art into provinciality'.[16]

It is significant that British critic Peter Fuller, who saw *Recent Australian Painting* as a 14-year-old schoolboy, remembered it as a landscape exhibition (Fig. 20).[17] Years later (but before he travelled to Australia), Fuller would write of his intuition of the 'dreadful *otherness* of Australia':

> flickering image[s] of a second creation of strange flowers, trees, birds, and marsupial beasts, clinging to a habitable, coastal ribbon which fringed vast, uncultivated expanses of desert dust, emptiness, and natural dereliction.[18]

These are words that exactly echo those used by Robertson, Clark and Colin McInnes in 1961.[19] More than a decade earlier, Clark's first experience of Australia had seemed to confirm the arguments he was then formulating into a book, *Landscape into Art*, where landscape painting is defined as the pictorial expression of human values.[20] In the preface to the exhibition catalogue for *Recent Australian Painting*, he reiterated the same view: 'the scenery is not painted for its own sake, but as the background of a legend and a reflection of human values'.[21] Peter Fuller would use landscape paintings by Drysdale and Nolan (both artists championed by Clark) as evidence to support his symbolic quest for a 'higher landscape' for modern times: a redemptive landscape that could convey symbolic values.[22]

The idea of a 'higher landscape' was, Fuller willingly conceded, both 'profoundly conservative' but also 'deeply radical'.[23] Inspired by the philosophy of John Ruskin, Fuller built his thesis on the shifting sands of the Australian desert and paintings of Australian desert landscape. The industrial revolution in Britain, Fuller contended, had led to a loss of innocence, a fall from grace. Britain had forsaken the God-given garden until, paradoxically, the devastation of two world wars brought about a 'redemption through form' through the new vision of war artists Moore, Nash, Piper and Sutherland, who looked upon a landscape torn apart by war.[24] Fuller uses Nolan's 'lyrical and tragic' drought paintings (1953) as another example of this 'redemption through form': imagery of 'dehydrated corpses of cattle in seductive ripolin paint ... that was in itself brutal and about death, gained another kind of life through the decorative way it was painted' (Fig. 21).[25] It is interesting to compare Fuller's words with those of his erstwhile mentor John Berger, who, in a 1953 review for *Meanjin*, had used the same Nolan *Drought* paintings to reinforce his Marxist interpretation of Australian art. The underbellies of these calves were seen as a:

> scaleless landscape of sand dunes … subjects express[ing] a spirit which *is* typically Australian … a determination to harness the forces of Nature—for all her vastness, a physical directness between men and their jobs.[26]

After his return to Australia from Europe in 1951, Nolan began to see the bush increasingly in terms of quasi-religious imagery. 'The burnt bush is black up to a certain height', he wrote to Clark in December 1951, 'the foliage in sharp contrast is scorched to an almost white ash … the sun coming through the smoke and haze produces an impression of a tangible religious atmosphere'.[27] Influenced by *Landscape into Art*, Nolan began to interpret the Australian landscape through Clark's writings, to whom he would later write: 'When I read your *Landscape into Art* I realised for the first time that even the Australian landscape was already an imaginative construction. Even in the case of the remote desert which I painted'.[28]

Smith considered the critic Herbert Read a more sensitive person than Clark, but when Read visited Australia in 1963 he was 'a tired and ageing man' who failed to see the country's possibilities—that Australian art might develop a different trajectory of values from those in Europe, where Smith perceived the optimism of early modernism had hardened to become part of a 'philistine establishment', 'turn[ing] in upon itself to cultivate nihilism and despair'.[29] Reed saw in the forms of late modernism 'excess' and 'the denial of life', but, like Clement Greenberg, whom Smith invited to Australia in 1968 to deliver the inaugural Power Lecture in Contemporary Art, he took no interest in Australian art as either a tradition or an alternative way forward.[30] In his lecture, entitled 'Avant-garde Attitudes', Greenberg formally announced the death of abstract expressionism, *art informel* and tachisme. Speaking as of an aged and much-loved relative, he announced:

> Abstract Expressionism collapsed very suddenly back in the Spring of 1962 … It is true that it had begun to lose its vitality well before that, but nevertheless it continued to dominate the avant-garde scene, and by the time of its final retreat from that scene it had led art for close to twenty years. The collapse of Abstract Expressionism was as sudden as it was because it was long overdue, but even had its collapse come five or six years earlier (which is when it should have come) the span of time over which Abstract Expressionism held its leadership would still have been over the average for art styles or movements within the last century and a half.[31]

The Greenberg that Smith describes in 'Some Northern Critics' is a man supremely confident in his own judgements, an engaging if somewhat intimidating figure: 'the leading prophet of late modernism in its condition of decline'.[32] At the same time he displayed all the signs of preferring figurative expressionist 'antipodean painting' to the 'second-hand' work of the young Australian colour-field painters who flocked about him in adulation.[33] Smith had already guessed that 'Greenberg's commanding influence was almost finished' and, in inviting him to Australia, was able to witness, in 'Avant-garde Attitudes', what amounts to a requiem for American abstract expressionism.[34] 'Avant-garde Attitudes' marked the point of Greenberg's separation from the academic world that had put its trust in the principle of a perpetual avant-garde. As Greenberg put it: 'if everyone is out front, who lags behind?' The funereal quality in Greenberg's 1968 address finds an interesting parallel in a conversation between Peter Fuller and Sidney Nolan, published in *Modern Painters* twenty years later. Nolan described how, in coming to Europe after the war, he felt that he had come 'to witness the decline of the West':[35]

> When I saw the first exhibition of abstract expressionist painting sent out by the Museum of Modern Art, in the late 1950's, I saw that it was a funereal decorative art ... the fear and trembling which was once in those American pictures has evaporated, too; you are left with the decorative thing. I think a lot of people realised that when they saw the Rothkos in the Tate Gallery last year.[36]

Just as Western civilisation's inevitable decline into decadence is a theme running through Fuller's 1988 interview with Nolan, so does the final chapter of Clark's *Landscape into Art* encapsulate the zeitgeist of the immediate postwar period and betray Clark's own deep sense of fatalism about the recent horrors of concentration camps and the atomic bomb. Clark found historical precedent for it in chiliasm, a fear that the world is coming to an end, and which is supposed to be connected with the Millennium.[37] 'Our belief in chiliasm has come fifty years early', he wrote, 'but then our new religion has provided a great deal better grounds for it than the old one did'.[38]

To Fuller, decline into decadence was evident in the pluralities of late modernism and the 'mega-visual' culture of advertising and commercial imagery which had created a 'sort of anti-art ... favoured by the "international" institutions and magazines of art'. It colluded, in his view, 'with the destruction of aesthetic potentialities', and evoked George Orwell's 'negative vision of an anaesthetic future ... the advent of a world such as that described in *1984*'.[39] Fuller was profoundly depressed by the 1982 *Eureka* exhibition that he had seen in London—and which he considered a 'profoundly regressive and potentially deeply destructive' exhibition which demonstrated that Australia had followed the 'kind of Late Modernism which dabbled with mass media techniques, and aped the new technologies'.[40]

When Smith met Fuller in Australia later that same year, he found him a grumpy and beleaguered man. Fuller had long since rejected John Berger, the 'intellectual father and personal mentor of his youth', and was now well into his Ruskin period, Smith recalled.[41] Julian Stallabrass has shown how Fuller somehow managed to take elements of Marxist theory ('materialism', 'structures of feeling' and 'the aesthetic dimension') and graft them onto a political position on the Right, where they became 'stripped of all connection with the critical theories in which they had originated'. Fuller, almost by sleight of hand, managed to undergo a radical political shift from Left to Right while maintaining the same aesthetic ideology. To Stallabrass, Fuller:

> was a self-conscious eccentric ... an irascible and uncompromising writer, who, while never forgetting to court a public, journeyed from Marxist to conservative, from materialist to quasi-religious views, barely touching the middle ground.[42]

Bernard Smith and Peter Fuller had Marxism in common, although in Fuller's case it was a Marxist youth later rejected, while in Smith's case it was what Peter Beilharz describes as a lightly but insistently worn 'soft or warm' Marxism.[43] The two men also shared the same basic aesthetic philosophy, at least to the extent of Fuller's radical critique of late modernism. Nevertheless, it is surprising to find Smith in so much sympathy with Peter Fuller, since he so often found himself in disagreement with his writings.[44] Significantly, Smith was interested in Fuller's capacity for rejection, which he believed had begun with the rejection of his father and developed to become a core trait in Fuller's critical faculties. Opposition is the key to understanding their academic relationship. Both took up oppositionist positions in their relationship to the prevailing art movements of the times. To Beilharz, Smith was a *Gegner*:

> an oppositionist [who] wanted to stand against the current, when necessary, but ... did not expect the current to subside. The object of his politics was less to change the world than to stop it getting worse.[45]

The clarity that Smith strove for in his own writing was the same quality that he admired in Fuller's criticism. 'Perhaps it is because Fuller takes such pains to make his position clear that so many feel that it must be reactionary', Smith suggested. 'But far from being a reactionary, Fuller is in the process of fashioning one of the most radical critiques of late modernism that we have witnessed in a generation.'[46] Above all else, Smith acknowledged Fuller as one of the first to think of Australian art in terms of a tradition. 'I admired him as a person capable of independent thought about art.'[47] He alone had the 'determination to work out a fully-fledged aesthetic for himself'.[48]

Smith did not simply admire Fuller as an independent mind, a fellow *Gegner*, swimming against the tide; there was another fundamental point of agreement between them. In his essay 'The Myth of Isolation', Smith argued against internationalism in Australian art:

> This desire to keep up at all costs with the international Jones's of the art of the moment is in my view an infallible sign of the provincial mind, of artists and critics uncertain of what they are doing or where they are going.[49]

Writing in 1986, Fuller echoed Smith's argument in declaring that the development of Australia's 'great vision had been stunted and occluded by the enthusiasm, since the late 1960s ... for the latest fads and fancies of the late modernist "international" art'.[50]

> I believe that the Australian achievement in painting would have been greater still if, during the 1960s and 1970s, Australian artists had not been so greviously deflected by their desire to keep up at all costs with 'the international Jones's of the art of the moment'. The exhibitions that have been coming out of Australia in the 1980s and visiting London, Paris, New York and Edinburgh have been, in Bernard Smith's sense, infinitely more 'provincial' than that great 1961 [Whitechapel] show.[51]

'Actually, to call this 'provincialism', Fuller went on, 'is to give the provincial vision a bad name':

> Rather I'll refer to it as Biennale-International-Club-Class-Art, or BICCA, for short … Actually, this much-vaunted 'internationalism' of the fashionable modern art world, though hardly 'conservative' … is deeply reactionary. It is really no different from the corporate 'internationalism' of MacDonald's, Playboy, or the Hilton Hotel. And it meets exactly the same all-American tastes whether or not the Biennale is held in Rio de Janeiro, Timbuctoo [sic], or Alice Springs.[52]

Smith and Fuller shared a rejection of the hegemony of American culture. Fuller considered modernist formalism particularly appropriate to the 'the thin and ugly climate of modern American "cultural" life' where 'In New York, at least, the relation between the social, the political and the aesthetic was transparently readable'.[53] In 1959 Smith had used 'The Antipodean Manifesto' to oppose the proselytes of CIA-sponsored American abstract expressionism—an art that was 'insufficient for our time' and revealed 'a death of the mind and spirit'.[54] Even Nolan, in an interview with Fuller, revealed that he was in favour of Smith's attack on the promotion of the American school but was opposed to a theoretical stand *per se* against abstract art. Nolan's description of the 'funereal decorative' qualities in the first exhibition of abstract expressionist painting he saw in the late 1950s even finds some parallel in 'The Antipodean Manifesto', to which he was fundamentally opposed, which foretold of the death of art 'after an Indian summer of decorative luxury'.[55] To Fuller, a process of *kenosis* or self-emptying, prevalent in Western art since the 1880s, had reached crisis point in late modernism. Paintings and sculptures had acquired 'an ever more drained out, vacuous character, as if artists were voluntarily relinquishing the skills and techniques which they had previously possessed'.[56] Even the high sentiments of Mark Rothko, acknowledged by Fuller as 'the great master of this ultimate radicalness … collapsed into the "blinding square" and "dead blank" of anti art [and] within a few months … [the artist] lay dead in a pool of blood on his studio floor'.[57]

At face value, 'Some Northern Critics of Southern Art' gives us Smith's opinion on some of the most influential art critics of his time. We might well question whether his picture of Clement Greenberg as a critic who preferred Pro Hart to Australian abstract painting is an entirely fair or accurate one. Smith's failure to secure the Whitechapel Gallery for an Antipodeans exhibition undoubtedly tainted his view of Robertson, to the point where it was detrimental to his judgement, although in later years Smith's opinion of *Recent Australian Painting* would mellow somewhat. While admitting that it was 'a splendid selection of contemporary Australian art ... the only exhibition of Australian painting abroad that has ever evoked anything more than a smothered yawn', he still considered its presentation, in nationalistic and primitivistic terms by Robertson and Hughes, 'a disaster'.[58] To Fuller, *Recent Australian Painting* had been a revelation, and he later lamented that the paintings shown had not done more to encourage 'the best British artists to refuse that pseudo-international, BICCA, anti-culture, which, during the 1960s, began at first to obsess, and later to consume, them'.[59]

In 'Some Northern Critics', written in the postmodernist era, Smith found affirmation for views he had expressed many years earlier, during his formative period as an art critic in the late 1940s and 1950s. 'As I read Fuller', he wrote, 'I gain the impression frequently that I am traversing my own past'.[60]

In staging the *Antipodeans* exhibition in 1959, Smith would later reveal:

> I was hoping to develop a discourse about the relative merits of figural and abstract art at a time when the U.S. State Department [had] decided to promote American abstraction as an export [and] political weapon against the socialist realism of the USSR and Eastern Europe. I could not spell that out in the Manifesto but that was the hidden reason why I felt that it was necessary to act. I could live comfortably with abstraction as one genre of art among others but not as the only legitimate form of 20th century painting.[61]

It is interesting to compare 'In Defence of Art', Peter Fuller's early essay of 1979, in which arguments run parallel to, and sometimes intersect with, those used in Smith's defence of the image in 'The Antipodean Manifesto', published twenty years earlier.[62] It must have been with some satisfaction, therefore, that Smith saw the 'trans-national implications' of the *Antipodeans* exhibition and its manifesto reaffirmed and re-asserted through the authority of Fuller's own later writings.[63]

NOTES

1 Bernard Smith's essay first appeared as the foreword to Peter Fuller, *The Australian Scapegoat: Towards an Antipodean Aesthetic*, University of Western Australia Press, Nedlands, WA, 1986, pp. ix–xv. It was republished under the title 'Some Northern Critics of Southern Art' in *The Death of the Artist as Hero: Essays in History and Culture*, Oxford University Press, Melbourne, 1988, pp. 273–81.

2 Smith, 'Some Northern Critics of Southern Art', p. 274.

3 ibid., p. 273.

4 Sidney Nolan, interviewed by Peter Fuller, 'Sidney Nolan and the Decline of the West: A *Modern Painters* interview with Sir Sidney Nolan', *Modern Painters*, vol. 1, no. 2, Summer 1988, p. 41.

5 Kenneth Clark's 'The Idea of a Great Gallery' was subsequently published in Franz Philipp and June Stewart (eds), *In Honour of Daryl Lindsay: Essays and Studies*, Melbourne University Press, Melbourne, 1964, pp. 8–19.

6 Kenneth Clark, 'Foreword', in *Recent Australian Painting*, exhibition catalogue, foreword by Kenneth Clark, with introduction by Robert Hughes and preface by Bryan Robertson, Whitechapel Gallery, London, 1961, p. 4.

7 Kenneth Clark, in Kenneth Clark, Colin MacInnes and Bryan Robertson, *Sidney Nolan*, Thames & Hudson, London, 1961, p. 8.

8 See Bernard Smith, *A Pavane for Another Time*, Macmillan, Melbourne, 2002.

9 Smith's *Place, Taste and Tradition: A Study of Australian Art Since 1788* was published by Ure Smith, Sydney, in 1945. See also Simon Pierse, *Australian Art and Artists in London 1950–1965: An Antipodean Summer*, Ashgate, Farnham, UK, 2012, p. 29.

10 Pierse, *Australian Art and Artists in London*, p. 85, n. 26.

11 Bernard Smith, interview with Simon Pierse, Melbourne, 22 December 2005.

12 Bernard Smith, 'The London Myth about Art in Australia' [book review], *The Age*, 24 August 1963, p. 19 (review of John Douglas Pringle, *Australian Painting Today*, republished in 1989 in *The Critic as Advocate*).

13 See Sheridan Palmer, 'The Lone Antipodean: Bernard Smith's Post-War Modernism', *Eyeline: Contemporary Visual Arts*, nos 78–9, 2013. See also Pierse, *Australian Art and Artists in London*, pp. 85–6.

14 Pierse, *Australian Art and Artists in London*, p. 102.

15 Elwyn Lynn, 'Australia Rediscovered: The Whitechapel Gallery Exhibition', *Meanjin Quarterly*, vol. 20, no. 3, September 1961, pp. 337–9.

16 Smith, 'Some Northern Critics of Southern Art', p. 277.

17 Peter Fuller, 'Art and Post-Industrialism', in *The Australian Scapegoat*, p. 31.

18 Peter Fuller, 'The Antipodes and I', in *The Australian Scapegoat*, p. xix.

19 Clark, MacInnes and Robertson, *Sidney Nolan*.

20 Kenneth Clark, *Landscape into Art*, John Murray, London, 1949. Smith, who was in London researching European painting in the South Pacific when *Landscape into Art* was published, wrote to Clark, surprised at how 'the different qualities of vision at the root of painting were the very ones I had been seeking to track down in my own piece of work. It was, indeed, the relation between the landscape of fact, the natural vision, and the ideal landscape, that I sought to elucidate'. Bernard Smith to Kenneth Clark, 14 May 1950, Tate Gallery Archive, London, Kenneth Clark Papers, TGA 8812.1.2.6063. See also Pierse, *Australian Art and Artists in London*, p. 10.

21 Clark, 'Foreword', p. xx.

22 Fuller, 'Art and Post-Industrialism', p. 32.

23 ibid., p. 32.

24 Fuller, 'The Antipodes and I', p. xx.

25 Fuller in an interview with Nolan, 'Sidney Nolan and the Decline of the West', p. 42.

26 John Berger, 'London Exhibition of Australian Art', *Meanjin*, vol. 12, no. 3, Spring 1953, pp. 276–8.

27 Sidney Nolan to Kenneth Clark, 18 December 1951, Tate Gallery Archive, London, Kenneth Clark Papers, TGA 8812.1.2.4769.

28 Sidney Nolan to Kenneth Clark, 14 January 1960. See Nancy Underhill (ed.), *Nolan on Nolan: Sidney Nolan in His Own Words*, Penguin/Viking, Melbourne, 2007, p. 192.

29 Smith, 'Some Northern Critics of Southern Art', p. 274.

30 ibid., pp. 274–6.

31 The lecture was given on 17 May 1968. See Clement Greenberg, *Avant-garde Attitudes: New Art in the Sixties*, The John Power Lecture in Contemporary Art, Delivered at the University of Sydney on Friday 17 May 1968, Power Institute of Fine Arts, University of Sydney, Sydney, 1969.

32 Smith, 'Some Northern Critics of Southern Art', p. 275.

33 According to Judith Pugh, in 1968 Greenberg spoke of erstwhile Antipodean Clifton Pugh as the artist in Australia with the most potential. In 1979 he would add: 'But sometimes, Judith, it's your job to shoot him in the head when he's halfway through a painting'. See Judith Pugh, *Unstill Life: Art, Politics and Living with Clifton Pugh*, Allen & Unwin, Sydney, 2008, p. 65.

34 Smith, 'Some Northern Critics of Southern Art', p. 276, where he writes: 'I doubt whether I would have invited him to give the first John Power Lecture in Contemporary Art had I thought otherwise'.

35 Nolan interviewed by Fuller, 'Sidney Nolan and the Decline of the West', p. 41.

36 ibid., p. 42.

37 See Clark, *Landscape into Art*, p. 142.

38 ibid. The 'new religion' that Clark refers to here is presumably science, epitomised by recent developments such as the electron microscope and the splitting of the atom.

39 Fuller, 'The Antipodes and I', p. xxi.

40 *Eureka*, Serpentine Gallery, London, 13 March to 25 April 1982, described by Fuller as 'a pathetic exhibition of very recent Australian art'. See Fuller, 'The Antipodes and I', *The Australian Scapegoat*, p. xxi.

41 Smith, interview with Pierse.

42 Julian Stallabrass, 'Success and Failure of Peter Fuller', *New Left Review*, no. 207, September–October 1994, pp. 87–102.

43 Peter Beilharz, 'Bernard Smith 1916–2011: Marxism and Politics', speech delivered at the National Gallery of Victoria on 28 November 2011, later published in *Art Monthly Australia*, no. 250, June 2012, p. 68.

44 In an interview with Simon Pierse (22 December 2005), Smith revealed: 'I was rather critical of him in *The Scapegoat* for moving away from his influences ... my introduction was rather critical ... but he took it rather gently and when asked to reply in kind he didn't really ... I asked him how long will Ruskin last?'

45 Beilharz, 'Bernard Smith 1916–2011'.

46 Smith, 'Some Northern Critics of Southern Art', p. 277.

47 Smith, interview with Pierse.

48 Smith, 'Some Northern Critics of Southern Art', pp. 276–7.

49 Smith, 'The Myth of Isolation', in *Australian Painting Today*, The John Murtagh Macrossan Lectures, 1961, University of Queensland Press, Brisbane, 1962 (republished in Bernard Smith, *The Antipodean Manifesto: Essays in Art and History*, Melbourne University Press, Melbourne, 1975, here citing p. 58).

50 Fuller, 'The Antipodes and I', p. xxi.

51 Fuller, 'Art and Post-Industrialism', p. 32.

52 ibid., pp. 32–3.

53 Peter Fuller quoted by Julian Stallabrass in 'Success and Failure of Peter Fuller', in John McDonald (ed.), *Peter Fuller's Modern Painters: Reflections on British Art*, Methuen, London, 1993, p. 111.

54 Bernard Smith, 'The Antipodean Manifesto', foreword to *The Antipodeans 4th–15th Aug 1959*, exhibition catalogue, Victorian Artists' Society, Melbourne, 1959 (republished in 1975 in Smith, *The Antipodean Manifesto*, here citing pp. 165–7).

55 Nolan interviewed by Fuller, 'Sidney Nolan and the Decline of the West', p. 42. See also Smith, 'The Antipodean Manifesto', p. 167.

56 Peter Fuller, 'Fine Art after Modernism', *New Left Review*, no. 119, January–February 1980. See also Fuller, 'Aesthetics after Modernism', in *The Australian Scapegoat*, p. 11.

57 Fuller, 'Aesthetics after Modernism', p. 12.

58 Bernard Smith to Simon Pierse, 25 September 2003.

59 Fuller, 'Art and Post-Industrialism', p. 33.

60 Smith, 'Some Northern Critics of Southern Art', p. 278.

61 Smith to Pierse, 25 September 2003.

62 Peter Fuller, 'In Defence of Art (1979)', in Peter Fuller, *Beyond the Crisis in Art*, Writers & Readers Publishing, London, 1980, pp. 230–64.

63 Smith, 'Some Northern Critics of Southern Art', p. 278.

The life and the work: Australian art biography

JOHN CLARK

There is very good reason for looking at some of the biographical and autobiographical writing of Bernard Smith in order to understand the complexities of Australian art history from the 1920s to the 1960s, and to see where artists of different cohorts may fit within it. This is because Smith was actively engaged in criticising contemporary tendencies in Australian art, chiefly painting, and had definite opinions about which directions it should move in. Perhaps I could add a personal note, that, as an immigrant who arrived here some twenty-six years ago, I am interested in the way a reading of Smith allows me to enter art worlds in Australia I could not otherwise have known.

Firstly, Smith's autobiography, *The Boy Adeodatus: The Portrait of a Lucky Young Bastard* (1984),[1] is about the first part of his life, up to the age of twenty-four, and concerns the experiences of a politically engaged school art teacher who chose to abandon becoming an artist, or rather decided not to make further efforts to become one. Reading it may produce an understanding about the difference between making art and doing art history.

Secondly, he wrote, or rather wrote up, the biography-autobiography of an important but largely ignored artist, Noel Counihan (1913–1986): *Noel Counihan: Artist and Revolutionary* (1993).[2] This biography was clearly intended to reclaim a part of the history of Australian art and to regain understanding of some largely

Marxist positions about the link between art practice and purposive behaviour represented through the 'humanist' stylistic of some artists. These had been pushed aside by other kinds of historical conflicts and their winners. It is worth considering Smith's approach in Counihan's biography, therefore, for what it might tell us about how an artist's life may be used to construct art history.

Thirdly, writing an artist's biography or assembling materials about artists and their generation seems to be a particular genre of art writing in Australia. What do its existence and its various types tell us about Australian art and its histories? There are quite a few examples to draw upon, among which I have chosen Humphrey McQueen's *Tom Roberts* (1996),[3] Drusilla Modjeska's *Stravinsky's Lunch* (1999)[4] and Janine Burke's *Australian Gothic: A Life of Albert Tucker* (2002).[5] All of these post-date both of Smith's biographies.[6]

In *The Boy Adeodatus*, two peculiar strategies are in play before we even get to Smith's own life 'in art', as one might call it. He tries to excavate the whole prehistory of his family forebears in Ireland, even though he was not brought up by his mother: how his mother left Ireland, why his mother did not or could not abort the infant who became Bernard, and why he was nonetheless subsequently sent away to be fostered. For Smith, the causations of his life lie in an extended genealogy from Ireland, through England and Scotland, to several distant parts of Australia. The style of his narrative and the almost imperceptible blending of surviving letters and hearsay anecdotes is to carry forward a narrative technique, mostly applied in the early part in the third person or written from an observer's point of view. It is not clear why this should be particularly revealing of the formative elements of his life, apart from the description of how he actually lived.

Furthermore, a second line of enquiry is opened up through the self-reflective palimpsests of the Roman Catholic religion whose citations stud Smith's texts. It is as if such textual nodes were the explication of his life, or at least the concentration points from which its twists—and by extension his artistic knowledge as a sort of resistance—were to be seen. This textual referencing procedure is by turns illuminating and stultifying: we learn how a certain consciousness can be carried by the loved but abandoned child. Yet we do not, on the other hand, learn the full range of his later philosophical and political objections to the practices and beliefs that these textual references carry. This might lead us to conjecture that perhaps the transgenerational and transcontinental genealogy and the broken narrative are so important to the text precisely because the continuity of life seen from outside is in other respects fractured and lacks its own natural, accepted and inherent dynamic and historical authority.

Part of Smith's frustrations that lead to his abandoning art practice are due to his self-perceptions about the gap between Australian subjects and their actual representation in art forms. He says: 'How he would like to be able to paint it all. Nobody had painted the Australian rain forest. Too difficult, no doubt'.[7]

I don't know why Smith in the 1980s should have put forward this view of his own in the late 1930s. It is an art-historical view, not an artistic one about previous practice, and is one for which even a non-specialist can immediately think of counter examples. It is also, curiously for a person who subsequently became an art historian, a-temporal. He does this elsewhere:

> His interests turned increasingly to drawing and painting. He had not abandoned his ambition to become an artist. On 24 April *that year* [my italics] he had confided to his diary: 'A joiner of Erskineville (Wilson) won the Travelling Scholarship'.[8]

Only later on the same page does he give the information that allows the reader to deduce that the year referred to was 1937. Smith buys into an argument that European Australian artists up to a certain unspecified point in time didn't or couldn't paint the landscape, the light, the rainforest around them. The reason—not adumbrated, but made clear by his citations elsewhere from Marcus Clarke—is because the land didn't in some profound sense 'belong' to them, despite their culture dominating it.[9]

Here lies one of the dangers of using art biography as material for studying art history: the confusion of the established attitudes of the artist or art historian with the material facts needed to document them.

The confusion lies in the intention of the text. Smith later discusses the purposes of the Sydney Teachers' College Art Club, based on his perception of the need to improve the status of art and art teachers, to expand the audience for art, and to increase the range of materials, principally books, to inform ideas of what modern art was.[10] We learn that surrealism was the major art movement in which Smith, and no doubt others, felt it necessary to educate themselves in 1937, and by

November 1938 the critic Basil Burdett wrote in *Art in Australia* that 'in Australia "surrealism was practically non-existent"'.[11] This citation runs slap up against the limitations of biography for unstructured art-historical analysis or as a documentary statement, by the citation of Smith's other materials as 'he noted in his diary', when what this means is, 'as I, Bernard Smith, then wrote in my diary, and which was my opinion at that time', that is:

> It is noticeable that most of the so-called modernism is linked with a goodly quantity of pretty little things the public like. Artists as a race seem pretty well extinct in this country. Criticism amounts to back-slapping. The only value that is taken as a reliable standard on which to judge a work is the amount of money the 'art-loving public' is willing to pay for it.[12]

Why then should we think the sort of generalisation Smith cites from his diary is valid, or rather, for what purposes is it valid? Clearly it is so, as a non-public appraisal of a public situation in the Australian art world. It is also valid as a secondary statement about the sort of situation that made Smith give up painting in favour of broadening the field of discourse about art:

> He did draw the trunk of another tree that he had burned down when they had cleared the playground of dry grass, for fear of summer bushfires; its great branches, black and dead, spread all around it, like a huge circus tent after the canvas had been rolled away, for it possessed a macabre beauty. His good intentions had destroyed the tree. It was *only a painting now* [my italics].[13]

We are unsurprised to learn, several pages later, that Smith gave up painting because 'What Australia lacked was not artists but an informed audience for art'.[14]

And Smith was to become the observer, and increasingly informed educator, who was to construct that information, however much he still remained a third-person subject:

> At least they taught him more than they all realised. That was the sadness of it: for they had made him one of them and yet not one of them. A stranger within their gates; a child among them taking notes.[15]

Smith's second exercise in biography is *Noel Counihan: Artist and Revolutionary*

(1993), a massive work of 558 pages. It could not have been written to this extent and in such detail without the collaboration and provision of material by the deceased artist's wife, Pat Counihan, which Smith acknowledges. In the book there is so much documentation and direct first-person statement by the artist, or its close paraphrase, that any reader will conclude it is more like an autobiography, ghost-written by Smith, who states:

> It seemed appropriate therefore because he wrote well and self-reflectively, to allow his own voice to be heard as much as possible. So in one sense, this book is an autobiography within a biography.[16]

Smith's claim that *Noel Counihan: Artist and Revolutionary* took five years to write, with two breaks of six and three months,[17] indicates that the author has been trawling through a very large amount of material, whose sovereignty over his biographical task he acknowledges several times. Indeed, he immediately denies what might be one task expected of an artist's biography, by avoiding the assessment of the artist's work. This stratagem possibly obviates the need to make considered judgements that might confuse moments in a life with stages in the production of works. It also removes the need to illustrate the biography on a grander scale, and, despite Smith's self-denial, many important Counihan works are illustrated, although without the attention to plate quality or colour demanded by a catalogue.[18]

This authorial standpoint might be understood as due to Smith's sympathy for the humanist artistic positions adopted by Counihan, and because Smith opposes many abstractionist, non- and anti-figurative tendencies in modern art, which he elsewhere defined as the 'Formalesque'.[19] It is also due to a confusion between 'social realism' and 'socialist realism' maintained by many of Counihan's opponents:

> Socialist realism is not a realism at all but an instrumental art addressed to winning and maintaining political power (which is not to say that it is impossible to produce socialist realist art of high aesthetic value; far more good art has been produced through history in the service of power than as a voice of liberation). Social realism on the other hand addresses itself to the social evils of the day irrespective of outcomes. It seeks to tell the truth as seen and experienced. This essential distinction is further confused by the fact that most artists who practice social realism are socialist in their politics.[20]

The conflation of social realism with socialist realism is also important because, from 1939 to 1951, Smith was a member of the Communist Party of Australia,[21] whose debates on the social function of art and on the relationships between modernism and Marxism Smith observed. Counihan was an important progenitor of these debates, chiefly with Albert Tucker through the pages of the magazine *Angry Penguins*. Counihan and Smith were caught up in what now appears to have been an inter-generational factional fight for organisational dominance of the Contemporary Art Society, waged between realists and the 'modernist' group around John Reed, to which Tucker belonged.[22] This took place in a social context of extreme conservatism in the Australian art world, in which a Sydney–Melbourne rivalry over the future course of an embattled modernism at times surfaced. The isolation of Counihan's work during the 1950s and early 1960s was partly to do with the categorisation of his work as realist in the context of a post-1945 Cold War art criticism practised assiduously in Sydney. But when newspaper critics saw Counihan's actual work, they could respond to it positively, despite differences in political opinion. Curators and art historians, however, 'tended to lock his reputation into his war-time work, the "realism" rubric blinding them to his formal achievements'.[23]

Smith's apology for the consequences of his own intellectual rigidity in categorising Counihan's work also allows him to understand the differences between a 'Depression' communist and a 'War-time' communist. Smith sympathetically understands the former's greater difficulty on 'breaking with the Australian party's petty intolerances' and in shaking off their 'belief in Soviet "democracy"'.[24] Smith in any case regards biography as an exercise in empathy, in seeing what choices artists have to make. For him, biography is written out of 'curiosity, not envy' of a life that the author, in different circumstances, could have led. Autobiography, 'however skilfully it may be distanced from the self of the author, inevitably delivers him or her up as a hostage of conceit'.[25]

The work of Counihan had escaped proper understanding, and it was Smith's decent task to see that gap filled. This was because communists were anathema for the political right, all the way up to Prime Minister Robert Menzies, who had gone so far as to found a short-lived Australian Academy of Art in 1937 on conservative principles. This loss of duly recognised significance was compounded by the conflicted loyalties of Counihan to three sometimes opposed goals: he declined to remove political content from his art, he tried to make an art that had popular reference, and his work was produced with handcraft technique that could be enjoyed by a broad public. Beyond this, the neglect his work suffered was no doubt due to the factionalisation of the art world along realist–modernist lines which, when the modernists won the battle, led to the neglect and suppression of the realists.

Noel Counihan the biography has, for this later observer at least, reclaimed a part of the history of Australian art, and it has provided links between art practice and the 'humanist' stylistic of some artists. But can this material be used, as it is, to construct art history? Smith himself hints at its limitations in his explicit wish to sympathise with Counihan's Marxist humanism, and his lack of denigration of an inherited handcraft technique. Counihan's Marxist sympathy is with the Depression-forged resistance to a kind of capitalism, but this resistance was found on many sides, from the un-Marxist John Maynard Keynes to the reform Marxist Joseph Schumpeter. Smith himself withdrew from the Communist Party of Australia after his Czechoslovak experiences in 1949. I think this drive to reconstruct and sympathise with a leading humanist is too close to its subject, despite their differences of position about Marxist understanding of the state. Nowhere is this clearer than in Smith's excessively even-handed treatment of Counihan's reaction to the Hungarian uprising, when Counihan even upbraided his friend Jack Lindsay for signing an ill-advised letter to the *Daily Worker*.[26] Smith rehearses the to-and-fro of these Left debates, without pointing to the obvious contradiction between Counihan's selective social realism, which won him prizes in Australia, and his political partisanship in interpreting the bloodied national-patriotic face of an uprising against Soviet rule as a mere difference of political line in party conflict.

In a sense, the biography of an artist that takes up only some of the issues of their life and does not counterpoint them against their work, as Smith explicitly states, is always going to end up taking the subject of the biography's position as a given, especially if it is well articulated by documents they have left behind. But the main problem with a biography that does not make analysis of the work an intrinsic part of the life is that the loop is cut between the artist's reactions to the way their work is received and the motivations for their technique in order to receive the reaction they desire, whether this be in financial recompense or in reputation.

The writing of long artistic biographies is well established in Australia, perhaps beginning with R. H. Croll's biography of Tom Roberts, which, like Counihan's, was strictly dependent on the materials provided by the artist's widow.[27] Roberts was also the subject of a massive (784-page) biography by Humphrey McQueen in 1996.[28] But McQueen takes two positions that differ from Smith's: he documents every single reference to an identifiable source—one art historian has bemoaned to me that 'he cites every damn thing'. McQueen shows no compunction in introducing analytical appraisals about the artist's works, discussion of the contexts in which his work was produced, and speculations about the artist's psychodynamics, sometimes of a Freudian kind. If McQueen's approach is more hammer-and-anvil compared to Smith's stitched palimpsest, his judgements are explicit and his use of sources transparent. Indeed, beyond its biographical treatment I found McQueen's biography a valuable background to thinking about many issues concerning art and society in Australia in the 1880s and 1900s. In some ways Smith provided such a background for 1930s and 1940s left-wing art movements in Australia, but a reader would still have to go outside *Noel Counihan* to understand the currents of ideas and stylistic exemplars at that time. In this respect, Smith adopts Counihan's position on Haese's *Rebels and Precursors*,[29] but without really specifying what is wrong with the book, other than that it adheres to a Melbourne-centred view around Albert Tucker.[30] In particular Smith very uncritically accepts Counihan's idea that he was not an unblinking supporter of the Stalinist Zhdanov line imposed by J. D. Blake of the Communist Party of Australia in June 1946.[31] Smith interprets Counihan to have thought that 'neither Blake, nor any other party functionary, had any answers to the problems implicit in relating art to the people'.[32]

That for a critical period Counihan was indeed a supporter of the Soviet Communist Party line of 1934 applied to art by Zhdanov (1896–1948), even if not a wholly committed one, is implied by his positions and actions in later visits to Eastern Europe and the Soviet Union. Smith does not remark on this.

An arguably more balanced and informative biography of an artist active at the time is Janine Burke's biography of Albert Tucker, despite Tucker being directly opposed to Counihan during a polemic in 1943.[33] Burke's book accumulates personal detail, art positions and keen observations of the particular avant-garde art society of John and Sunday Reed in a fully flowing narrative which does not have, and perhaps does not need, the obfuscations of the ideological gap between party line and personal practice and belief required in *Noel Counihan*. It is to Burke's credit that this book is clearer on some of the ideological issues relating to art practice and artworks than is *Noel Counihan*, particularly in the discussion of the social function of art.[34] In her examination of the life of one artistic personality, and maybe because Tucker moved from a position of Marxist social critique to a Jungian defence of surrealism, rather than maintaining ideological conformity through his creative life, we actually learn more about both sides of the Melbourne art debates than we do from Smith's ventriloquising of Counihan's autobiographical defence. Art-historical value in artist biography is therefore sometimes more richly and usefully mapped if there is a certain complexity to the life lived and the movements of thought through it. In a way this value is found more significantly in Smith's own construction of an historically distributed, many-layered and differentially sited biography, *The Boy Adeodatus*. It is found there more than in *Noel Counihan*'s examination of a monological and, despite his clashes with party authority, a much more ideologically conformist Counihan. The profoundly redeeming quality of Counihan's art, which I first saw in a print in 1988 and in a small painting in about 1994, is his deep respect for facture and the brilliance of his fusion of artistic sympathy with a distanced subject. It is endowed by the humanist traditions he so deeply loved, and exists beyond their framing by those suppositions of social philosophy or historical causation that he could imagine. If Counihan's work was so much more than the particular characteristics and limitations of the artist who made it, why did Smith decline to consider the work properly?

There is a view in art history that art work must escape from the maker and go beyond him or her into another world of value, that it should be assessed, critiqued and historically emplaced in a different order from the series of causations that interact with the characters or historical contexts of its maker. This is a reaction in part against the use of a notion of 'natural genius' as the first cause of the work's origination, rather than any given ingrained skill interpreted as being a last or subordinate feature residual to its making. The separation of the life from the work is intended, I suppose, to make the work aesthetically enjoyable and assessable in an order of knowledge that does not depend on intractable and untraceable peculiarities of the skill or personality of the maker. McQueen and Burke get around this dilemma by interspersing analyses of actual works with biographical details of where the artist—Roberts or Tucker—was at the time of the making, and of which personal characteristics or psychodynamics contributed to a turn towards 'the real' or 'the surreal' in either case. I think Smith tries to avoid this at all costs by his distancing third-person stance in autobiography, a stance that he adopts even when he is describing in intimate detail his sexual experiences, for example, or which is in other respects evident in his acceptance of the artist's position or textual documentation when doing a 'biography' of Counihan.

To answer my question at the end of the previous paragraph, I suppose Smith, in a particular Marxian trajectory, wanted at all costs to preserve the legitimacy of class analysis as a way of presenting the artist's generation of his or her work. Class analysis—or a perspective based on it—could provide a method of interfacing with external social forces that had their correlates in political pressures, hostile or sympathetic, that were applied by Left or Right political parties or particular politicians at a given time or historical situation. They also had their stylistic correspondence in realism, and not in the surrealism or modernist abstraction that Smith clearly thought were alienating and thus against the class interests of the working people Counihan portrayed.

Another technique of biography is to put the biography of the woman artist and her works into a series of overlapping narratives about women's lives. These are far more variegated and intertwined than a concentration on 'the artist' or 'the work' would allow. This was done perceptively and elegantly in Drusilla Modjeska's double biography of Stella Bowen and Grace Cossington-Smith *Stravinsky's Lunch*, which rather indirectly also suggested an alternative method to approaching an artistic life. It did so by overlaying a kind of boundary trope for the creative situation and its authorised habits in Stravinsky's demanding silence from his family during lunch when he was working on a composition. This was coalesced by Modjeska with the needs of a woman artist or writer for a separate income and a space of her own, as outlined in Virginia Woolf's *A Room of One's Own*:

> For it is not only a room of her own and an income that a woman needs—though that is often hard enough to come by—but the place in herself, the space in her soul from which she can withstand the onslaught of a world that cannot, or will not, take her seriously.[35]

Modjeska doesn't quite accuse class analysis or creative genius theories of masculinism, although there is a whiff of that position throughout her book, which it might have been better to make more explicit. Smith's isolation of life from work is not in itself masculinist, but it does allow much more room for the monumental and the indicative super-work, which have echoes of the male artist as genius hero, an emphasis that one might have thought he would be trying in other respects to avoid.

If the narrative intermixings of *Stravinsky's Lunch* seem to allegorise the situation of a woman artist and thereby seek narrative strategies as a way out of a gender trap, then Smith's allegorical figures are those of the male artist as national hero. Apart from the significant issue of art-historical evaluation as to who have actually been the major artists in Australian art history, that of which artistic careers actually mark 'the Australian-ness of Australian art', the artistic biographies I have chosen are all concerned with, or are allegories for, what art means to be seen as Australian. Short of prescriptively or denotationally defining this, they have all chosen to skirt the issue by use of allegory, or by overlapping narrative, or by historical extension back into pasts that might not really seem that relevant—McQueen takes Roberts back into Dorset, Smith takes his own life back into the far distant past of his Irish forebears. These strategies might suggest to the reader of these texts something about the Australia that they denote: namely, insecure characters, who are unsure of their presence and are prone to heroic poses, who remain caught in gender traps from which escape is difficult but that can nonetheless be construed by narrative decomposition. The biographies in question also contain positive prescriptions of the lived structure of Australian-ness: valued friendships between cohorts of men and women; being brave, sometimes intrepid, sometimes foolhardy; travelling to unlock buried pasts and oppressive structures experienced at home but derived from foreign transfers; a love of a specific light and flora; a plenitude to be shared.

How these contrastive and conflicted domains find themselves articulated in works and their makers remains a central topic that art history needs to address.

NOTES

1 Bernard Smith, *The Boy Adeodatus: The Portrait of a Lucky Young Bastard*, Allen Lane, Melbourne, 1984.

2 Bernard Smith, *Noel Counihan: Artist and Revolutionary*, Oxford University Press, Melbourne, 1993.

3 Humphrey McQueen, *Tom Roberts*, Pan Macmillan, Sydney, 1996.

4 Drusilla Modjeska, *Stravinsky's Lunch*, Pan Macmillan, Sydney, 1999.

5 Janine Burke, *Australian Gothic: A Life of Albert Tucker*, Random House, Sydney, 2002.

6 Among many other such biographies and autobiographies are Robert Henderson Croll, *Tom Roberts: Father of Australian Landscape Painting*, Robertson and Mullens, Sydney, 1935; Stella Bowen, *Drawn From Life*, Collins, London, 1940; George Mann, Maidestone, UK, 1974; Ann Galbally, *Arthur Streeton*, Lansdown, Melbourne, 1969; rev. edn 1979; Lloyd Rees, *Peaks and Valleys: Lloyd Rees, An Autobiography*, Collins, Sydney, 1985; Christopher Wray, *Arthur Streeton: Painter of Light*, Jacaranda Wiley, Milton, Qld, 1993; Brenda Niall, *The Boyds: A Family Biography*, The Miegunyah Press, Melbourne University Press, Melbourne, 2002.

7 Smith, *The Boy Adeodatus*, p. 196.

8 ibid., p. 234.

9 See his citations in Bernard Smith (ed.), *Documents on Art and Taste in Australia: The Colonial Period, 1770–1914*, Oxford University Press, Melbourne, 1975, pp. 134–6.

10 See Smith's relationship with the Country Lending Service, as detailed in *The Boy Adeodatus*, p. 234–6.

11 ibid., p. 253.

12 ibid.

13 ibid., p. 265.

14 ibid., p. 297.

15 ibid., p. 300.

16 Smith, *Noel Counihan*, p. 4. Among other works on Counihan are Max Dimmack, *Noel Counihan*, Melbourne University Press, Melbourne, 1974; Robert Smith, *Noel Counihan Prints, 1931–1981: A Catalogue Raisonnée*, Hale & Iremonger, Sydney, 1981.

17 Smith, *Noel Counihan*, p. 1.

18 ibid., p. 7.

19 Bernard Smith, *Modernism's History: A Study in Twentieth-Century Art and Ideas*, University of New South Wales Press, Sydney, 1998. Smith gave an earlier public version of these views in his lecture 'Modernism, Postmodernism and the Formalesque', delivered at Monash University and published in *Editions* (no. 20, Winter 1994, pp. 9–11). I made an invited and unpublished response to his paper at the Power Institute seminar in Sydney to honour Smith on 18 October 1994, 'Bernard Smith: Postmodernism and the Formalesque'.

20 Smith, *Noel Counihan*, p. 5.

21 Smith, *The Boy Adeodatus*, p. 280. Smith doesn't here say exactly when he joined the Communist Party of Australia, as he would in *Noel Counihan*, p. 542, and he left it in 1951 after a disillusioning visit to Czechoslovakia in the summer of 1949; Smith, *Noel Counihan*, p. 543.

22 Smith, *Noel Counihan*, p. 195–7.

23 ibid., p. 541.

24 ibid., p. 542.

25 ibid., p. 544.

26 ibid., p. 318. Among others who signed the protest letter to the *Daily Worker* were E. J. Hobsbawm, Christopher Hill, Doris Lessing and E. A. Thompson.

27 Croll, *Tom Roberts*.

28 McQueen, *Tom Roberts*.

29 The best guide to these years is Richard Haese's *Rebels and Precursors: The Revolutionary Years of Australian Art*, Penguin Books Australia, Melbourne, 1981. A good survey, all the more clear because it was designed for an untutored British audience, is Max Harris et al., *Angry Penguins and Realist Painting in Melbourne in the 1940s*, South Bank Centre, London, with Australian National Gallery and Australian Bicentennial Authority, Canberra, 1988.

30 Smith, *Noel Counihan*, p. 523.

31 ibid., p. 209–10, 523.

32 ibid., p. 211.

33 Burke, *Australian Gothic*, p. 223–31.

34 ibid., p. 77–9.

35 Modjeska, *Stravinsky's Lunch*, p. 18.

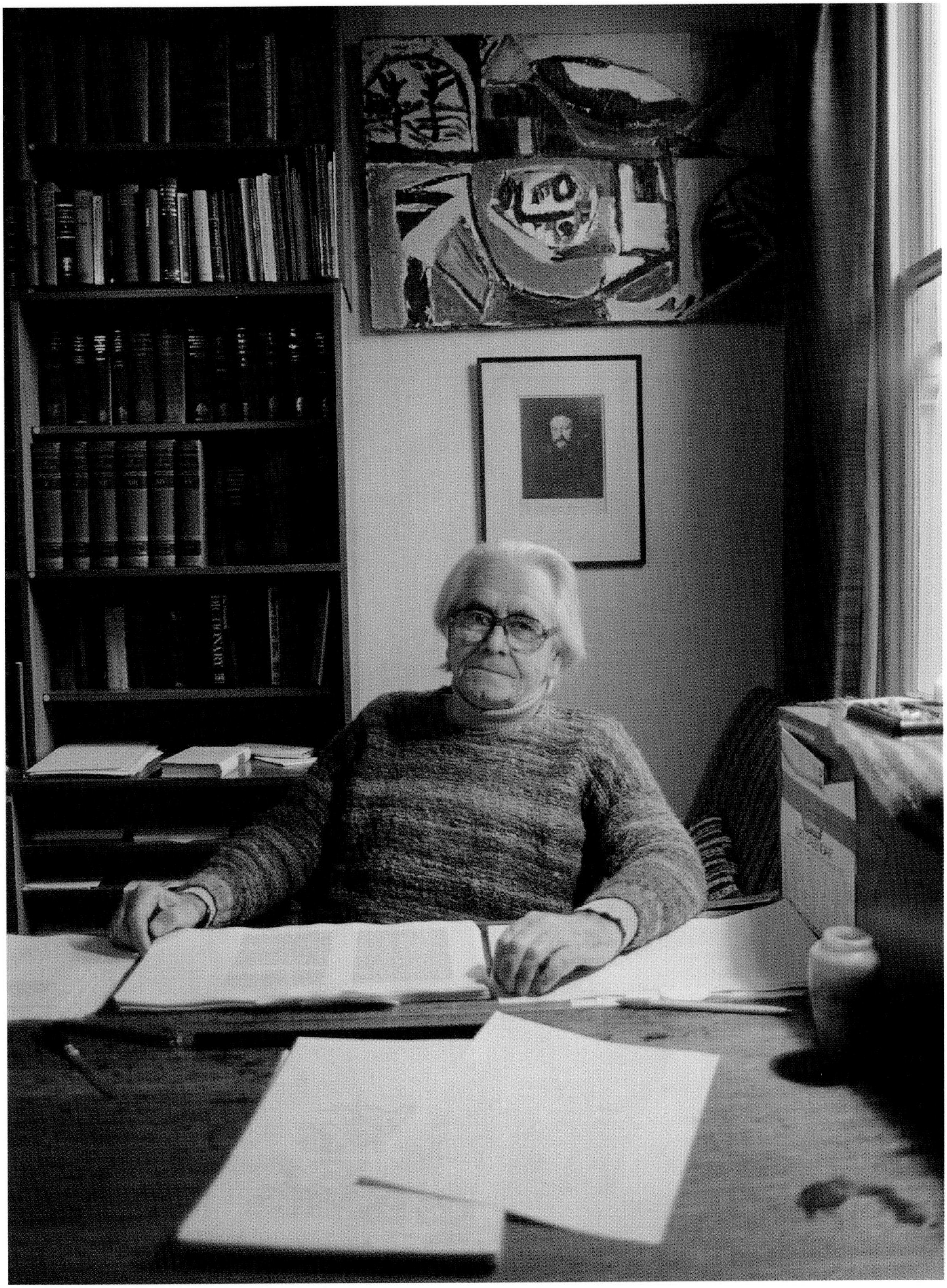
DICTIONARY

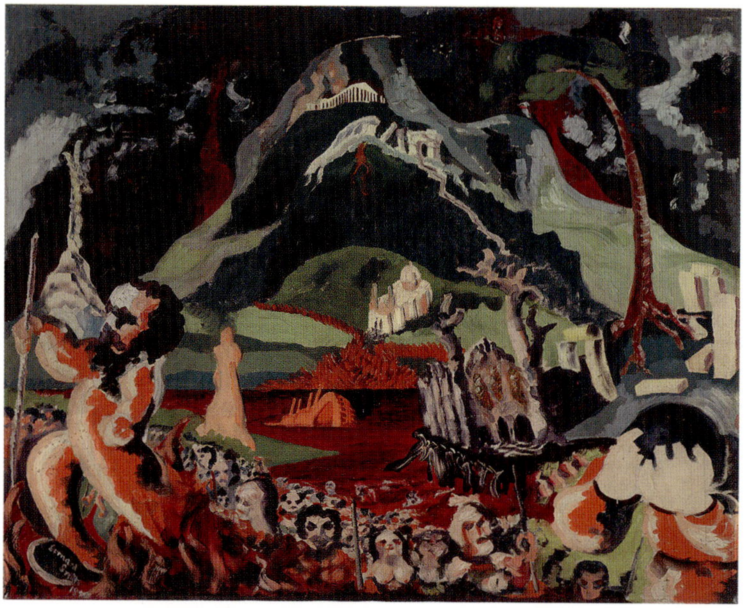

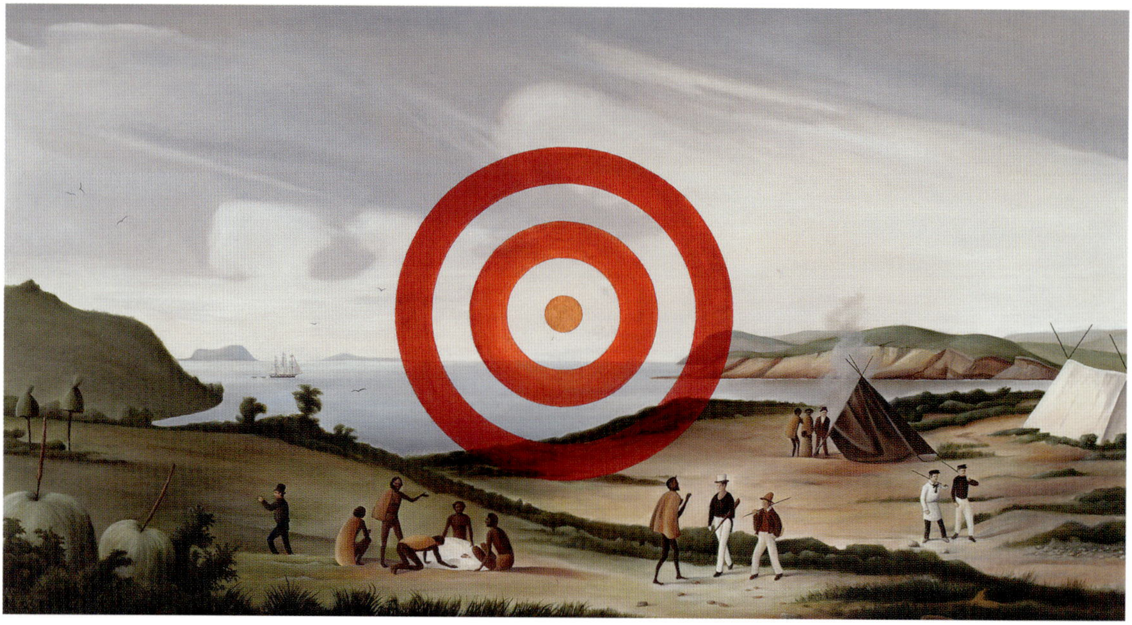

previous page:
Alec Bolton, Portrait of Bernard Smith, Fitzroy, 1987
Courtesy National Library of Australia, Canberra

1. Bernard Smith, *The advance of Lot and his brethren*, 1940.

2. Christopher Pease, *Target*, 2005.

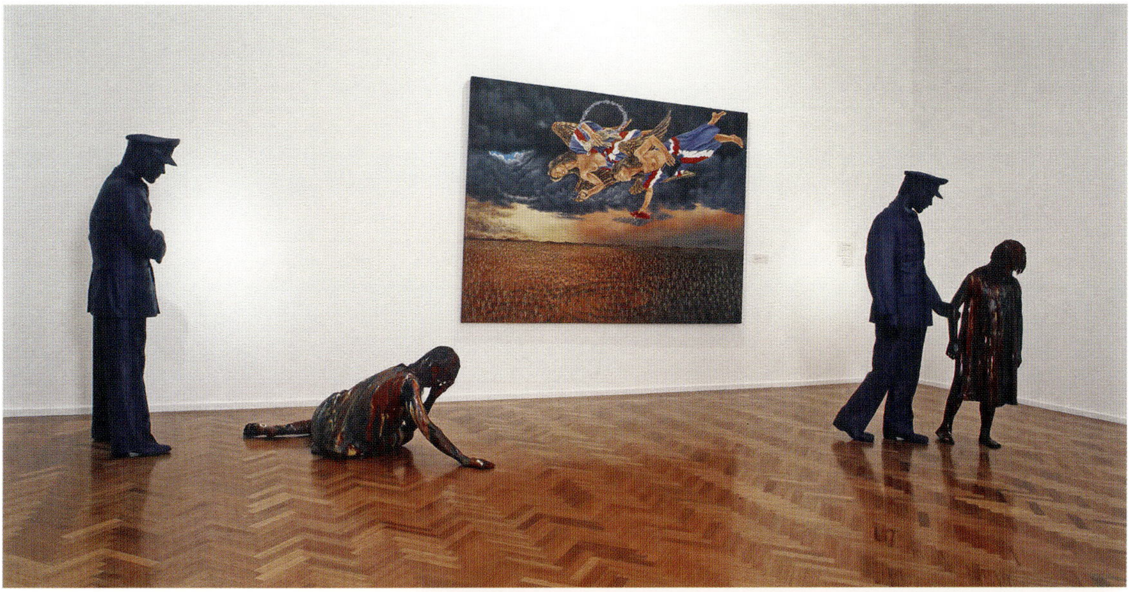

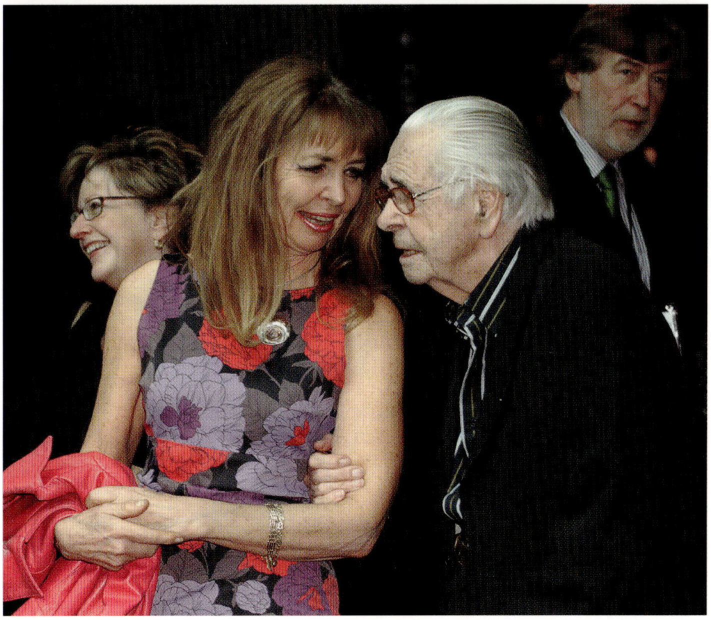

3. Lin Onus, *They took the children away*, 1992. Onus won the 1993 RAKA Award with this work, a political statement about the separation of Aboriginal children from their parents.

4. Bernard Smith with his daughter Elizabeth Heathcote, and in the background Gail Feigenbaum (Getty Research Centre, Los Angeles) and Rüdiger Joppien (Hamburg), at the Comité International d'Histoire de l'Art congress 'Crossing Cultures: Conflict, Migration and Convergence', Government House, Melbourne, January 2008.

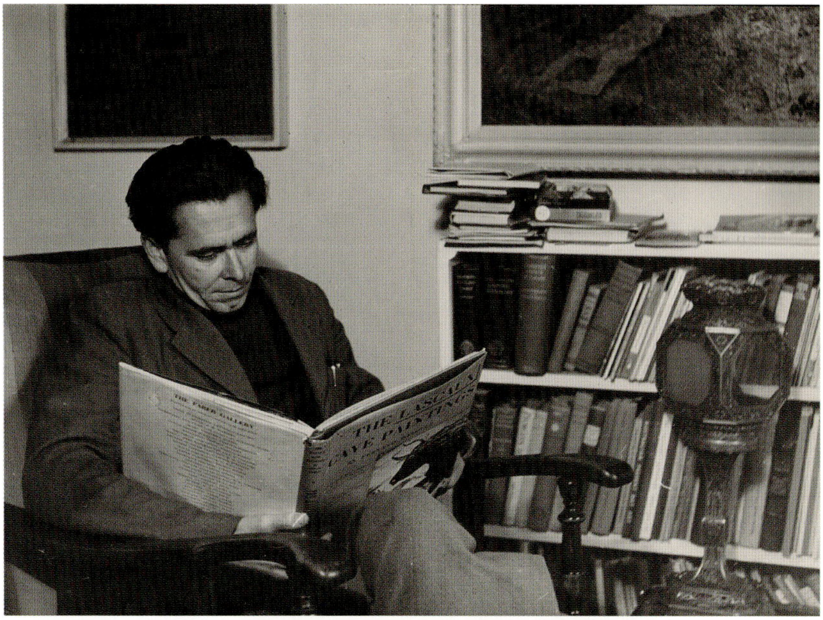

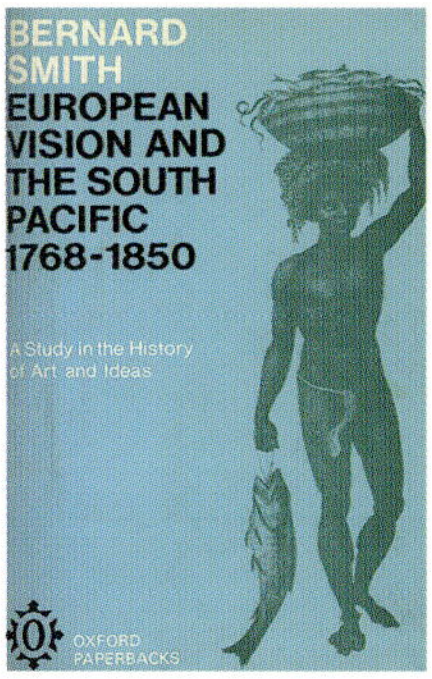

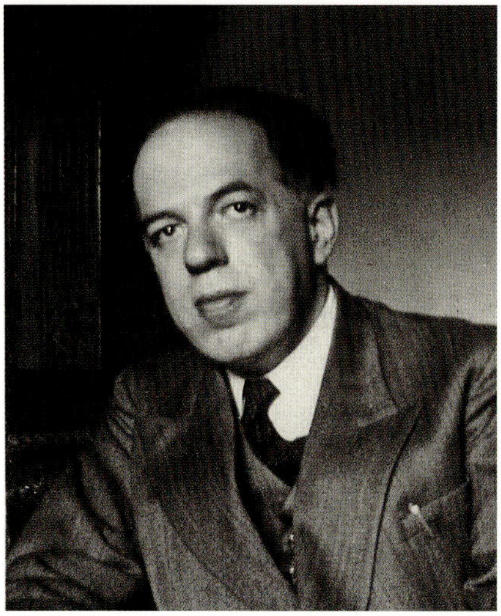

5. Bernard Smith in his study in the Abbey Art Centre, 1950. Below: first edition cover of *European Vision and the South Pacific 1768–1850.*

6. E.H. Gombrich, Smith's eminent colleague at the Warburg Institute, in London in the 1950s.

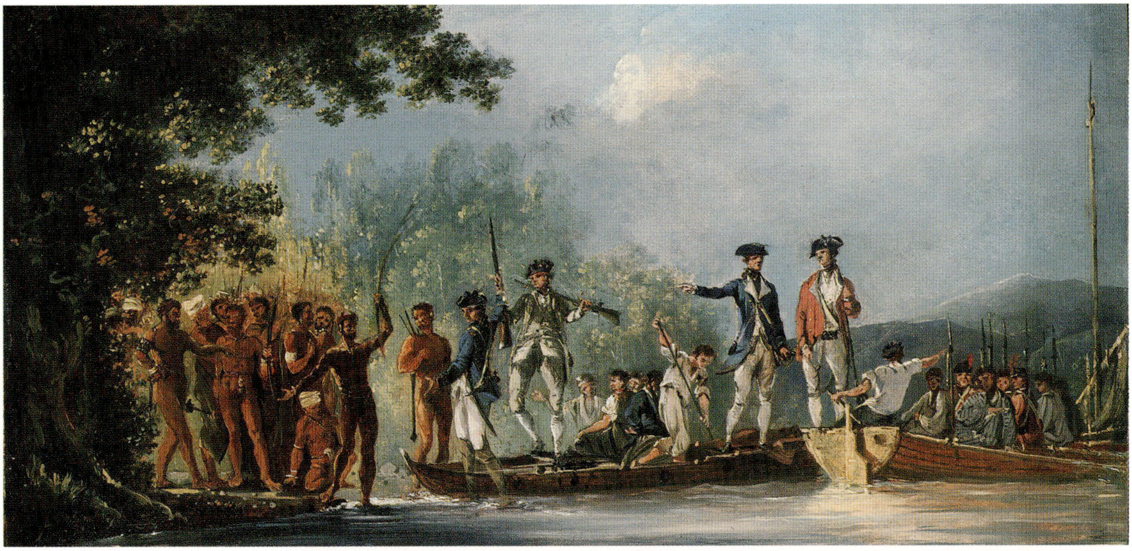

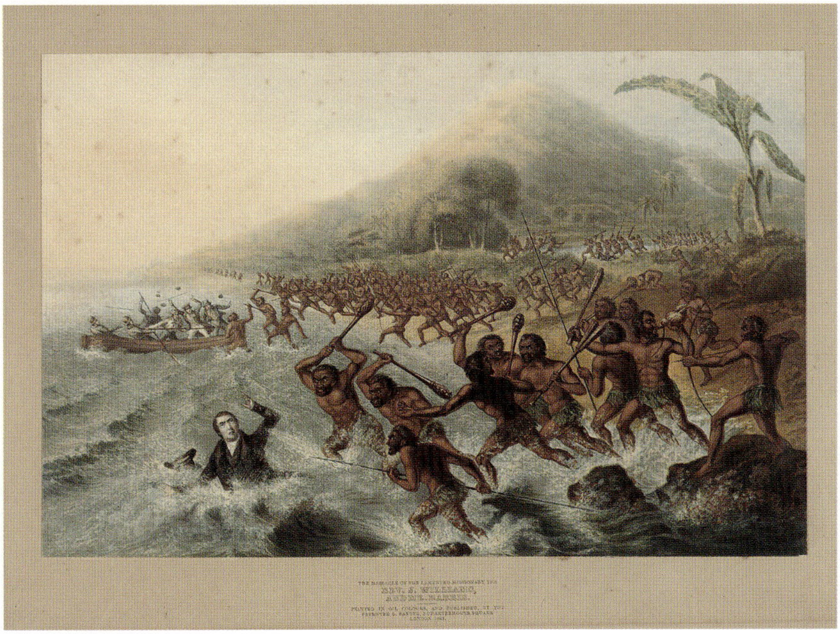

7. William Hodges, *Landing at Mallicollo [Malakula], one of the New Hebrides*, c. 1776.

8. George Baxter, *The massacre of the lamented missionary the Rev. J. Williams and Mr Harris*, 1841.

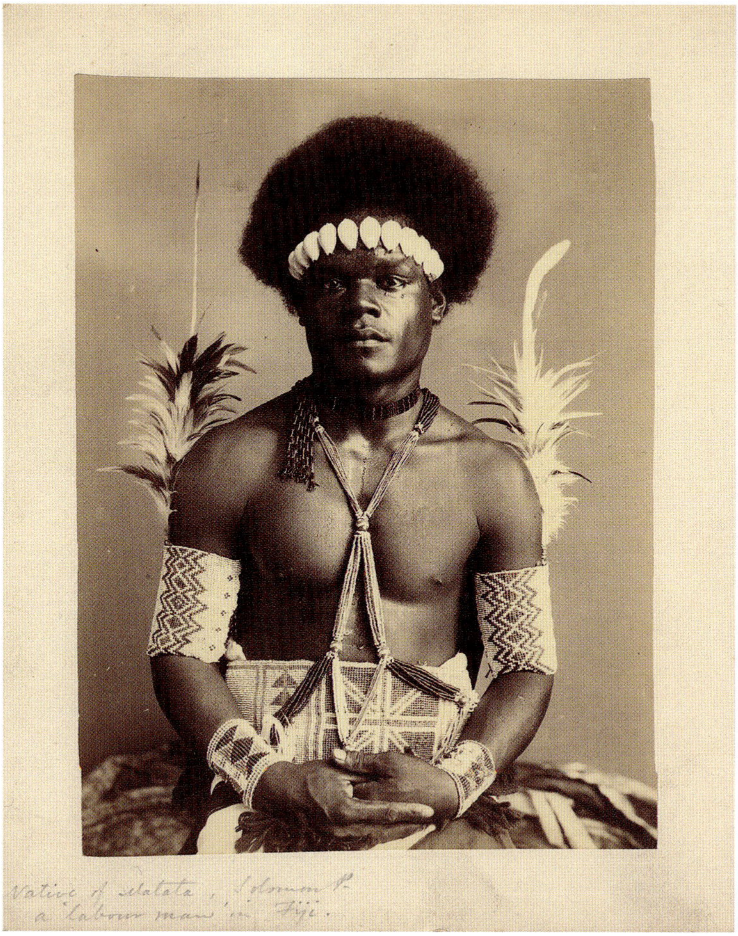

9. *Labour recruit from Malaita, Solomon Islands, wearing ceremonial dress with bead belt featuring the Union Jack, photographed in Fiji*, c. 1880s.

10. *Sculpture known as the 'Blue man', Malo, Vanuatu,* collected during the voyage of the *Korrigane* in 1935.

11. Tene Waitere, *Pouhaki*, c. 1922.

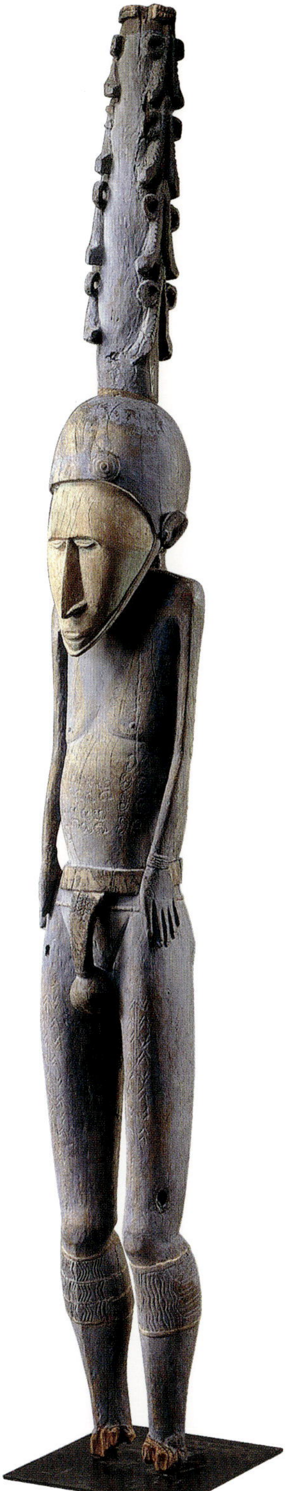

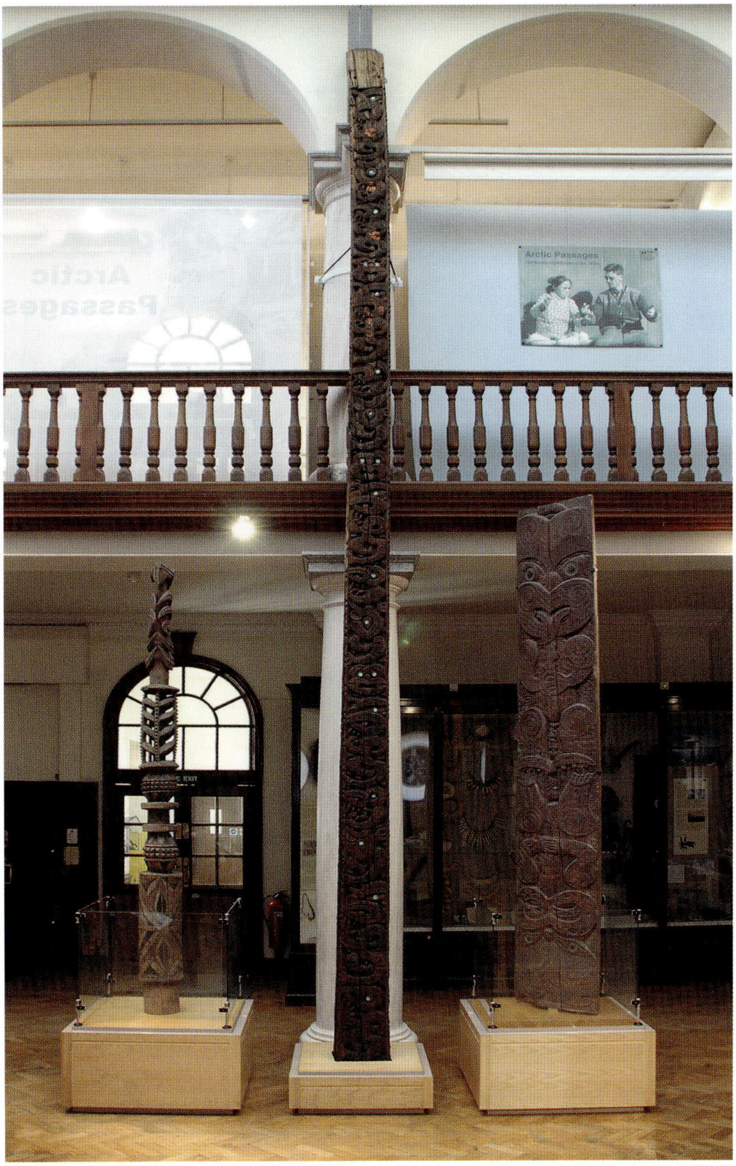
Arctic Passages

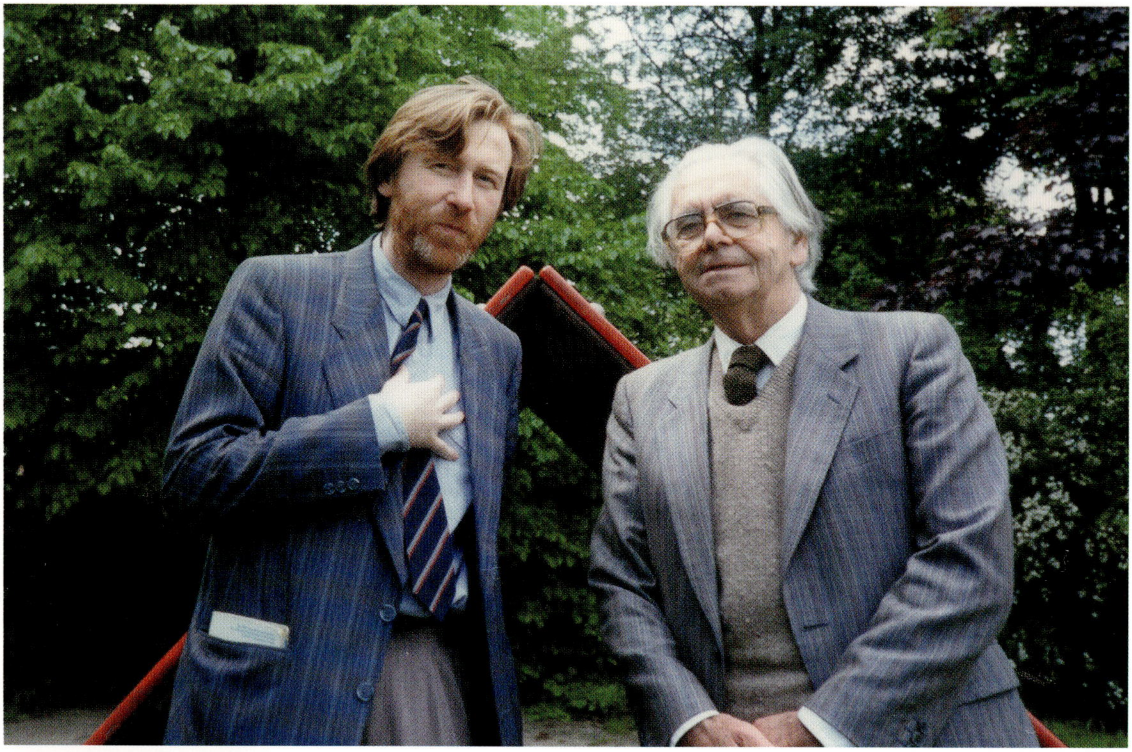

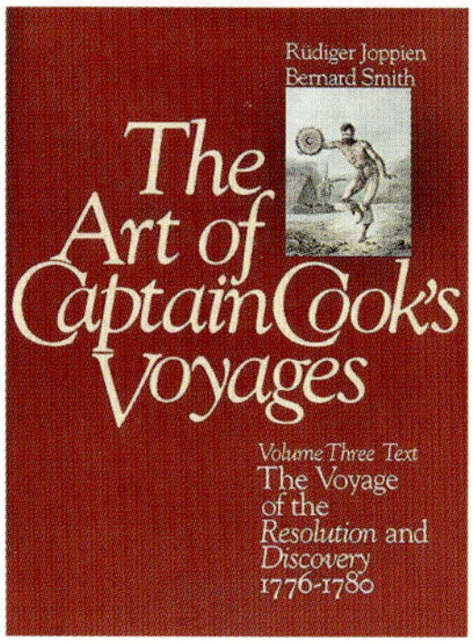

12. Rüdiger Joppien and Bernard Smith in Hamburg after the publication of the third volume of *The Art of Captain Cook's Voyages*, 1988. Below: cover of *The Art of Captain Cook's Voyages*, 1985.

13. Léveillé (after Bisson Brothers), *Kaour & Kaour-Iga natives of Torres Strait*, 1846.

14. Henry Barnes, *Echidna skeleton and natural history specimens sent from the British Museum to the Australian Museum*, c. 1864.

15. John McGregor, *James Hector*, c. 1863.

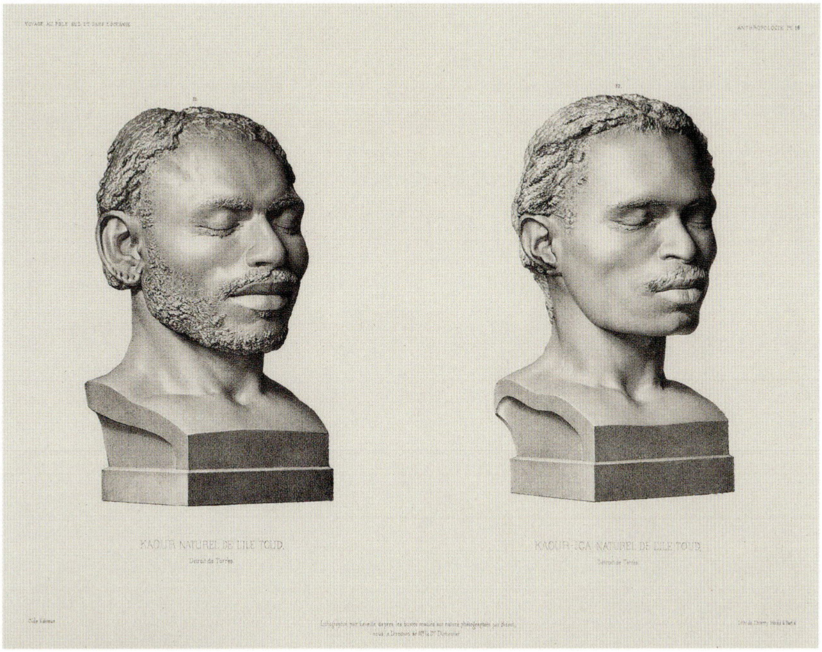
KAOUR NATUREL DE L'ILE TOUD.
Détroit de Torrès
KAOUR-IGA NATUREL DE L'ILE TOUD.
Détroit de Torrès

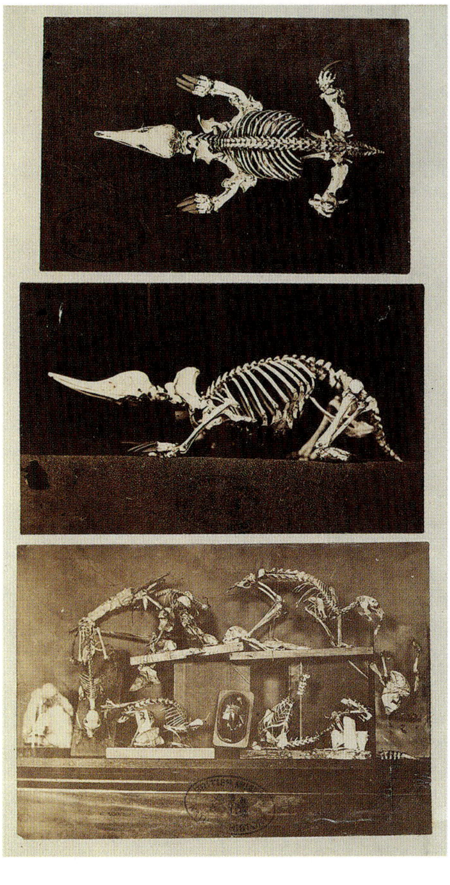

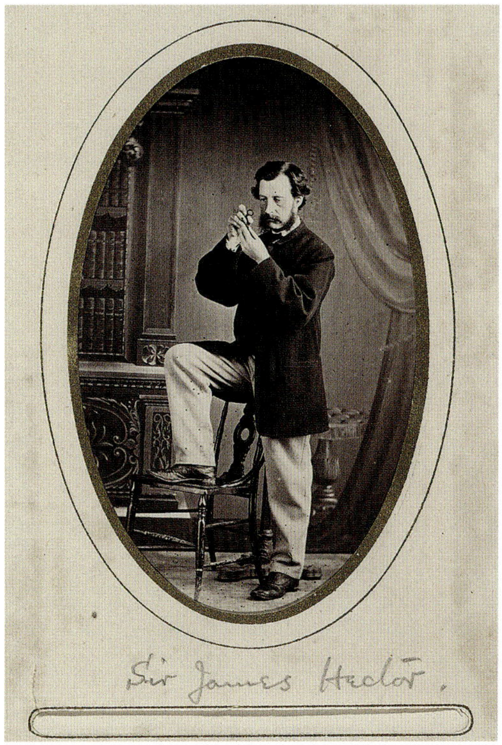
Sir James Hector.

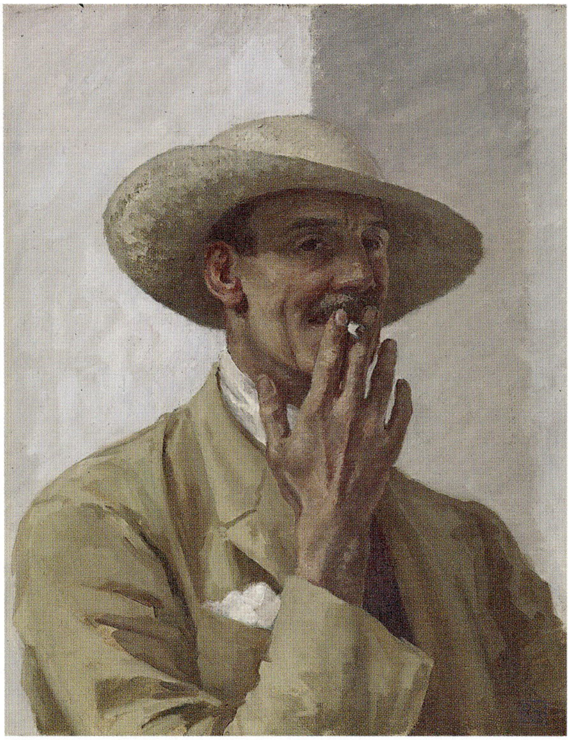

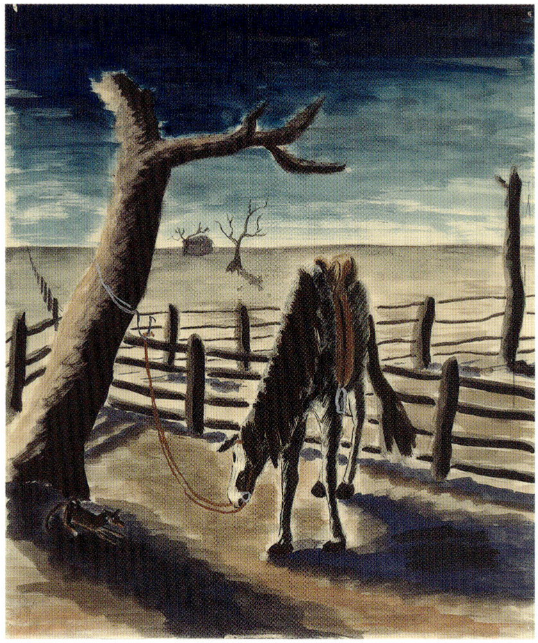

16. Rupert Bunny, *Self-portrait*, c. 1920.

17. Peter Purves Smith, *Drought*, 1939/40.

18. Ola Cohn, *Head of a virgin*, 1926.

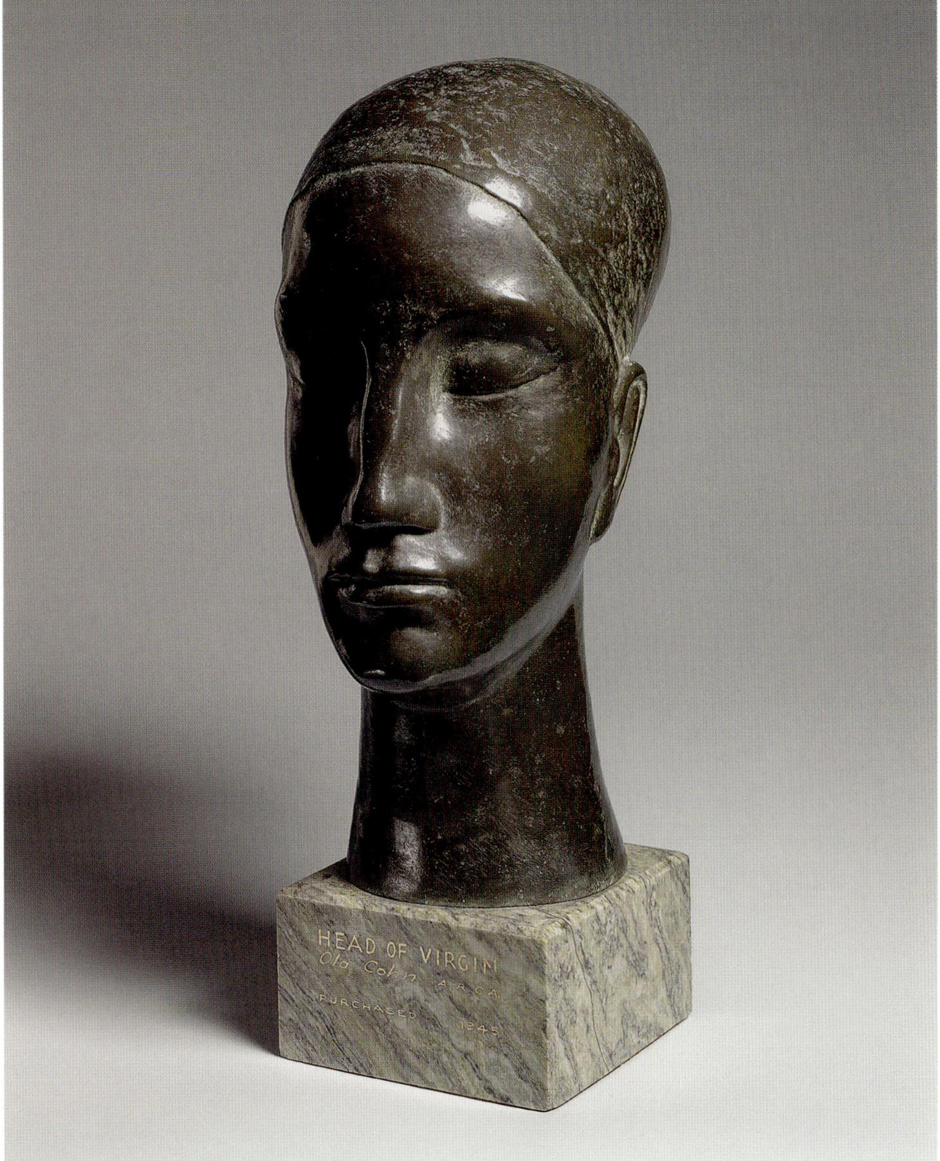
HEAD OF VIRGIN
Ola Cohn A.R.C.A.
PURCHASED 1945

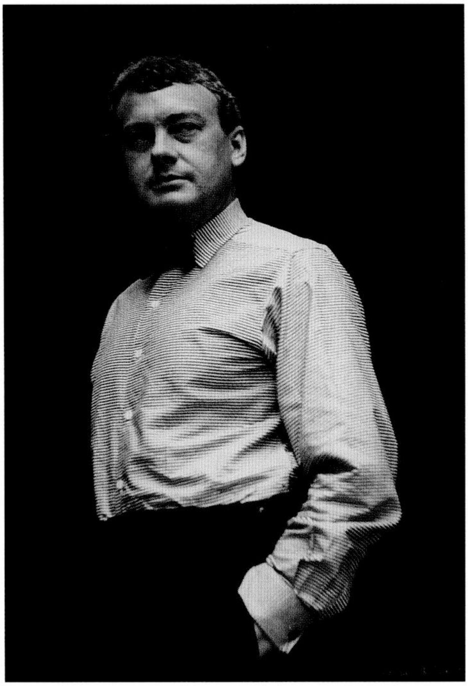

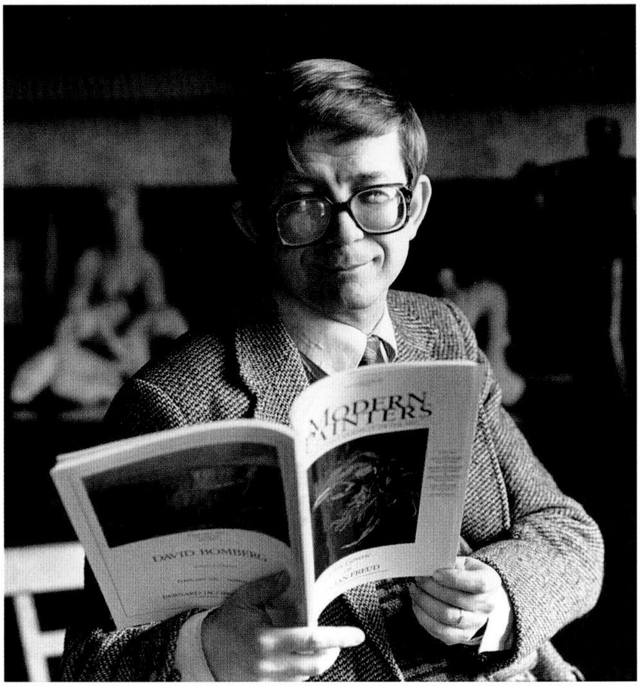

19. Ida Kar, *Bryan Charles Francis Robertson*, 1958. As director of the Whitechapel Art Gallery (1952–69), Robertson declined Smith's proposal for an exhibition of the work of the Antipodeans. Smith developed a strained relationship with Robertson, who Smith satirised as the 'Chief Celtic midwife to our London Australiana'.

20. The British art critic Peter Fuller, photographed in 1988 by Jane Bown. He holds a copy of *Modern Painters*, the art journal he founded in 1987.

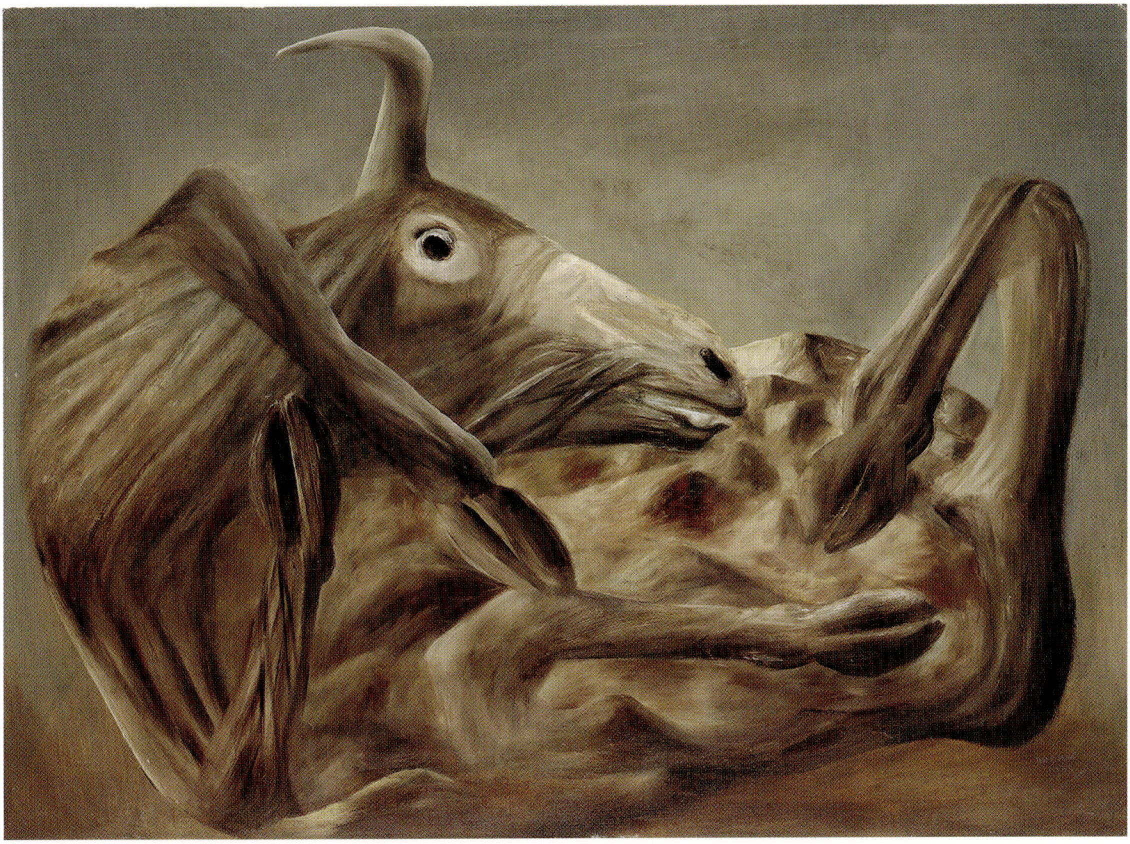

21. Sidney Nolan, *Carcass*,
1953.

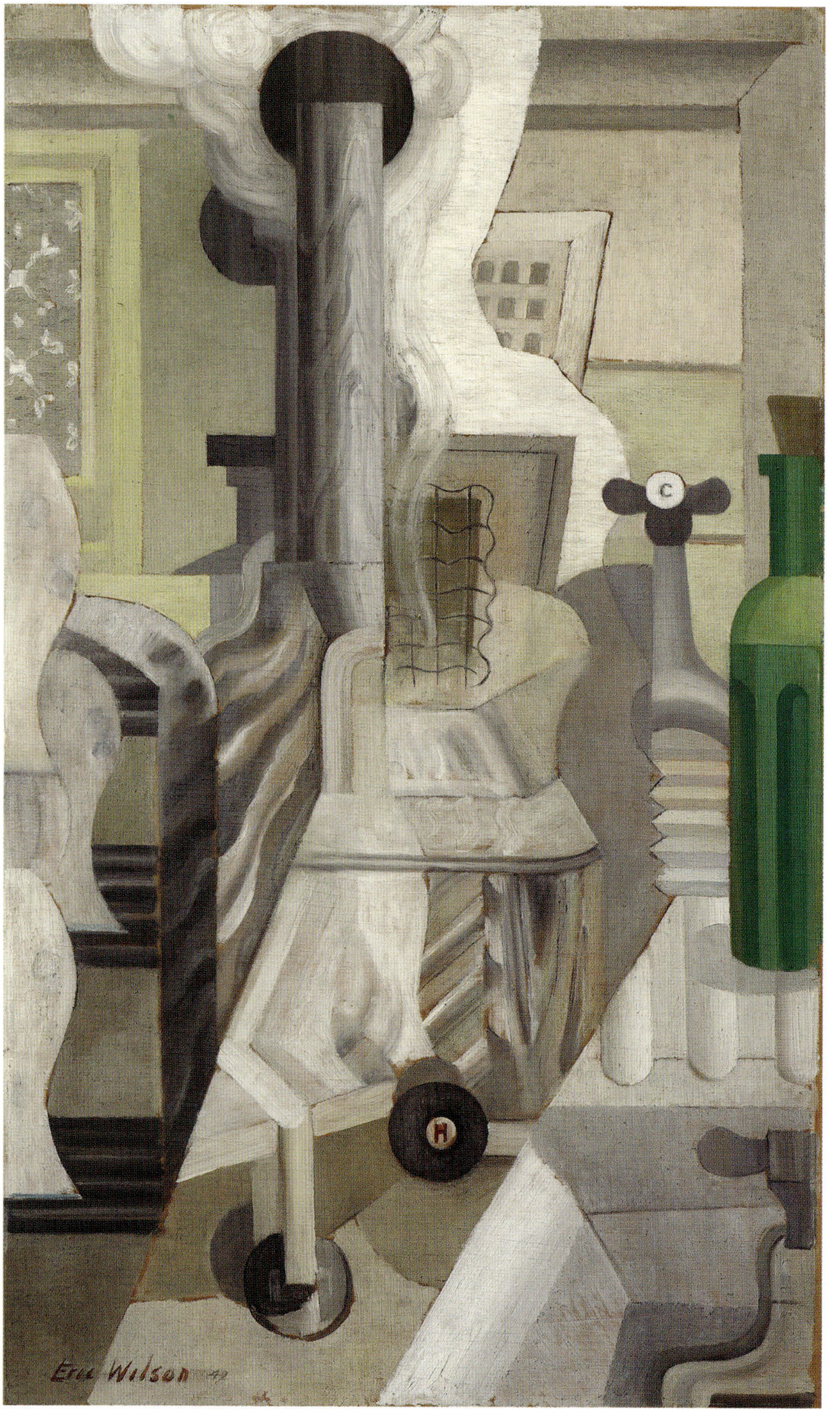
Eric Wilson

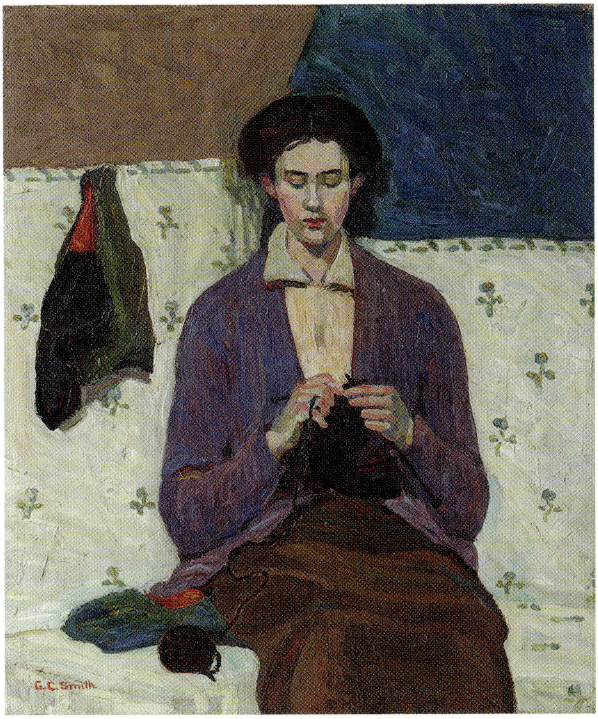

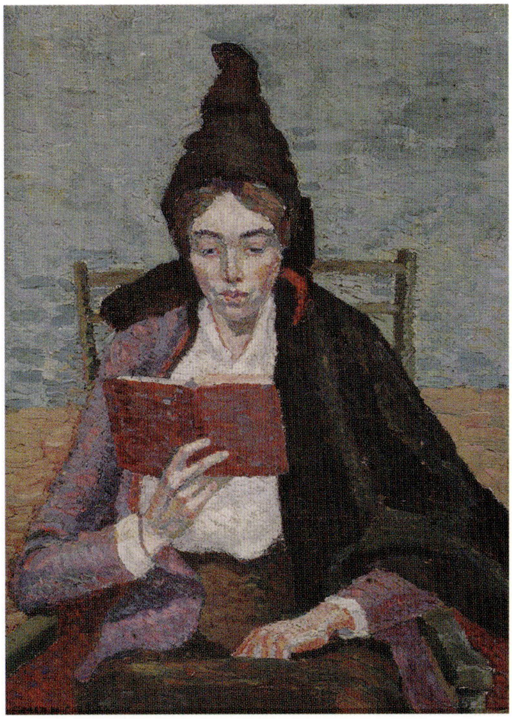

22. Eric Wilson, *Hospital theme—the sterilizer*, 1942. The National Art Gallery of New South Wales purchased this work in 1945 after it had been recommended for acquisition by Smith's Travelling Art Sub-Committee.

23. Grace Cossington Smith, *The sock knitter*, 1915. In June 1960 Smith wrote to Art Gallery of New South Wales curator Daniel Thomas to recommend the gallery purchase the work, the first post-impressionist work exhibited in Australia.

24. Grace Cossington Smith, *The school cape*, 1916.

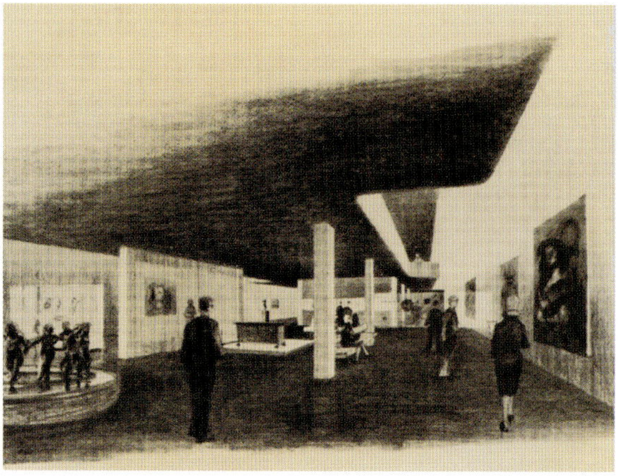

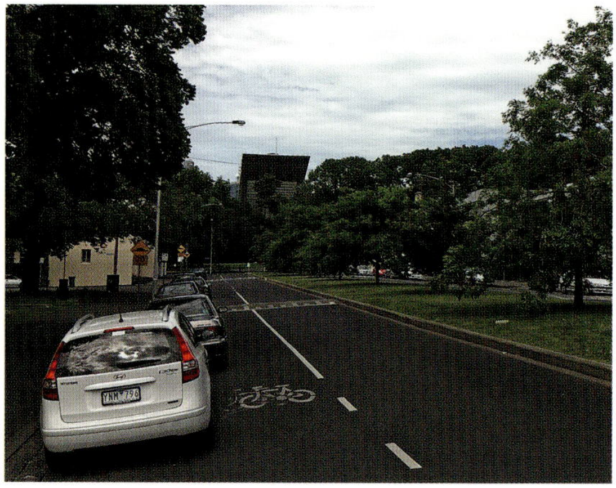

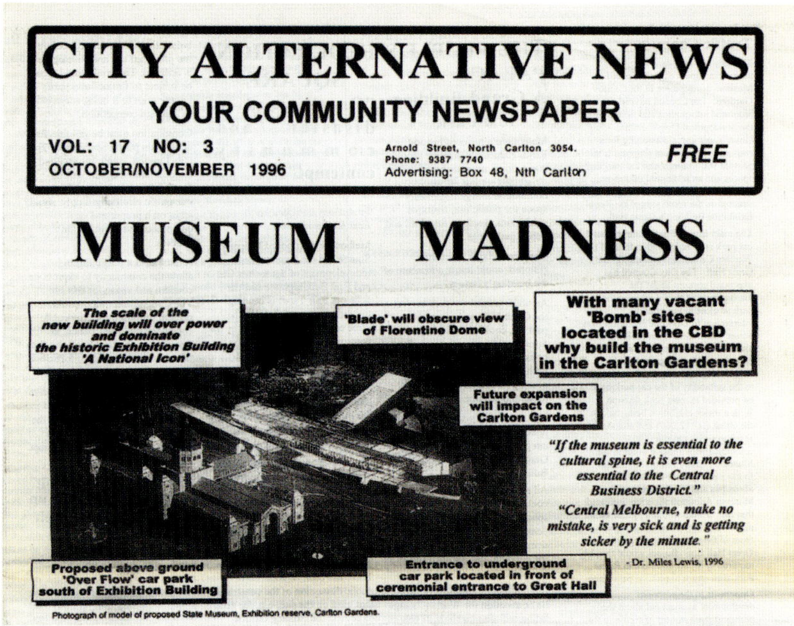

CITY ALTERNATIVE NEWS

YOUR COMMUNITY NEWSPAPER

VOL: 17 NO: 3
OCTOBER/NOVEMBER 1996

Arnold Street, North Carlton 3054.
Phone: 9387 7740
Advertising: Box 48, Nth Carlton

FREE

MUSEUM MADNESS

The scale of the new building will over power and dominate the historic Exhibition Building 'A National Icon'

'Blade' will obscure view of Florentine Dome

With many vacant 'Bomb' sites located in the CBD why build the museum in the Carlton Gardens?

Future expansion will impact on the Carlton Gardens

"If the museum is essential to the cultural spine, it is even more essential to the Central Business District."

"Central Melbourne, make no mistake, is very sick and is getting sicker by the minute."

- Dr. Miles Lewis, 1996

Proposed above ground 'Over Flow' car park south of Exhibition Building

Entrance to underground car park located in front of ceremonial entrance to Great Hall

Photograph of model of proposed State Museum, Exhibition reserve, Carlton Gardens.

25. Paul Wallace (illustrator), *Typical display gallery*, 1960, for planned National Gallery of Victoria.

26 . 'Museum madness', criticism of the plans for the Melbourne Museum in the *City Alternative News*, October–November 1996.

27. View towards the Melbourne Museum across the Carlton Gardens from Canning Street, Carlton, showing the obstruction caused by the Melbourne Museum's 'blade' to the Royal Exhibition Building's dome.

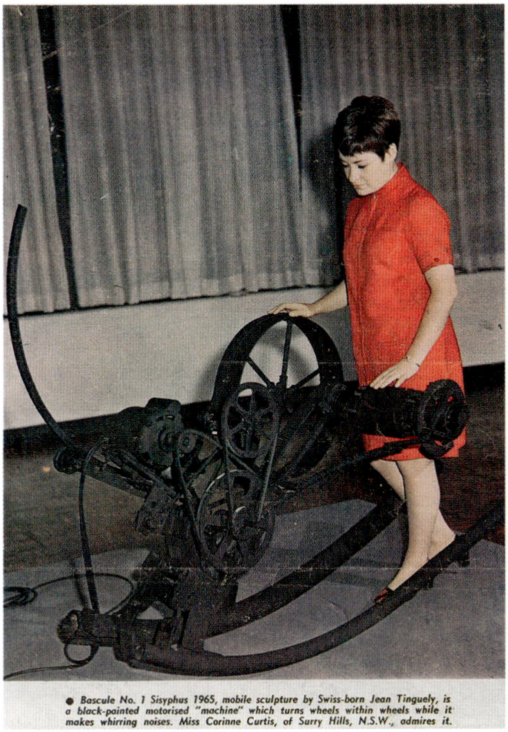

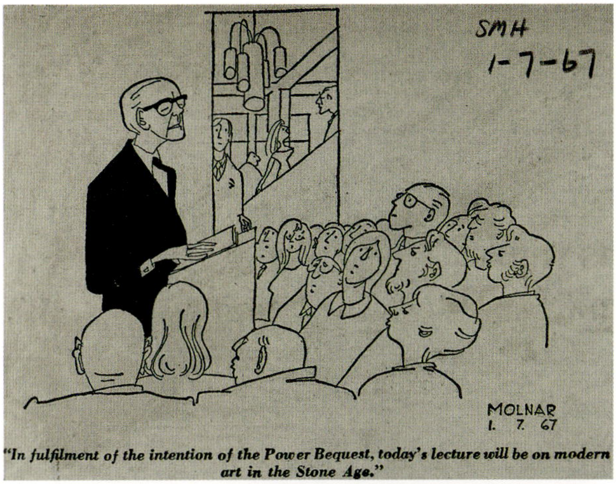

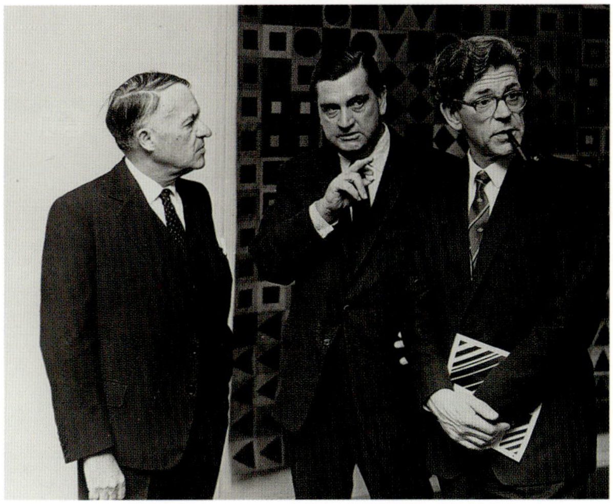

28. Jean Tingueley, *Bascule no. 1 Sisyphus*, 1965.

29. George Molnar, Caricature of newly appointed Professor Bernard Smith delivering a lecture, *The Sydney Morning Herald*, 1 July 1967.

30. German Consul-General W. C. Brückmann, Elwyn Lynn, newly appointed Power Curator, and Professor Bruce Williams, University of Sydney Vice-Chancellor, at Power Collection exhibition opening, at Farmer's Blaxland Gallery, July 1969.

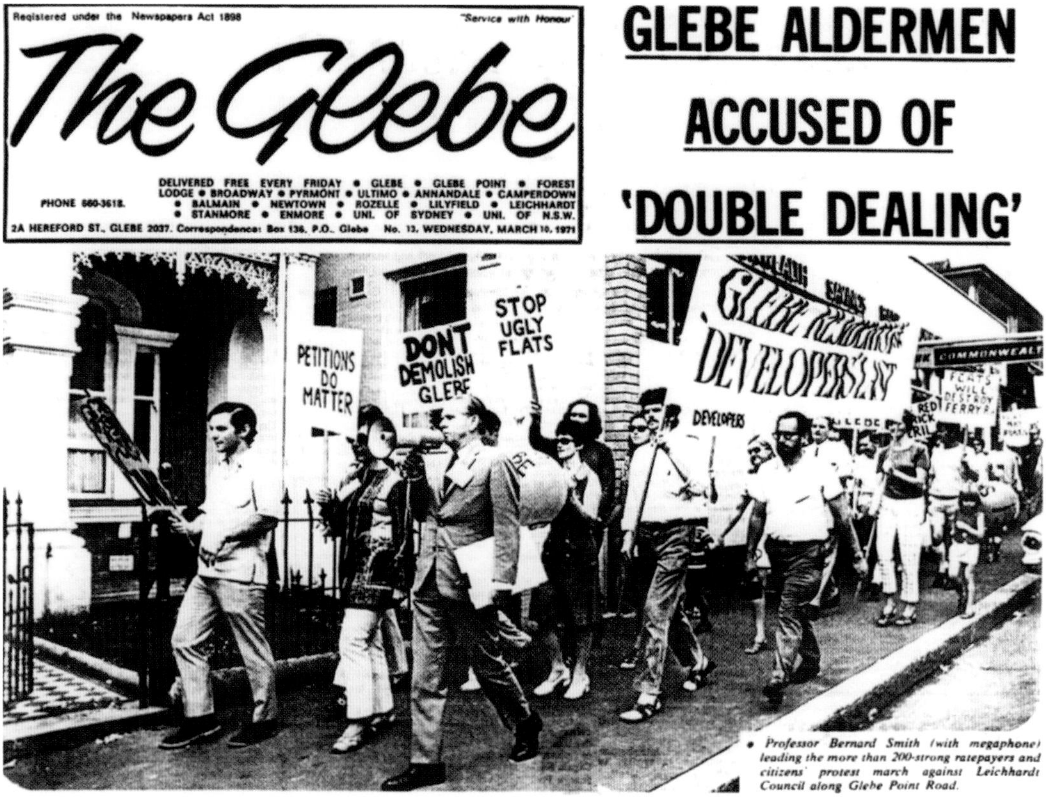

Registered under the Newspapers Act 1898 "Service with Honour"

The Glebe

PHONE 660-3618.

DELIVERED FREE EVERY FRIDAY • GLEBE • GLEBE POINT • FOREST LODGE • BROADWAY • PYRMONT • ULTIMO • ANNANDALE • CAMPERDOWN • BALMAIN • NEWTOWN • ROZELLE • LILYFIELD • LEICHHARDT • STANMORE • ENMORE • UNI. OF SYDNEY • UNI. OF N.S.W.

2A HEREFORD ST., GLEBE 2037. Correspondence: Box 136, P.O., Glebe No. 13, WEDNESDAY, MARCH 10, 1971

GLEBE ALDERMEN ACCUSED OF 'DOUBLE DEALING'

• *Professor Bernard Smith (with megaphone) leading the more than 200-strong ratepayers and citizens' protest march against Leichhardt Council along Glebe Point Road.*

31. Professor Bernard Smith (with megaphone) leading the more than 200-strong ratepayers and citizens' protest march against Leichhardt Council along Glebe Point Road, *The Glebe*, 10 March 1971.

32. Bernard Smith with Gerard Dillon's *Boys catching crabs in Connemara*, 1949–50.

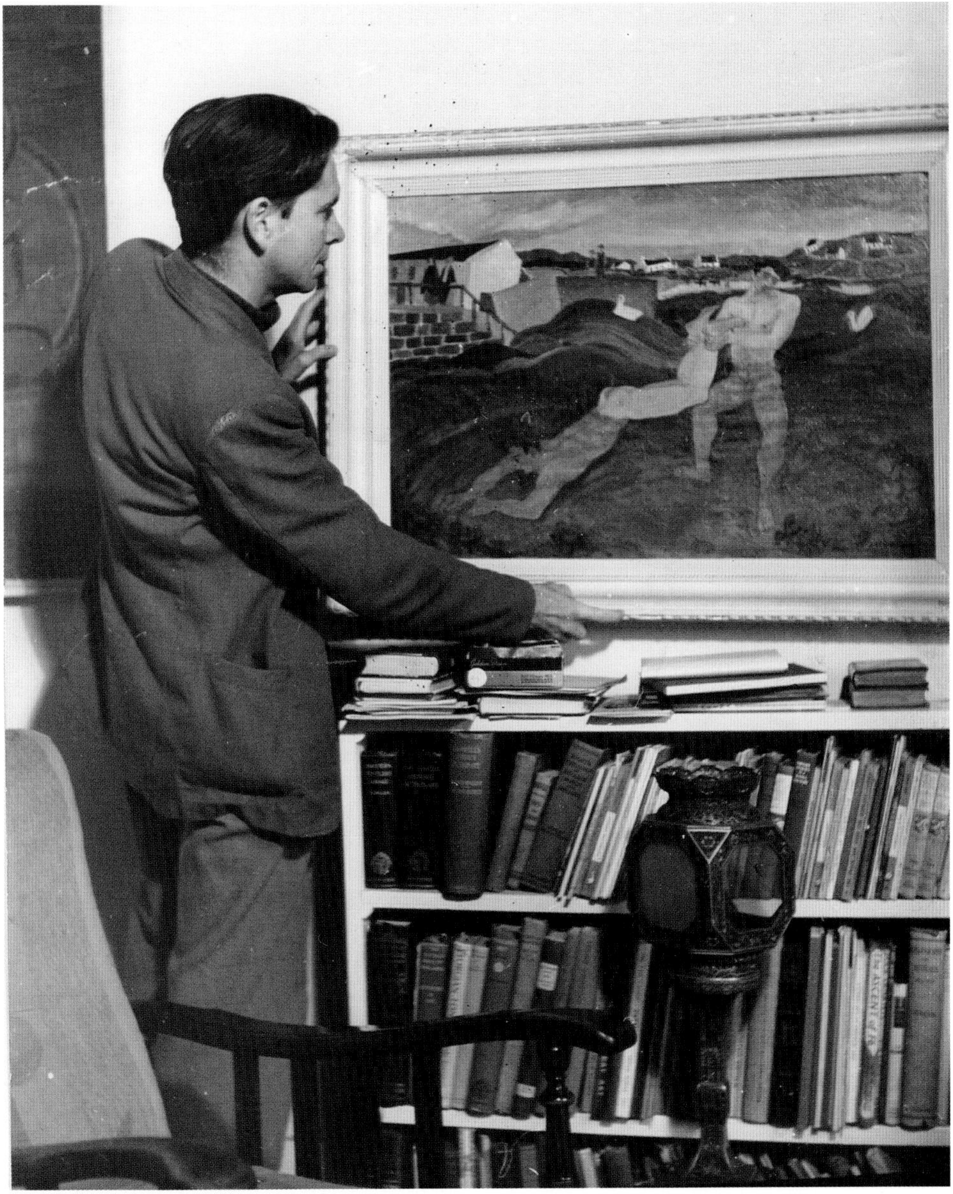

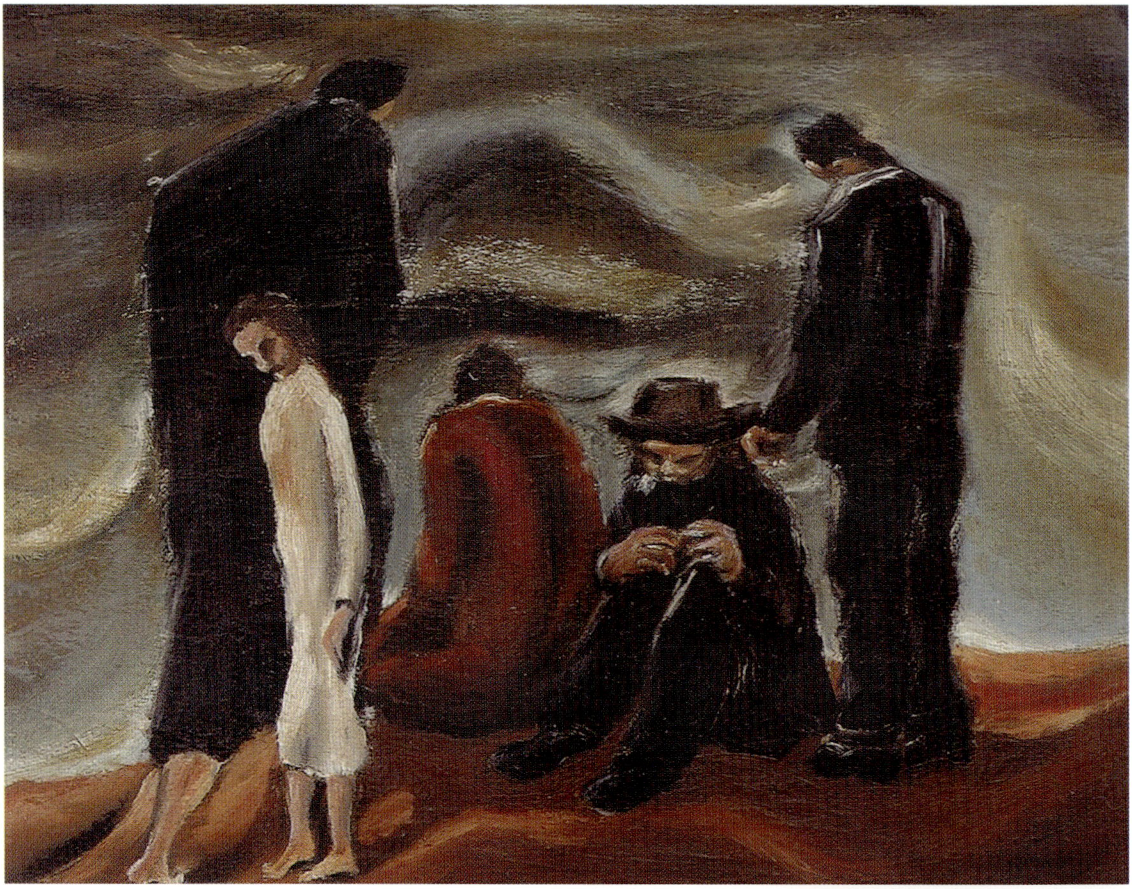

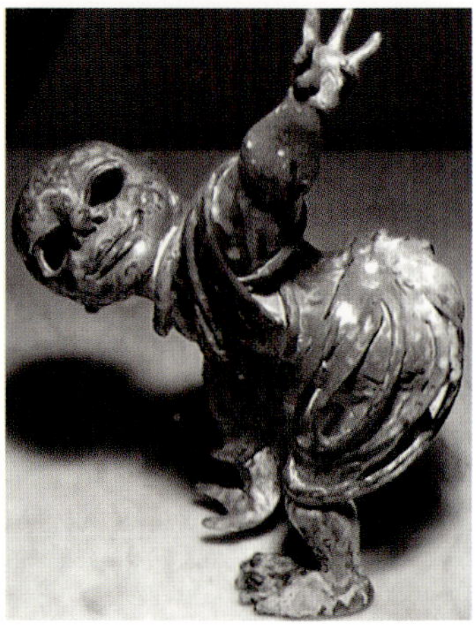

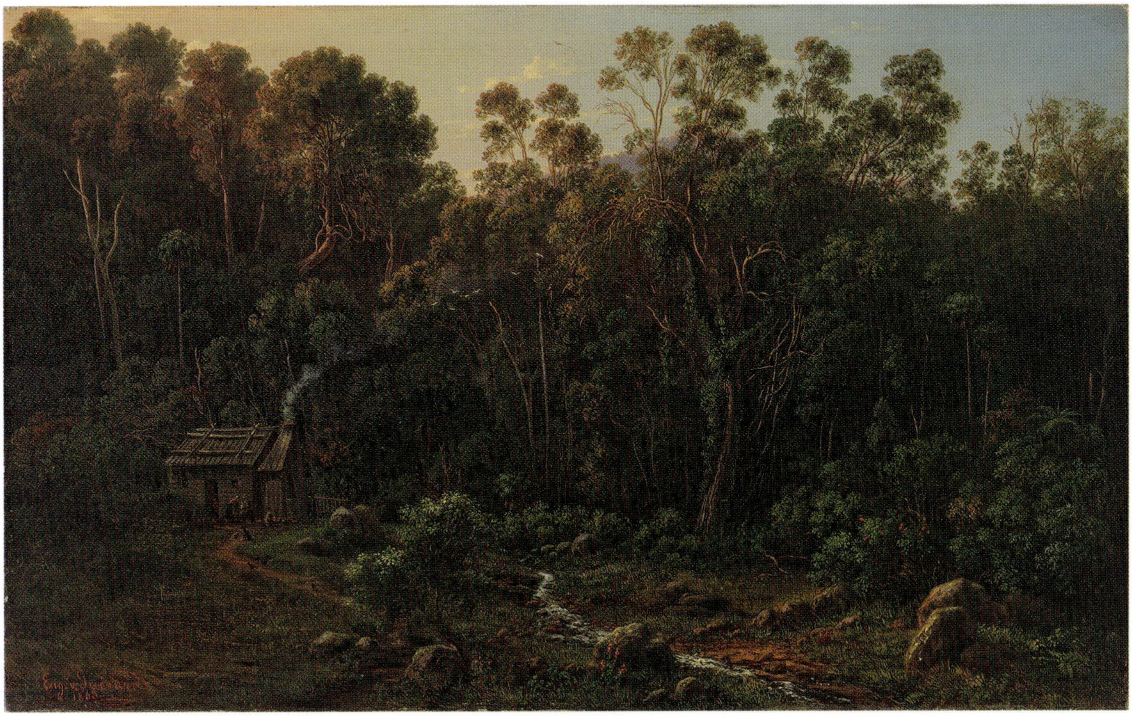

33. Vic O'Connor, *The refugees*, 1942.

34. John Perceval, *Angel learning to walk*, c. 1958.

35. Eugene von Guérard, *Forest scene near Kiama*, 1863.

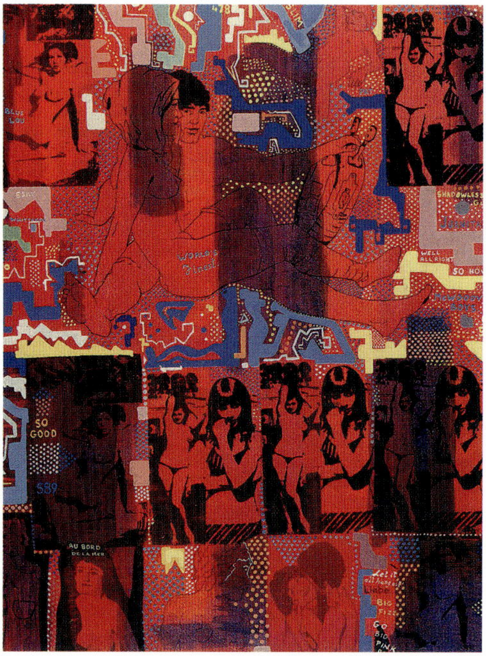

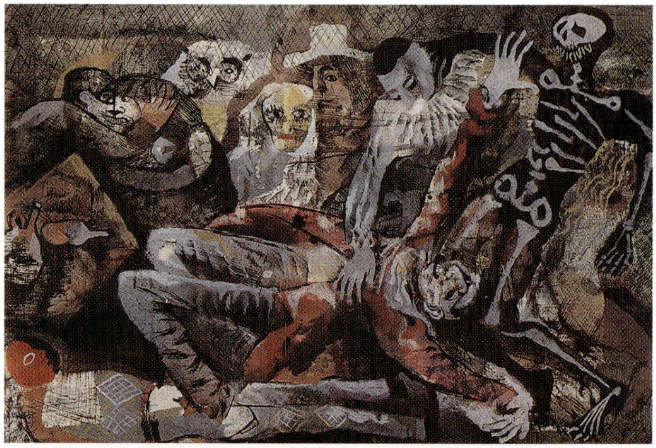

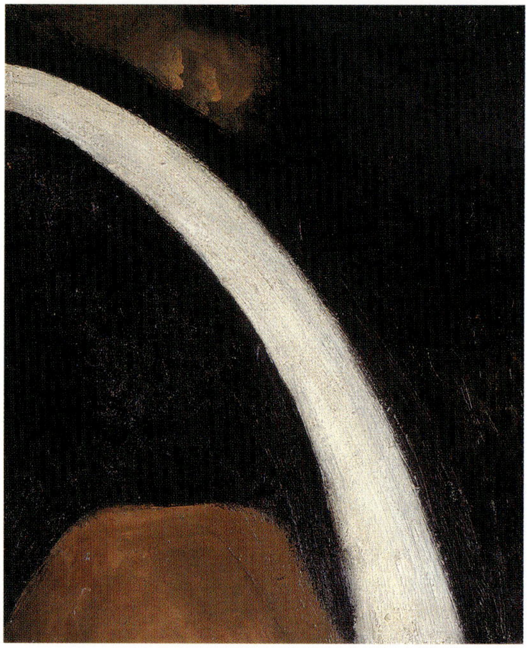

36. Richard Larter, *Well all right, so how*, 1970.

37. Donald Friend, *John Bell's party*, c. 1964.

38. Colin McCahon, *Waterfall*, 1964.

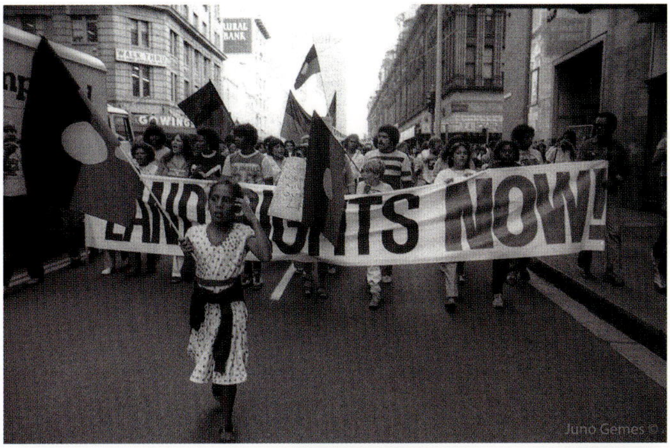

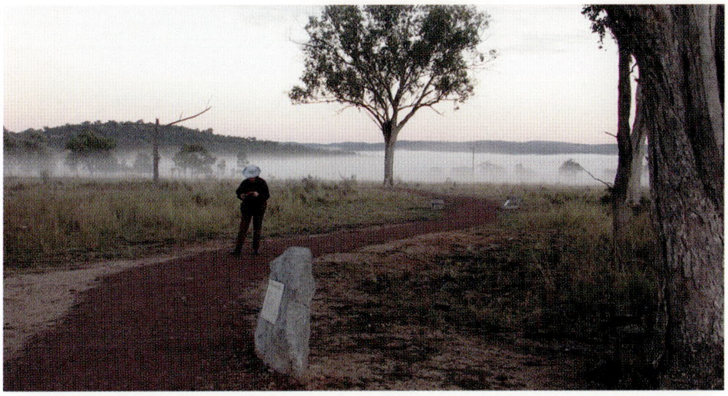

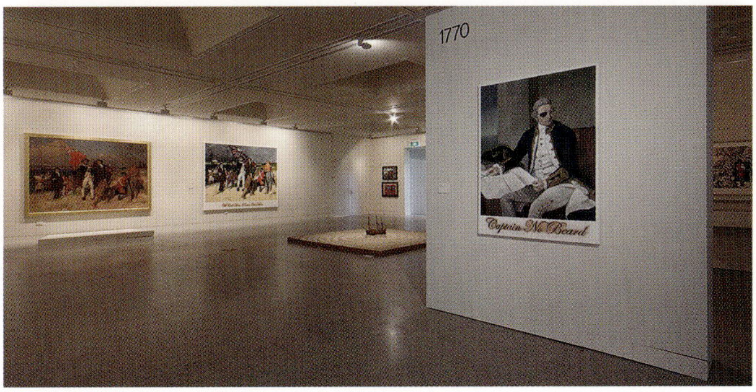

39. Juno Gemes, *Land rights march, NADOC Day Sydney*, 1981.

40. Myall Creek Massacre Memorial (near Bingara, NSW), 2000. The image shows a section of the project, one of seven plaques detailing the story of dispossession and massacre in 1838. In early June each year, descendants of perpetrators and survivors lead a procession of young and old along the path to a large plinth where participants reflect on 'the truth of our shared history'.

41. Installation view of Ace Bourke's exhibition *Lines in the sand*, 2008.

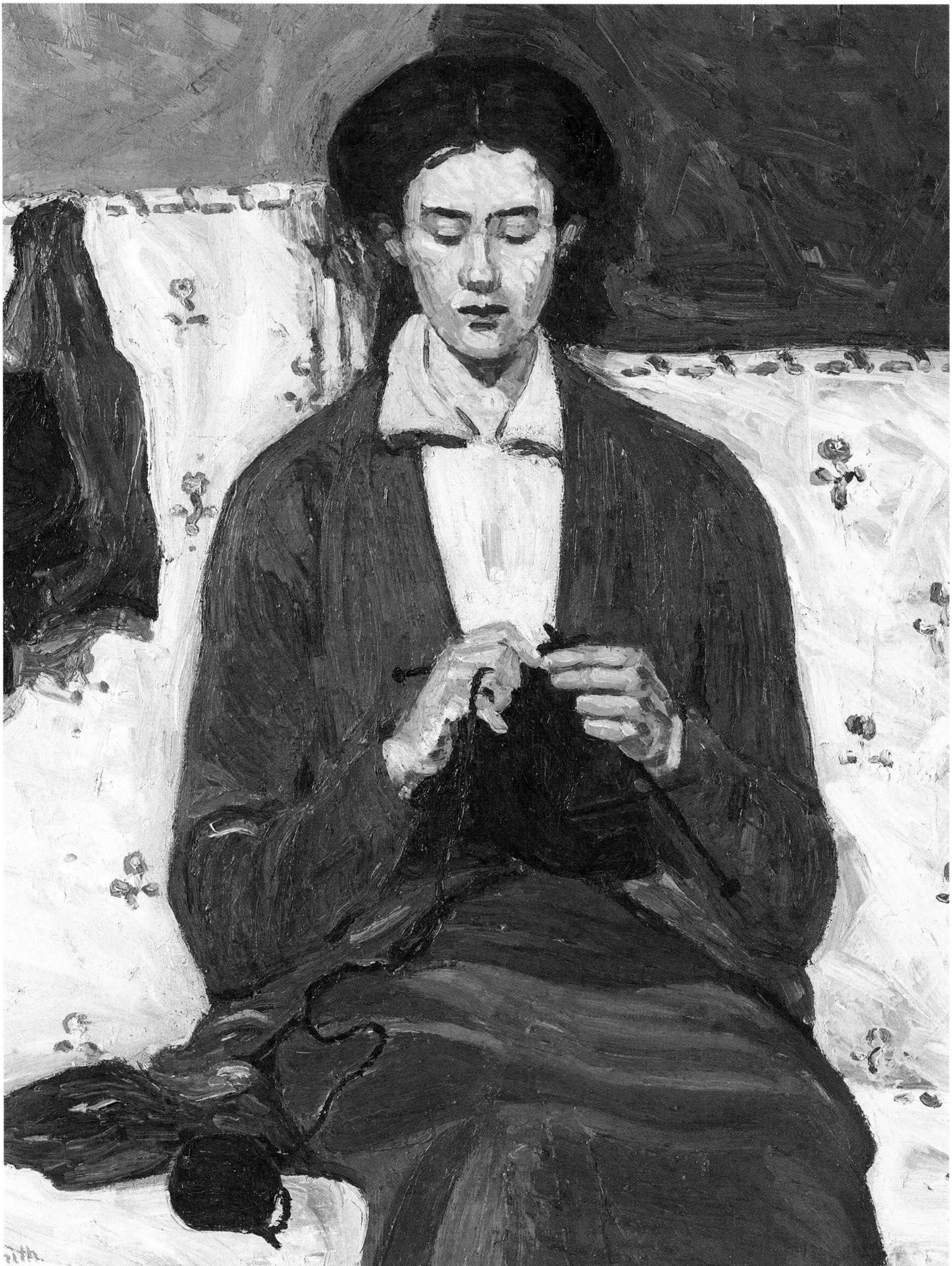

3

BERNARD SMITH AND THE ART MUSEUM

Contingency as the guard dog of history:

Bernard Smith at the National Art Gallery of New South Wales, 1944–48

STEVEN MILLER

In the August 1990 issue of *Art Monthly*, Bernard Smith wrote a lively reply to his critics—namely the authors of *The Necessity of Australian Art*—challenging their 'revisionary history of Australian art' and their interpretation of Smith's own work as an art historian.[1] Among other things, he objected to the claim that the second edition of his book *Australian Painting* gave unqualified endorsement to the 1960s avant-garde, an endorsement signalled by his choice of an abstract work by Trevor Vickers for a cover image.[2] Yet this choice of imagery was not Smith's, he revealed; it was a design and marketing decision made by the publishers:

> I was quite surprised when I first saw the new reprint and recall feeling that I might at least have been consulted. But I was busy with other work at the time and let the matter pass. It is contingent factors such as this that the authors of *The Necessity*, writing always at a theoretical level, tend to ignore. Contingency is the guard dog of history that protects it from invasion by theoretical fictions.[3]

By invoking contingency in this context, Smith was not suggesting that historical events are merely random, a perspective taken by some historians who stress the contingent factor in history over the necessary, the universal or teleological.[4] He was making the commonsense observation that in many situations people are forced to make the best of what is available and to work with structures over which they do not have control nor of which they are even fully aware. This was particularly true of his experience at the National Art Gallery of New South Wales (NAGNSW).[5] He worked there when the institution was changing from a provincial nineteenth-century museum, staging two or three exhibitions a year, to one aspiring to be modern and professional, with a fuller program of exhibitions and educational activities.

Smith objected to the criticism made in *The Necessity of Australian Art* that his account of Australian art, grounded in stylistic description and analysis, undervalued the contexts in which art is produced. To counter this, he cited articles he had written and courses he had taught which he believed demonstrated his sensitivity to context and to the relation of art institutions to art practice. He could have also cited the first-hand experience he had of museum work during the seven years he was associated with the NAGNSW. This work saw him engaged both practically and theoretically with issues of art patronage, the market and institutional culture.

Smith's time at the gallery fell into two distinct periods. The first was from mid-1944, when he was seconded to the gallery for the 'encouragement of art', as the official dossier put it, which meant organising a series of art exhibitions designed for circulation throughout regional New South Wales, until September 1948, when he left to take up a British Council travelling scholarship. The second was from 1951 to 1953, when he returned to Australia and to the gallery to compile the first scholarly catalogue of its Australian oil paintings. The focus of this paper is on the first period.

ART FOR REGIONAL AUSTRALIA

Smith began work at the NAGNSW on 3 July 1944. He gives a full account of the events leading up to his appointment in *A Pavane for Another Time* and elsewhere.[6] Smith notes that the aim of bringing original artworks to rural New South Wales had been part of the platform that brought William McKell's Labor Party to power in the May 1941 state election. Mary Alice Evatt, wife of the attorney-general, and publisher Sydney Ure Smith, a trustee at the gallery, devised a plan for achieving this by having Smith seconded from the Education Department. Bernard Smith and

Sydney Ure Smith knew each other from the War Art Council, where they were secretary and president respectively.[7] Nancy Underhill has described Bernard Smith as 'the last major beneficiary' of Ure Smith's patronage.[8]

Records show, however, that Bernard Smith was just as active in placing himself at the centre of this new scheme, calling upon the support of his friends. On 28 April 1944 he took the initiative and wrote to the board of the gallery, asking that Mary Evatt attend a meeting in connection with a proposal to establish a travelling art exhibition. In June, Ure Smith reported on that meeting to the board. A subcommittee was then established to act in association with the Education Department, Evatt moving that 'Mr Bernard Smith (be) appointed to take charge of the work'.[9]

Smith wrote of the opposition that the Travelling Art Scheme initially encountered, from the lack of enthusiasm from the director-general of education, to outright hostility from some members of the art gallery board. Yet it could be argued that Smith exaggerated the nature of this hostility and that the board was in no way opposed to a scheme for circulating art in the country. What many of them objected to was Bernard Smith himself and his—as they saw it—machinations. Lionel Lindsay wrote to fellow trustee James McGregor that Smith was 'clearly a book read and too cock sure'.[10] Lindsay went further when writing to print dealer Harold Wright in London: 'that damned understrapper, his name is Bernard Smith, in case you may have dealings in future with him … I shall not forgive his intolerance, priggishness and vanity'.[11]

Smith cast trustee John Maund as his nemesis at the gallery. He nicknamed Maund 'Johnnie the terror', characterising him as an interfering, die-hard conservative.[12] Director Hal Missingham shared Smith's dislike of Maund, writing that he was 'the most callous and insensitive man I ever had the misfortune to meet'.[13] Maund, from a working-class background like Smith, was a political conservative. In these years of escalating Cold War tension he was vigilant about what he saw as the infiltration of Australia's institutions by communists and communist sympathisers—by people like Smith and Missingham. It was at his insistence that Missingham had to resign from the committees of all art societies, including the Left-leaning Studio of Realist Art (SORA). In Maund's opinion, many of the other trustees were naive about the real threat that communism posed to Australia. He forced debate on the issue at board meetings, bringing, for example, an article from *The Sydney Morning Herald*—'How Communism is Infiltrating Cultural Organisations'—to the August 1948 meeting.[14]

It was not surprising that Maund should take an interest in art education programs at the gallery. The board minutes reveal that this was an area of particular concern to him and in the early 1930s he had been appointed by the state government to investigate complaints of 'wasteful expenditures, over-staffing and ineffective control' made against the art school at East Sydney Technical College. He came out strongly in support of the school, criticising its critics.[15]

The suggestion that trustees like Maund were opposed to travelling exhibitions in the country is difficult to credit, given that they had been supporting a Mobile Art Scheme from 1939.[16] This was put together by Valentine Crowley and the artist George Finey. It operated for three years, but Smith completely discounted it. Crowley was a member of the nationalist Australia First Movement, and a close friend of P. R. Stephensen, and so from the other end of the ideological spectrum to Smith. He was also an ex-communist, as were many of the ultra-nationalists associated with the magazine *The Publicist*. When it was proposed to amalgamate the two art schemes, Smith opposed it, as he thought the quality of the works that Crowley was circulating was not sufficiently high. This, at least, is what he told Missingham some years later when both Crowley and Finey complained that their work had not been duly acknowledged.[17]

Ideological and personal prejudices probably informed Smith's hostility to the Mobile Art Scheme, as the quality of works circulated was not as low as he suggested. The scheme included Grace Cossington Smith's *Orchestral concert* (c. 1939), now in the collection of the National Gallery of Australia, along with a good representation of Margaret Preston, Thea Proctor and Antonio Dattilo-Rubbo. It is interesting to note that 'Johnnie the terror' appeared as Crowley's lawyer during the trial concerning his internment in March 1942 under national security regulations.[18]

Apart from Crowley and the Mobile Art Scheme, another precursor to Smith's work whom he failed to acknowledge was Gwen Sherwood, who had been employed at the gallery since 1937 as the director's secretary. She also lectured on art and was the resident producer for the Public Service Musical and Dramatic Society. A year before Smith came to the gallery, Sherwood was sent to the country to make an inventory of works already on loan and to draw up proposals for how the loan of works could be more effectively managed. At this time more than 500 works were already on loan. Country loans had in fact increased during the war, as this was seen as a way of securing the collection.[19]

After the war an *ad hoc* program of loans continued.[20] The trustees wanted to extend this but were concerned that many institutions requesting works were run by volunteers. The trustees needed to be assured that a public body would accept responsibility for the safe custody of works loaned. Requests for loans also coincided with a focus on art education after the war. The gallery increased its program of art lectures as well as broadcasts on the ABC, often funded by money from the Carnegie Corporation. In 1941 trustee Charles Lloyd Jones submitted a memorandum to the board entitled 'Art in our time'. This included proposals for the gallery that have only recently been adopted, such as opening late one evening each week, regular film screenings, and Saturday mornings dedicated to children, using appropriately trained guides.

This was the background to Smith's travelling art exhibitions, little of which he acknowledged when writing about the period. Gwen Sherwood did the groundwork for him. In Bathurst, Orange, Parkes and Forbes, she visited schools and the local councils and drew up guidelines for an improved program of travelling art exhibitions. Perhaps Smith failed to mention her because of tension between them. The board minutes hint at this. In July 1945, for instance, Sherwood informed the board that the gallery's press-cutting book was 'being depleted by Mr Bernard Smith'.[21] It seems that Smith was removing clippings of use to him for his studies and writing.[22]

THE 'ENCOURAGEMENT OF ART'

So far this paper has focused on placing Bernard Smith's early work at the NAGNSW in a wider context than the one given by him in his own writings. In doing this it is difficult to dismiss criticisms often voiced of him, namely, that he could be blinded by ideological convictions (particularly in his early years) and that he undervalued the contribution of women. This chapter will now look at Smith's considerable achievement in organising twenty exhibitions during four years, which were held in 100 different venues and visited by over 150,000 people. Many of these shows were mounted in difficult circumstances. Local councils were rarely supportive. 'I have seen the Mayor Mr Collins, an ironmonger', a letter from Tamworth records, 'and he point blank refused to open the show or have anything to do with it. He added that the people would agree with him for not wasting his time on such things'.[23] Even some of Smith's colleagues, such as Contemporary Art Society secretary Peter Bellew, attempted to sabotage his program. Smith later wrote:

> Bellew was employed by the Fairfax Press and as editor of the war-time *Art in Australia* had run a powerful campaign for the reform of the Sydney gallery. As a professional journalist, he preferred high-profile confrontationist tactics and did not want to see anything of a worthwhile nature issuing from the gallery.[24]

Smith found that audiences varied considerably from town to town. School groups typically made up half of the attendances, but Smith had to be careful that his program was not seen as being too closely associated with the State Board of Education, as this could lead to Catholic schools boycotting the shows. For the success of the schools program he was dependent on the artists being willing to travel with the shows as lecturers. They were never paid enough and so it was hard to convince them to give up three or four weeks of their year.[25] Notwithstanding this, the list of artist lecturers is impressive, including Arthur Murch, James Cant, Desiderius Orban, Jean Bellette, Jeffrey Smart and Noel Kilgour.

Lecturers had not only to be knowledgeable about art and capable public speakers, but morally upright as well. Sali Herman, who was a good friend of Smith's and lived in the same apartment building in Potts Point, was a popular lecturer until barred in February 1949. The incident that led to this occurred at Wynyard Railway Station in central Sydney, where Herman, allegedly suffering from a bout of diarrhoea and not being able to locate the men's toilet, ran into the women's. He was arrested when a woman saw a man's shoes under the cubicle door. Despite William Dobell vouching for his character, Herman was fined £5 for indecent behaviour and the trustees resolved that 'in view of recent publicity on this artist's behaviour he should not be asked to visit country centres as a guide-lecturer'.[26]

Although the recompense was not great, lecturing with the Travelling Art Scheme was a useful supplement to artists' incomes. It also gave them an opportunity to develop a market for their work outside the metropolitan centres. Many of Smith's exhibitions were in fact a hybrid between a museum show and a selling commercial exhibition. His program relied on artists lending their work. Initially he developed a group of seven separate exhibitions, to be held in forty country centres from July 1944 to June 1945.[27] He began organising this program by writing to eighty-five artists resident in New South Wales, asking for the loan of pictures for a period of seven months. Within a week of writing, he had secured ninety works, including ten from Margaret Preston and thirty from husband and wife George Duncan and Alison Rehfisch.

When it was finally put together, the first exhibition of the scheme, *150 Years of Painting in Australia*, was made up of twenty-seven works from the gallery's collection, three from the Mitchell Library and twenty-one loaned by artists and collectors. The second exhibition, *Some Recent Australian Painting*, was shown in Canberra in December 1944 and included 100 works. Smith deliberately made this second show more challenging than the first, showcasing paintings by Sydney modernists Grace Crowley, Ralph Balson and Frank Hinder and works by James Gleeson, Eric Wilson, Mary Webb and others. Quite a few of the works were sold; in Canberra alone three paintings by Frank Hinder, one by Herbert McClintock and one by Roland Wakelin were sold for over 96 guineas. Stimulating the art market was a conscious aim of Smith through his travelling art exhibitions. He wrote: 'if artists were to have a reasonable chance of living professionally from their work, a massive education programme had to be undertaken in the schools, colleges, universities and public galleries'.[28]

One important outcome of Smith's travelling exhibitions was the profile they gave to art in rural centres.[29] At the time, New South Wales lagged behind Victoria, with its web of regional galleries, many of them established in the nineteenth century. Smith's exhibitions supported regional centres in their push to establish their own galleries. At the very first exhibition in Wagga Wagga, the newspapers noted that the council exhibited with the show plans for a local art gallery. In Newcastle, where exhibitions were normally held at the Trades Hall, Smith reported that the need for an art gallery was featured in the press and over the air. The 1948 annual report for the Department of Education noted:

> The success of the [scheme] has encouraged a number of municipal and shire councils to view favourably the principle of establishing local art galleries in

> conjunction with libraries and museums. This has gone beyond the proposal stage at … Albury, Wagga, Newcastle, Wollongong and Lismore.[30]

As it turned out, it took another twenty to thirty years before galleries were established in these centres. A regional art prize often came first, such as in Albury from 1947, which was acquisitive and eventually led to the establishment of a gallery.

Although the travelling art exhibitions stimulated art in the country and helped promote New South Wales artists beyond Sydney, their most lasting legacy was probably at the NAGNSW itself, and in an area with which they are not normally associated, namely, acquisitions. From the start Smith wanted to include modern works in his travelling exhibitions; where these were not available from the gallery's own collection he borrowed them. He even planned to purchase artworks as part of a travelling art exhibition collection. Some members of the gallery's board saw this, quite accurately, as a criticism of their buying policy. Nonetheless, at the January 1945 board meeting, Charles Lloyd Jones moved that:

> owing to the need to include some examples of recent Australian painting in the exhibitions arranged for country centres … [it is moved that] the trustee members of the Travelling Exhibition Committee be empowered to purchase paintings to an aggregate sum of £500.

With Mrs Evatt seconding the motion, this astonishing resolution was pushed through by a narrow majority.[31]

This is how the first works by Sali Herman came into the gallery's collection. The committee immediately bought his *Kincumber* (1945) and *House, North Sydney* (1944). But the committee's power to purchase works directly was short lived. John Maund saw this as a method of bringing contemporary works into the collection through the back door. At the April 1945 board meeting he argued against the legality of the resolution and had it rescinded. From then on a Travelling Art Sub-Committee could choose works, which would then need to be submitted to the board for final approval.

Nonetheless, Eric Wilson's *Hospital theme—the sterilizer* (1942) was put up and got through, surprisingly, in September 1945 (Fig. 22). One of the most abstract works to come into the collection at the time, it was part of a submission of ten works.

Others that were considered, but eventually rejected, included Russell Drysdale's *A football game* (1943), now in the collection of the Ballarat Art Gallery, and James Gleeson's *The pretext of accident*, now in the National Gallery of Australia.

An unexpected result of the Travelling Art Scheme was that it eventually brought additional funding to the gallery for acquisitions. This funding came from the Department of Education rather than from the Treasury, which traditionally funded acquisitions. Any money left over after all the operating expenses of the program had been paid could be used to buy works. In February 1952, when Smith had returned to the gallery for the second time, the trustees found that they had almost £2000 in unspent funds from the program. They purchased James Gleeson's *The oracle* (1948), Frank Hinder's *Painting* (1946), Rod Shaw's *Cable layers* (1946) and Ralph Balson's *Painting* (1951).

In June 1948 Smith wrote to the board, informing them that he could no longer manage the Travelling Art Scheme, as he was going overseas in September to study on a British Council scholarship. Although Smith later in life made much of the hostility that he had encountered from the trustees, there were many who were disappointed to lose him. Director Hal Missingham, at the request of the board, wrote thanking him for his 'great efforts in establishing, maintaining and developing this important side of gallery activities'. Missingham had always appreciated Smith's exceptional abilities, as had trustees Charles Lloyd Jones, Mary Alice Evatt, Professor Eben Gowrie Waterhouse and William Dobell.

When he came to the NAGNSW in 1944 to work 'for the encouragement of art', Smith could not have guessed what this would eventually entail. In a short period he had gained a surprisingly wide experience of the museum and commercial gallery worlds. He worked as an education officer, organising lectures and public programs, as a curator, both of touring exhibitions and of some in-house gallery ones, as a critic, preparing art-historical notes for the catalogues to his travelling art exhibitions, and as a de facto commercial dealer for those artists from whom he borrowed works for his travelling exhibitions. He even acted informally as director over two periods and helped shape, albeit for a short time, the gallery's collection of Australian art.

NOTES

1 Bernard Smith, 'A reply to my critics', *Art Monthly Australia*, no. 33, August 1990, pp. 3–6. The authors of *The Necessity of Australian Art: An Essay About Interpretation* (Power Institute of Fine Arts, Sydney, 1988), were Ian Burn, Nigel Lendon, Charles Merewether and Ann Stephen.

2 As the cover to the second reprint of the second edition in 1978.

3 Smith, 'A reply to my critics', p. 4

4 From his many years of engagement with Marxist thought, for example, Smith was aware of the continuing tension between the contingent and the necessary in accounting for human activity, and the need for Marxists to account for the fact that modes of production usually begin from presuppositions which are not produced by them but are presupposed by them.

5 The gallery dropped 'National' from its name in 1958.

6 Bernard Smith, *A Pavane for Another Time*, Macmillan, Sydney, 2002; Bernard Smith, 'Taking Art to the Country: How it Began', in Peter Timms and Robyn Christie (eds), *Cultivating the Country: Living with the Arts in Regional Australia*, Oxford University Press, Melbourne, 1988, pp. 33–46.

7 In late 1943 Bernard Smith had also submitted a manuscript of his *Place, Taste and Tradition* to Sydney Ure Smith for publication.

8 Nancy Underhill, *Making Australian Art, 1916–49: Sydney Ure Smith, Patron and Publisher*, Oxford University Press, Melbourne, 1991, p. 121.

9 Art Gallery of New South Wales Archive, Sydney (hereafter AGNSW Archive), National Art Gallery of New South Wales Board Minutes, 23 June 1944, p. 2668.

10 Lionel Lindsay to James R. McGregor, 6 February 1945, Mitchell Library, Sydney, Lindsay Family Papers, MLMSS1969/4, p. 302.

11 Lionel Lindsay to Harold Wright, 15 May 1945, Mitchell Library, Sydney, Harold J. Wright Papers, MLMSS515/4, p. 337.

12 Bernard Smith, interviewed by Nancy Underhill, 3 December 1983, National Library of Australia, Canberra.

13 Hal Missingham, *They Kill You in the End*, Angus & Robertson, Sydney, 1973, p. 31.

14 Jean Campbell, art critic and daughter of the founder of Sydney's Macquarie Galleries, knew Maund since she was a girl. She remembered him as a person who did not mince his words, but who was kind and humorous. A professional rugby player in his youth, Maund was unusually talented and went on to study law. It was Maund who privately purchased Tom Robert's *Bailed up* in 1928, as the NAGNSW vacillated about the work. He immediately loaned it, until the gallery eventually purchased it, years later.

15 *Sydney Morning Herald*, 'Fine Art Classes: Honorary Commissioner's Investigations', 4 September 1933, p. 8.

16 The first of these exhibitions opened at Sydney Girls' High School on Friday 29 September 1939. The state director of education intended that seven groups of twenty to thirty paintings be circulated continuously in eighteen high schools for one year. At the end of the year every school would have viewed every set. The original group of twenty-four pictures was collected from the Macquarie Galleries by Crowley and offered on loan to the Education Department for exhibition in the metropolitan area. Will Ashton, then director of the NAGNSW, cooperated with the Department of Education by writing to artists and galleries, inviting them to contribute works to the Mobile Art Scheme. He also wrote some critical notes that were hung beside the works when exhibited. The scheme continued in 1941 and 1942, with paintings lent by the NAGNSW, Macquarie Galleries, the Grosvenor Gallery and the Fine Arts Gallery. In August 1942 the scheme was discontinued.

17 State Records NSW, Sydney, Travelling [Country] Art Exhibitions, file 6/23146.7.

18 Crowley was one of the sixteen people from Sydney interned in March 1942 as part of the right-wing Australia First movement. See 'Internment Appeal Dismissed', *Canberra Times*, 4 September 1942, p. 3. He was released in September 1942.

19 Before the war, country centres were asked to contribute half of the costs incurred in exchanging artworks. This fee was dropped during the war for, as the board minutes noted, 'the distribution of works to country centres now serves the dual purpose of removing works in the National Collection to centres less vulnerable to air attack, and at the same time allowing them to be seen by the people'. AGNSW Archive, National Art Gallery of New South Wales Board Minutes, 25 September 1942, p. 2449.

20 Throughout the early 1940s, the trustees had received requests to borrow works, from such bodies as the Moree School of Arts, the Young School of Arts and the Goulburn Technical College.

21 AGNSW Archive, National Art Gallery of New South Wales Board Minutes, 27 July 1945, p. 2803.

22 As archivist for the Art Gallery of New South Wales, I have often wondered why the gallery's press books, so ample for the 1920s and 1930s, are depleted in the early 1940s. I had assumed that this was the result of wartime disruption, rather than a pilfering Bernard Smith.

23 State Records NSW, Sydney, Travelling [Country] Art Exhibitions, file 6/23146.23d.

24 Smith, 'Taking Art to the Country', p. 44.

25 At first they were paid three guineas a day as a flat rate. They had to give a minimum of nine talks to children and three to adults, spread over three days.

26 AGNSW Archive, National Art Gallery of New South Wales Board Minutes, 25 February 1949, p. 3063. Some reports in the press said that he was loitering in the toilet for over an hour. Herman gave various reasons, including that he had lost his way or that he was canvassing potential models for his studio. 'Charge against artist', *Daily Telegraph*, 12 February 1949, n.p.

27 Exhibition 1: *150 Years of Painting in Australia*; Exhibition 2: *Some Recent Australian Painting*; Exhibition 3: *Since Conrad Martens*; Exhibition 4: *History of American Painting*; Exhibition 5: *A Group of Australian Paintings*; Exhibition 6: *Mortimer Menpes Reproductions of Old Masters*; Exhibition 7: *Twenty-One Australian Painters*.

28 Smith, 'Taking art to the Country', p. 36.

29 Some young artists living in the country remembered the encouragement they received from Smith's travelling exhibitions, including artist Earle Backen, who saw Smith's exhibitions in Wagga Wagga. Backen eventually became a teacher at the National Art School and the City Art Institute, Sydney.

30 *Report of the Minister for Public Instruction 1948*, Department of Public Instruction, Sydney, p. 7.

31 AGNSW Archive, National Art Gallery of New South Wales Board Minutes, 26 January 1945, p. 2741.

Bernard Smith and the professional art museum

JOANNA MENDELSSOHN

In July 1971 the University of Sydney student newspaper, *Honi Soit*, ran a special issue devoted to career opportunities for graduates. In a back-page article on careers in fine arts, Bernard Smith wrote that 'the demand for professional officers in art museums seems likely in the next five or six years at least, to considerably outrun supply'.[1]

He knew that a combination of the recent expansion of the National Gallery of Victoria, the soon to be re-opened Art Gallery of New South Wales (AGNSW) and the fledgling Australian National Gallery collection would be increasing their numbers of professional staff. He was also aware that in rural New South Wales there was growing community agitation in the larger centres as they aspired to at least equal Victoria by providing what Smith called 'provincial art galleries'. At a time when the once amateur museum profession was beginning to establish professional standards, Smith saw possible career paths for his graduating students. As well as canvassing possible careers in commercial galleries, school teaching and academic life, he especially urged new graduates to consider art museums, where:

> A University degree is sought for normally, although non-graduates have been accepted in the past for the simple reason that graduates, in most cases, have not been available. A pass major in the subject is desirable, but anyone with an

> Honours degree in the subject would be rather unlucky should they decide for professional work in museums and not to find a job fairly soon.[2]

The University of Sydney's first fine arts graduates had completed pass degrees at the end of 1970, and in 1971 nine students were undertaking the first honours year. As director of the Power Institute of Fine Arts, Smith structured the program so that the Power Curator, Elwyn Lynn, taught what was the first formal Australian university subject in museology to these students. In this context it does not matter that the course was woefully inadequate and consisted mainly of Lynn reminiscing on travelling to Europe and the United States to purchase works for the Power Collection. It was the start of a general recognition that universities were the appropriate places to teach those who would wish to be curators; this understanding would effectively supersede the tentative training courses begun by the Art Galleries Association of Australia (now amalgamated with Museums Australia).

In another lecture from about the same time, possibly for the Art Galleries Association's annual conference, Smith expanded on his claim for the importance of art museums, because 'the improvement of the public taste would lead to moral betterment and the emergence of a more cultivated and civilised society'.[3] Because of this there was a direct parallel with the nineteenth-century creation of universities as instruments of civilisation through education. This meant that 'we of the Art Museums and the University Art Departments have broadly common origins and a broadly common purpose' and so should come together on occasion for the common good of scholarship and of art. The partnership he advocated was hardly novel. At the University of Melbourne, Joseph Burke had established a close connection with the National Gallery of Victoria with his appointment to the Herald Chair of Fine Arts in 1946, but Smith saw an opportunity to take this further at Sydney with 'the establishment of a course in Museology, including museum administration, the assembling of exhibitions, the principles of conservation, cataloguing, museum and exhibition design'. Later, in 1976, he established that university's diploma of museum studies, the first of many postgraduate qualifications in museum studies and related fields throughout the country. His advocacy for this qualification extended to its graduates. Smith's initial contribution to the 1977 inaugural meeting of the Australian Gallery Directors' Council was to tell the delegates that 'several graduates from the Museums Studies course at the University of Sydney were still available for employment'.[4]

There is a remarkable consistency in Bernard Smith's concerns in establishing professional standards and scholarship in art museums. As has been well recorded, he came to scholarly writing and Australian art via both a public lecture program and Ure Smith's publication of *Place, Taste and Tradition* in 1945. The same year he applied for the position of director at the National Art Gallery of New South Wales (NAGNSW), which was at that time best described as primitive in its administrative structure. The position was awarded to Hal Missingham, whose intellectual generosity was combined with a well-recorded animosity to the bureaucracy of the Public Service Board and the gallery's trustees.[5] Smith's publisher, Sydney Ure Smith, the gallery trustee who had been Smith's main advocate for the position of director, was subsequently able to arrange for Bernard to be seconded from the Department of Education to the gallery in order to organise travelling art exhibitions throughout rural New South Wales. The NSW State Archives hold the records of the numerous layers of bureaucracy that both enabled this transition of Smith's career from primary-school teacher to *de facto* curator—and stymied it.

On 28 December 1945, J. W. Hayes, superintendent of primary education in New South Wales, wrote to Smith with an implied rebuke of this career direction: 'a perusal of your diaries shows that you spent an extraordinary amount of time at the National Art Gallery during the year'.[6] This brought an immediate response from Smith, which detailed, over two pages, twenty-six points on exactly what was entailed in organising a properly administered travelling art exhibition, and why so much time was needed with the art he was preparing for display:

1. Research for biographical material concerning artists for inclusion in catalogues of travelling art exhibitions.
2. Preparation of historical introductions etc, for catalogues of exhibitions.
3. Preparation of publicity material for use by country press in connection with travelling art exhibitions.
4. Preparation of talks to be given to children and to adults at country centres visited with exhibitions.
5. Preparation of talks to be given to Rotary clubs etc, and over country broadcasting stations during visits to country centres.

6. Discussing with Director nature of format, layout and material to be used in catalogues for country exhibitions.
7. Arranging suitable exhibitions and, with the advice of the Director, assembling art exhibitions for country circuits.
8. Approaching artists with the view to their lending pictures for country exhibitions.
9. Arranging for collection of pictures on loan from artists by carrier and their return when country circuits are completed.
10. Keeping lists of paintings on loan and providing for their insurance, safety, repair to frames where necessary etc.
11. Interviewing country visitors interested in country art exhibitions.
12. Interviewing artists who assist the scheme by guide lecturing in the country, in order to explain the nature of the procedure at a centre, or to review work completed.
13. Drafting preliminary itineraries at the beginning of each series of exhibitions.
14. Arranging for guide lecturers to attend country centres.
15. Arranging details concerning railway tickets, times of travelling, hotel accommodation for lecturers.
16. Keeping in communication with Town Clerks, Secretaries of art committees concerning organisation of exhibitions in country centres. A preliminary survey reveals that an average of six letters have to be framed and sent to each centre in order to finalise preliminary arrangements. Forty eight exhibitions were held during last year, an average of almost one a week.
17. Arrangements concerning the packing of pictures at Gallery, and continual supervision of freight movement of paintings from one centre to another. Making out of consignment notes etc. for this purpose.
18. Checking of returned catalogues, catalogue sales etc.
19. Printing and forwarding of invitation card-arrangements.
20. Arranging for the printing and forwarding to each centre of publicity display posters for shop windows etc.
21. Following up developments which arise out of country art exhibitions. Enquiries concerning later exhibitions, local exhibitions, proposed galleries, etc.
22. Arrangements with other galleries for the loan of paintings from other galleries, etc. to supplement the exhibition scheme. During the present year these have included, David Jones' Art Gallery, The Dixson Gallery of the Public Library,

The Commonwealth Library, Canberra, The Macquarie Galleries, Bligh St, Sydney, The American Offices of War Information.

23. Forwarding advice to country centres concerning methods of hanging paintings, lighting, colour of walls, etc.
24. Preparation of reports on travelling exhibitions for the Travelling Exhibitions Committee meetings.
25. Preparation of annual report on Country Art Exhibitions.
26. Reading materials and articles concerned with the organisation of travelling art exhibitions in England (English C.E.M.A.) and America.

> These include the regular items. It is apparently not appreciated that I was not seconded to the National Gallery to guide lecture country art exhibitions but to bring into existence and to direct a satisfactory country art exhibition scheme, and to guide lecture to the advantage of the scheme. It should be realised that the scheme requires regular and consistent centralised organisation. The scheme is not a travelling circus and I cannot organise from Albury what is taking place at Lismore.[7]

It is clear that Smith was even at this stage beginning to create the framework that later enabled his further research. It is also clear that he saw the value of the travelling art exhibitions not as a way of educating the taste of people in rural New South Wales, even though he deliberately (and sometimes provocatively) chose contemporary works for these country tours, but to give them a sense of the history of art in their own country:

> I said that I felt that I had a duty to show people in the country how art began here in this country, how it had changed, and let them see what was being done now.[8]

One of the long-term consequences of the travelling exhibitions was to encourage people in local centres to hold local art prizes and, in time, begin to lobby for their own arts centres. Unlike in the Victorian gold rush towns, there were few regional art galleries in rural New South Wales, and the travelling art exhibitions were very much a novelty.

As well as organising the travelling exhibitions, Smith used his years at the gallery to begin an arts degree at the University of Sydney. It is reasonable to assume that the subtext of the bureaucratic complaints about his activities was resentment at this educational ambition. In the 1940s teacher training in New South Wales was a two-year college program, followed by further internal testing. It was not usual for a primary-school teacher to undertake a university degree. However, in order to lift the educational level of the country, the NSW Public Service Board had enacted a policy to encourage public servants to enrol as part-time university students. Smith was therefore allowed five hours a week 'to permit your attendance at the University, in terms of their circular of 25th May 1945, subject to two hours per week being made up at a time convenient to the Department'.[9] Although he was officially only part-time, his first-year subject choice of English, history and archaeology reads suspiciously like a full-time load. In *A Pavane for Another Time*, Smith repeats the advice he received from Joseph Burke to 'regard your posting as a grant for research'.[10] It is very much to Smith's credit that his university studies became two-way traffic, so that the gallery ultimately benefited from his scholarship. He was at that time the only member of the gallery staff with any form of university education. The director, Hal Missingham, had trained as an artist, but his education had been entirely studio-based. The contrast between the necessarily *ad hoc* improvisations of his colleague and the rigour of academic study served to indicate to Smith the value of a university education for those wishing to work in art museums.

In 1982, in an address to the Art Museums Association and the Art Association, Smith obliquely drew on his own experiences when making a case for a continuing close relationship between universities and art museums. He argued for 'an essential identity of interest between the Art curatorial profession and the teaching of art history'. In what was more likely than not a comment on the recent development of highly commercialised blockbuster art exhibitions, he claimed that curators should not 'lower the status of their profession, by viewing themselves as popularisers'.[11] He also claimed that a 'period of years employed in a gallery in a curatorial capacity is of the greatest value in the training of any art historian', so he urged that the two institutions—art museums and universities—needed to recognise their mutual interdependence.[12]

Smith was writing at a time when the educational value of art museums was less recognised as a part of public policy than it is today, and his paper is in part advocacy for education through art. Despite the educational value of exposing students to collections and exhibitions, his substantial argument was that the most important value of art museums to universities was as a research tool:

> We would all be much better art historians and curators if we knew far more than we know at present why all those objects have been brought into our museums, for our enjoyment and admiration. What is their individual history, who and why were the[y] purchased [*sic*], and under what conditions were they purchased. We need to know more than we do about the moral, social, political and religious attitudes of the people, both acting individually or in committee responsible for the accessions.[13]

This was not an argument for the varied and complex administration of a series of travelling art exhibitions, as useful as that experience may have been for developing his broader understanding of the protocols of exhibition management. Rather it was a ringing endorsement of the research that underpinned *Australian Painting, 1788–1960*, which is a far more comprehensive account of Australia's art history than *Place, Taste and Tradition*.[14] In claiming the significance of catalogues to art historians, and the urgent need for all public museums to open access to detailed records of all their collections, he was again referring back to his own experience when he created the catalogue of Australian oil paintings in the NAGNSW.

In 1948, after completing only two years of an undergraduate degree, Smith applied for, and was granted, a British Council scholarship to the Courtauld Institute in order to study 'the English contribution to the beginnings of art in Australia'.[15] The awarding of this scholarship to someone without a degree was unusual, to say the least. Dates come into play here. In the years immediately after World War II, when former soldiers were resuming their academic studies, the world was in a state of flux. Internationally there was a reordering of priorities to educate the generation damaged by both the Great Depression and war. At a time when many were underqualified it was easier for someone with a certain degree of self-confidence to take opportunities as they were offered. In Smith's case there was another reason for his success. The publication of *Place, Taste and Tradition* meant that he was one of Australia's few art historians, and he was also able to give due emphasis to his work as the gallery's travelling art education officer. His application was well supported by Daryl Lindsay, director of the National Gallery of Victoria, and Hal Missingham. His only academic referee was Professor Dale Trendall, curator of the Nicholson Museum of antiquities at the University of Sydney. Smith does note that he was strategic in failing to mention in his application that he was a current undergraduate student: 'I was becoming adept at weaving my way through the labyrinths of bureaucracy'.[16]

Smith returned to Sydney in January 1951, having spent some months educating himself by immersion in the great art of Europe and having published the essay version of his seminal research, 'European Vision and the South Pacific'.[17] He had studied under the great art historians—Blunt, Wittkower, Gombrich and Summerson—and he had a vision of what should be possible: to create art histories in the provincial backwater of Sydney.

As a previously active Communist Party member, Smith was especially vulnerable in the political climate of the Cold War. His longstanding patron Sydney Ure Smith had died in 1949. Hal Missingham, who was a member of the communist front artists' group, the Studio of Realist Art (SORA), had to defend himself against public accusations of being a communist.[18] The gallery trustees' minutes reveal that anti-communist attacks on the gallery had preceded Smith's departure for Europe. In August 1948 one of the trustees expressed concern about a *Sydney Morning Herald* article on 'How Communism is Infiltrating Cultural Organisations', which had led to Missingham being warned to 'be more circumspect in statements not dealing directly with normal gallery activities'.[19] In this climate it is understandable that Smith's employer, the Department of Education, wished to see him out of the public eye, with his most likely destination being the Newcastle Teachers' College, over 180 kilometres north of Sydney. This would have had the exquisite advantage of officially promoting him out of the classroom but placing him in a communist-dominated working-class cultural backwater, a ghetto for dissident teachers where he could never complete his degree.

There are slightly varying accounts of how the newly returned scholar managed to avoid being relegated to the provinces by creating one of his most important publications, the catalogue of Australian oil paintings in the NAGNSW. In *A Pavane for Another Time* Smith wrote that when he returned to the gallery he found someone else was running the travelling art exhibitions program and Tony Tuckson was the new assistant to the director.[20]

From the perspective of the Public Service Board, Tuckson had a number of advantages as an employee. He was English, had been educated at Christ's College, and was therefore from a superior social class to the proletarian Missingham or Smith. Most importantly, in the cultural context of postwar Australia, Tuckson had seen active service as a Spitfire pilot, while Smith had successfully avoided active military service.

Smith wrote that in order to pre-empt any move the department might make against him, he paid a visit to the president of the trustees, E. B. Waterhouse, and described his idea of producing a scholarly catalogue of the gallery's Australian oil paintings, based on Martin Davies' catalogues of the National Gallery collection in London. He did this because 'Australian public collections were quite unknown in Europe, mainly because of the lack of scholarly catalogues'. Waterhouse had admired Smith's earlier work on the travelling art exhibitions and appreciated his skill, so he 'promised to give his support to my idea'. In Smith's mind this support was also coloured by the traditional antagonism between the Public Service Board and the gallery trustees.[21] Once Waterhouse's support was secured, Smith then called on the Evatts, because Mrs Evatt was one of his longtime supporters among the trustees, while Dr Evatt was leader of the Labor opposition. Dr Evatt gave him the necessary introduction to another trustee, J. P. (Jack) Glasheen, who was a recent right-wing Labor Party political appointment to the Public Service Board. Smith suspected Glasheen of being a Grouper, a part of the anti-communist movement that would later form the Democratic Labour Party, but this did not prevent Glasheen from helping him:

> I suspect that Glasheen intended to get me out of the Gallery if he could, convinced that in my capacity as organiser of the country art shows I had been corrupting the taste and morals of country children. Sitting quietly at a desk compiling a catalogue I would be less of a nuisance.[22]

A Pavane for Another Time is a memoir, and memoirs are documents in which the patina of time mutes the tones and softens the edges of the past. One of the problems with Smith's interpretation of events is that, even in his old age, he saw everything through a filter of faction fights and personal power struggles. So in his explanation as to why Waterhouse supported his proposal, Smith claims that 'he himself probably resented the pressure then being put upon the Trust by the Public Service Board and the Education Department'. This may well be true, but Waterhouse had earlier written a congratulatory letter when *Place, Taste and Tradition* was first published, calling it 'a fine contribution'.[23] There was another reason why the erudite and scholarly Waterhouse would have welcomed a keen young scholar able to write a complete catalogue of the gallery's poorly recorded collection. The June 1941 minutes of the trustees recorded that the director of the gallery, at that time Will Ashton:

> submitted a number of biographical notes on Australian artists and a description of their paintings. The general idea embodied in the notes submitted by the Director was approved, but it was deemed preferable to defer the matter until the Director returned from America. He would then be able to inform the Trustees as to the method adopted there.[24]

Ten years later the war was over and it was time to think again of optimistic projects. In doing so the trustees were keen to adopt the best, internationally approved methods. Smith's appointment was confirmed at the board meeting of 23 February 1951, a relatively swift decision by the standards of the New South Wales public service.[25] For the next two years he worked in an alcove at the far end of the boardroom in what is now a gallery exhibiting Australian art.[26] Here he combined catalogue worksheets, archival research, and correspondence with living artists, to create one of the most significant documents in Australian art history.

A Catalogue of Australian Oil Paintings in the National Art Gallery of New South Wales was not the first publication on the gallery's collection. There had been a series of illustrated catalogues in the 1880s and 1890s, as well as a picture book in 1931, but the information contained in them is scant.[27] The limitation of Smith's publication is that it is confined to oil paintings. In his final report, submitted for the trustees' meeting of 18 December 1953, Smith wrote of a second volume:

> The manuscript of this catalogue comprising 468 items and 87 brief biographies (of artists not represented in the oils catalogue) is as complete as I can make it. Five paintings have not been located and it has not been possible to obtain facts about a few minor artists. The form of the catalogue follows the oils catalogue but

> I have added in almost every case a brief verbal description of each painting. The manuscript will be ready for the typist at the end of the year.[28]

Even though Smith offered 'to act in a consultative capacity if necessary while the two catalogues are in the press provided the time involved is not excessive', the offer was not taken up and the watercolour catalogue remained unpublished. Nevertheless this catalogue of Australian oil paintings still stands as a benchmark to enable future histories of Australian art, and its scholarly significance cannot be overestimated. The introductory note states:

> No attempt is made in this catalogue to define the frontiers of Australian painting. The inclusion of a painting has been determined by a practical consideration; can it be said to be of Australian interest?[29]

This is why the catalogue included expatriate works by Roy De Maistre, who had permanently relocated to England in the 1920s, as well as paintings by Charles Conder and Girolamo Nerli, who spent only a few short years in Australia before returning to Europe. All had a profound influence on the narratives of Australian art, so all belonged in the canon of Australian art history. Smith also incorporated paintings that the trustees had transferred to the Mitchell Library in the 1920s at a time when history was not seen as a part of the gallery's brief. These included Sydney Long's paintings of old Sydney, painted as a part of a project to record a city that was about to vanish. They are now seen as central to Australia's art history. Although they were no longer in the gallery's collection, the catalogue treated them with respect, giving a full provenance, referring to exhibition history, media commentary and a condition report.[30]

A catalogue of a collection is a democratic document in that it treats both well-known and little-known works in a similar manner. Even though there are no images in Smith's catalogue, the result provided the basis for a more nuanced picture of Australian art—albeit one with a strong bias towards New South Wales artists. In order to write a catalogue entry, the art historian needs to physically examine the work in question. This close connection with the materiality of art, as well as the intellectual exercise of linking art to archive, helped temper Smith's approach to the past.

For the modern reader, it is the biographies that accompany each entry that make this catalogue outstanding. Here is the first publication of accurate biographical material on many Australian artists, including newspaper references from critiques when the works were first exhibited and collected. In this Smith was aided by the gallery's archive, which earlier generations of trustees had ensured included comprehensive press cuttings, annotated catalogues and old illustrated journals. Smith describes the room where they were kept as a place where 'old minutes of Board meetings and kindred documents lay in heavy leather-bound volumes, shrouded in layers of the silent dust of the past'.[31] His respect for this material helped the gallery continue to archive both its records and those of Australian artists, an act that has encouraged further research.

Smith wrote of his biographical notes that they were 'fairly detailed. These have been considered desirable in the absence of any comprehensive dictionary of Australian artists'.[32] Perhaps it was the context, but in this description Smith was being uncharacteristically modest. The only previously published collections of biographies on Australian artists were brief notes in the second volume of William Moore's 1934 *The Story of Australian Art*,[33] and some seriously inaccurate anecdotes in Herbert Badham's *A Study of Australian Art*,[34] published in 1949 as a rejoinder to *Place, Taste and Tradition*.[35] Smith's biographies are distinguished from these others by their detailed referencing of primary sources. As well as compiling bibliographic material, he created foolscap worksheets, which he sent to artists so that he could collate their chronologies. These entered the artists' files in the gallery's records, providing an invaluable record for future researchers. It could almost be argued that in these biographical notes he started the first draft of his later project to create a dictionary of Australian artists.

The data for the biographies had another consequence. In 1959, when Smith was writing *Australian Painting* for Oxford University Press, he was able to contact Grace Cossington Smith, who is named by Moore as one of the early followers of post-impressionism in Australia, and is a minor figure in *Place, Taste and Tradition*.[36] By the early 1950s four of her minor recent works were in the gallery's collection. As she exhibited with the Society of Artists, Badham, who had also noticed her and with characteristic incompetence had conflated her radical 1915 paintings with her more conventional 1940s paintings, downplayed her achievement as 'apt rather than searching ... although her colour sense is personal, fresh and delicate and her key is high and appropriate to her schemes'.[37] Smith believed in primary sources. As discussed in this volume by the younger Kate Challis, he wrote to Cossington Smith, then visited her in her Turramurra home, where he saw *The sock knitter*, that most radical of all early modernist works, which had remained unseen by all except family and friends since 1915 (Fig. 23). Smith was no longer connected to the gallery, but wrote to the new curatorial assistant, Daniel Thomas, to tell him about this treasure trove, an act that led directly to the gallery's magnificent holdings of Grace Cossington Smith's works. Bernard bought *The school cape* for himself (Fig. 24). In 1989 he sold this and other works from his collection to establish the RAKA to honour his late wife.[38]

Throughout the rest of his career Bernard Smith saw the nexus between art in the studio, art in the museum and art history as taught by the university. When he was appointed the first Power Professor in 1967 he realised that the AGNSW needed to have the same fruitful relationship with the University of Sydney as the National Gallery of Victoria had with the University of Melbourne, and he worked to foster those connections.[39] Gradually, organically, graduates from both this degree and other university degrees in art and art history joined the professional staff as the gallery transformed so that academic and curatorial traditions could continue to inform each other.

NOTES

1 Bernard Smith, 'Careers in Fine Arts', *Honi Soit*, July 1971, p. 32.

2 ibid.

3 Bernard Smith, 'The Art Museum and the University', National Library of Australia, Canberra, Bernard Smith Papers (hereafter NLA, BSP), MS8680, Folder 27, Item 12. There is an amusing crossed-out reference to Brian Finemore's taste for fine dining. Finemore was curator of Australian art at the National Gallery of Victoria. I have kept Smith's spelling and capitalisation.

4 Minutes of Inaugural Meeting of the Australian Gallery Directors' Council, 21–22 February 1977, inserted in the 1977 volume of the Minutes of the Trustees of the Art Gallery of New South Wales.

5 Hal Missingham, *They Kill You in the End*, Angus & Robertson, Sydney, 1973.

6 J. W. Hayes to Mr B. Smith, 28 February 1945, State Records NSW, Sydney, Travelling [Country] Art Exhbitions, File 6/23146.7.

7 State Records NSW, Sydney, Travelling [Country] Art Exhibitions, File 6/23146.7.

8 Bernard Smith, 'Art Galleries and the Teaching of Art History', keynote address to the Art Association of Australia and the Art Museums Association of Australia Annual Conference, 7 August 1982. NLA, BSP, MS8680, Folder 36, Item 14, p. 9.

9 N. L. Salmon to Mr B. Smith, 23 July 1946, State Records NSW, Travelling [Country] Art Exhibitions, File 6/23146.7.

10 Bernard Smith, *A Pavane for Another Time*, MacMillan, Melbourne, 2002, p. 152.

11 Smith, 'Art Galleries and the Teaching of Art History', p. 1.

12 ibid., p. 1.

13 ibid., pp. 4–5.

14 Bernard Smith, *Australian Painting, 1788–1960*, Oxford University Press, Melbourne, 1962.

15 Smith, *A Pavane for Another Time*, p. 156.

16 ibid., p. 157.

17 Bernard Smith, 'European Vision and the South Pacific', *Journal of the Warburg and Courtauld Institutes*, no. 13, 1950, pp. 66–100.

18 Missingham, *They Kill You in the End*, pp. 11–12.

19 Minutes of the Trustees of the National Art Gallery of New South Wales, 27 August 1948, p. 3039

20 Smith, *A Pavane for Another Time*, p. 454.

21 ibid., p. 455.

22 ibid., p. 456.

23 Information from Steven Miller, Archivist, Art Gallery of New South Wales, 7 November 2012.

24 Minutes of the Trustees of the National Art Gallery of New South Wales, 27 June 1941.

25 State Records NSW, Travelling [Country] Art Exhibitions, File 6/23146.7.

26 Smith, *A Pavane for Another Time*, p. 458.

27 The earliest is *Catalogue of the National Art Gallery of New South Wales*, John Sands, Sydney, 1884. There is no author cited, but the director, 'E. L. Montefiore and others' are credited with the line drawing illustrations. *New South Wales Art Gallery Pictures*, with an introduction by J. S. MacDonald and published by the Trustees in 1931, also has no named author.

28 Loose page inserted into the minutes of the Trustees of the National Art Gallery of New South Wales, 18 December 1953.

29 Bernard Smith, *A Catalogue of Australian Oil Paintings in the National Art Gallery of New South Wales, 1875–1952: With Annotations, Biographies and Index*, National Art Gallery of New South Wales, Sydney, 1953, [p. 6.].

30 ibid., pp. 126–7.

31 Smith, *A Pavane for Another Time*, p. 458.

32 Smith, *A Catalogue*, [p. 6].

33 William Moore, *The Story of Australian Art*, Angus & Robertson, Sydney, 1934.

34 Herbert E. Badham, *A Study of Australian Art*, Currawong Publishing, Sydney, 1949.

35 Bernard Smith, *Place, Taste and Tradition*, Ure Smith, Sydney, 1945.

36 Moore, *The Story of Australian Art*, vol. 1, p. 229; Smith, *Place, Taste and Tradition*, p. 182.

37 Badham, *A Study of Australian Art*, pp. 116–17.

38 Joanna Mendelssohn, 'A Gift for Utopia', *The Bulletin* (Sydney), 25 July 1989, pp. 98–9.

39 In 1972 and 1973 Smith arranged for Daniel Thomas, then senior curator, to give a series of introductory lectures on Australian art to second-year undergraduate students.

Mind the gap!

Bernard Smith versus the museum, 1961 to 1995

CHRISTOPHER R. MARSHALL

Throughout his career, Bernard Smith manifested a characteristically complex attitude towards the idea of the museum as institution. On the one hand, his political sensibilities made him profoundly suspicious of any lingering association that the museum might have then had with the legacies of authoritarianism and elitism. In 1946 he accordingly denounced 'the futility of art museums' for maintaining an exclusionary attitude towards their audiences—an attitude that was anathema to his own more socially inclusive commitment to full public programming and art education:

> National galleries, to put the matter bluntly, have been expressions of pride rather than expressions of the love of art ... These galleries with their towering Roman façades, their 'palace of art' courts, and finally their temporary galleries which degenerated into outhouses and slum-like oddities in the rear, became excellent examples in themselves of most of the qualities of bad art. The haphazard planning was evidence of haphazard thinking, a product of the inability to decide whether an art museum should be a civic monument or should perform a specific educational function. Art museums, that is to say, have not fulfilled the intentions of their founders. At least not if we take them seriously.[1]

It is characteristic of the complexity of Smith's thinking on the museum—as on so many of the topics explored in this volume—that he was able to accommodate a number of different perspectives—even at times seemingly contradictory ones. Thus, while he remained wedded to a socially progressive view of the importance of full public participation in museums, he was also committed to a traditional—and in its own way also elitist—model of the curator as specialist keeper whose worth was to be judged on the basis of a deep and abiding specialised research into the permanent collections. As a result, Smith published frequently on the need for curators to remain fixed, not so much on the superficial distractions of populist temporary exhibitions, as rather on their long-term commitment to producing impeccably researched permanent collection catalogues based on the model of Martin Davies' postwar publications on the National Gallery, London.

Smith's major intervention into this field was in his championing of the need for Australian museums and galleries to produce well-researched catalogues raisonnés of the works in their collections, following the model of his own *Catalogue of Australian Oil Paintings in the National Art Gallery of New South Wales* (1953). As noted elsewhere in this volume, his contribution in this area was significant, but in many ways it did not bear long-lasting fruit. Smith's own subsequent comments reflect his ultimate disillusionment with subsequent Australian museum scholarship:

> When I published *A Catalogue of Oil Paintings in the National [Art] Gallery of New South Wales* in 1953 I had hoped that similar sectional catalogues would appear within a few years from most of the other state galleries. But the lack of interest in cheaply priced, scholarly catalogues has been shattering. Scholarly work is directed excessively to current exhibitions. Perhaps the Internet will eventually solve the problem and curators of Australian art and other kinds of art in our museums will at last become experts in the whole field of what it is they curate, instead of experts in dreaming up novel frameworks for ephemeral shows.[2]

This chapter will examine this complex attitude as it manifested itself in two noteworthy instances of Bernard Smith's public agitation against high-profile museum redevelopment projects.

The first case study dates to early 1961, when Smith chose to speak out publicly against the prevailing mood of civic pride and optimism that otherwise characterised the release of initial information about the proposed design for the new National Gallery of Victoria, formulated by Roy Grounds in close consultation with the gallery's modernising director, Eric Westbrook.[3]

As is well known from the official histories of the National Gallery of Victoria (NGV), plans to move the gallery out of its original cramped location in the old Swanston Street complex comprising the State Library of Victoria, National Gallery of Victoria, Applied Science Museum of Victoria and National Museum of Victoria had been gathering pace since the late 1950s. Roy Grounds had been appointed architect in December 1959, and both he and Eric Westbrook had left Melbourne in the second half of 1960 for a study tour of European and American galleries and museums. The presentation drawings of the new museum prepared by Grounds' office, and Westbrook's enthusiastic descriptions of its innovative design features, had been released to the public as part of a major fundraising campaign in late 1960, following their return.

One aspect of the new designs attracted particular attention and caused growing ripples of concern to spread among the Melbourne cultural circles of the day. Eric Westbrook initially explained this feature in positive terms in a media interview of early 1961:

> To allow natural light to filter down the walls of the gallery to illuminate works of art, the first, second and third floors will not extend the full 50-foot width of the galleries. Instead they will be cantilevered 'floating' platforms. The gallery will be the first in the world to use these 'floating' floors and it will solve a natural lighting problem that has defied experts throughout the world. Many of the works of art will be illuminated by a combination of daylight and artificial lighting.[4]

Grounds' and Westbrook's solution to the problem of how to bring natural top-lit illumination into the lower levels of the new gallery was thus as ingenious as it soon proved to be contentious. They proposed to construct a floating upper floor that created a gap between the viewer and the paintings on the walls. In fact, it did not take long for misgivings about this idea to circulate in the press. The first criticisms were voiced by the Adelaide-based architect and academic David Saunders, who published a critical review of the proposal in *The Nation*. In it, he characterised the idea of a five-foot gap between viewers and artworks in memorable terms as constituting a 'cultural gap'.[5] In an otherwise studiously even-handed review of the project, published in *Meanjin* in April 1961, Franz Philipp, lecturer in art history in the Department of Fine Arts, University of Melbourne, also expressed his misgivings, stating that 'The most serious apprehension arises over the proposal to separate paintings and viewers by a gap of about five feet'.[6]

It was at this stage that Bernard Smith entered the debate. Seizing on the 'cultural gap' idea presented in Saunders' earlier article, Smith expanded on the notion of an ensuing sense of cultural alienation that would potentially be created in the mind of the viewer as a result of this proposal. In a long article published in *The Nation* in April 1961 he accordingly drew out an extended and overtly Marxist metaphor of contemporary Australian art audiences being made to feel like cowed, neo-colonial convicts in a new gallery that should do everything in its power, rather, to make them feel at home. He began by noting the fundamental importance of closely studying paintings in order to appreciate their technique, observing that:

> if they [the public] should dare to study painting technique at all closely on the upper display floor of the new Cultural Centre they will tumble over the balustrade into a chasm twenty or more feet deep. I can think of no better way of discouraging the public from the full enjoyments that painting can provide.[7]

Perhaps more revealing of Smith's political sensibilities was his picking up on one of the points raised by the director of London's National Gallery and all-round influential arbiter of cultural taste, Kenneth Clark, during an earlier visit to Melbourne in 1949 to publicise the idea of a new museum for the city. On that occasion, Clark had noted that a good gallery should present artworks in a manner that encourages viewers to feel a sense of intimacy with them—almost as if he or she were visiting works in their own collection.[8] Smith's riposte to this was to note that:

> a balustrade and chasm five feet wide and twenty feet deep will not make the visitor feel in the least like a private collector with his possessions. It will make him feel more like a potential vandal, a proto-convict from whom the treasures of the state must be protected at all cost.[9]

In voicing these concerns, Smith would have been encouraged by knowing that many others in Melbourne's close-knit institutional arts scene were experiencing similar misgivings—not only Franz Philipp and his colleague Ursula Hoff, but also the painter John Brack (soon to become director of the National Gallery Art School)[10] and, most influentially of all, Professor Joseph Burke—Herald Chair of Fine Arts at the university. Burke was not only a recent trustee and current member of the Felton Bequest Committee, but was also at that stage a member of the Cultural Centre Building Committee charged with supervising the commission.

The archived Cultural Centre Building Committee documents contain a revealing exchange of letters between Burke and Grounds, dated to this same month of April 1961. These are stated as having been written in direct response to the issues raised in Smith's article and were forwarded to the committee, evidently in order that they be tabled and discussed as indications of the differing positions in the debate about the design.[11] The first document of the group is a letter from Grounds to Burke dated 13 April 1961. In it, Grounds attempted to assuage Professor Burke's concerns by suggesting that the degree to which the galleries would be truly free-floating had been overstated in the press. Grounds wished to emphasise, in this respect, the following key points:

> The display galleries are on two floors, the ground floor and one other. On the ground floor, there is no fixed physical obstruction to the public's inspection of pictures at close quarters. That takes care of half of the total display area. On the other floor, there is no balustrade, gap or obstruction between the viewer and the picture for 60% of the area. In the total display areas, that makes 80% of the space, wall and floor areas with unrestricted access for examining pictures at close quarters, i.e., bang on. The remaining 20% is to provide a facility for the gallery staff to show works of art of any kind, if they so desire, under conditions where the public cannot touch them, but can study them from a distance of five feet or more.

These comments appear somewhat disingenuous, in fact, given that the only design published of the interior had, in fact, featured the balustrade prominently and that Westbrook had, as previously noted, further stressed the significance of the balustrade as a major innovative emphasis of the new plans (Fig. 25).

In his tabled response, Professor Burke chose to take the high moral ground and refused to engage with the architect on specifics. Rather, he took issue with Grounds on the more fundamental basis of a supposed failure to listen to the 'experts' with whom he felt Grounds should have consulted prior to formalising his designs. As he put it:

> The principle is that the architect of an art gallery should consult with the professional experts ... The professional experts in this case fall into two groups. There are the general experts with a first-hand knowledge of the collections, namely Eric Westbrook, Gordon Thomson, Sir Daryl Lindsay and, overseas Sir Kenneth Clark, Dr Boase, Professor Pevsner and Dr Milliken. Secondly there are the specialists in particular periods, again with a first-hand knowledge of the collections. These are Franz Philipp for the late Middle Ages and Renaissance, Dr. Hoff for the seventeenth century, myself for the eighteenth century and Bernard Smith for the nineteenth century and Australian art.

He goes on to note that Grounds had agreed to this principle but then did not consult with them—and he finishes: 'I regard it as essential that the Committee should reassure public opinion that no pictures will be separated from any class of spectator by a barrier of five feet'.[12]

This concerted opposition seems to have had the desired effect of forcing Grounds (and Westbrook, who supported Grounds' plans) to modify his thinking. An additional exchange of letters archived in the Cultural Building Committee documents indicates that a number of other members of the committee, including Leonard Cox, the Building Committee's chairman as well as chairman of the gallery trustees,[13] also came to share Burke's views. Grounds' reply to the Building Committee's CEO, John David Rogers, dated 31 May 1961, witnesses him backtracking yet further by suggesting that his initial design with the free-floating galleries was merely an early idea to give a basic concept of the galleries. He accordingly notes that the sketches that prompted the debate were only meant to be indicative and:

> were not prepared for consideration by the Building Committee or for critical study by professionals or semi-professionals. They bear as much relationship to the likely finished design as does the poster produced for fund raising purposes.[14]

The criticisms made by Smith, Professor Burke and other members of the Department of Fine Arts, and other figures from among the Melbourne cultural elites, accordingly forced Grounds and Westbrook to modify their plans and retract the idea of the 'floating balcony'. However, Smith and the other critics did not entirely subdue Grounds' and Westbrook's desire to find some other means of creating continuous top-to-bottom lighting stretching down from the third to the ground floors. In fact, a second round of more internalised controversy on this point subsequently erupted, when it was discovered in late 1963 that Grounds had changed his plans to incorporate a modified plan for a series of zig-zag screens—or triangular gaps—on the walls of the upper second-floor galleries (the galleries dedicated to European and Australian art). As planned, these gaps would effectively have created channels running down from the second to the first floor to allow light from the ceiling to reach the galleries on the lower floor below. Ultimately Grounds and Westbrook (who continued to support the aesthetic integrity of his architect's conception on this point) were also defeated in this modified version of their plans by a concerted push by the staff of the gallery (including, most notably, Ursula Hoff) with the continued support of members of the Building Committee, who ultimately referred the issue to the trustees. The trustees strongly recommended a rethinking of Grounds' and Westbrook's plans.[15]

So, in this first case study, we see an unpopular architectural design element proposed for a museum being overturned by the concerted efforts of Bernard Smith acting in alliance with a united and closely convergent group of artists, museum professionals and academics. The second case study, dating to the end of Smith's career, presents the reverse of this process.

In the early 1990s the Museum of Victoria finally found itself in a position to secure its own migration and relocation out of its cramped original location in the State Library complex. The museum's solution to its modernisation and redevelopment imperative, however, was much more fraught and politically turbulent than that of the National Gallery of Victoria some thirty years earlier.[16] The initial plans for relocating the museum had involved its removal to the south bank of the River Yarra. By 1992 this proposal had been formally adopted—following many delays and iterations—and planning had gone as far as the creation of a finished design and laying-in of concrete foundations for the Daryl Jackson-commissioned new museum building to be erected on this site.

In October 1992, however, this scheme was thrown into disarray by the election of a new Liberal–National Coalition state government, which proceeded to cancel the south bank museum project as part of its longstanding opposition to the previous Labor government's plans for the museum's renovation. With the Southbank site to be reserved instead for a new revenue-generating casino and nearby exhibition and convention centre, the Coalition government moved quickly to identify the area adjoining the 1880 Royal Exhibition Building in Carlton Gardens as a more appropriate site for the new museum. In 1994 the architectural firm of Denton Corker Marshall (DCM) was awarded the contract for the museum as part of its broader brief during this period to act as the government's preferred architects, responsible for a number of its major infrastructure projects, including the Melbourne Convention and Exhibition Centre and the Melbourne International Gateway to the CityLink Freeway.[17]

It was inevitable that Bernard Smith, as a long-term inner-city resident living close by the Carlton Gardens, would be drawn to join ranks with those opposed to this project. Smith's opposition was based, in part, on a continuation of many of the same principles of locally based, grass-roots activism directed against state government and big-business-led inner-city urban development that had characterised his earlier time agitating against inappropriate development in the inner-Sydney suburb of Glebe during the late 1960s to mid-1970s (as described in this volume by Max Solling).[18] In this case, Smith and his fellow Melbourne activists opposed what they saw as an inherently inappropriate encroachment of the museum onto the cultural heritage and public amenity of the neighbouring Carlton Gardens on the one side of the museum, and the heritage-listed Royal Exhibition Building of 1880 on the other. They also opposed what they saw as the museum's problematic location on the outskirts of the city, away from major public transport infrastructure, and they immediately began to circulate a spirited series of arguments against the museum in media and local publications (Fig. 26).

Bernard Smith joined with Miles Lewis, professor of architecture at the University of Melbourne, to become one of the most outspoken and influential critics of the project. He wrote no fewer than three substantial letters to the editor, together with a stand-alone article, which were all published in *The Age* between 25 November and 27 December 1995.[19] His criticisms followed the major points raised by the opponents of the project. But the feature that particularly drew his opprobrium and over which he particularly crossed swords with his opponents was the 80-metre-long roof of the new Forest Gallery. This central element of the museum was conceived by DCM as the new building's major design feature. While much of DCM's museum as built is noteworthy for its relative functionality and minimalism of design, this feature, by contrast, seeks to break free of its surrounds and impress itself upon the viewer as an iconic architectural feature stretching diagonally high above the main building and acting as a prominent inner-city marker, visible from many kilometres' distance.

Smith was strongly opposed to this, seeing it (correctly as it transpired) as a major visual intrusion that would significantly block views of the 1880 Exhibition Building—particularly the long-established vista along the archetypal Victorian streetscape of Canning Street, for which the Exhibition Building had always acted as the culminating point of visual reference (Fig. 27). He was accordingly particularly outspoken in his denunciation of this capstone feature of DCM's new design:

> We have been informed that the Blade thrusting up from the Northern centre of the building is 11 metres lower than the dome of the Royal Exhibition Building, that it will obscure the dome at only two degrees of the circle, and that it will complement the dome agreeably. What irrelevant nonsense! Both dome and blade will be seen from perspectives at ground level. At all points on the Northern side of the gardens, wherever dome and blade can be glimpsed through the trees, the tumescent penis-like blade will be nudging, or juxtaposed to, the breast of the dome. From many aspects it will be seen poking up its head in the air much higher than the dome itself, like the grab end of a bulldozer. What an optical triumph that will be for the male ego! The present handsome vista of the dome all the way down Canning Street Carlton will be destroyed. What ignorance! What insensitivity! Perhaps it's time that architects and designers, even here in Australia, began to think more seriously, not only about the visual symbolism of architecture and its implicit sexual connotations, but their own ambitiously wayward unconscious drives as well.[20]

Smith revived his gendered and quasi-psychoanalytical metaphor in a final article, published in the arts section of *The Age* on 27 December:

> Now a gigantic 'blade', misbegotten stairway to nowhere, will be perched on the roof of the DCM erection to compete with the Dome from all sides. In my view

> it will also effect a devastatingly symbolic change. Juxtaposed to the blade, the dome, with both seen high in the sky, will be transmogrified symbolically from a breast into a scrotum. The new museum, if built as presently designed, may come to be admired not as a triumph of 21st century modernity, but as the cock and scrotum exhibition.[21]

The essential points of Smith's criticisms regarding the visually obtrusive elements of the new museum were well taken. However, the colourful nature of his gendered metaphor of the blade proved distracting, eliciting a number of responses, not all of them positive. In particular, Norman Day, lecturer in architecture and design at the Royal Melbourne Institute of Technology, as well as architecture critic for *The Age*, took issue with Smith's ideas, labelling the sexualised metaphor as a 'corrupt and passé notion'. Day argued: 'It is plainly not so that buildings necessarily take on these characteristics and to imply that somehow the old girl is to be violated by the new boy is arrant nonsense'. In Day's opinion, the museum's design was, rather, to be applauded as 'a building for this time … to be respected, enjoyed and protected by future generations'.[22]

Undeterred by this rebuttal, Smith, in order to cap off his campaign, then acted as co-signatory to a more formal group letter of 23 May 1996 that rearticulated the group's major criticisms of the project. The letter was also signed by Professor Miles Lewis, together with a number of other influential members of the Melbourne cultural and political landscape: Barry Humphries (of Dame Edna Everage fame), Trevor Huggard (former Lord Mayor of Melbourne), Rosemary Stott (Melbourne City Councillor), Professor Evan Walker (former Cain state Labor government minister for planning), and Professor David Yencken (president of the Australian Conservation Foundation).[23] By this stage, though, the momentum of opposition to the project had passed. The Melbourne Museum formed one important item on the newly elected government's ambitious agenda to re-brand Melbourne as an entrepreneurial and business-friendly city—'on the move'—characterised by boldly designed, contemporary infrastructure developments. Indeed, many of these were by DCM, whose jutting 'blade' trademark would come to be synonymous with this period, appearing not only on the Melbourne Museum but also at the Melbourne Gateway to the CityLink Freeway, and the Melbourne Exhibition Centre. This new government was, moreover, fully in the ascendancy and in no mood to countenance any opposition to its reformist agenda. It 'took decisions with breathtaking speed' —as the official history of the museum puts it:

> and brooked no argument. It not only believed it had a mandate, it also had, thanks to the projected revenue from the new Casino, money to spend on public works beyond the wildest dreams of any previous Victorian Government.[24]

A further significant point of difference between Bernard Smith's museum agitation of 1961 and his push against the Melbourne Museum during the 1990s was that the latter opposition, of which he formed part, was divided among itself. Moreover, it lacked the internally based influence and convergence of interests that, as we saw, were so effective in the case of the National Gallery of Victoria. In particular, the staff and board of the Melbourne Museum were in no position to protest effectively, having been worn down by years of funding shortfalls and setbacks to their decades-long plans for relocating the museum. In addition, the National Trust, whom one might otherwise have assumed to be a natural ally in the cause against the new building, was, in point of fact, significantly unresolved on the matter. After months of anguished discussion, the Trust ultimately came out in support of the project—a highly controversial decision that won it many enemies but that it took on the grounds that it would stop, in its opinion, the Royal Exhibition Building from becoming a 'white elephant' and that would create instead a 'viable, long term use for the building that would ensure that it would be preserved in perpetuity'.[25]

So it was that on 21 October 2000 the Melbourne Museum opened to the public, at a final cost of $300 million. In a perhaps emblematic footnote, the new Premier of Victoria, Steve Bracks—the Labor Party having only recently overthrown the Coalition government in a surprise election win—was hit by a cream pie. This was not thrown by an individual protesting against the museum's siting on the Carlton Gardens, but rather by a youth who had earlier taken part in the protests against the World Economic Forum held in Melbourne in September 2000—those protests forming an early instance of the anti-global corporate protests that gathered pace significantly in the years thereafter.[26]

All of this contrasts markedly with the more effectively self-contained protest that characterised Bernard Smith's 1961 tilt against the National Gallery of Victoria's contentious new gallery designs. That earlier protest demonstrated the very great distance that the museum sector had travelled between the 1960s and the turn of the millennium. In 1961 a museum controversy could be handled 'in house' by the museum staff and the cultural elites that supported their activities. As an influential academic commentator and lecturer in the Department of Fine Arts, Bernard Smith was very much part of this small and influential insiders' group—as witnessed also by the strong convergence of views between himself and his university colleagues Joseph Burke, Franz Philipp and Ursula Hoff—in other words, between the entire Department of Fine Arts as it then stood.

By the 1990s, by contrast, the concept of the museum had evolved towards a much more outwardly oriented—and also more uncertain—terrain. The museum of the millennium was beholden instead to a more complex and wide-ranging group of stakeholders, external interest groups, and political and media alliances. It was no longer possible for an academic commentator like Bernard Smith, or Miles Lewis, or Joseph Burke, to wield the internally consistent influence that they had been able to achieve in earlier decades. These two case studies accordingly provide rare insight into the public discourse surrounding Australian museums. At the same time, though, they are also revealing for the different ways that the museum has come to present itself to the public between the 1960s and now.

NOTES

1 Bernard Smith, 'The Art Museum Today', *Meanjin Papers*, vol. 5, no. 2, Winter 1946, pp. 129–32, republished as 'The Social Role of the Art Museum', in Bernard Smith, *The Death of the Artist as Hero: Essays in History and Culture*, Oxford University Press, Oxford, 1988 (here quoting p. 162).

2 Bernard Smith, 'Introduction: A Biographical Memoir', in John Spencer and Peter Wright (eds), *The Writings of Bernard Smith: Bibliography 1938–1998*, Power Institute, Foundation for Art and Visual Culture, Power Publications, Sydney, 2000, pp. 10–11.

3 For this project, see Philip Goad, 'An Oriental Palazzo: Roy Grounds and the National Gallery of Victoria', *Backlogue: Journal of the Halftime Club*, vol. 3, 1999, pp. 72–99; and Emily Gray, 'Spirit and Purpose: Eric Westbrook and the Modernization of the National Gallery of Victoria (1956–73)', PhD thesis, University of Melbourne, 2009, pp. 117–60.

4 Eric Westbrook, quoted in *Christian Science Monitor*, 28 March 1961, copy located in Public Record Office Victoria, Melbourne (hereafter PROV), VPRS 12730/P0002/Unit 1: National Gallery and Cultural Centre Building Committee April–December 1961. The significance of this feature is also stressed in an internal planning document, found at this same archival location, which formed the basis for 'The National Gallery and Cultural Centre' publication that was sent out to publicise the scheme. See 'Victorian National Gallery and Cultural Centre', n.d. [c. 1960], p. 5: 'The second major development will be in the design of the galleries themselves. These will be so arranged that some floors stand away from the walls so that light from the roof can pass down beside them, giving both floors top lighting. By this means the whole building can be kept very flexible and, according to the requirements of each department, in some sections there will be four floors and in other places two.' In the finished publication this description appears without the last sentence, as: 'The second major development will be the design of the galleries themselves. These will be so arranged that some floors stand away from the walls so that light from the roof can pass down beside them, giving both floors top lighting.'

5 David Saunders, 'Spire and Chasms: A Five Foot Cultural Gap in Roy Grounds' Design?', *Nation*, 11 March 1961, pp. 13–14.

6 Franz Philipp, 'The Cultural Centre', *Meanjin*, vol. 20, no. 1, April 1961, p. 81.

7 Bernard Smith, 'Design for Vandals: More Protest Against the Five-Foot Cultural Gap', *Nation*, no. 66, 8 April 1961, p. 17.

8 Kenneth Clark, 'The Idea of a Great Gallery', in Franz Philipp and June Stewart (eds), *In Honour of Daryl Lindsay: Essays and Studies*, Oxford University Press, Melbourne, 1964, pp. 12–13.

9 Smith, 'Design for Vandals', p. 17.

10 For Brack's opposition to the plans, see *The Age*, 'Critic of Art Plans', 22 April 1961, p. 2.

11 The exchange between Grounds and Burke is to be found at PROV, VPRS 12730/P0002/Unit 1, National Gallery and Cultural Centre Building Committee April–December 1961.

12 PROV, as above, Professor Joseph Burke to Roy Grounds, 14 April 1961.

13 Phip Murray, *The NGV Story: A Celebration of 150 Years*, National Gallery of Victoria, Melbourne, 2011, p. 88.

14 Roy Grounds to Leonard Cox, 31 May 1961, PROV, VPRS 12731/P0001/Unit 3, National Gallery and Cultural Centre—Miscellaneous papers 01 Jan 1960 to 01 Jan 1970.

15 For this aspect of the discussions surrounding Roy Grounds' plans for the building, see Leonard B. Cox, *The National Gallery of Victoria, 1861 to 1968: A Search for a Collection*, National Gallery of Victoria Publishing, Melbourne, 1970, pp. 331–41.

16 For the official history of the Museum of Victoria's long and drawn-out renovation and rebuilding project, see Carolyn Rasmussen, *A Museum for the People: A History of Museum Victoria and its Predecessors*, Scribe Publications, Melbourne, 2001, pp. 340–3, 360–84.

17 For DCM and the Melbourne Museum/Exhibition Centre projects, see Haigh Beck and Jackie Cooper, *Denton Corker Marshall: Rule Playing and the Ratbag Element*, Birkhäuser, Basel, 2000, pp. 40–63, 188–9, 194–209. For the Melbourne International Gateway CityLink project, see ibid., pp. 232–7.

18 For which see Bernard Smith and Kate Smith, *The Architectural Character of Glebe, Sydney*, University Co-operative Bookshop, Sydney, 1973; Max Solling, *Grandeur and Grit: A History of Glebe*, Halstead Press, Sydney, 2007.

19 Bernard Smith, 'This (s)exhibition Goes Over the Top' [letter to the editor], *The Age*, 25 November 1995, p. 22; Bernard Smith, 'Museum Project Displays Contempt' [letter to the editor], *The Age*, 30 November 1995, p. 10; Bernard Smith, 'Sic Transit Gloria: Planners Try Euphoria' [letter

to the editor], *The Age*, 7 December 1995, p. 12; Bernard Smith, 'A Question of Sensitivity', *The Age*, 27 December 1995, p. 19.

20 Smith, 'This (s)exhibition'.

21 Smith, 'A Question of Sensitivity'.

22 Norman Day, 'New Museum is a Building for its Time' [letter to the editor], *The Age*, 28 December 1995, p. 14.

23 Trevor Huggard, Barry Humphries, Bernard Smith, Rosemary Stott, Evan Walker, David Yencken and Miles Lewis, 'A Call to Reconsider Site of New Museum' [letter to the editor], *The Age*, 23 May 1996, p. 14.

24 Rasmussen, *A Museum for the People*, p. 368.

25 Simon Molesworth [National Trust Chairman], quoted in Dugald Jellie, 'Are the Cracks Starting to Show in the National Trust?', *The Age*, 11 November 1996, p. B5.

26 Padraic Murphy, 'Pie in Face Mars Museum Opening Day: Birth of a Cultural Landmark', *The Age*, 22 October 2000, p. 2.

Documenting art:
Bernard Smith, academic art history and the role of the curator

JIM BERRYMAN

Returning from study in London in 1951, Bernard Smith set himself the task of cataloguing the collection of Australian paintings in the National Art Gallery of New South Wales (NAGNSW).[1] Ambitiously, Smith modelled his methods on Martin Davies' scholarly catalogues of the Old Masters in the National Gallery, London. The influence of academic education on the role of the art curator would concern Smith throughout his long career. As a teacher and art historian, he was instrumental in the professionalisation of the discipline in Australia. Although supportive of the shift from connoisseur-collector to academic-professional in matters of curatorship, Smith was not totally happy with the intellectual and art-historical results. This chapter charts Smith's interest in art museum scholarship in Australia, with reference to his critique of art-historical accounts of modernism and its institutional legitimacy in Australia's public galleries.

Bernard Smith had a complex relationship with art curators. As a teacher, he was responsible for their training, helping to produce the first generation of professional curators schooled in academic art history. On some occasions he commended the great advances in curatorial practice, citing improvements in public programs, exhibition presentation and scholarship. However, on other occasions, especially in the 1980s, Smith also became the profession's greatest detractor. In 1985 he voiced some of his most disapproving comments about curators, among them these trenchant lines:

> Far too many younger curators, and some not so young, are strong on opinion but weaker in that disinterested intellectual curiosity which makes for the tone of a good art museum. They will tell you, even before you ask, that in their personal view, most of the collection is tripe and might better be sold or perhaps burnt. People with such views should never be appointed to be curators of anything at all, let alone precious objects.[2]

Bernard Smith was a British Council scholar at the Courtauld and Warburg institutes from 1948 to 1949. This experience was his first formal education in art history. There the young art historian met the big names of Anglo-European art history, including Ernst Gombrich, Rudolf Wittkower and Anthony Blunt. In London he encountered the discipline's classical European tradition, a tradition ensconced in the German-speaking academic arena since the mid-nineteenth century.[3] In mature age he would write: 'after two years at the Courtauld and Warburg institutes, I sought to write art history with a better awareness of distance'.[4] This was in contrast with the juvenilia of *Place, Taste and Tradition*, 'which was not so much art history as passionate rhetoric in support of social realism'.[5] Throughout his long intellectual life, Smith defended art history as an autonomous discipline with clearly delineated knowledge boundaries. This outlook is implicit in his own scholarship. And from the 1980s, with the professionalisation of art history in the art museum setting, it is also explicitly stated in his numerous critiques of curatorship as practised in Australia's art museums.

To understand the basis of this criticism, it is first necessary to explore Smith's philosophy of art history and his understanding of the role of the professional art curator. By highlighting his growing anxiety over the influence of international modernism, I contend that Smith's interest in this matter is important because it anticipates his final—and most controversial—intellectual project. Bernard Smith's art historiography of modernism, which resulted in his contested period style called the 'Formalesque', had its origins in his analysis of the role of the modern curator.

Upon returning to Australia in 1951, Smith put his newly acquired skills and training to practical use. Inspired by Martin Davies' National Gallery catalogues, he catalogued the collection of Australian oil paintings at the NAGNSW.[6] What did this scholastic exercise reveal about Smith's new appreciation of academic art history? Catalogues are products of empirical observation and method—the tools of disciplined practice. Not unlike taxonomy in the natural sciences, where organisms are classified as types or classes, artworks are systematically grouped into medium or school, or some other art-historical category, including by period style. Davies, keeper of paintings at the National Gallery, had set new scholarly standards with his catalogues of the national collection's Old Master paintings. As models of professional practice and scientific precision, they set benchmarks for museum-based research, which Smith was keen to emulate.[7]

Smith advocated art history as a humanistic science, a discipline shaped by empirical and rational methods. Until the very end of his career, and despite the blurring of traditional knowledge boundaries in the postmodern humanities, he defended art history as a sovereign field of enquiry, informed by historical consciousness and disinterested analytical criticism. Smith summarised his views on disciplinary autonomy in 2007; published in *The Formalesque*, this became his final statement on art history:

> Art history is not philosophy, anthropology, or sociology—though it may bear significant lateral *relationships* to them and to other disciplines. It is taught as a distinct discipline because it has developed for itself its own body of knowledge and practice, and a degree of independence from a family of kindred disciplines. Like other disciplines, it is grounded in a deep respect for evidence by means of which it seeks to understand and interpret the life and work of creative artists. It is an art itself, like science, but in the general sense only, not in the special sense. It is neither ideology nor fiction.[8]

While not advocating a dry positivism, Smith did emphasise an epistemology that challenged the arbitrary value judgements of the amateur connoisseur. Early in his career, when employed as an exhibitions officer at the NAGNSW, Smith realised that academic expertise was needed to modernise the insular culture of Australia's public galleries. This meant confronting the old regime of lay trustees as well as the authority of artist-directors, whose claims to exclusive 'craft' knowledge had precluded non-practitioners from directorship positions. Before 1956, the year in which Eric Westbrook was appointed as director of the National Gallery of Victoria (NGV), it was customary for local artists to occupy executive roles.[9] J. S. MacDonald had been director of both the NAGNSW (1928–36) and the NGV (1936–41). Even in retirement, he remained a steadfast defender of the artist's privilege in matters of aesthetic opinion. MacDonald's hatred of modernist art was infamous. Another target of his scorn was the new breed of art academic:

> What D. S. MacColl, a painter, who in turn was Keeper of the Wallace Collection and Director of the Tate Gallery, has called 'art reporters', now began to rule; and they still dominate Britain in the matter of art criticism and governance. They have far less interest in paintings and the craft-methods that brought them about, and the opinion of those who created them, than in the writings about them by men of their type and the catalogues produced by unimaginative drudges who are oblivious to their raison d'être.[10]

As a new branch of learning, keen to legitimate its position among the established academic disciplines, art history had to demonstrate a methodological robustness. This trend was consistent with international precedents and followed experiences in Britain, which in turn had followed earlier experiences in the United States.[11] In 1933, in his inaugural lecture as Slade Professor of Art at Cambridge University, Roger Fry made the point that art history's future in the academic curriculum rested on its ability to formulate objective criteria, 'in which scientific methods would be followed wherever possible, where in all events the scientific attitude may be fostered and the sentimental attitude discouraged'.[12]

The international standards of academic art history would influence the discipline's formative development in Australia. First established at the University of Melbourne in 1946, this pioneering course was based on established international examples. According to Ursula Hoff, who taught part-time at the university, the Viennese School and the Warburg Institute provided the teaching models at Melbourne.[13] This environment was highly conducive to Smith's academic interests. He was appointed lecturer in the Department of Fine Arts at Melbourne in 1955, before taking his PhD at the Australian National University in 1957. Between 1955 and his retirement from the Power Institute in 1977, Smith oversaw the education of Australia's first generation of academically trained curators. The establishment of an integrated and professional art museum sector in Australia thus resembled earlier international experiences, where academic art history provided the intellectual foundations for applied art history in the museum. Smith followed this development with interest and, generally speaking, he was satisfied with the outcomes. In a report to the Australian Academy of the Humanities on the state of Australian art-historical research and publishing, he praised the achievements of the new academia–museum nexus. As evidence, he cited 'the considerable improvement in the quality of exhibition presentation and the preparation of catalogues, together with an expansion of museum educational activities'.[14] Smith continued:

> Undoubtedly the greatest single factor affecting art historical research in Australia, as in other countries, is in the *tone* of the relationship established between art history departments in the universities on the one hand and the managerial and curatorial staffs of the national, state, and provincial art museums on the other.[15]

The institutionalisation of art history in Australia's public galleries revolutionised the intellectual and corporate culture of these parochial organisations. This development was directly related, Smith wrote, to an 'increasing number of young art history graduates gaining curatorial and management positions'.[16] How did Smith acknowledge the passing of the old regime? He saw the decline of the unqualified curator as a major improvement. In 1984, at the height of his authority in Australian art history, Smith caricatured the older generation as the 'charming and attractive amateur with the "good eye", impeccable taste, and monumental prejudices, but lacking professional training, drive and competence'.[17] And yet, at the same time, a tone of ambivalence is detectable in Smith's appraisal of the new professionalism.

While Bernard Smith never regretted the passing of the old establishment, which had been based on Edwardian attitudes and artists' lore, his support for the new regime was not unequivocal. Throughout the 1980s he grew increasingly preoccupied with modernism, focusing on its commanding status in the Australian institutional setting. For someone as progressively minded as Smith, this critical tension was somewhat ambiguous. As he explained:

> Modernism in the gallery has brought structural changes with it. The old trustees who were painters or played at being connoisseurs and true gentlemen of taste have largely gone, or if not, their power has gone. Curators acting in consort with the director now play a greater part in the role of acquisition. On balance, I think this has been a considerable advance. But the desire to acquire, to play a part in

> the acquisition process, has begun to bulk [*sic*] largely in the activities of curators in comparison with their more traditional roles, such as cataloguing and the mastery of a knowledge of their collections.[18]

Bernard Smith had been a key player in the campaign to establish the credentials of modern art in Australia. But, unlike his contemporaries, Smith was in a unique position. He had witnessed these developments through the prism of academic art history. Most importantly, when Smith described 'the introduction of art history into Australian universities as a by-product of the modernist debate',[19] he raised the possibility that art history and modernism were historically related developments. This insight revealed a unique awareness of the discipline and its theoretical and historical origins. Though at this point he lacked a coherent theory of modernism as it related to art history's epistemological program, Smith's criticism anticipated the speculative art historiography of Hans Belting; Belting's project would come to explore the nineteenth-century origins of art history and the parallel trajectory of modernism, both of which were centred on the continuity of style and the idea of unilineal progress.[20] Importantly, Smith's remarks in this area foreshadowed his future work on the Formalesque.

As Smith grew more concerned about pervasive modernist attitudes and influences, especially in the arena of art curatorship and public gallery administration, his thinking about international modernism became more critical. Smith was among the first historians of modernism to identify a dialectical connection between avant-gardism and mass culture. This internal dynamic was manifested in the drive towards newness, obsolescence and novelty. In 1983 he wrote:

> Modernism created a new image for the art museum. To get the public into galleries it had to stress, it was asserted, the new. Even if it were old, it had to be presented to the locals in the guise of the new.[21]

Another negative consequence of the new paradigm was the tendency, as he saw it, towards aesthetic trend-setting and taste-making:

> But in all this flurry of attention to the passing scene, one wonders whether curatorial work is not becoming an increasingly complacent appendage of the commercial world, enhancing the market values of the art of the living or the recently dead.[22]

Of course, whenever Bernard Smith debated modernism, contesting the supremacy of abstraction was always high on his agenda. Since the early 1940s, his art criticism and narrative accounts of Australian painting had revealed a strong intellectual sympathy for realism. But while Smith's longstanding interests had previously focused on the influence of modernism on contemporary art practice, a pivotal event in 1981 prompted him to formulate a new critical position. This concerned the effects of modernist attitudes that applied to art history. The catalyst of this debate was the publication of Richard Haese's book *Rebels and Precursors: The Revolutionary Years of Australian Art*.[23] This influential and popular publication, which provided a whiggish account of modernism's progress in Melbourne and Sydney, positioned the artists of the Angry Penguins circle as the heroes of Australia's artistic battles; the book celebrated the achievements of Sidney Nolan and Albert Tucker in particular. According to this narrative, the Angry Penguins were the avant-garde of Australian progressive culture, triumphing over the reactionary Australian Academy of Art, local post-impressionism and social realism. Not only did *Rebels and Precursors* challenge Smith's contemporary account of the period, first published in *Place, Taste and Tradition* in 1945, Smith also thought Haese downplayed the progressive exploits of the social realists. To Smith's dismay, the *Rebels and Precursors* narrative gained art-historical orthodoxy, supported by a wave of exhibitions mounted by the public galleries.[24] Worst of all, he feared Australian art history had misrepresented the social realists as *socialist* realists, doctrinaire artists programmatically aligned with the Communist Party of Australia.

Smith reproached this outlook whenever the opportunity arose, in catalogue essays, art journals and the mainstream media. His growing anxiety about modernism, and art history and curatorship, touched on in earlier writings, was explicitly stated in a catalogue essay written in 1988. *Angry Penguins and Realist Painting in Melbourne in the 1940s* was a travelling exhibition organised by the Australian National Gallery for the Australian Bicentenary. This international event presented the ideal opportunity for Smith to confront the Heide account of Australian art history. Smith rejected *Rebels and Precursors* as a book imbued with cultural politics, one that reflected the encroaching influence of a hegemonic modernist ideology. Rather unfairly, he wrote that *Rebels and Precursors* 'is best viewed, despite its documentary value, as a product of aesthetic values generated by the Cold War'.[25] On the status of social realism, he wrote that:

> the book has given an air of historical legitimacy to an implicit attitude that has marginalised realist art from the contemporary art market and the curatorial art world since the late 1940s.[26]

Smith perceived curators primarily as the custodians of art history's material artifacts and secondly as adjunct art historians. But before curators could write art history based on their collections, they had to first understand the intellectual and material origins of the collections with which they were entrusted, hence the premium he placed on collection catalogues and the importance of cataloguing as a core professional responsibility. Collection catalogues were important to Smith because they recorded art that was critically unfashionable and art that fell outside the parameters of prescriptive art history, which according to Smith was precisely how modernism viewed the art of realism: 'Modernism developed its own peculiar modes of aesthetic censorship. The realists were marginalised almost to extinction and today only their wartime art is much sought after by collectors and curators'.[27]

Constructing aesthetic fashion was one thing, but re-interpreting art history to fit an ideological worldview was something more serious. Modernism, in seeking a pedigree to legitimate its place in the art museum (and in art history), imposed its providential mission on the art of the past. Smith's response to the celebrated *Golden Summers: Heidelberg and Beyond* exhibition of 1985 is significant in this respect because it foreshadows his Formalesque thesis. His review of this exhibition, originally published in *The Age Monthly Review*, is a fascinating exercise in metacriticism—in this case, a critique of curators who themselves were critiquing conventional accounts of Australian art history. Smith had named a chapter in *Place, Taste and Tradition* 'Impressionism in Australia' and had used the term 'impressionism' liberally in *Australian Painting*. He was therefore wary of revisionist scholarship that questioned the art-historical validity of an Australian school of impressionism. The argument being mounted against the impressionist label, which received considerable documentary support in the *Golden Summers* catalogue, dominated his review:

> Yet one of the most interesting facts to emerge from the splendid *Golden Summers* exhibition is the manner in which so many curators and art historians are now seeking to qualify the existence of an Australian school of impressionist painting virtually out of existence.[28]

Smith was alarmed that Australian impressionist painting was being reframed in the context of the modernist tradition of Impressionism as exemplified by Monet and his circle. To this end, *Golden Summers* drew attention to the differences in technique and style that differentiated Tom Roberts from Claude Monet. In other words, when measured against the features of textbook Impressionism, Australian impressionism was not Impressionism. Although Smith was happy to challenge this interpretation on technical grounds, he was forced to confront the art-historical consequences of modernism's institutionalisation in both the academy and the art museum. Smith's opinions on this matter were insightful:

> In seizing upon those components of French impressionist technique: rainbow palette, divided colour, etc, which were driving impressionism away from naturalism towards the anti-naturalism of modernist paintings, our curators and art historians reveal just how much they themselves are the children of modernism. This is, from an historical point of view, all too understandable. But it also provides a way for misunderstanding Australian impressionism.[29]

If Australian curators were indeed the children of modernism, their intellectual grandfather was Alfred H. Barr Jr. The pioneering curator and foundation director of the Museum of Modern Art (MoMA) in New York, Barr was among the first art historians to formulate a reflexive history of modernism. Contradicting the efforts of avant-garde artists, and contrary to popular perceptions, modern art did not represent a radical break with the past. Instead, in the hands of dominant institutions like MoMA, modernism was reframed as a continuation of art history, or if not continuation, culmination. This idea was widely expounded in Barr's authoritative exhibition catalogues. In the postwar decades, this narrative gained art-historical orthodoxy worldwide, promulgated by travelling exhibitions mounted under the auspices of MoMA's International Council, including *Two Decades of American Painting* and *Modern Masters: Manet to Matisse*, which toured Australia in 1967 and 1975 respectively.

While Smith respected the scholarship of Barr, his Modern Master catalogues were not comparable to Martin Davies' Old Master catalogues. Unlike Davies' *collection* catalogues, which used evidence to analyse and understand an artwork's value as a historical artifact, Barr's *exhibition* catalogues propounded an official narrative of modernism. Despite their use of scholarly method, the evangelising rationale behind MoMA's catalogues compromised their impartiality. In short, they lacked critical and temporal distance. Smith expressed his concerns on this matter as early as 1964:

> it is to be noted that the institution which has undoubtedly achieved the highest scholarly standards in the consideration of most recent contemporary art has been the Museum of Modern Art of New York. This has been due to the fact that Alfred H. Barr, its versatile Director during the greater part of its existence, insisted upon scholarly standards, in which the historical disciplines play an important role ... My only criticism is that the Museum, by the very nature of its foundation being involved in the *cause* of contemporary art, has not succeeded in developing a high standard of dispassionate and evaluative criticism. Its aims are essentially interpretative.[30]

And yet, in *Modernism's History*, when Smith dubbed Barr the first historian of the Formalesque, he acknowledged the powerful new role of the museum curator in the modern art system.[31] Supplanting that of academic historians, curators had acquired the authority to legitimate emerging trends and developments *as* art history. For Smith, the balance of power had shifted. The art museum ought to be, first and foremost, a museum of history. To paraphrase Smith's position on these professional matters: curators lay the foundations and prepare the groundwork upon which others build.[32]

It also pays to remember that Smith's foray into this area coincided with his own research for *The Art of Captain Cook's Voyages*, a remarkable example of museum scholarship produced in collaboration with Rüdiger Joppien. Highly empirical, this multi-volume catalogue raisonné was built upon primary collection-based research. Drawing on material from dozens of international collections, the venture depended on the availability—and indeed the existence—of collection catalogues. These catalogues were written for a community of scholars, not a popular audience. In response to the absence of up-to-date catalogues for Australian public collections, Smith would further rebuke curators for wasting their time on the production of ephemeral exhibition catalogues, especially those of the blockbuster variety:

> Instead [of collection catalogues], we have opted for the 'Selections from' or the 'Masterpieces (?) in' type of catalogue. No doubt these catalogues fulfil a useful

> function, as popular keepsakes, and we all possess them; however, they are of limited professional use.[33]

What started as a critique of professional practice grew to preoccupy Smith in the final decades of his life. Modernism, a revolutionary ideology, had been responsible for reshaping the public galleries. The art-historical consequences of this revolution would drive Smith to investigate modernism's own conceptual origins. This would culminate in his magnum opus *Modernism's History* and his contentious re-evaluation of the art historiography of the modern movement. This investigation produced the theory of the so-called Formalesque, Smith's construct of a twentieth-century period style. These matters are related: some of Smith's earliest formulations of modernism's historiography are discernible in his critical responses to institutional art history.[34]

However, before concluding, it would be wrong to suggest that Bernard Smith was a lone dissenting voice, decrying the influence of modernism on the role of the art curator. In the 1980s, Smith's critique belonged to a global backlash against the hegemonic agenda of modernism. His concerns at this time were not entirely incompatible with broader debates in contemporary art theory and practice. In the art world, postmodern pluralism had challenged the monolithic authority of international modernism. And in the academy, the so-called New Art History was debating the ideological premises of the discipline; this amalgam of interpretative, and largely anti-formalist, perspectives comprised feminist, semiotic and Marxist social-historical insights.

From the 1970s, Australia's public art institutions became powerful new champions of international modernist values. To quote Ian Burn, modernism was 'internalised as the corporate aesthetic' of Australia's public galleries.[35] For Smith, and other opponents of the international modernist agenda, *The Field* exhibition of 1968 was a symbolic turning point. But this event—the opening exhibition at the new National Gallery of Victoria—did more than consolidate a contemporary vogue for colour-field abstraction. Ian Burn and Nigel Lendon have viewed the significance of *The Field* exhibition in broader historical terms. This event established a new role for international avant-gardism in the Australian art institutional setting. The legacy of *The Field* greatly exceeded the influence of the style for which it is known:

> The rhetoric of 'the new' and the 'logic' of an institutionalised avant-garde was legitimised by *The Field* exhibition and subsequently reproduced in the survey exhibitions, project shows and the Sydney Biennales of the 1970s, in the acceptance of the idea of an avant-garde by the major institutions, in the Australia Council, and in the collecting policies of the Australian National Gallery. To concentrate therefore on the 'look' of the exhibition is misleading. Rather, the institutional sponsorship of an 'avant-garde' context for contemporary art in Australia was itself the major historical initiative of *The Field*.[36]

Bernard Smith's idea of the professional scholar-curator was closer to the Martin Davies model than that of the Alfred H. Barr model. Whereas one documented art history, the other dictated art history. As the Barr model prevailed in Australia's public galleries, Smith grew more agitated and outspoken on professional matters. Exploring the art-historical implications of the art of the modern era was his ultimate preoccupation; maybe, one day, this will be his most important legacy. Earlier in his career, when called upon to defend the teaching of modern art in the university setting, Smith summarised his philosophical position. In 1964 he wrote:

> This will be the challenge, to fashion an honest critical style that can approach the present without shedding the values of the past; to bring dispassionate and responsible evaluation grounded in tolerance and the scholarly disciplines of the humanities to the disturbing and complex art of our own time.[37]

Unfortunately, however, this was a challenge that Bernard Smith never fully met.

NOTES

1 The gallery dropped 'National' from its name in 1958.

2 Bernard Smith, 'The Art Museum and Public Accountability', in *The Death of the Artist as Hero: Essays in History and Culture*, Oxford University Press, Melbourne, 1988, p. 169.

3 Elizabeth Mansfield (ed.), *Art History and its Institutions: Foundations of a Discipline*, Routledge, London, 2002.

4 Bernard Smith, *The Formalesque: A Guide to Modern Art and its History*, Macmillan, Melbourne, 2007, p. 10.

5 ibid.

6 Bernard Smith, *A Catalogue of Australian Oil Paintings in the National Art Gallery of New South Wales, 1875–1952: With Annotations, Biographies and Index*, National Art Gallery of New South Wales, Sydney, 1953.

7 Smith, 'The Art Museum and Public Accountability', p. 173.

8 Smith, *The Formalesque*, p. 19.

9 Westbrook's four predecessors were artists Daryl Lindsay, James S. MacDonald, Bernard Hall and George Frederick Folingsby.

10 James S. MacDonald, *Australian Painting Desiderata*, Lothian, Melbourne, 1958, p. 9.

11 Alice Goldfarb Marquis, *Alfred H. Barr Jr: Missionary for the Modern*, Contemporary Books, Chicago, 1989, p. 36.

12 Roger E. Fry, *Art-History as an Academic Study*, Cambridge University Press, Cambridge, 1933, p. 10.

13 Ursula Hoff, 'Observations on Art History in Melbourne, 1946–1964', *Australian Journal of Art*, vol. 3, 1983, pp. 5–9.

14 Bernard Smith, 'Art Historical Studies in Australia with Comments on Research and Publication Since 1974', in *The Australian Academy of the Humanities: Proceedings*, no. 12, 1982–83, Australian Academy of the Humanities, Sydney, 1984, p. 55.

15 ibid.

16 ibid.

17 ibid.

18 Smith, 'The Art Museum and Public Accountability', p. 174.

19 Smith, 'Art Historical Studies in Australia', p. 46.

20 Hans Belting, *Art History After Modernism*, University of Chicago Press, Chicago, 2003.

21 Bernard Smith, 'Where Are Our Gallery Catalogues?', *Art in Australia*, vol. 21, no. 1, Spring 1983, p. 27.

22 Smith, 'The Art Museum and Public Accountability', p. 170.

23 Richard Haese, *Rebels and Precursors: The Revolutionary Years of Australian Art*, Penguin Books Australia, Melbourne, 1981.

24 *Joy Hester*, National Gallery of Victoria, Melbourne, 1981; *Sidney Nolan: Landscapes and Legends: A Retrospective, 1937–1987*, National Gallery of Victoria, Melbourne, 1987; *Angry Penguins and Realist Painting in Melbourne in the 1940s*, South Bank Centre, London, and Australian National Gallery, Canberra, 1988; *Albert Tucker: A Retrospective*, National Gallery of Victoria, Melbourne, 1990.

25 Bernard Smith, 'Realist Art in Wartime Melbourne', in *The Critic as Advocate: Selected Essays, 1948–1988*, Oxford University Press, Melbourne, 1989, p. 369.

26 ibid., p. 374.

27 ibid.

28 Bernard Smith, 'An Australian Impressionism', in *The Death of the Artist as Hero*, p. 241.

29 ibid., p. 248.

30 Bernard Smith, 'Sir Herbert Read and the Power Bequest', in *The Antipodean Manifesto: Essays in Art and History*, Oxford University Press, Melbourne, 1976, p. 74.

31 Bernard Smith, *Modernism's History: A Study in Twentieth-Century Art and Ideas*, Yale University Press, New Haven, 1998, pp. 188–94.

32 Smith, 'The Art Museum and Public Accountability', p. 173.

33 Smith, 'Where Are Our Gallery Catalogues?', p. 27.

34 Jim Berryman, 'Bernard Smith's Formalesque and the End of the History of Art', *Thesis Eleven*, vol. 123, no. 1, August 2014, pp. 3–16.

35 Ian Burn, 'The Art Museum More or Less', *Art Monthly Australia*, November 1989, p. 3.

36 Ian Burn and Nigel Lendon, 'Purity, Style, Amnesia', in *The Field Now*, exhibition catalogue, Heide Park and Art Gallery, Melbourne, 1984, p. 21.

37 Smith, 'Sir Herbert Read and the Power Bequest', p. 83.

Bernard Smith as curator:

soixante-huitard or Grand Tourist?

ANN STEPHEN

Over two months during the northern hemisphere summer of 1968, the newly appointed Power Professor of Contemporary Art and Director of the Power Institute at the University of Sydney, Bernard Smith, visited the Venice Biennale, *documenta 4* at Kassel, and Paris and London, where he would acquire some sixty contemporary artworks for the recently established Power Collection. How did Smith interpret the vision of artist-benefactor J. W. Power, whose remarkable will challenged the University of Sydney to collect 'the most recent contemporary art of the world … so as to bring the people of Australia in more direct touch with the latest art developments'?[1]

Political demonstrations and student unrest in the late 1960s would ricochet round the world and had unexpected consequences for art institutions. For instance, in his book *The Rise of the Sixties*, art historian Thomas Crow writes that 'the proliferation of dissent and the fragmentation of voices propelled advanced art to new levels of desirability for wealthy individuals, corporations and great civic museums'.[2] In Australia this paradoxical response to protest and avant-garde provocation was largely invisible, as the state art museums rarely actively acquired contemporary art at this time. The exception, however, was the Power Collection, which leads us to ask: what was collected and how was it received at the time? How well, in retrospect, does it map the contemporary cultures of these years?

For instance, how did Smith, the Marxist art-historian-turned-curator, respond to the political upheavals of that year, from student occupations at the Sorbonne, to the Prague Spring in Czechoslovakia, and international anti-war demonstrations?

Historically it has proven difficult to assess the extent and significance of this iceberg of a collection for, without a permanent home, only a few of the more spectacular of its over two thousand works are regularly seen. By 1969, when Elwyn Lynn became curator, the third in as many years, the university was already planning a gallery for the Power Collection, with Smith directly involved in extensive negotiations with major architects. Over the next fifteen years Lynn would continue to purchase regularly from the Venice and São Paulo biennales as well as *documenta*, and in the 1980s Bernice Murphy continued this project of contemporary acquisition, with the Museum of Contemporary Art as its base.[3] Yet, forty-five years on, the Power Collection is consigned to storage, a time capsule yet to be unlocked. By looking at a short period in its initial phase, I hope to make visible not only perennial questions associated with contemporary collecting, of astuteness and relevance, but also to discuss the specific challenges of this period, divided as it was between late modernist battles over the formalist aesthetics of Clement Greenberg, and the wider cultural and political crises. By making a critical reading of the art and its reception, it becomes possible to assess Smith's contribution to the Power Collection.

THE INTERREGNUM

Smith had stepped into the breach following the departure of the first Power Curator, Gordon Thomson. The year before his trip, Smith in his capacity as the newly appointed Power Director had released plans for the collection amid robust public debate. At a rowdy meeting of the Contemporary Art Society, Sydney artist John Olsen accused him of betraying the spirit of Power's will. Smith felt compelled to defend his new position and answered his critics by arguing:

> The sum of $20,000 which I mentioned recently at the CAS meeting as being available annually for purchase has caused considerable comment. [It was

> recommended that] ... 25 per cent of the gross income of the Bequest is allocated exclusively to works of art ... The great challenge of the bequest ... is to purchase the work of the Jasper Johns of this world before the cost of their work passes beyond our budget ... What is relevant is that at the time of purchase a sound case can be made that they represent the most recent contemporary art of the world. That is a challenging task, but I believe that Mr Thomson and his overseas advisors will make a good showing. He is hoping to return with about 20 works.[4]

In fact, Thomson as the first Power Curator spent $31,000 on thirty works, his only acquisitions before retiring from the fray to return to his previous position as deputy director of the National Gallery of Victoria.[5] In early 1968, Thomson's acquisitions were displayed at the newly completed Australia Square tower in central Sydney. This building provided a glamorous stage-set for launching the Power Collection, with an Anthony Calder sculpture at its entry and a foyer ringed by Vasarely and Le Corbusier tapestries. It fell to Harry Seidler, as the architect of Sydney's modernist skyline, to install the show in a temporary gallery on the first floor of his circular tower. To dramatise the luminous kinetic art, he planned 'to darken [the gallery] ... completely and make people walk into an artificial atmosphere'.[6] Jean Tinguely's *Bascule no 1: Sisyphus* (1965) proved to be a hit, as its metal see-saw was fitted with an interactive mechanism inducing bouts of frenetic rocking at the touch of a foot pedal (Fig. 28).

The exhibition was widely covered in the press. *The Australian Women's Weekly* ran a double-page colour report entitled 'Power Gallery Purchases Dazzle', which included Smith's opening speech at the launch. He had declared that it was 'the most important and truly international exhibition in Australia since 1939 ... Contemporary art should be international. In this exhibition we have 27 artists from 13 countries represented'.[7] Smith's comparison invoked Australia's landmark exhibition of European modernist painting, the *Herald Exhibition of French and British Contemporary Art* of 1939, when Paris was the undisputed centre, yet, three decades later, exactly what 'international' meant was a subject of much debate. Melbourne art critic G. R. Lansell was critical of the emphasis given to kinetic art:

> not, to my mind, one of the most important (so far) much less central, strands of contemporary art at the moment, Kinetic art is still a minor, rather adolescent

> movement, unfortunately blown up out of its true, humble proportions several years ago.[8]

John Henshaw, writing for *The Australian*, was much more positive, explaining that:

> representation from South Americans in the *Groupe de Recherche* in Paris is heavy no doubt because the superb *Lumiere et Mouvement* exhibition at the Musée National d'Art Moderne, which Mr Thomson saw last year, had a lot of their work.[9]

George Molnar, one of Smith's colleagues at the university (in the architecture faculty), who doubled as a cartoonist for *The Sydney Morning Herald*, captured the prevailing scepticism about the academy's capacity to realise Power's vision in a series of mocking cartoons and caricatures (Fig. 29).[10] Smith was depicted as a prophet in a suit on a hapless mission to convert the bemused masses. Another of Smith's colleagues at the Power Institute, Donald Brook, who was then also art critic on that same Sydney broadsheet, staunchly defended the exhibition:

> as a remarkable event introducing ideas and movements that are only familiar to a very few people in this country ... the group of kinetic art could scarcely come closer to the spirit of Dr Power's insistence upon the most recent and the thoroughly international ... the recent American exhibition that had people queuing in the Domain was a fine one, but relatively narrow and unhappily a returnable loan.[11]

Lansell disagreed with Brook, arguing that 'certain American works ... would have been within the ambit of Thomson's budget, as the price-list for some of the works in the *Two Decades of American Painting* indicated'.[12]

Thomson's acquisitions were attacked as Eurocentric. Sydney sculptor Ian McKay was one of the many who responded in the letters page of *The Sydney Morning Herald*, observing:

> It was most refreshing to see students demonstrating against Prof B Smith at the Art Gallery last Wednesday ... he said that the American/British section of the art world was of somewhat minor importance. This was incredible when right next door was an exhibition of exciting, adventurous and enlightening works of art. It may however explain his attitude that it is to France and Italy [that] we must look.[13]

McKay was referring to the blockbuster *Two Decades of American Painting*, which had been seen in Tokyo, New Delhi and Melbourne over 1966–67, before its final destination in Sydney. Although this was a Museum of Modern Art (MoMA) touring exhibition, the majority of the paintings were for sale, though none would be acquired for the Power Collection. In fact, among the dozen acquisitions made by Thomson from the Galerie Denise René in Paris, most were by Latin-American émigrés from Venezuela (Carlos Cruz-Diez) and Argentina (Martha Boto, Gregorio Vardanega, Julio Le Parc, Hugo Demarco and Luis Tomasello).

When Smith stepped into Thomson's shoes the following year, despite his notorious battles against abstraction, he had meetings with several key American architects of late modernism on the final stop on his international tour. They included Waldo Rasmussen, curator of *Two Decades*, Kynaston McShine, newly appointed to the department of painting and sculpture at MoMA, and critic Clement Greenberg, who had accompanied the *Two Decades* tour to Tokyo and Calcutta, but not to Australia. On the international stage Smith shelved his antagonisms and invited Greenberg to deliver the first Power Lecture the following year. In fact he would find in him an unexpected ally, when Greenberg subsequently launched an attack on the art of the 1960s and its 'eccentric styles, trends, tendencies, schools', listing 'Assemblage, pop, and Op … Hard edge, Colour Field, and Shaped Canvas … Neo-Figurative, Funky and Environmental … Minimalism, Kinetic and Luminous … Computer, Cybernetic, Systems … Participatory—and so on'.[14] But in 1968, how did Smith himself navigate these turbulent waters, at a time when the very terms of what counted as contemporary were profoundly contested, and art institutions were themselves in crisis?

SMITH'S GRAND TOUR

As Smith left for Europe he would have been acutely aware of the public scrutiny of his mission as the acting Power Curator. Although he had attended the Venice Biennale five times, and provided advice to the Art Gallery of New South Wales (AGNSW) on potential acquisitions of Australian art, he had never acquired contemporary art for a public collection. Moreover, he would confront unprecedented difficulties with the escalating protests of the international student movement.

During his visit, demonstrations spilled over into the major art events at Kassel and Venice, and led to exhibition boycotts, closures and strikes. He had arrived in the middle of the Venetian summer after a notorious opening, when the Giardini's exhibition gardens had been closed down by police, following protests about the 'Biennale of capitalists' with threats to torch the pavilions.[15] After a day of visiting commercial galleries, Smith recorded in his diary on Saturday 22 June:

> Arrived at Arsenale at about 12.30.
>
> It had been opened in the morning from 9. We were told it would be opened at 2pm. Wandered in the gardens outside. Some coffee. The gardens were very heavily garrisoned both by troops and the police who were hanging about a good deal. At 2 a group of students and visitors had gathered at the entrance. Shortly after 2 a notice was posted up … to say that the Biennale has been closed for the day because of lack of staff and would open at 9am tomorrow. About this time large numbers of attendants came filing out the gates. They had apparently come out in sympathy with the students who are opposing the opening of the Biennale. The police and the military were heavily armed.
>
> … Student leaders and others pointed out that all university students here are poor, there are few scholarships. Met one anarchist who has embraced Chinese Communism in opposition to the Russian line of the local Communist Party … The Triennale closed in Venice by similar student activity. The Kassel Documenta may suffer similarly. The wife of the artist Sergio Fergola was beaten up … although she protested that she was an American and not a student the police did not believe her.[16]

In support of the students, many of the exhibiting artists had withdrawn works, pavilions were closed and the program of official prizes was abandoned. The influential Swedish museum director Pontus Hulten subsequently reflected on these circumstances: 'There was a general sense of hope that the future could happen only via the necessary destruction of the past'.[17]

Smith made little commentary on the protests, possibly because there was a parallel Australian movement against the war in Vietnam, with which he was familiar and indeed supported. However, the demonstrations would have disrupted any attempt at collecting, which might explain why he acquired only three works from exhibiting artists in the Venice Biennale, and all were minor figures: a Brazilian printmaker, Anna Quadros; and two Eastern Bloc sculptors, the Czech Vladimír Preclík and the Romanian Ovidiu Maitec. It may have been certain connections to early twentieth-century modernism that intrigued Smith, for instance Maitec's *Column* (1967), a monumental wooden obelisk that recalls the Romanian origins of his precursor Brancusi, though drilled with a grid of holes to create an op art effect. He also purchased more than a dozen Italian prints from the Biennale of Contemporary Italian Engraving in Venice; none was political in any direct way, though as Smith noted in his diary, that exhibition had also been closed down. When the prints were subsequently exhibited in Sydney most critics agreed with the verdict of the Italian newspaper *La Fiamma*, which complained that 'the pictures exhibited are graphic works of second rate importance'.[18]

It was outside Venice that Smith found more interesting work, which later prompted him to observe that 'the decentralised state of Italian culture … bears some similarity to the situation in Australia', concluding that 'Milan is probably the most active centre of contemporary art'.[19] There he acquired a refined group of earlier Italian kinetic and op art, including Getulio Alviani's aluminium grid *Superficie a testura vibratile, opera programmata no. 3142* (Surface with vibrating texture, programmed work no. 3142) of 1963, and Enzo Mari's prefabricated module *Structure no. 725* (1962). Mari was a Milanese designer whose exhibition *Luce e Movimento* (Light and Movement) had been featured in the design magazine *Domus*. In the Power Collection, his work could make an interdisciplinary link to the kinetic art already acquired. Smith commented that these artists worked largely with 'virtual movement', and thus could be regarded 'as a continuation and development of the investigations into pictorial dynamics initiated by the Futurists'.[20] Smith's historicist bent led him to seek earlier art-historical themes in contemporary art, a tendency that informs his otherwise eclectic selection. In Milan, Smith met Gio Pomodoro, one of the artists who had withdrawn from the 1968 Biennale, and purchased his work *Quasi quadrato* (Almost square) of 1964, from his series *Surfaces under tension*, constructed by moulding and casting stretched canvas. At the time Pomodoro described the highly polished distorting surfaces of his bronze pieces in metaphoric terms as representing 'societal tensions'.[21]

Smith was also drawn to the Milanese pop art of Enrico Baj and Valerio Adami. Baj had organised the 1950s *Movimento Nucleare* group, which included Pomodoro, and in the 1960s he continued making socially critical art, like the anti-militarist *General* series, from which Smith acquired *Il Barone Robert Clive de Plassey, Gouverneur de Bengale* (1966). His parody of the eighteenth-century British colonial ruler of India was collaged from felt, braid, badges and brocade, akin to the anarchic humour of the *Sgt. Pepper's Lonely Hearts Club Band*—in fact the 'eyes' are Beatles fan badges. When Smith invited Baj to lecture in Australia the following year, six of his prints were added to the Power Collection. By contrast, Adami's figurative forms are refined studies in sexual fetishism, like blown-up X-rated cartoon cells, heighted by flat, astringent enamel paint, outlined in black, with an occasional drop shadow indicating a stage-like space. The Power work, *F. Lensky at the International Dance Studio* (1968), portrays a renowned male dancer of Carnegie Hall fame. Beyond the pointed limbs and genitals, the flesh-toned shapes that are sliced into cubist arcs resemble nothing but tightly bound energy. Framed by doubled mirrors, feet, and the barres of the studio, this frozen dance might have been considered by Smith as a fitting legacy of Futurism.

When these Italian acquisitions were singled out for exhibition in April 1969 at the commercial Bonython Gallery in Sydney, Donald Brook's enthusiasm had noticeably cooled. In reviewing the exhibition for *The Sydney Morning Herald* he noted:

> the ubiquitous appearance of high skill, professionalism or fine finish ... in the entire range of styles from Alviani's polished virtual-kinetic surfaces in aluminium through to Baj's satiric-comic pop ... perhaps especially in the graphic works—and one wonders to what extent these features may be identified with the elusive 'quality' that Prof Smith declares to have been the first consideration in his choice of purchases.[22]

Brook's contention was that Smith's formalist defence in fact masked a conservative preference for the highly crafted art object, more like a latter-day William Morris than a Greenbergian. As Brook knew, such skills were assailed by a shift towards an impersonal aesthetics of minimal and conceptual art. Smith's successor, Lynn, also stonewalled critics when faced with critical debate, arguing that 'One does not purchase to represent the latest movement or its vicissitudes, but one seeks quality in the most recent art'.[23] The problem of such a position was that much art of the late 1960s disavowed the very idea of quality and the refined eye of a spectator, in favour of participation, critical scrutiny or dialogue.

DOCUMENTA 4

After three weeks in Italy, Smith travelled on to West Germany, as that year the Venice Biennale coincided with *documenta 4* in Kassel. Unlike Venice, *documenta* was always a curated exhibition, rather than one primarily based on national pavilions. Art critic and then AGNSW curator Daniel Thomas noted that 'anything bought at Kassel is well and truly pre-tested for quality'.[24] However, that year controversies had dogged the preparation of *documenta 4*, the swansong of its founding director, Arnold Bode, who had responded to criticism by establishing a committee to select artists. Instead of having a retrospective character, like its precursors, *documenta 4* focused exclusively on the art of the 1960s. Yet the dominance of American art in the exhibition provoked much criticism and demonstrations. The American military intervention in South-East Asia, combined with two decades of dependency orchestrated through the Marshall Plan, fuelled this opposition. 'In a volatile and internationalised art economy', as Crow points out, there was much resentment, as 'America remained largely closed to imports from the Continent'.[25] Indeed, a sense of exclusion was experienced by any non-American artist who aspired to make international art in the 1960s.

Smith arrived in Kassel on 4 July and met with Bode, inviting him to visit Australia in October as a guest of the Power Institute, though this invitation was not taken up. Of the nineteen purchases made in Kassel (about one-third of his total acquisitions) only one was by an American artist, a Kenneth Noland serigraph on linen, produced in an edition of 150 by the *documenta* Foundation and sold for a modest $115. In fact, many of Smith's acquisitions were multiples. A few years earlier, gallerist Denise René had coined the term when she began marketing editions of kinetic art. Smith was interested in how industrial designers like the Dutch artist Jos Manders could apply processes associated with plastics and industrial technologies to multiples. Manders' three-dimensional monochrome wall piece entitled *General communication* is distinctly European, with its title and organic shapes, compared to the industrial order of Donald Judd's specific objects. Others, like the Greek sculptor Takis, who had worked with the Paris-based *Lumière et Mouvement* group, himself commissioned the *Signal Series* in 1968 as an unlimited edition of manufactured kinetic light works for *documenta 4*. Inspired by railway signals, the artist spoke of refining machinery, such that 'in their economy they became objects fit to be produced'.[26] Smith acquired three of these elongated metal rods topped by variously coloured flashing lights.

Smith chose several prints by French pop artists Arman, Ramon and Alain Jacquet, who had all been associated with the group *Nouveaux Réalistes* from the early 1960s. Once again Smith selected artists whose work self-consciously referenced early (French) modernism, which gives their work a rarefied retrospective feel compared to the embrace of mass culture by American pop artists. For instance, while Jacquet's silkscreens are based on enlarged photo-mechanical dots *à la* Lichtenstein and are mass-reproduced *à la* Andy Warhol, his subjects refer back to the art of museums. His *Portrait d'homme (red, yellow, blue)* of 1964, now in the Power Collection, comes from a re-enactment of Manet's iconic modernist masterpiece *Déjeuner sur l'herbe*, in a modern setting but camouflaged by off-register screening. It singles out the head of the Manet's central seated male figure, but is only one sheet of over 250 that would constitute the total work. Other multiples issued by the *documenta* Foundation that went into the Power Collection included works by British pop artist Joe Tilson, *The software chart* (1968), and Italian Lucio Fontana, *Concetto spaciale* (1968). The latter translated his pierced and cut surfaces into mechanically perforated holes in a serigraph.

Fontana, who would be dead before *documenta 4* ended, had also installed a major luminous labyrinth, *Ambienti spaziali*, culminating in a wall cut by a single slash. His act of opening up space to create, in his words, 'a new dimension, beyond the flat surface or the image', influenced a generation of (particularly European) painters. For instance, Germany's Gotthard Graubner would develop his 'cushion paintings', which extend into literal space while his restrained use of paint employs virtual 'bodies of colour space'.[27] He spoke of them as 'mirrors of light … [with] light … reflected through the stretched skin of the painting'.[28] In her account of the evolution of the Museum of Contemporary Art, Bernice Murphy singled out 'the most enduringly interesting works' from Smith's acquisitions as the German artists' works, noting Graubner's as:

> a strong example of the early phase of this artist's work, before he moved into the larger, more dense and mature phase of the 'padded paintings' that have occupied his attention for years since, giving him a high profile within German art.[29]

She also mentions Günter Fruhtrunk and Rupprecht Geiger, though 'these remain more regional figures related to the Munich area'.[30] When reviewing Smith's *documenta 4* selection in July 1969, Daniel Thomas characterised these artists as 'first rate peripheral mainstreamers', arguing that 'since Germany doesn't make any claim to be an art centre, like Paris, London or New York, its critical distance from the mainstream is just right'.[31] His account tends to simplify the complicated postwar art world of a divided Germany, but it would have resonated with an Australian audience when looking at the painting by Dick Watkins in *The Field* exhibition in 1968, which also referenced constructivism. Fruhtrunk's painting *Von Rot zu Rot* (From red to red) was a more reductive form of hard-edge painting, which, with its tightly controlled diagonals and minimal use of colour, creates effects of rhythmical optical pulsing. The differences and common ground between European and American late modernist painting were teased out in an extended comparison between Fruhtrunk and Nolan by Terry Smith in the University of Sydney student newspaper *Honi Soit*.[32]

Smith added a Victor Vasarely porcelain relief multiple, *Laika* (1964), to one that Thomson had acquired in 1967, claiming that the artist was the most important living representative of the constructivist tradition in painting. Another work he singled out 'in view of his importance for twentieth century art' was a drawing by Hans Hartung, associated with the postwar Parisian group *Art Informel*.[33] Like all the artists Smith selected, these were European, of his generation or older, and all but two were men.

THE MIXED LEGACIES OF TRANSMISSION

When the second group of Smith's acquisitions was shown in July 1969 in Sydney's Blaxland Gallery (Fig. 30), more than half were from *documenta 4*. It was in that catalogue that his most overt political comments are to be found. He states in the brief introduction that '1968 should not pass without the Power Gallery (supporting) the avant-garde art of Czechoslovakia'. To this end he had acquired the work of three Czech artists: Vladimír Preclík, Mikuláŝ Medek and Jiří Kolář. The latter's work, *Anthropodiak—hommage à Larousse* (1966), previously shown in *documenta 4*, was made from collaged fragments of a nineteenth-century encyclopaedia, described by Smith as an art 'deeply committed to exploring in visual terms the predicament of man in history'.[34] When the Prague Spring was suppressed by Soviet tanks in May 1968, Kolář's torn surfaces came to be read as a testimony to the struggle against the Stalinist state. For Smith, it offered a realism without the 'proletarian mock-heroics of official Russian art'.[35]

For the short time that he was a curator, Smith was able to select works that reveal his views on the relations between art and politics. Such ideas were shaped more by Marxist debates and allegiances of the 1940s and 1950s than by the New Left cultural politics of the *soixante-huitards*. His acquisitions can be seen in a European humanist tradition and reveal a predilection for craft skills, whether casting, carving, printmaking or collage. As Smith's art history was shaped by a model of dependency that traced a linear development through European modernism, so his internationalism was likewise not receptive to North or South American late modernism. As a result he did not engage with the critique of abstraction mounted by minimal and conceptual art in the 1960s. In fact, as his introduction to the exhibition catalogue of 1969 suggests, while he claimed to interpret the cosmopolitan terms of Power's bequest, writing of a 'process of assembling a representative collection of the contemporary art of countries other than Australia',[36] his purchases were almost entirely European. Thus, just as he had a decade earlier sought to articulate an antipodean movement for his own country, his acquisitions of 1968 were conceived to represent national currents and characteristics in contemporary European art.

In spite of its limitations, the early Power Collection does offer the all too rare possibility of tracing different, often overlooked, strands in the art of this period. For instance, Susan Best recently used the early collection to single out 'the transmission of constructivism to South America and its "altered" after-life there'.[37] Such a project re-examined kinetic art, as part of the wider reassessment of this much-disparaged genre. For example, art historian Pamela Lee has recently argued, in the context of new media, that automatons such as Tinguely's 'spoke to the rise of a hybrid technological media' because they plunged 'modernist medium specificity into a murky impurity'.[38] Yet Lee's argument does not have much force in a peripheral culture like Australia, where the impure and murky are inextricably part of its modernism. More potentially productive is Best's proposal for revising the mechanistic aesthetic associated with kinetic art, proposing an expansion to 'other terms that suggest biological rhythms, like pulse, throb, quiver or shudder to sit alongside the more mechanical form of repetition suggested by vibration, flicker and oscillation'.[39] So could we in fact see, in the excitement generated by Tinguely's machine in 1968, not so much the impure but a form of identification by the audience with the catatonically disempowered body politic that, Sisyphus-like, threw itself, again and again, in front of what was called in the 1960s the military-industrial complex?

NOTES

1 J. W. Power, Will, 1939, University of Sydney Archives, 094/0004/00110. All citations from contemporary newspaper and magazine reviews are taken from 'The Power Gallery Records', scrapbook volume 1, 1963–73, held in the Schaeffer Library, University of Sydney (n.n.).

2 Thomas E. Crow, *The Rise of the Sixties: American and European Art in the Era of Dissent 1955–69*, George Weidenfeld & Nicholson, London, 1996, p. 12.

3 Bernice Murphy gives a comprehensive, though partisan, account of the history of the Power Bequest in her institutional history, *Museum of Contemporary Art: Vision and Context*, Museum of Contemporary Art, Sydney, 1993.

4 Bernard Smith, 'The Power Art Bequest', *Sydney Morning Herald*, 15 July 1967, p. 2.

5 An approximate conversion to 2014 currency values would be about $200,000.

6 Harry Seidler, 'Architect to Plan Exhibition', *Sydney Morning Herald*, 12 January 1968, n.p.

7 Anne Olsen, 'Power Gallery Purchases Dazzle', *Australian Women's Weekly*, 27 March 1968, n.p.

8 G. R. Lansell, 'Fun and Games', *Sun Telegraph*, 3 March 1968, n.p.

9 John Henshaw, 'Crucial Showing for a Gallery Without Walls', *Australian*, 2 March 1968, n.p.

10 George Molnar, cartoon, *Sydney Morning Herald*, 1 July 1967, n.p.

11 Donald Brook, 'Art at the Burgeoning Edge of Change', *Sydney Morning Herald*, 2 February 1968, n.p.

12 Lansell, 'Fun and Games'.

13 Ian McKay, Letter to the Editor, *Sydney Morning Herald*, 25 July 1967, n.p.

14 Clement Greenberg, 'Avant-garde Attitudes: New Art in the Sixties', in *Clement Greenberg: The Collected Essays and Criticism*, ed. J. O'Brian, vol. 4, University of Chicago Press, Chicago, 1993, p. 294.

15 Vittoria Martini, 'A Brief History of the Venice Biennale Seen from the Giardini', Jennifer Knaeble (transl.), www.artandeducation.net/.../a-brief-history-of-i-giardini, viewed 1 September 2014.

16 Bernard Smith, 1968 Diary, National Library of Australia, Canberra, Bernard Smith Papers, Manuscripts, Box 1, Bag 2.

17 Pontus Hulten interviewed by Marco Minuz, in L. M. Barbero, *Venice 1948–1986: The Art Scene*, Skira, Milan, 2006, pp.126–7.

18 P.T., 'Arte italiana d'avantguardia alla Galleria Bonython', *La Fiamma*, 16 April 1969, n.p.

19 Bernard Smith, 'Introduction', in *Power Bequest Exhibition No. 1, 1969*, exhibition catalogue, Power Institute of Fine Arts, University of Sydney, Sydney, 1969, n.p.

20 ibid.

21 ibid.

22 Donald Brook, 'Art Review', *The Australian*, May 1969, n.p.

23 Elwyn Lynn, 'Introduction', in *Power Bequest Exhibition, 1971*, exhibition catalogue, Power Institute of Fine Arts, Sydney, 1971, n.p.

24 Daniel Thomas, 'Acts of Protest', *Sunday Telegraph*, 6 July 1969, n.p.

25 Crow, *The Rise of the Sixties*, p. 145.

26 Takis, quoted in *Power Bequest Exhibition 2*, exhibition catalogue, Farmer's Blaxland Gallery, Sydney, 1969, p. 13.

27 Gotthard Graubner, quoted in *Power Bequest Exhibition 2*, p. 5.

28 ibid.

29 Murphy, *Museum of Contemporary Art: Vision and Context*, p. 163.

30 ibid.

31 Daniel Thomas, 'Acts of Protest', *Sunday Telegraph*, 6 July 1969, n.p.

32 Terry Smith, 'The Responsive Eye', *Honi Soit*, 18 July 1969, p. 8.

33 Smith, 'Introduction'.

34 ibid.

35 Bernard Smith, 'The Power Bequest Exhibition', *Art and Australia*, vol. 5, no. 4, March 1968, p. 630.

36 Smith, 'Introduction'.

37 Susan Best, *Vibration, Vibração, Vibración: Latin American Kinetic Art of the 1960s and '70s in the Power Collection*, University Art Gallery, University of Sydney, Sydney, 2012, p. 5.

38 Michelle Kuo, 'Art's New Media', *Artforum International*, vol. 51, no. 1, September 2012, p. 67; Pamela M. Lee, 'Media Specificities', ibid., p. 403; Eric C. H. de Bruyn, 'Ghost Story: Kinetic Art and New Media', ibid., pp. 526–33.

39 Best, *Vibration, Vibração, Vibración*, p. 3.

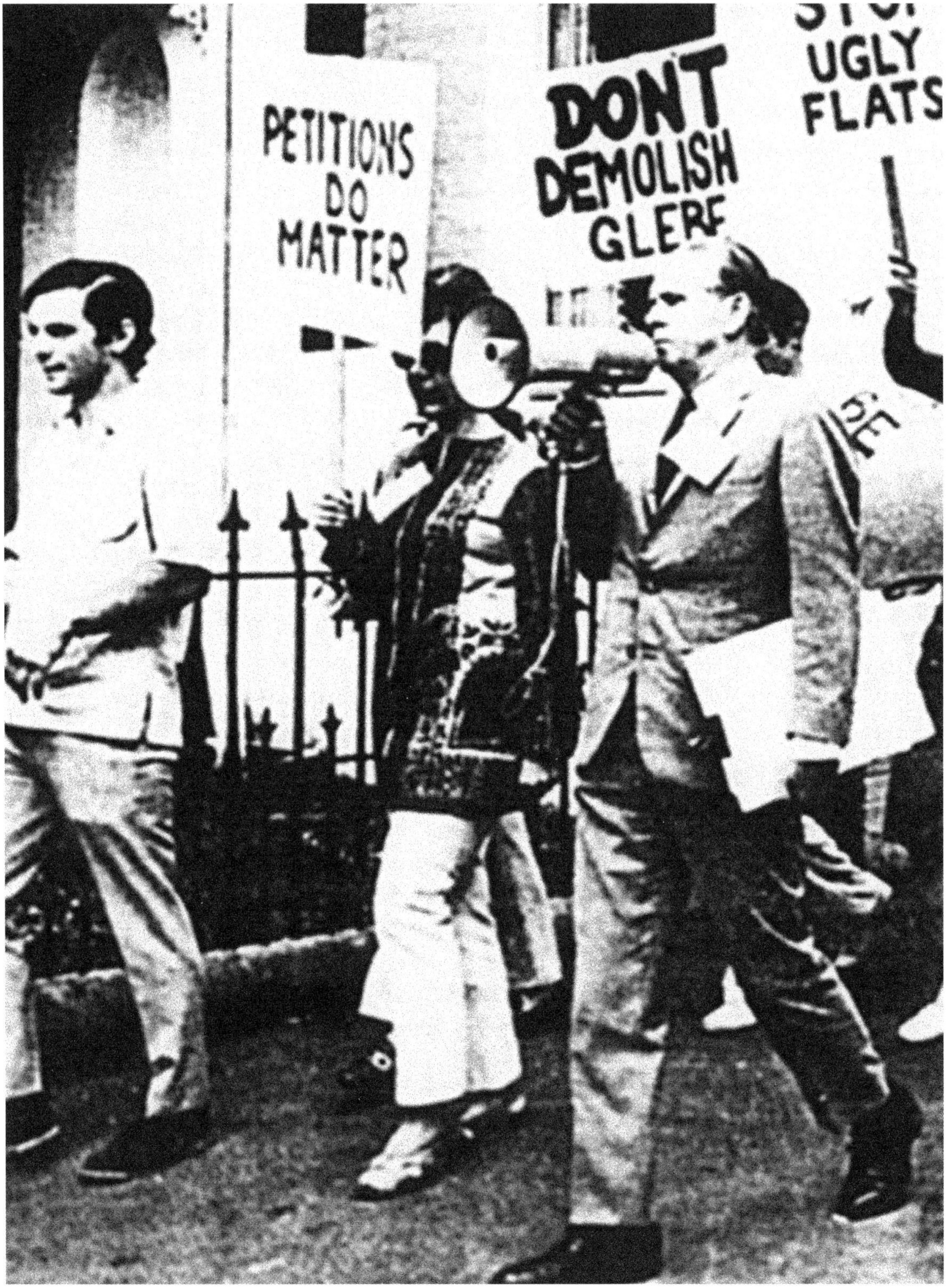
PETITIONS DO MATTER
DONT DEMOLISH GLEBE
UGLY FLATS

4

BERNARD SMITH'S CULTURAL POLITICS

Bernard Smith as activist

MAX SOLLING

The following is based on the text of an address delivered by Max Solling at a 'wake' for the late Professor Bernard Smith, organised by the Power Institute of the University of Sydney and held at the Toxteth Hotel, Glebe, on 9 November 2012.

I recall Kate Smith knocking on the door of my Boyce Street, Glebe, lodgings in 1968, where I'd lived for eight years with other students. Somehow she'd found out I was writing a thesis on nineteenth-century Glebe. It was the beginning of an enduring friendship with Bernard and Kate. Glebe was my sort of place, its earthy friendliness, and lack of pretence, not dissimilar from small towns in rural New South Wales where my parents spent their lives.

The Smiths bought a residence in Glebe after Bernard's appointment on 9 January 1967 as foundation Power Professor of Contemporary Art and Director of the Power Institute at the University of Sydney. Before examining Bernard's activism, I think it's important to understand something of the way in which the social pattern of Sydney's inner industrial suburbs, of which Glebe was a constituent part, was set in the first half of the twentieth century. Henry Lawson in his poem 'Faces in the Street' identified the working class as the traditional peasantry, with its own manners, morals, customs and rituals, concentrated in the early years of Federation in an inner Sydney increasingly invaded by industry.[1] And the insights of a relatively small but distinct group of social realist novelists—Louis Stone, Kylie Tennant, Ruth Park and Dorothy Hewett—capture the very essence of crowded neighbourhoods encircling the city, the residents' feeling of belonging and sense of place.[2]

In 1944 when Sali Herman's painting of McElhone Stairs at Woolloomooloo won the Wynne Art Prize, the *Bulletin* described it as 'a melancholy account of one of Sydney's slummiest aspects'. Bernard wrote that 'practically everyone agreed in those days, whatever their political persuasion, that the inner suburbs of Sydney were slums and that after the war, with post-war reconstruction, the slums must go'.[3] The combination of the Depression, World War II and rent control contributed to the decay of neighbourhoods near the city. The newly created Cumberland County Council condemned inner Sydney in 1948 as 'totally substandard areas requiring replacement', and accompanying an agenda to replace housing, not improve it, its report generalised about the morals and behaviour of inner-suburban residents.[4] Its residents lived with the slum stigma, a negative image that cast its shadow onto the 1950s and 1960s.

But Sali Herman did not see these suburbs in that way and continued to paint their terraces with a new warmth and affection; in Herman's phrase he could see into 'the character of things'. 'Historical perception deepens the temporal perspective', Bernard observed; 'things that were once seen as merely old and obsolescent are seen in a new light as human heritage'.[5]

The postwar upsurge in preservationism saw the creation of the National Trust of New South Wales in 1947; its initial *raison d'être* in public campaigns was to save and restore the nation's 'stately homes'. Its membership was originally 'by invitation only', and its principal offices remained in the hands of lawyers and well-established landed families.[6] The members inherited from Hardy Wilson both their enthusiasms and an exclusively patrician point of view, and a sense of history that did not extend much beyond Georgian and Regency buildings. The National Trust remained the only voice of preservationist sentiment into the 1960s, with preservation efforts centred on its register: buildings compiled mainly by architects on the basis of whatever information they could glean from research.

The economic structure of the Sydney central business district (CBD) began to change in the 1960s, signalling the city's transformation from an industrial city to a corporate one. Closely tied to CBD development was the rapid expansion of capital-intensive, service-based industries.[7] Professional, technical and administrative people employed in these new industries often preferred older, architecturally interesting housing close to the city, and an upward shift in professional and technical workers moving in represented a gradual change of class relations. The landscapes of Paddington and Balmain were the first areas to experience change with a new awareness of their environment and history, and these suburbs formed inner-city resident action groups in 1964 and 1965.[8] The role of resident action groups paralleled that played by trade unions in the workplace, and they became the political voice of the conservation movement.

Between 1965 and 1971 there was a massive inflow of private capital into Sydney, and the New South Wales Askin Liberal Government was committed to massive redevelopment of the inner city. The scale of speculative redevelopment threatened the very existence of a number of traditional working-class residential neighbourhoods.[9]

Bernard and Kate Smith came to Glebe when a new energy and enthusiasm pervaded the suburb, with communities forming opinions of their own about the quality of their environment. A small group of like-minded people gathered together at 23 Avenue Road, Glebe, the Smiths' home, on 27 February 1969, concerned about serious threats to the character of Glebe's townscape, and began organising the inaugural meeting on 24 April 1969 of what became the Glebe Society.[10] The first general meeting of the Glebe Society at Glebe Town Hall, on 19 June 1969, was an animated occasion chaired by Kemp Fowler. Its first newsletter spelt out its aims:

> The Society will concern itself with the problems threatening Glebe as a pleasant place to live. Our approach will be two-pronged, to ensure that adequate thought and planning goes into new projects in the area and to preserve and conserve what is good in the already existing buildings and places of historic interest.[11]

Bernard, elected as the society's first president, found resident action a new and exciting experience, and the society's first social activity, a walk around Glebe in July 1969, was designed to savour what it was fighting for. Bernard wrote:

> The new sense of historical values, which the residents discovered for themselves and transmitted to others should do much towards making the suburb a more neighbourly place to live in and preserve the environmental fabric of traditional buildings for posterity.[12]

Two immediate threats to Glebe's townscape—urban radial expressways and the building of flats—preoccupied the new society. Kate, an indefatigable pedestrian, stopped and talked to everyone on her daily errands (the Smiths never owned a car), and no one recruited more members to the Glebe Society than Kate in the formative period, using skills acquired as a schoolteacher, and later rallying the troops for demonstrations.

Residential zoning under the existing planning scheme permitted unfettered construction of flats in Glebe; the society's first initiative in July 1969 appeared in the *Local Leader*, under the heading 'Society Formed to "Save" Glebe'. Bernard told them there was insufficient control on unit development, and developers needed to set aside areas for landscaping.[13]

The Department of Main Roads (DMR) began resuming properties in Glebe in 1969 to create a pathway for the proposed expressway. In December 1969 Smith wrote to P. H. Morton, minister for local government and highways, expressing concern that creating an open-cut section in Glebe, to stretch from Lombard Street to Maxwell Street, to facilitate the North Western Expressway, 'will effectively destroy the natural unity and amenity of a highly valued and historic suburb'.[14] A meeting was hastily arranged with DMR officials at my office in the Maritime Services Board (MSB) building in February 1970. One month later the society was delighted to receive a letter from the minister saying that the section of the expressway would be a bored tunnel, not open-cut.

Bernard immediately posed the question 'How vitally necessary is the North Western Expressway?', and its appropriateness was now challenged by the Glebe Society.[15] Albert Mispel, Glebe Society planning convenor, conducted an extraordinarily focused anti-expressway campaign, writing and printing a newssheet, *Moving and Living*, from his Cardigan Street home in the evenings, disseminating information and lobbying the authorities.[16]

As local industries were encouraged to leave land zoned industrial along Glebe's waterfront, Bernard questioned the zoning of this land, seeking the MSB's plans for it. At a public meeting about Glebe's waterfront in August 1970, and at a protest at the end of Leichhardt Street on 12 September 1970, local aldermen pledged their support to change the waterfront zoning. The MSB considered the waterfront might be needed in the future, and was adamant the industrial zoning would remain. Smith expressed the view to society members that Glebe was 'an ideal spot for much-needed student housing. The harbour and inner city suburbs are already polluted enough. More industry would only add to the problems',[17] and then argued the case for waterfront rezoning in 'Will Black Wattles Bloom in Blackwattle Bay?', published in *The Sydney Morning Herald* in September 1970.[18]

Anxious to influence planning policy, the Glebe Society completed a master plan in April 1970, expressing the need for conservation and preservation, and presented it to Leichhardt Council in September 1970. Three months after the plan had been returned to council from the State Planning Authority, the authority's recommendations had not been considered by council nor released to the society.[19] Smith recalled that an official study of Glebe by the State Planning Authority in 1970 advised the Glebe Society that, in its view, the only buildings in the suburb worth preserving were a group of bungalows built in the 1930s.[20]

A protest against proposed high-rise development at 59–61 Ferry Road, Glebe, attracted 200 residents who, led by Bernard Smith armed with a megaphone, marched down Glebe Point Road on 6 March 1971 to a rally in a small park in Ferry Road (Fig. 31). The Glebe Society had presented a petition to ward alderman Dr H. J. Foley, who failed to pass it on to council as promised. Smith was reported in the press as saying 'Ratepayers and citizens of Glebe would no longer tolerate Council's double dealing, their betrayal, or their arrogance. Foley let us down'.[21] Though Leichhardt Council rejected the Ferry Road proposal on 16 March 1970, Smith's views brought a swift response from the ward alderman. At Leichhardt Council chambers, Bernard reported that Dr Foley gave 'a hell-fire and damnation type of speech', castigating the Glebe Society and president Smith 'as a gang of larrikins and dastardly plant-tramplers'.[22] The rough and tumble of inner-city machine politics at Leichhardt Town Hall was not something Bernard had previously encountered. After being subjected to their ridicule Smith quietly enquired whether councillors were afforded the same legal immunity that parliamentarians enjoyed.

Confronted by an unsympathetic Labor-controlled council that made decisions behind closed doors, and attempts within Australian Labor Party (ALP) branches to proscribe Glebe Society members, the society decided to actively support candidates under the banner of Campaign for a Better Council (CBC) at elections on 18 September 1971.[23] Six CBC councillors in coalition with independent Balmain councillors Origlass and Wyner controlled the new council (1971–74), which adopted a conservation, anti-expressway and open-council platform. Council implemented more stringent zoning restrictions for Glebe, prohibiting uncontrolled apartment-block development and incursions of non-residential land uses.[24]

Sydney's expressways were planned at a time when the inner suburbs were coloured in as 'zones of blight' on planning maps, and because of their low status their residents were to bear the brunt of the 'greater good'; in the 1970s the DMR assumed inner-city housing would continue to decay. The two proposed expressways effectively sliced Glebe into three sections and would displace about 2500 residents. The historic house 'Lyndhurst', in the pathway of the North Western Expressway and threatened with demolition, became a symbol of the anti-expressway movement. Bernard met the commissioner of main roads, urging the preservation of Lyndhurst, and *The Herald* provided him with the opportunity to argue his case in February 1972 in 'A House with a History'.[25] But the DMR pressed ahead, with bulldozers moving into the Darghan Street area in April 1972, demolishing houses. They were confronted by residents and squatters in DMR-affected properties. After several confrontations with police and demolishers, the Builders Labourers Federation (BLF) was called on to impose a 'Green Ban' on the North Western Expressway, which it did, and the DMR withdrew from Glebe. But the battle was far from over. The Green Bans were very much a response to insensitive official attitudes, especially towards predominantly working-class people close to the city.

The Askin Government was unwilling to abandon the expressway network—local Labor state parliamentarian Pat Hills was in favour of it—but Leichhardt Council under Mayor Nick Origlass actively opposed it and led a paint-in by the Leichhardt Anti-Expressway campaign in Bridge Road, Glebe, in February 1972. The Green Bans, imposed by the communist-led BLF with Jack Mundey, Joe Owens and Bob Pringle its most prominent figures, took on the classic features of an urban social movement: it was sudden, unexpected and spontaneous, and relatively short lived (from 1972 to 1974). But its impact was dramatic, shutting down a series of construction projects.[26] Bernard, Society president in 1974, wrote: 'we must develop the widest possible public opposition to both the Western and North-Western Expressways, and co-operate closely with the increasing number of anti-expressway groups'.[27]

The federal ALP government led by Gough Whitlam, elected in December 1972 with a program of social reform and open government, was also the first federal government to produce explicit urban policies. After this government acquired control over urban arterial roads (those it had funded), the Askin state government gave the DMR orders to move into Fig Street, Ultimo, in October 1974 with its bulldozers, and begin demolition work. They were confronted by the BLF and a miscellaneous collection of people from across the spectrum, united in their opposition to urban radial expressways: the Glebe Anti-Expressway Group, Leichhardt Council, Anti-Urban Radial Expressways, Glebe Society members and others.[28] The confrontation and vigil at Fig Street received national coverage, halting further demolition. Later reflecting on this political campaign, Bernard was diffident about moving too far out front on this issue, as the disappearance in 1975 of Juanita Nielsen, after waging a campaign against the redevelopment of Victoria Street in Kings Cross, was ample testimony that opposing powerful interests could be a dangerous business.

A representative of the Glebe Administration Board told the Glebe Society in September 1969 about its plans to redevelop the Anglican Church's Glebe Lands, to include giant office blocks and town houses, but when these plans were submitted to Leichhardt Council they were rejected.[29] After making a topographical survey of the Glebe Lands, the Society had sufficient research material to prepare a pamphlet, *The Glebe Lands of Bishopthorpe and St Phillips: The Case for Preservation and Restoration*, when the Anglican Synod announced plans in October 1972 to sell off part of the Glebe Lands.[30] A submission was made to the Glebe Administration Board, lobbying it to retain its land in Glebe. The paper contained two main strands. Firstly the Glebe Lands' cottages and terraces of the period 1860 to 1880 formed a continuous townscape, representing a valuable cross-section of Australian domestic architecture. And secondly it argued for retention of a tract of Glebe inhabited for more than a century by low-income families, a vibrant community possessing a coherence and identity of its own.

Leichhardt's Mayor Origlass urged the federal government to buy the Glebe Lands. The newly created federal Department of Urban and Regional Development under minister Tom Uren changed the face of urban planning. It appointed Jackson Teece Chesterman Willis & Partners Pty Ltd to carry out a feasibility study on the proposed acquisition of the Glebe Lands, and the federal government acquired the lands for $17.5 million under the *Glebe Lands (Appropriation) Act 1974*, a unique venture by government to rehabilitate rather than redevelop.[31] It demonstrated that terraces could be refurbished for considerably less than the cost of a single high-rise unit.[32] Halting redevelopment of the Glebe Lands was fundamental to retention of Glebe's social mix.

On a number of occasions I walked with Bernard around Glebe's streets, often on Saturday afternoons, discussing how and when development took place from neighbourhood to neighbourhood, and anomalies on the landscape. After Bernard had soaked up the built environment and an immediate sense of the past, his acute original thinking was on display, open to ideas and possibilities, able to make complex connections. Our conversations ranged across a broad spectrum, with Bernard's intellectual vigour and insights opening up new ways of looking at things; few thought Glebe had anything worth writing about, but we did, and it was great to share my enthusiasms with kindred spirits.[33]

Bernard later urged a broader base for local history to develop: a historical society, a local history journal, photographers to create a visual inventory, a museum for local antiquities, archaeological digs, and so on. The first issue of the *Leichhardt Historical Journal* in 1971 was greeted enthusiastically by the Smiths.[34] An unformed collection of materials was being melded in the crucible of Bernard's mind, where the idea of an architectural history was taking shape, and I was happy they found my Glebe thesis of some value for their planned book.

At the end of 1948, when Glebe lost its municipal identity and came within the enlarged boundaries of the Sydney City Council, its municipal records fared badly. Most of its correspondence was destroyed and other records ended up in diverse locations. The minute books later went from Glebe to Leichhardt; its rate books, crucial for dating local houses, were located unkempt in the bowels of Sydney Town Hall, and a submission was made for their transfer to the then Archives Office of New South Wales. Photographs of Glebe aldermen were recovered from a disused Darlington air raid shelter. Once these sources were tracked down, other complementary research materials—Sands' directories, Sydney subdivision boxes, tenders, land titles and a miscellaneous collection of plans—were evaluated in the quest for accuracy in house dating.[35] Kate worked through the Glebe rate books in a systematic way, filling her notebooks with data, her painstaking labour meticulously recorded in the footnotes and printed sources.

Bernard wrote the text of the Glebe book in close collaboration with Kate, locating buildings in a taxonomy of styles—Colonial Georgian, Regency, Victorian Gothic, Italianate and the notion of a fifth style, Federation, which he promulgated, flourished in the country immediately before the Federation of the Australian colonies in 1901.[36] Their *Architectural Character of Glebe*, published in 1973, was a seminal work tracing the stylistic evolution of the Australian terrace house. But the work did more than define and defend the architectural fabric of Glebe. The book's introduction was a polemical defence of a threatened inner-city neighbourhood, a form of consciousness-raising, designed to show us the rich heritage we had all but taken for granted.[37] It urged legislative protection for Glebe as part of safeguarding 'a future and more civilised Australia', and the book gathered together hard evidence for the National Trust to list Glebe as a conservation area in 1974. The idea of a historic building, one to be restored as far as possible to its original state and shored up against the ravages of time, is a comparatively recent concept. The first piece of Australian legislation was Victoria's *Historic Buildings Act 1974* and in 1977 New South Wales passed the *Heritage Act*.

As the migration of more affluent workers into Glebe increased in tempo, some traditional residents were being pushed out; Bernard urged preservation of Glebe's social mix because, he wrote, 'it provides a more diversified style of life than suburbs styled to only one or two income-strata of the community'.[38] Years later, on his return to Glebe in December 1989 for Oxford University Press's reissue of the Glebe book, Bernard told *The Sydney Morning Herald* that 'public ownership of a large part of Glebe had prevented working class people being moved out'.[39]

Smith's lifelong concerns about fraternity and community linked directly to these virtues Glebe celebrated, and, as Terry Smith recalled, he 'was acutely sensitive to the politics of the unequal exchange: in life, in culture, in art'.[40] In his determination to chart the relations between art, society and politics, Bernard was a cultural activist. The Glebe Estate Workshop, in which he was involved, brought together a group of artists, workers and craftspeople under one roof on the corner of Derwent and Mitchell Streets in 1976, providing an opportunity for the community to participate in the creation of artwork. Bernard hoped the project would be self-supporting; however, he said, 'if it doesn't serve the local people then the idea has not worked'.[41]

Campaigns by inner-city residents to protect their neighbourhoods occupy an important place in this embryonic time for heritage and heritage conservation, and in his role as president of the Glebe Society (1969–71 and 1974–75) Bernard Smith brought to the debate a highly developed sense of history and the environment. Articulate, open to ideas and possibilities, he relished defending his suburb against threats that would irrevocably change the townscape of Glebe—expressways, high-rise units and industrial development. And, as he was a prominent public figure, articles he wrote for Sydney newspapers in defence of inner Sydney presented a compelling case for the conservation movement.

Council's rejection of high-rise buildings in Ferry Road in 1971 was an important win for grass-roots agitation, but the crowning glory, the resident confrontation at Fig Street, Ultimo, in October 1974, ultimately meant there would be no expressway construction through Glebe. Under enlightened initiatives of the Commonwealth Department of Urban and Regional Development the new expressway system was re-routed through Pyrmont and Glebe Island, preventing Glebe and other suburbs from 'being dehumanised and scarred with a wide swathe that would cut them in two'.[42] Glebe's willingness to engage in a 'good stoush', embodied by its 800 World War I diggers, was revived in a time of environmental crisis. The BLF and a miscellaneous collection of resident groups turned up in force at Fig Street, where Bernard, confronted by bulldozers, chains and police, addressed protesters; within a short time the Whitlam Federal Government withdrew funding for arterial roads.

A conglomeration of circumstances between 1972 and 1974 came together to ensure the physical fabric and character of Glebe remained intact, and, as we have seen, Bernard fought the good fight and was an integral part of this resident activism. On his retirement in 1977 Bernard and Kate moved to 168 Nicholson Street in Fitzroy, Melbourne, to be near their children, but they retained fond memories and a deep affection for Glebe.

NOTES

1 Henry Lawson, 'Faces in the Street', first published in *The Bulletin*, 28 July 1888.

2 H. J. Dyos, 'The Victorian City in Historical Perspective', in H. J. Dyos, D. Cannadine and D. A. Reeder (eds), *Exploring the Urban Past: Essays in Urban History*, Cambridge University Press, Cambridge, 1982, pp. 3–18.

3 Bernard Smith, 'On Perceiving the Australian Suburb', in Rosemary Dobson (ed.), *Australian Voices: Poetry and Prose of the 1970s*, Canberra Fellowship of Australian Writers in association with Australian National University Press, Canberra, 1975, p. 107.

4 Cumberland County Council, *Report of the Planning Scheme for the County of Cumberland, New South Wales*, Cumberland County Council, Sydney, 1948, p. 33.

5 Smith, 'On Perceiving the Australian Suburb', p. 116.

6 Graeme Davison, 'A Brief History of the Australian Heritage Movement', in Graeme Davison and Chris McConville (eds), *A Heritage Handbook*, Allen & Unwin, Sydney, 1991, p. 18.

7 Kevin O'Connor, R. J. Stimson and Maurice T. Daly, *Australia's Changing Economic Geography: A Society Dividing*, Oxford University Press, Melbourne, 2001, p. 27.

8 Anthony Strachan, Elias Duek-Cohen and Harold Johnston, *Local Civic Groups and Planning*, Civic Design Society, University of New South Wales, Sydney, 1971, p. 13.

9 Andrew Jakubowicz, 'The Green Ban Movement: Urban Struggle and Class Politics', in C. Paris and J. Halligan (eds), *Housing In Australia*, Macmillan, Melbourne, 1984, p. 59.

10 *Sydney Morning Herald*, 25 April 1969.

11 *Sydney Morning Herald*, 20 June 1969, p. 13; *Glebe Society News Bulletin*, vol. 1, no. 1, July 1969, p. 1.

12 Smith, 'On Perceiving the Australian Suburb', p. 117.

13 'Society Formed to "Save" Glebe', *Local Leader*, 9 July 1969, p. 1.

14 *Glebe Society News Bulletin*, vol. 1, no. 7, January 1970, p. 4.

15 *Glebe Society News Bulletin*, vol. 1, no. 9, March 1970, p. 1.

16 *Glebe Society News Bulletin*, vol. 2, no. 3, September 1970, p. 3.

17 *Glebe Society News Bulletin*, vol. 2 no. 3, September 1970, p. 2.

18 Bernard Smith, 'Will Black Wattles Bloom in Blackwattle Bay?', *Sydney Morning Herald*, 26 September 1970, p. 21.

19 Robert Johnston, 'Participation in Local Government: Leichhardt 1971–1974', in Richard Lucy (ed.), *The Pieces of Politics*, 2nd edn, Macmillan, Melbourne, 1979, p. 245.

20 Smith, 'On Perceiving the Australian Suburb', p. 117.

21 *Glebe Weekly*, 10 March 1971, p. 1.

22 *Glebe Society Bulletin*, no. 3 of 1971, p. 1; *Sydney Morning Herald*, 17 March 1971, p. 7.

23 *Glebe Weekly*, 21 July 1971, p. 2; *Glebe Society Bulletin*, no. 6 of 1971, p. 1.

24 Johnston, 'Participation in Local Government', pp. 245–8, p. 1.

25 Bernard Smith, 'A House with a History', *Sydney Morning Herald*, 26 February 1972, p. 20.

26 R. J. Roddewig, *Green Bans: The Birth of Australian Environmental Politics*, Hale & Iremonger, Sydney, 1978, p. 30.

27 *Glebe Society Bulletin*, no. 7 of 1974, p. 1.

28 R. Cain, Transportation, Planning and Conflict in Sydney: A Case Study of Inner City Expressways, BSc Thesis, University of New South Wales, Sydney, 1975, pp. 85–6.

29 *The Glebe Society News Bulletin*, vol. 1, no. 3, September 1969, p. 2.

30 *Australian*, 14 October 1972, p. 9; *Sydney Morning Herald*, 19 October 1972, p 15.

31 Jackson Teece Chesterman Willis & Partners Pty Ltd, *The Church of England Lands, Glebe: A Report to the Department of Urban and Regional Development*, Jackson Teece Chesterman Willis & Partners Pty Ltd, Sydney, 1973.

32 C. Wagner, 'Sydney's Glebe Project: An Essay in Urban Rehabilitation', *Royal Australian Planning Institute Journal*, vol. 15, no. 1, February 1977, pp. 3–24.

33 Max Solling, *Grandeur and Grit: A History of Glebe*, Halstead Press, Sydney, 2007, pp. 265–6.

34 Smith, 'On Perceiving the Australian Suburb', p. 118.

35 Peter Balmford and J. L. O'Brien, 'Dating Houses in Victoria', *Historical Studies: Australia and New Zealand*, vol. 9, no. 36, 1961, pp. 379–80; Max

Solling, *Source Materials for Local History*, self-published typescript, 1970.

36 Bernard Smith, 'Architecture in Australia', *Historical Studies*, no. 14, 1969, pp. 90–1.

37 Mark Thomas, *Australia in Mind: Thirteen Influential Australian Thinkers*, Hale & Iremonger, Sydney, 1989, p. 61.

38 Bernard Smith and Kate Smith, *The Architectural Character of Glebe, Sydney*, University Co-operative Bookshop, Sydney, 1973.

39 Bernard Smith, quoted in 'Old Glebe Meets New', *Sydney Morning Herald*, 4 December 1989, p. 4.

40 Terry Smith, 'Vale Bernard Smith', *Power Institute News*, 16 February 2012.

41 *Leichhardt Local*, 26 October 1976, p. 7.

42 Tom Uren, *Straight Left*, Random House Australia, Sydney, 1994, p. 282.

The Marxist collector:
the art collection of Bernard and Kate Smith

KATE CHALLIS

In memory of my grandmother, who after almost thirty years is still missed.

One of the first theories I recall my grandfather teaching me was that of 'speculative consumption'. He shunned luxury and consumerism all his life. Wealth, or rather its pursuit, he believed corrupted. The notion of owning things as status symbols both perplexed and, at times, enraged him. My grandparents' house was filled with books, and their lives with experiences, and yet over their lifetime Kate and Bernard Smith amassed an extensive collection of art. This chapter looks at what they collected and how Bernard reconciled the collection's escalating monetary worth with his own moral compass.

Being the consummate historian, Bernard compiled two inventories of his art collection, the first made on 12 June 1977, following his retirement as Power Professor and before his move to Melbourne.[1] It itemises the collection at their Glebe home and lists some eighty framed works, thirty-one artifacts including sculptures, ceramics, carvings and textiles, as well as 176 works on paper in his print cabinet. The second inventory, made twenty years later, only records the works hanging on the walls, which totalled 127 framed pieces.[2]

A broad overview of these inventories reveals the Smiths' interests and tastes. Not surprisingly, many of the works were by their contemporaries and friends, such as John Perceval, Vic O'Connor, David and Arthur Boyd, Donald Friend and their neighbour Sali Herman. But not exclusively so: early Australian modernists were represented, including Max Meldrum, Thea Proctor, Margaret Preston, Roland Wakelin and Grace Cossington Smith. Provocative political works by Richard Larter, Mike Brown and Mandy Martin hung beside historical pieces by Frederick McCubbin, Eugene von Guérard and convict painter William Buelow Gould. Despite Bernard's reputation for being a champion of figurative art, he and Kate also owned numerous abstract pieces, including an early Peter Booth and a Tony Tuckson.

While paintings, prints and drawings by Australians prevailed, a few international artists were also collected. The Italian surrealist Enrico Baj and New Zealander Colin McCahon were acquired (Fig. 38), alongside an array of miscellaneous items such as two Tibetan prints on rice paper, a Chinese watercolour of a cherry blossom, two Hogarth prints, a large Tongan tapa cloth, an original woodcut from a 1562 edition of the Bible, and posters from the May 1968 student protests in Paris. They bought ceramics, including a Boyd coffee service and pieces by Les Blakebrough and Peter Travis, which was an interest largely encouraged by Kate.[3]

Bernard was the primary purchaser of the art. Nevertheless, Kate's influence is stamped on the collection. In fact, the foundation of their collecting was the four works she brought with her from England in 1938: a *Winchester script lettering prepared for Ruth Adeney* (1921) by the father of modern typography, Edward Johnston, and three works by Eric Gill: a woodcut of her best friend's mother, *Clare Pepler*, a sculpture of the Madonna and Child and a pencil drawing of the same subject.[4] Kate grew up in Ditchling, a small village in East Sussex, surrounded by art and craftsmen of the Guild of St Joseph and Dominic, an artistic community founded by Gill.[5] Her adoptive father, Cuthbert Adeney, was a surgeon; her adoptive mother, Hilda, a child from the bohemian Ruskinians. They supported the arts by purchasing works from their neighbours and friends. Kate, like Bernard, had strong views about what she liked and what she did not. While he usually consulted her on the purchase of works of art, he did not always listen.

The first major piece Bernard acquired was Vic O'Connor's *The refugees* (1941), which he bought from the artist's studio while on a trip to Melbourne in 1945 (Fig. 33). In a letter back home to Kate he wrote 'which I am sure you will like'.[6] She did not. While she admired its intention, the painting haunted her. Until the end of his life it was one of the pieces Bernard was proudest of owning. While Kate was alive it always hung in Bernard's study—in part due to Kate's feelings, and in part because it embodied that which Bernard admired most about visual arts: the relationship between morality and beauty. O'Connor's painting was, and given the current political climate still is, a challenging statement about humanity, or rather the lack thereof, towards the dispossessed.

Indeed, while Bernard championed political art, Kate had a penchant for more intimate domestic subjects and she was the force behind the acquisition of one of Perceval's ceramic angels (Fig. 34), their Grace Cossington Smith (Fig. 24) and a Margaret Olley still life. The circumstances of this last purchase are not clear, but what is vivid is Bernard's position about it. He refused to have the painting in their house; Kate, ever the peacemaker, complied with his wishes. Domestic scenes and landscapes by historically significant artists, such as William Buelow Gould's *Still life with dead game* (c. 1845, now in the Geelong Gallery) seemed to be exempt from Bernard's staunch stance.

A work Bernard bought on a whim was *Boys catching crabs in Connemara* (c. 1948) by Irish artist Gerard Dillon, whom he met at The Abbey Arts Centre and Museum, an alternative artists' community in New Barnet on the outskirts of London, where Bernard and the family lived between 1949 and 1950 (Fig. 32).[7] It must have been quite a place to be, with James Gleeson, Leonard French, Inge and Graham King, Douglas Green, Noel Counihan and their families all residing there.[8] The artists focused on their work while the children played in the garden and Bernard wrote his seminal paper 'European Vision and the South Pacific'.[9] Some fifty years later Bernard recalled that Dillon's *Boys*:

> possessed a gay sense of humour and folksy charm … I felt it would be easy to live with in a life that was being increasingly devoted to the tough problems of scholarship. A reminder of my origins.[10]

Indeed, this was quite a contrast to the bleak, politically charged Vic O'Connor he had bought only three years earlier.

Bernard maintained that he never collected, but simply bought works by friends who needed help. There is no doubt that altruism was a strong motivator in his decisions on both what art to buy and when to buy it. During his 1945 sojourn in Melbourne, in which he purchased the Vic O'Connor, he also visited Noel Counihan to look at his most recent works, which he described in a letter back to Kate as 'magnificent … If he continues in this manner he will become one of the most important painters in the country'.[11] Yet Bernard did not acquire anything. It was only when Vance Palmer was raising money to send Noel abroad several years later that he purchased a series of twelve lithographs called *War or peace* (1950) which stayed wrapped up in Bernard's print cabinet for the remainder of his life.[12] There are numerous examples demonstrating Bernard and Kate's sensitivity to the financial predicament that plagued many artists, and this also influenced their acquisitions.[13] Shortly after buying Rick Amor's woodcut *The ship* in August 1988, Bernard recalled that the artist 'called in unannounced at lunchtime to seek payment … he was then obviously short of cash'.[14]

Indeed, Bernard felt that he had a moral obligation to help those who were 'a bit hard up' and especially those who treated him with a smudge of disdain. In July 1961 John Perceval wrote to Bernard accusing him of publicly 'embarrass(ing) … undermin(ing) and underrat(ing)' him. Perceval signs off: 'Best wishes anyway "Brother"', but not before saying, 'With your help (I am sure, unknowingly) you are keeping me back—at least psychologically',[15] even though Bernard had described Perceval's 1958 *Angels* exhibition at Heide as 'one of the most important one-man shows held in Australia since the war'.[16] From this exhibition he had purchased *Angel learning to walk* for 80 guineas.[17] Unlike the Vic O'Connor, this mischievous toddler was adored by Kate, and she was heartbroken when it was stolen from their Glebe home some ten years later. They owned two other works by Perceval: a 'muffin dish' and *Romulus and Remus* (oil on paper).[18] Five years later Bernard sent to Sydney University Press a draft of a monograph on Perceval.[19]

In the years leading up to 1960, the Smiths' serious collecting began. Bernard now held senior positions, his children were adults and he had more discretionary income. In 1959, the year of the infamous *Antipodeans* art exhibition and manifesto,[20] he purchased Eugene von Guérard's superb *Forest scene near Kiama* (1863) from McClelland Galleries, Melbourne, for 35 guineas, equivalent to $958 in 2013 (Fig. 35).[21]

His collecting intensified during his time as *The Age* art critic (1963–66) and reached its peak during his tenure as the inaugural Power Professor and Director of the Power Institute, University of Sydney (1967–77). He believed that with these positions came a role as cultural advocate, and this he wholeheartedly embraced. While acting as Power Professor, Bernard was actively involved in the protests against the demolition of Glebe (Fig. 31), was a constant at contemporary art exhibitions, and was a regular visitor to the radical Yellow House artists' collective in Macleay Street near Kings Cross. In October 1969 both Kate and Bernard worked alongside Christo and Jeanne-Claude and some hundred students, artists and teachers to wrap 2.5 kilometres of the south-east coastline in fabric.[22] During these years in Sydney, Bernard acquired works by some of the most controversial artists of the time, such as Mike Brown's *Standing still, it outpaces the runner* and Richard Larter's *Well all right, so how* (1970) (Fig. 36),[23] but he did not do so to the exclusion of other art. In 1973, he finally bought a major work by his longtime friend Noel Counihan, *Woman with candle* (1972) from Counihan's solo show in London.[24] The following year saw the acquisition of *Preparing for the North Shore Bridge* (1925) by John Moore.[25] Once Bernard retired in 1976, the collection continued to expand and in 1978 Bernard purchased works by a number of historically significant artists including *The blue Mediterranean* by Frederick McCubbin, painted in 1907 on the artist's only trip abroad, and *Sydney coastal landscape* (c. 1914–15) by Emanuel Phillips Fox.[26] At the same Christie's auction he successfully bid for *Landscape and farm house* (1925) by early modernist Roland Wakelin, whose work he had admired since the 1940s.[27]

Kate always regretted not having bought one of Arthur Boyd's *Bride* series. When Boyd was painting these, the families saw a lot of each other, while living in what were then the bohemian Melbourne bayside suburbs of Beaumaris and Sandringham. Nevertheless, they enjoyed looking after Boyd's paintings in the late 1950s while Arthur and Yvonne were abroad. As late as 1981, Boyd was finally represented in their collection when Bernard purchased his still life *Mackarel*.[28] Reviewing the works Bernard owned, and when they were purchased, it is hard not to argue that he was building a collection of sorts.

Naturally a number of the pieces were gifts from the artists, such as Sali Herman's *Dead parrot* (1961) and Clifford Bayliss's *Surrealist bird* (1945),[29] or they were bought from the artists directly or at exhibitions, sometimes those that Bernard reviewed or opened. In his review for *The Age* he wrote that Jean Bellette's 1964 exhibition at South Yarra Gallery 'lifts the heart and rouses the spirit of all who love good paintings. I cannot recall an exhibition in Melbourne of this quality since I began to write this column'.[30] From this exhibition he bought *Above Fornalutz*.[31] Charles Doutney's *Rue de Macleay* (c. 1953) he purchased when he opened Doutney's 'first one man show at Macquarie Galleries'.[32] Thomas Gleghorn's *Crucifixion* he purchased from Gleghorn's 1959 exhibition, which he opened.[33]

My grandparents believed it was the responsibility of individuals to actively support the arts by purchasing works. I recall as a child and teenager being taken to avant-garde productions at La Mama and the Pram Factory theatres. Even if we could not attend or the play was not to their liking, their attitude was that creative experimentation should be supported, regardless of the end result. These were the days when visual art had not yet been substantially monetised, so it was still affordable. On their wedding day, Bernard and Kate did not have enough money for a celebratory dinner, 'as they had spent £10 buying a beautiful "Negroid" vase by Muriel Medworth'.[34]

Although Kate and Bernard consistently supported the arts, they rarely spent vast sums. Adjusting for inflation, many pieces, such as the von Guérard, Jean Bellette and Roger Kemp, cost them less than the equivalent of $1000 in 2013.[35] A significant number were priced below $5000, including the Colin McCahon, Phillips Fox, McCubbin, Thomas Gleghorn, Lyndon Dadswell and Perceval.[36] Reflecting on the prices for contemporary art today, these are modest sums. The only outlier is Donald Friend's *John Bell's party* (Fig. 37), which cost them $2500 in 1975; adjusted for inflation this is approximately $15,000 in 2013.[37] Investment and capital gain were never part of their decision-making process; in fact, any suggestions of these motives would have appalled them both.

Nevertheless, soon after Bernard's retirement and return to Melbourne he wrote to gallery owner Joseph Brown to renew their acquaintance:

> I have never regarded myself a serious collector, but I have bought a few things from time to time which are of interest and have become valuable … [and] would like to avail myself of the new income tax provisions which allows concessions to income tax for works given to public institutions.[38]

Then he mentioned that the Hamilton Art Gallery, a public art gallery in south-east Victoria 'may be interested in a gift of one or two from my collection'. Four days later Brown did visit Bernard.[39] While no while official valuation exists and the Hamilton offer came to nothing, the von Guérard must have caught Brown's eye, and within a fortnight it was at his gallery.[40] This is not surprising, given that two years earlier the sale of von Guérard's *View of Purrumbete Station* fetched an unprecedented $22,000.[41] Initially Bernard's painting was to be offered at Joseph Brown's autumn show,[42] but a month later Brown wrote to inform him that the Australian National Gallery had reserved it.[43] On 16 June 1978 Bernard wrote to Joe, saying:

> I'm in no great hurry for the money ... I would certainly like it to go to an Australian public collection, if possible. But I should be willing to sell the painting to you now for the $8,000 agreed upon on the understanding that you would only offer it to a public collection, ie state or provincial within the first six months after purchase.[44]

Nine days later Brown sold the painting to the Australian National Gallery for $10,500.[45] Bernard's letter indicates a level of impatience, which was a typical characteristic of his: once he had made his mind up about something he wanted it done immediately. He would have been content with $8000 rather than chase a higher figure, especially if that work would end up in a public institution.

Bernard had a keen sense of wanting important works to go to galleries. Towards the end of his life, Bernard was determined to secure a permanent home for his *The advance of Lot and his brethren* and *Pompeii*, which he had painted in 1941. With the help of Daniel Thomas a deal was brokered in 2008: Bernard would donate *Lot* to the now National Gallery of Australia on the proviso that the gallery would purchase *Pompeii*. Bernard was also instrumental in the Art Gallery of New South Wales acquiring Grace Cossington Smith's *The sock knitter* (1915) (Fig. 23). In June 1960 Bernard wrote to Daniel Thomas at the gallery:

> As the Sydney Gallery seems to be in the process of buying paintings by the early Sydney moderns, it might well consider Miss Grace Cossington Smith's *The Sock Mender* [*sic*] ... It is an exquisite painting ... and it would make a fine acquisition

> to the Sydney Gallery. I bought *The Reader* [*sic*] of hers myself and would love to own *The Sock Mender* [*sic*] too but I do think it should be in a public collection. If you don't want it I shall mention it to the Melbourne Gallery.[46]

Thomas responded a few weeks later, saying that he had gone to see the painting and a recommendation for its purchase would be submitted to the next board meeting.[47]

The sock knitter had been part of the 1915 exhibition of the Royal Art Society of New South Wales, and is considered to be the first post-impressionist painting to be shown in Australia.[48] Bernard and Kate's painting, known as *The school cape,* not *The reader* as Bernard had referred to it, was painted a year later, and in many ways is its companion piece (Fig. 24).[49] Madge, Grace's sister, is depicted in both, seated while absorbed in the traditional female activities of knitting and reading. My grandmother, an avid reader and knitter, absolutely adored this painting.

While there is no further extant documentation about the purchase of this piece, I can only imagine that my grandmother had a persuasive influence on the decision to acquire it. Not only would the style have appealed to her, but also the gender of the artist and the subject matter—doubly so. It is likely Bernard saw these works at Cossington Smith's Turramurra home when he interviewed her while researching *Australian Painting, 1788–1960*, the first edition of which was published in 1962; *The sock knitter* was one of the few colour plates in the volume.[50]

It was not until Kate's death in 1989 that Bernard began liquidating his collection, and for a very specific purpose. The first painting sold was Cossington Smith's *The school cape*, only four months after my grandmother died. It was a painting she loved and Grandpa told me that she would have never let him sell it. Fetching a staggering $93,500 at Sotheby's in April 1989, it was the most valuable work from his collection.[51] Heartened by the success of this sale, he went on to sell another eight paintings the following August, including his Colin McCahon (Fig. 38), Peter Booth, Harold Weaver Hawkins, Donald Friend, Margaret Preston, William Frater and Roland Wakelin; together they raised a further $98,200.[52] The proceeds of these two sales, made from his most valuable pieces of art, formed the capital base for the endowment of an Indigenous art prize.

This was an idea he had been thinking about for some time. On 19 April 1984 Bernard made a will bequeathing the majority of his estate to the Australian Academy of the Humanities for the purpose of setting up an annual Indigenous art award, to be known as the Tierney-Challis Award (Tierney being his mother's maiden name and Challis my grandmother's).[53] Six years later my grandmother died and he changed his mind: he would set it up immediately in her memory. I recall him telling me that he wanted to do it himself, to ensure it was done properly. In the meantime, the Australian Centre at the University of Melbourne had been established and to this institute he entrusted the running of the Kate Challis Ruth Adeney Koori Award (RAKA): Kate Challis was my grandmother's birth name and Ruth Adeney her adoptive name. Bernard's writings notably omit Indigenous art, and a similar absence is evident in his art collection, with the exception of two spears and one bark painting. His Boyer Lectures, presented in 1980, and the establishment of the RAKA were his attempts to make amends. He strongly believed one should accept one's shortcomings with humility. This is the main reason why, in spite of criticism, he did not revise *Australian Painting*. He would tell me that each generation needs to write their account of the past. Up until the establishment of the RAKA he felt he had not done enough to encourage Indigenous artists. Paradoxically, it is the establishment of the RAKA that may be my grandfather's most enduring legacy.

Although Bernard and Kate's collection was, by the 1980s, extremely valuable, the irony is that my grandparents did not seek wealth. In fact whenever Bernard won a prize with some monetary value he quickly gave it away. The prize money from the 1984 Premier's Award for Non-Fiction for the first volume of his autobiography *The Boy Adeodatus* went towards the founding of the Nuclear Disarmament Party. By supporting the community in which he was intimately involved, Bernard was able to become an important philanthropist. RAKA would not have been possible without the capital growth of their art collection.

Today, a successful artist must satisfy numerous conditions, many both onerous and highly competed for: secure gallery representation, win prizes, gain entry to prominent public and private collections, excite the interest of professional commentators and scholars. Requiring an entire industry of critics, dealers, academics and curators, these conditions push the monetary value of art well out of reach of today's equivalents of Kate and Bernard Smith. In other words, on a lecturer's or curator's salary today, one cannot assemble the sort of collection my grandparents did between the 1940s and 1970s. They were active in a world where art could be readily owned, but was considered esoteric by wider society; compare that to today where art literacy and general appreciation are at all-time highs, yet its ownership is narrower than it ever was. Most readers of this book are directly or indirectly part of a buoyant monetary art market, to which Bernard himself contributed, but is this the best set of cultural conditions for the production and consumption of art?

In Bernard's time, buying art was not motivated by capital gains, self-funded superannuation or being a philanthropist. He purchased art because he believed in artists. Bernard often quoted Ernst Gombrich's iconic opening of *The Story of Art*: 'There really is no such thing as Art. There are only artists'.[54] Bernard bought art from artists he believed had merit, but also from those he believed needed monetary and personal encouragement. This is evident when we read Bernard's letters and diaries, which are filled with a vibrant correspondence with numerous artists, some of whom are household names today, others long forgotten. With both, he communicated with the same amount of dedication and support. His Marxist values and beliefs caused him to collect for no other reason than that he could spend time, money and effort on personal interaction and fellowship with artists of his day. He never collected to increase his own wealth, rather he collected to foster culture.

Thank you to the following people for their help with this chapter:

Joan McClelland from the Joshua McClelland Print Room, Susan Thomas at the National Library of Australia, Dr Sheridan Palmer and Andrew Hollo.

NOTES

1 Bernard Smith, Inventory of drawings and paintings at 23 Avenue Road Glebe on 12 June 1977, National Library of Australia, Canberra, Bernard Smith Papers (hereafter NLA, BSP), MS Acc10.088, Box 32, Folder 436, Personal Collection—Paintings and Drawings.

2 Bernard Smith, Inventory of Artworks at Jeansville. 168 Nicholson St., Fitzroy. August 1997, NLA, BSP, MS Acc10.088, Box 32, Folder 436.

3 Bernard Smith, interviewed by Sheridan Palmer, 24 October 2008.

4 Ruth Adeney was Kate's adoptive name. Inventory 1977, pp. 2 and 8; Inventory 1997, pp. 13–14. These four works are now in private collections.

5 S. Falkner, 'Memories of a Ditchling Childhood', *Matrix*, vol. 13, Winter 1993, pp. 43–61.

6 Bernard Smith to Kate Smith, 13 August 1945, cited in Bernard Smith, *A Pavane for Another Time*, Macmillan, Melbourne, 2002, p. 138. *The refugees* was sold at auction: Deutscher Menzies, *Australian and International Paintings, Sculpture and Works on Paper*, 25 April 1999, Lot 26. The hammer price of $33,350 remains the highest paid for O'Connor's work. Australian Art Auction Records, www.artrecord.com.

7 Smith, *A Pavane for Another Time*, p. 389. Bernard eventually sold *Boys catching crabs* at auction: Deutscher Menzies, *Australian and International Fine Art*, 4–5 June 2003, Lot 42.

8 Smith, *A Pavane for Another Time*, pp. 343–86.

9 Bernard Smith, 'European Vision and the South Pacific', *Journal of the Warburg and Courtauld Institutes*, no. 13, 1950, pp. 66–100.

10 Smith, *A Pavane for Another Time*, p. 389.

11 Bernard Smith to Kate Smith, 18 August 1945, cited in Smith, *A Pavane for Another Time*, p. 140.

12 Smith, *A Pavane for Another Time*, p. 177. See Inventory 1977, p. 4. Eleven of the twelve lithographs are now part of NLA, BSP, MS Acc10.088, Box 75, Artworks 189–199.

13 Inventory 1977, p. 3; Inventory 1997, p. 8. In 1950 Bernard bought *Black sheep* from Carl Plate, who wrote thanking him for his interest and purchase, saying it was 'compensation for my financial extravagance of putting on a show in Melbourne'. Carl Plate to Bernard Smith, 29 September 1956, NLA, BSP.

14 Inventory 1997, p. 3. Bernard Smith, 'Gary Catalano's The Solitary Watcher: Rick Amor and his Art' [book review], *Australian Book Review*, vol. 234, 2001, p. 33.

15 John Perceval to Bernard Smith, 26 July 1961, Mitchell Library, Sydney (ML) Bernard Smith Papers, MSS 5202, Box 4.

16 Bernard Smith, 'The Antipodeans', *Australia To-Day* (special number of *The Australian Traveller*, Melbourne), no. 55, 14 October 1959, p. 104.

17 Approximately $2237 in 2012 values. RBA Inflation Calculator, www.rba.gov.au/calculator/annualPreDecimal.html. Museum of Modern Art of Australia, *John Perceval's Angels*, exhibition catalogue, Museum of Modern Art of Australia, Heidelberg, 1958, no. 16.

18 Inventory 1977, pp. 1, 8; Inventory 1997, p. 4. Sold at Deutscher Menzies, *Australian and International Paintings, Sculpture and Works on Paper*, 25 April 1999, Lot 47.

19 NLA, BSP, MS Acc10.088, Box 32, Folder 422, John Perceval.

20 *The Antipodeans* art exhibition, which included Charles Blackman, Arthur and David Boyd, John Brack, John Perceval, Clifton Pugh, Robert Dickerson and Bernard Smith, was held at the Victorian Artists' Society, 4–15 August 1959. Bernard Smith, 'The Antipodeans Exhibition: Notes for the Opening Address', in *The Critic as Advocate: Selected Essays 1948–1988*, Oxford University Press, Melbourne, 1989, pp. 130–4.

21 RBA Inflation Calculator, www.rba.gov.au/calculator/annualPreDecimal.html, 2012; Inventory 1977, p. 2; Joan McClelland, email to the author, 10 August 2012; McClelland Gallery, Melbourne, *Early Settlers*, December 1959, Lot 40a.

22 Bernard and Kate purchased a limited-edition, large-format photograph signed by Christo to commemorate the event. NLA, BSP, MS Acc10.088, Box 75, Artwork 133.

23 Inventory 1977, p. 1; Inventory 1997, p. 8. Smith sold both paintings at auction: Brown's *Standing still, it outpaces the runner* at Deutscher Menzies, 25 April 1999, Lot 31; Larter's *Well all right, so how* at Sotheby's Australia, *Australian and European Paintings*, 14 August 1990, Lot 207.

24 Commonwealth Institute to Bernard Smith, 27 November 1973, NLA, BSP, MS Acc10.088, Box 32, Folder 436, Personal Collection—Paintings and Drawings. Smith sold this painting at auction: Deutscher Menzies, 25 April 1999, Lot 46.

25 Inventory 1977, p. 1; Inventory 1997, p. 11.

Purchased for $300 from the John D. Moore exhibition, Macquarie Galleries, Sydney, 17–29 July 1974, Cat. 13; NLA, BSP, MS Acc10.088, Box 32, Folder 436. Smith sold the painting at auction: Deutscher Menzies, 25 April 1999, Lot 42.

26 Inventory 1997, pp. 4–5. Both purchased at auction: Christie's Australia, 20 March 1978, Lots 69, 70. Smith bought the McCubbin for $950 and the Phillips Fox for $650. See NLA, BSP, MS Acc10.088, Box 32, Folder 436. Sold by Smith at auction: Deutscher Menzies, 25 April 1999, Lots 38, 39.

27 Inventory 1997, p. 11. Purchased for $500 at auction: Christie's Australia, 20 March 1978, Lot 104. Sold for hammer price of $9,200 at Deutscher Menzies, 25 April 1999, Lot 43; Australian Art Auction Records, www.artrecord.com. Wakelin was included in the National Art Gallery of New South Wales exhibition *Some Recent Australian Painting* 1944, and in the exhibition that Smith curated at the Masonic Hall, Canberra, in December 1944. See Smith, *A Pavane for Another Time*, p. 115.

28 Australian Galleries, Melbourne, *Arthur Boyd*, 1981, Cat. 17. NLA, BSP, MS Acc10.088, Box 32, Folder 436. Sold at Deutscher Menzies, 25 April 1999, Lot 34, hammer price $21,275, Australian Art Auction Records, www.artrecord.com.

29 Inventory 1977, p. 1; Inventory 1997, pp. 3–4. Sold Deutscher Menzies, 25 April 1999, Lots 32–35, hammer price for Herman $6,900 and for Bayliss $2,185, Australian Art Auction Records, www.artrecord.com.

30 Bernard Smith, 'Paintings to Rouse Spirit of All', *The Age*, 19 August 1964, p. 5, republished as 'The Critic as Advocate', p. 193. South Yarra Gallery, Melbourne, *Jean Bellette*, August 1964, Cat. 14. Smith offered this painting at auction, but it remained unsold: Deutscher Menzies, *Australian and International Fine Art*, 4–5 June 2003, Lot 286.

31 Inventory 1977, p. 2; Inventory 1997, p. 4.

32 Newspaper cutting stuck on the back of the painting. Sold at auction, Deutscher Menzies, 25 April 1999, Lot 27.

33 Inventory 1977, p. 1. Gifted to John, his son, before the 1997 inventory and now in a private collection, Melbourne.

34 Kate Smith to her grandchildren, Christmas 1988, cited in Smith, *A Pavane for Another Time*, p. 18. According to the Macquarie Gallery sales book, they spent £2 on the vase. Art Gallery of New South Wales, Sydney, Macquarie Gallery Papers, MS 1995.9b.

35 Hermia Boyd's *Drawing of child with cat* was purchased from South Yarra Gallery on 6 August 1965 for 15 guineas ($362 in 2012); Roger Kemp's *Etching cat no. 1 sequence twelve* from Rudy Komon Art Gallery on 16 September 1972 for $75 ($475 today); Les Blakeborough's *Slab built pot cat. 2* from Bonython Galleries in 1972 for $40 ($367 in 2012); George Luke's *Two southern belles* for $600 ($1050 in 2012) in 1990 from Schubert Gallery; Joyce McGarth's *Tomatoes* for $580 in 1998 ($860 in 2012). NLA, BSP, MS Acc10.088, Box 32, Folder 436. RBA Inflation Calculator, www.rba.gov.au/calculator/annualPreDecimal.html.

36 He bought Phillips Fox's *Sydney coastal landscape* in 1978 for $650 ($3000 in 2012); McCubbin's *The blue Mediterranean* in 1978 for $960 ($3450 in 2012); John Moore's *Preparing for the North Shore Bridge* in 1974 ($2000 in 2012); Gleghorn's *Crucifixion* in 1959 for 60 guineas ($1643 in 2012); Perceval's *Angel learning to walk* for 80 guineas in 1958 ($2237 in 2012); a brass sculpture by Dadswell for $600 in 1974 ($4303 in 2012). Colin McCahon's *Waterfall* was imported into Australia in 1965, according the the Australian Customs Duty Receipt Book No. 650114; it was valued at £200 ($4500 in 2012). NLA, BSP, MS Acc10.088, Box 32, Folder 436. RBA Inflation Calculator, www.rba.gov.au/calculator/annualPreDecimal.html.

37 Inventory 1977, p. 2. *Donald Friend*, 18 March to 26 April 1975, Cat. 82, NLA, BSP, MS Acc10.088, Box 32, Folder 436. Sold at Sotheby's Australia, 14 August 1989, Lot 393, hammer price $19,800, Australian Art Auction Records, www.artrecord.com.

38 Bernard Smith to Joseph Brown, 23 January 1978, NLA, BSP, MS Acc10.088, Box 32, Folder 436.

39 Bernard Smith, Diary, 27 January 1978, NLA, BSP, MS Acc10.64, Box 2.

40 Joseph Brown, note to Bernard Smith, 5 February 1978, confirming receipt of the von Guérard oil painting *Fig tree near Kiama*. NLA, BSP, MS Acc10.088, Box 32, Folder 436.

41 Christie's Australia, *Australian Paintings*, 6 October 1976, Lot 298, Australian Art Sales Digest, www.aasd.com.au.

42 Joseph Brown to Bernard Smith, 5 February 1978, NLA, BSP, MS Acc10.088, Box 32, Folder 436.

43 Joseph Brown to Bernard Smith, 14 March 1978, NLA, BSP, MS Acc10.088, Box 32, Folder 436.

44 Bernard Smith to Joseph Brown, 16 June 1978, NLA, BSP, MS Acc10.088, Box 32, Folder 436.

45 The original agreement between Smith and Brown was 'ten thousand dollars (less 15% commission) and not less than the sum of eight thousand net to be paid to Prof Smith'. Joseph Brown, note to

Bernard Smith, 5 February 1978, NLA, BSP, MS Acc10.088, Box 32, Folder 436.

46 Bernard Smith to Daniel Thomas, 16 June 1960, NLA, BSP.

47 Daniel Thomas to Bernard Smith, 1 July 1960, NLA, BSP. The painting was purchased by the Art Gallery of New South Wales for 40 guineas directly from the artist; Art Gallery of New South Wales, *Acquisitions 1960–1965*, Art Gallery of New South Wales, Sydney, 1966, p. 28, no. 36.

48 Daniel Thomas, *Grace Cossington Smith*, Art Gallery of New South Wales, Sydney, 1973, Cat. 1.

49 This is not to be confused with Grace Cossington Smith's *The reader* (1916), in the Art Gallery of New South Wales, Sydney.

50 Bernard Smith, *Australian Painting, 1788–1960*, Oxford University Press, Melbourne, 1962, pl. 106.

51 Sotheby's Australia, *Fine Australian Paintings: Including the Dr John L. Raven Collection of Important Colonial Paintings*, auction catalogue, 17 April 1989, Lot 454. Sotheby's Australia to Bernard Smith, 'Sale advice 17 April 1989', Mitchell Library, Bernard Smith Papers, ML MSS 5202, add on 2022, Box 4.

52 Sotheby's Australia, *Fine Australian Painting Including Important Colonial Furniture, Silver and the J. and J. Altmann Art Reference Library*, 14 August 1989, Lots 107, 211, 247, 244, 398, 445 and 467. For sale price obtained: Sotheby's Australia to Bernard Smith, 'Sale advice 14 Aug 1989', Mitchell Library, Bernard Smith Papers, ML MSS 5202, add on 2022, Box 4.

53 '19 April 1984 Will of Bernard William Smith', pp. 4–9, NLA, BSP.

54 Ernst H. Gombrich, *The Story of Art*, 3rd edn, Phaidon, London, 1950, p. 4.

Ideological conduits and political coathangers:

Bernard Smith on Counihan and Courbet

SHERIDAN PALMER

The art of a class begins as a weapon and ends as a whip with a velvet thorn.

Bernard Smith[1]

Bernard Smith wrote this in his 1943 diary: romantic prose that reflects his early socio-political beliefs. These had developed from his deep reading of Marxism and in particular from having resided at the edge of society. His sense of class structure—formed by a lack of status as a fostered ward of the State—was so ingrained that as he matured it was difficult to separate the man from his political motives. By the late 1930s, as the European crisis reached a critical point, politics was driving his entire intellectual and emotional being. Karl Marx's famous dictum 'Every metamorphosis is to some extent a swan song, to some extent the overture to a grand new poem' captured Smith's fervent need to be a part of 'the great new political poem', one that integrated artistic growth into the lives of the working class.[2]

The political atmosphere during the late 1930s and 1940s in Australia, as in much of the Western world, was dominated by 'anti-Nazism, the Popular Front … the struggle between Stalin and Trotsky, between Marxism and anarchism' and was one in which 'literature play[ed] a central role in the dialectical process'.[3] At the time Smith joined the Communist Party of Australia in April 1939, cultural activity and literary criticism were important means of advocacy among workers and the civilian population. Smith's 'declaration of faith and hope' in a Marxist reform based upon proletariat idealism and democratic socialism found him joining the 'warm-hearted support' for the Soviet Union that swept Australia after Hitler's invasion of that country in 1941. Apart from his job as a primary-school teacher, he began to operate at the coalface of the party's cultural activities, and the slogan 'Today the Communist Party is the guardian of the Arts' captured his role as a communist cadre. He was active in party branch meetings and Aid Russia meetings, developed Communist Party study groups to deal with problems associated with Marxism and culture, and wrote articles and gave lectures designed to raise the cultural level of its members.[4] Smith was also the secretary of the War Art Council and on the executive of the Encouragement of Art Movement, as well as SORA—the Studio of Realist Art.

The importance for Bernard Smith of literary criticism as a vehicle for political projection was in keeping with international trends, and subsequently he established, along with Katharine Susannah Prichard and George Farwell, the literary magazine *Australian New Writing*, a small, quarterly journal financially backed by the Communist Party of Australia. *Australian New Writing* was modelled on the British socialist *New Writing* and the American *Left Review* and showcased short stories, poetry and criticism aimed at the realities of everyday life and the working class, and offered Australian and New Zealand industry workers, soldiers, allied servicemen and women the chance to be published. Moreover, because the party believed the magazine could serve 'as a valuable weapon in developing propaganda at the United Front', Smith was emphatic that it had to have a pervasive political component.[5] As he said: 'In this country we still have to develop a consistent Marxist aesthetic, which will speak with authority and develop a tradition in active struggle with present existent aesthetic positions'.[6] Four issues were published between 1943 and 1944, with resounding success; the first edition of 10,000 copies sold out and a second print run was made in spite of wartime restrictions. In Melbourne, Noel Counihan was similarly concerned with cultural unity during the war period, and established the Artists Unity Congress and organised the *Anti-Fascist Exhibition* in December 1942.[7] Through these initiatives Smith and Counihan first became aware of each other's political ideologies.

The 'modern movement', as it was called in the first quarter of the twentieth century, was a period of great ferment during which radical artists and intellectuals operated as moral, political and ideological condensers. T. J. Clark has written that 'politics is the form *par excellence* of the contingency that makes modernism what it is', and as a medium of cultural and political exchange, Bernard Smith epitomised that contingency.[8] In May 1940 Smith gave a lecture titled 'Art and Social Reflection: Goya, Courbet and Daumier'; it flagged his artistic heroes, men who painted with a street-level meaning that showed 'the complexities of modern life [and how] art retains its fundamental biological function: [a] social consciousness'.[9] Courbet the Communard stood out from his contemporaries with a provocative realism and political energy, and Smith identified him and, for that matter, Goya as politically and ideologically relevant to his own time.[10] It is why he chose the pseudonyms 'Goya' and 'Courbet' under which to publish his literary criticism, especially after he began working at the National Art Gallery of New South Wales (NAGNSW) in 1944. As a modernist and a communist, Smith said his 'movement into the Gallery was highly political in an art political sense'.[11] Certainly his criticism of Lionel Lindsay's narrow nationalism, trenchant racism and anti-modernism, in particular Lindsay's book *Addled Art* (1942), aggravated Smith's position among the conservative trustees at the gallery.[12] Later Smith admitted to Harry Gould, editor of the Communist Party newspaper the *Tribune*, that he had 'been obliged to hide under a pen name' in order to get the censored sections of his book *Place, Taste and Tradition* (1945) into print. These were published under the alias 'Goya' in the *Communist Review* of 1946 as 'The Fascist Mentality in Australian Art and Criticism', in which he accused men such as Lionel Lindsay and the former director of the NAGNSW, J. S. MacDonald, as retarding Australian modernist art. Another article in the *Tribune*, published under the pseudonym 'Courbet', was a political rallying call for social realism:

> True to form the capitalist press, chasing sensationalism, has written up the Contemporary Art Society's exhibition as a 'surrealist' show. This is quite false. Among the most vital painters, the death wishes, Oedipus complexes and skull-and-cross-bones salesmanship, are wearing thin. The trend towards realism that has grown up in face of strong opposition is today the most important factor.[13]

Such articles, Smith believed, provided a platform to 'further the Communist Party policy of encouraging art because these were important steps in our leadership of the cultural sphere'.[14] That cultural sphere was both national and global, and he endorsed artists who challenged elitist values and supported an emancipatory socialism. It was why Smith eventually set out to write on Gustave Courbet and felt obligated to write the biography of Noel Counihan, men dedicated to the working class and fearless critics of society, even when they were 'victims of politicised discrimination'.[15] As Smith wrote:

> England ... has its Hogarth, France its Daumier and Germany its Kollwitz and Australia its Counihan. Such artists are rare birds ... it does not surprise me that Counihan was singled out ... And not because he was a communist, but because he died one. Such people are not readily forgiven. Remember Courbet.[16]

Noel Counihan's art 'addressed the suffering, Modernity's victims, the worker, the women, the urban indigenous and the underdogs of society';[17] moreover, as Bernard put it:

> In holding to his faith [Counihan] had to face up to a lot of local punishment. He possessed not only the courage to paint but also to write directly against the mainstream of contemporary art opinion.[18]

Being a communist, Counihan failed to get secondary and tertiary teaching appointments during the Cold War decade of the 1950s.[19] Courbet was also discriminated against for his political beliefs; for example, he was wrongly accused of ordering the destruction of the Vendôme Column and imprisoned in 1871.

The eighteenth and nineteenth centuries gave politics its democratic values, and artists such as Goya, Hogarth, Millet, Delacroix, Daumier and Courbet helped to 'transform political space by replacing ... the traditional vertical ordering of God, king and subject with a horizontal opposition' of liberty and egalitarianism.[20] These were fundamental values to Bernard Smith, who had dispensed with God and adopted Darwin, Marx and Hegel. Moreover, if art was to be potent in times of upheaval, then it had to ask and answer questions of political urgency and social reality. It was Goya, Smith wrote, 'who went to the charnel-pits outside Madrid to record the truth of the Napoleonic invasion';[21] it was the revolutionist Courbet who made the first departure from romanticism and painted the realism of life; and it was Counihan who painted the universal and local shades of the human condition. These artists saw the social hoax of the 'historical present', what Fredric Jameson refers to as 'the administered world ... the institutionalised society, the culture industry'.[22] Goya, Courbet and Counihan were iconoclasts prepared to strip away the veil of bourgeois capitalism, mock imperial or elitist values and expose the struggle of the working classes. It is why these artists became such important conduits for Smith's political ideologies.

When Smith was finalising his first book *Place, Taste and Tradition* (1945), he sent Noel Counihan a section that dealt with the contemporary modernist period. Counihan's reply praised him for devoting so much space to 'Aestheticism & Nationalism [and] the development of a pre-fascist mentality'; he also offered an appraisal of Australia's cultural development:

> As everyone is aware Australian literature has been marked from the beginning by its plebeian and strongly rebellious character—its intimate relationship to the labour movement and its reflection of militant democracy. All our major poets and writers were rebels, but look at Australian painting—what a contrast. Our 'eminent' artists have been the servants of the bourgeoisie.[23]

When Bernard Smith began working at the NAGNSW in 1944 he was forced to subvert his political activism in order to survive in the conservative institution. By 1946 he had begun to 'soften' his Marxism, in part because he was attending the University of Sydney, where broader scholarly interests distracted him from political activities, but he was also gaining a reputation as an up-and-coming intellectual. This made Smith increasingly ambitious and, in December 1946, he applied, unsuccessfully, for the position of assistant director of the National Gallery of Victoria. About this time several Sydney gallery trustees, in particular Mary Alice Evatt, encouraged him to study abroad. That he was highly regarded intellectually there is no doubt, but this might also have been a way of removing him from the NAGNSW without creating a stir. Lionel Lindsay put it somewhat differently:

> Mrs Evatt is working for Bernard Smith and asked [Lionel's brother Daryl Lindsay] ... if he didn't think it would be a good idea to send him [Bernard] to London for experience. To Hell would be better ...[24]

In 1948 Smith succeeded in obtaining a British Council scholarship, which raises the question of Evatt's influence in this matter.

Bernard Smith, however, never abandoned the political Left and maintained contact with his comrades. Noel Counihan and the artist Vic O'Connor were vital links. From the beginning of their friendship Counihan's letters to Bernard were partisan and frank; one of his first pieces of advice to Smith was:

> not to let *Australian New Writing* fall into the bogs of intellectualism, expressing the outlook only of a small, mutually-admiring clique ... I hope all Australian publicists will learn from 'Comment' and 'Angry Penguins' just what must at all costs be avoided like the plague.[25]

Counihan considered these journals 'completely isolated from the Australian spirit, tradition and life', principles that Bernard respected. But whereas Counihan was a hardline communist, Bernard tempered his politics of nationalism with a cultural universalism.[26]

At the time of Counihan and Smith's correspondence several important issues were being hotly debated in the journals *Angry Penguins*, the *Communist Review* and *Australian New Writing*, as Bernard Smith wrote:

> the war exacerbated the debate between modernism and realism ... [and] as the war intensified many [communists] felt that some aspects of the modernist programme—abstract art, surrealism and the more mystically oriented modes of expressionism—had become increasingly irrelevant to the war time situation.[27]

Noel Counihan had delivered a scathing reply to Albert Tucker's article 'Art, Myth and Society', in which Tucker argued that art had become bankrupt under capitalism and that communism's cultural policy was inadequate to resolve the crisis.[28] Counihan accused Tucker of having 'perverted' Marxism and satisfied his 'own unprincipled individualism and cowardice'. Their clash triggered an avalanche of articles by other leading artists and commentators. John Reed's 'Signs of an "Infantile Disorder" on the Cultural Front', printed in the *Communist Review*,[29] elicited further replies from Herbert McClintock and another accusatory article by Noel Counihan, titled 'The Double Dealing of John Reed'.[30] Smith believed Counihan's polemic was brilliant, but that his demolition of Tucker was doctrinaire and, together with his attack on Reed, divisive to the art world and Communist Party politics.[31] This, however, did not stop Bernard from 'weigh[ing] into the debate' with his essay 'The New Realism in Australian Art', published in *Meanjin* in 1944.[32] In this he openly supported Counihan and the social realists, as well as revealing his pedagogic approach to global aesthetic politics. This essay was one of Smith's last political articles, at least for the time being. Once the war ended he began to withdraw from the party's cultural front, a timely decision as the threat of Cold War politics, Red-baiting and anti-communist campaigns escalated. One anonymous article on the 1948 SORA exhibition revealed:

> The Studio of Realist Art brings the class war into the Art field. Star of the exhibition is ... Noel Counihan, who earns a crust as a cartoonist for the Guardian, the Melbourne Commo paper ... the intriguing thing about the exhibition is that it is being held at David Jones Gallery. One would not expect D.J's to be active in helping along the revolution ...

It continued:

> There is a complete lack of reality in dealing with the subject of Communists and Communism in this country, which of course, helps Comrades immensely. They are allowed to hide behind more aliases than a professional bigamist, and one of the thickest smoke screens they throw up is that of 'culture'.[33]

Fortunately, Bernard Smith escaped this climate by leaving in September 1948 to take up his British Council scholarship at the Courtauld Institute of Art in London. Noel Counihan followed the postwar trail of Australian artists, arriving in London six months later. Both had been under surveillance by the Commonwealth Investigation Services (CIS), which notified the British Secret Service of their departure. As a 'suspected member of the ACP' (Australian Communist Party), Bernard Smith was monitored in his movements, as revealed in a report sent to the CIS: 'the Secret Service still follows him and reports that "this English summer he was planning a short trip to Prague and Italy"'.[34] Though heavily immersed in scholarly research, Bernard found time for political activity; he visited the British Communist Party headquarters in Covent Garden and attended public lectures, one by the Marxist expatriate Australian V. Gordon Childe. Together with Noel Counihan and Bob Gollan, Smith also participated in London party branch meetings, while at the artists' colony The Abbey in north London, where the Smith and Counihan families lived between 1949 and 1950, Counihan and Bernard were often heard arguing in Noel's studio about the future of communism, the Cold War climate or, as Terry Eagleton has put it, how power is crystalised and submission is bred.[35] Both men had independently visited the 'newly established Soviet satellite state of Czechoslovakia in the summer of 1949', but whereas Smith had witnessed the cold hand of communism and was disillusioned by the conditions of the workers, Counihan enthusiastically embraced 'the new world in the making' and remained 'permanently red'.[36] On his return to Australia in 1951 Smith resigned from the Communist Party.

One month before the opening of *The Antipodeans* exhibition in July 1959 at the Victorian Artists' Society in Melbourne, Bernard Smith gave a lecture to his students at the University of Melbourne on 'Courbet and the Barbizon School'. Realism and revolutionary art were very much on Bernard's mind, and *The Antipodeans* and its manifesto signalled the re-emergence of Smith's political persona. As the group's convener, Smith wanted to establish Australian figurative art as a vital regionalist style on the international postwar stage; indeed, he was determined that Australian artists should retain their autonomy, their difference. But Counihan was not invited to participate in the exhibition, because his overt communist affiliation would have attracted political attention away from a carefully selected and politically neutral group of artists. As a medium for political-cultural exchange, Smith masterminded an attack on abstraction, particularly the incursion of American abstract expressionism as an adjunct of cultural imperialism. While he couched this in terms of the Cold War tensions between the United States and the USSR, Smith had evidence that several major American exhibitions that had toured Europe during the 1950s were funded by the CIA, in conjunction with New York's MoMA (Museum of Modern Art).[37] With his concern about power and metropolitan centres, especially those that subordinated relations of exchange, Smith's willingness to stand alone and question cultural hegemonies is what made him such a distinctive and important critic. As David Boyd, one of the *Antipodeans* artists, said: 'Smith was a politician of the arts ... [who] had another agenda, which he did not lay on our table at the time'.[38]

The late 1950s and the 1960s were an extraordinary era for art and politics and Bernard Smith's political activism in the arts was in keeping with both the times and his socialist beliefs. Moreover, he considered it was *his* business to locate Australian art in such international transactions of cultural conquest. Whereas fascism and Nazism had ignited his political activism in the 1930s, and Cold War politics in the 1950s, it was to France, the cradle of modernism and incubator of politicised aesthetics, that Smith turned in the 1960s. The emancipation of the working class had been at its most heroic in France, and Gustave Courbet was seen as the artist who broke with tradition and chose the new realism of social relations and political change. Bernard Smith's project on the 'apostle of realism' was to be a biographical study and catalogue raisonné of Courbet's work. There were few books in English on this artist, apart from Meyer Schapiro's brilliant essay 'Courbet and Popular Imagery: An essay on Realism and Naïveté', written in 1941.[39] T. J. Clark published *Image of the People: Gustave Courbet and the Second French Republic, 1848–1851*, in 1973,[40] and Jack Lindsay published his Courbet biography that same year.[41] After Smith's failure to carry the Antipodeans further as a group and exhibit them in England, he decided to pursue another line of investigation that linked his support for figuration and realism and that gave meaning to humanity, not the whitewash of abstraction he so detested. Because Smith never wavered from his belief that art must communicate to the broad base of the people, Gustave Courbet, whose mentors in art were 'nature, tradition, work, and the public', was the perfect conduit for Smith.[42]

In his sabbatical year of 1962, Bernard Smith and his wife, Kate, went to France to research Courbet's art and life. Smith could not have embarked on this project without Kate, who was fluent in French, and she became his linguistic aide and translator, working with him in museums at Besançon, Montpellier and Ornans, the Bibliothèque National in Paris, and the Witt and Conway libraries at the Courtauld Institute, where she transcribed hundreds of letters and papers on Courbet. On Smith's 1966 sabbatical they continued working on Courbet in France and were preparing to embark on a third research program in 1967 when Bernard was invited to apply for the position of Power Professor and Director of the Power Institute at the University of Sydney. He was successful and the biography of Courbet was shelved. In 1968, when Smith returned to France on a buying trip for the Power Institute's fledgling art collection, he witnessed the revolutionary aftermath of the student riots and the great general strike. Not only had 'Marxism come out of the cold', but this revolutionary event displayed a historical similarity to what Gustave Courbet had experienced in the mid-nineteenth century, and confirmed for Bernard how repetition is part of humanity's theatre.[43]

When Noel Counihan died in 1986, Bernard Smith decided to write the biography of Australia's own 'stormy petrel of art'. Counihan had already written some 20,000 words on his early life, so superbly written and in such a clear and fresh style that Bernard largely used this in its original state.[44] There had also been a strong *esprit de corps* between the two men during the 1940s; reflecting on that period, Bernard wrote:

> Why was it that so many of us became communists or communist sympathisers during the 1940s? ... The 1930s alerted many of us to the profound vacuities of capitalism under stress. But it was the march to power of Hitler, the destruction of the Spanish republic and the programmed extermination of Europe's Jewish community and its political radicals which convinced us that the western capitalist democracies possessed neither the will [n]or the capacity to defeat Hitler.

He continued:

> Those who joined late and left early are to be commended. Those who steered clear of politics, like Drysdale and Nolan, the wisest of all. They were certainly the most prudent. But there is also a paradox here. Where, one must ask, would the revolutionary years have been at all without this involvement in communism.[45]

Bernard Smith admitted that one of the reasons he wrote Counihan's biography was 'to redress a situation for which [he] was in part responsible'.[46] He was referring to his role in cementing Counihan's reputation as a social realist. Counihan, however, was quite capable of managing his own artistic reputation and political career. One compelling reason may have been Smith's own sense of political alienation, particularly after his resignation from the Communist Party and then later in his retirement. By writing Noel Counihan's 'life' he was able to redress his own political history, even stating 'there's no history until it's written. That's why the memoirs of Noel [are] important'.[47] Moreover, the biography was a coathanger that enabled Bernard to be an authorial participant and write about *his* contemporaries; after all, he had known them all too: Dobell, Bergner, O'Connor, Jack Lindsay, the Evatts, Eric Westbrook, the Boyd brothers, Tucker, Gleeson, Nolan, Perceval … The biography was as much a historical document as another political mask that allowed Bernard Smith to wield the whip with the velvet thorn.

As Richard Haese suggests, 'The reader who comes to this book with some sense of Smith's own ideological history will find considerable interest in the interweaving of the lives of both biographer and subject'.[48] I recall Bernard Smith saying that Marxism was a complex business, but I think it is fair to say that Courbet and Counihan operated as conduits for Smith's own deep political and humanist convictions, particularly when he needed to disguise or deflect political heat elsewhere.

NOTES

1 Bernard Smith, Diary, 1943, National Library of Australia, Canberra, Bernard Smith Papers (hereafter NLA, BSP, MS 8680), Acc10.064, Box 4. Where MS 8680 is given only, these papers were recently deposited and have not yet received accession details.

2 Karl Marx, quoted in Bernard Smith, 'Reversion and Growth in Art', lecture given at the New South Wales Teachers' Federation Art Society, 16 September 1942, NLA, BSP, MS 8680, Box 1, Folder 5.

3 Fredric Jameson, *Marxism and Form: Twentieth-Century Dialectical Theories of Literature*, Princeton University Press, Princeton, 1971, pp. ix, xi.

4 Smith's lecture at the 'Cultural Conference' held in Sydney in November 1941 was published as 'Art', in *Soviet Culture: A Selection of Talks at the Cultural Conference, November 1941*, The N.S.W. Aid Russia Committee, Sydney, 1942, pp. 57–63. See also Bernard Smith, Some Problems Connected with the Marxist Approach to Art Criticism, NLA, BSP, MS 8680, Box 1, Item 12.

5 Bernard Smith, *A Pavane for Another Time*, Macmillan, Melbourne, 2002, p. 101.

6 Bernard Smith to George Farwell, 28 February 1943 (copy), NLA, BSP, MS 8680.

7 Held at the Athenaeum Gallery, Melbourne, 8–18 December 1942.

8 Timothy J. Clark, *Farewell to an Idea: Episodes from a History of Modernism*, Yale University Press, New Haven, 1999, p. 21.

9 Smith gave this lecture to the New South Wales Teachers' Federation Art Society on 15 May 1940.

10 Smith bought a book in 1940 containing reproductions of Goya's eighty-five etchings *The Disasters of War*.

11 Bernard Smith, interviewed by N. K. Meaney, 6 November 1986, NLA, Oral History Collection, TRC–2053/17.

12 Smith published an article on Lindsay's *Addled Art* in the *Communist Review* in 1943.

13 Smith names Bergner, Counihan, O'Connor, McClintock, Dalgarno, Cant and Harry MacDonald as his chosen realists; see 'Realists Challenge Surrealists', *Tribune*, 1944. Newspaper scrapbook, NLA, BSP, MS 8680.

14 National Archives of Australia, Canberra, Item 09/6869/, Series A6126 (A6/126/XM1, Item 86).

15 Bernard Smith to Colin Badger, 16 August 1990, NLA, BSP, MS Acc10.088, Box 13.

16 Bernard Smith, Angry Penguins ..., NLA, BSP, MS 8680, Box 7, 49/100, p. 16.

17 Bernard Smith, The Dark Years, NLA, BSP, MS 8680, Box 8, 57/62, p. 3.

18 Smith, *Noel Counihan: Artist and Revolutionary*, Oxford University Press, Melbourne, 1993, p. 221.

19 Smith to Badger, 16 August 1990. The Melbourne Working Men's College, now RMIT University, discriminated against Counihan.

20 Sunil Khilnani, *Arguing Revolution: The Intellectual Left in Postwar France*, Yale University Press, New Haven, 1993, p. 7.

21 Smith, Reversion and Growth in Art, lecture notes, 16 September 1942, NLA, BSP. MS 8680, Box 1/5.

22 Jameson, *Marxism and Form*, p. 53.

23 Noel Counihan to Bernard Smith, 26 January 1944 (copy), NLA, BSP, 8680. Counihan sent biographies and photographs of Bergner's, O'Connor's, Ailsa Donaldson's and his own work to Smith for inclusion in *Place, Taste and Tradition*.

24 Lionel Lindsay to James McGregor, 10 April 1948, Mitchell Library, State Library of New South Wales, Lindsay Family Papers, MSS 1969/5.

25 Noel Counihan to Bernard Smith, 9 May 1943 (copy), NLA, BSP, MS 8680.

26 ibid.

27 Smith, *Noel Counihan*, p. 182.

28 Albert Tucker, 'Art, Myth and Society', *Angry Penguins*, issue 4, 1943

29 John Reed, 'Signs of an "Infantile Disorder" on the Cultural Front', *Communist Review*, July 1944, pp. 284–5.

30 Noel Counihan, 'The Double Dealing of John Reed', *Communist Review*, no. 37, September 1944, pp. 325–7.

31 Other articles included HM [Herbert McClintock], 'Comment on John Reed's View', *Communist Review*, no. 30, February 1944, pp. 206–7; HM [Herbert McClintock], 'A Further Reply to John Reed's Views', *Communist Review*, July 1944, pp. 285–6; Vic O'Connor, 'A Criticism of Adelaide's "Angry Penguins"', *Communist Review*, August 1944, p. 302; John Reed, 'Take the People to Art', *Australian New Writing*, vol. 2, March 1944, pp. 43–6.

32 Bernard Smith, 'The New Realism in Australian Art', *Meanjin Papers*, vol. 3, no. 1, Autumn 1944, pp. 20–5.

33 'Strange Boosters', in *Things I Hear*, Series 95, 23 August 1948, n.p.

34 National Archives of Australia, Series A 6126/XR Item 86, report in Bernard Smith file.

35 Terry Eagleton, lecture given at the University of Melbourne, 7 December 2007; see also Eagleton, 'Making a Break', London Review of Books, 9 March 2006, p. 25, on the virtue of necessity and negative utopianism.

36 Richard Haese, 'Permanently Red', *Meridian*, vol. 13, no. 1, May 1994, p. 66.

37 Bryan Robertson, director of the Whitechapel Gallery in London, mounted a Jackson Pollock retrospective in 1958, a Mark Rothko retrospective in 1961 and a Robert Rauschenberg retrospective in 1964. Robertson admitted he had been unaware that most big American shows circulating in Europe during the late 1950s and the 1960s had been backed by the CIA and MoMA.

38 David Boyd, interviewed by Sheridan Palmer, 2010.

39 Meyer Schapiro, 'Courbet and Popular Imagery: An essay on Realism and Naïveté', *Journal of the Warburg and Courtauld Institutes*, vol. 4, nos 3–4, April 1941 – July 1942, pp. 164–91.

40 Timothy J. Clark, *Image of the People: Gustave Courbet and the Second French Republic, 1848–1851*, Thames & Hudson, London, 1973.

41 Jack Lindsay, *Gustave Courbet: His Life and Art*, Jupiter Books, London, 1973.

42 Clark, *Image of the People*, p. 155.

43 Alex Callinicos, *Is there a Future for Marxism?*, Macmillan, London, 1982, p. 12.

44 Bernard Smith to Pat Counihan, 30 May 1986, NLA, Noel Counihan Papers, BSP, MS 9107, Box 7.

45 Bernard Smith, 'Communism and the Visual Arts in the 1900s', NLA, BSP, MS 8680, Box 5/35/8, draft notes published as 'Reds, and Other Colours', *The Age Monthly Review*, vol. 1, no. 6, October 1981, p. 7.

46 Bernard Smith, *Noel Counihan: Artist and Revolutionary*, Oxford University Press, Melbourne,1993, p. 541.

47 Smith to Pat Counihan, 30 May 1986.

48 Haese, 'Permanently Red', p. 66.

Bernard Smith, 'cultural convergence' and art history

CATHERINE DE LORENZO

In his 1980 Boyer Lectures, *The Spectre of Truganini*, Bernard Smith argued that settler Australians typically avoided tragedy because it disturbs 'the conscience' and requires reflection on 'moral values born of its own [cross-cultural] experience'.[1] Smith's words acted as a clarion call to those curators and art historians who sought to consider Aboriginal art as more than just an inspiration to settler modernism, or as solely grounded in issues of cultural and experiential knowledge. By examining some of the ways in which art writers frame their interpretation of the visual arts, especially photographic history, within a broader context of cross-cultural dispossession and convergence, this chapter analyses and questions the influence of Smith's insights into tragedy-avoidance in Australian curatorial and art-historical discourse.

My thinking on these issues began when I was writing something on Australian photo historiography and considering what, if anything, made it distinctive from other photo histories. So this perspective on Smith's *Spectre of Truganini* comes from considering a problematic in Australian photo historiography. In thinking about the histories of Australian photography, my interest was not in the subject matter found in photographic archives, nor really in trying to identify qualities that might constitute an Australian photographic style. Rather, I was keen to see whether anything had emerged in the literature that reflected some of the deeper cultural forces and complexities that have come to be embedded in Australian art history in general. One concern is the belated but wholehearted embrace of Aboriginal art by the art museum, the academy and society at large. How did the discourse on photographic history since the 1950s respond to broader cultural issues, such as Indigenous agency? For much of the period the results were not very heartening. Unlike Bernard Smith's seminal histories of Australian painting, the postwar texts on Australian photography by Jack Cato (1955)[2] and Keast Burke (1973)[3] are comprised largely of biographical and technological details that draw on the personal networks and professional know-how of the authors themselves. From the early 1980s a new wave of expertise, based on detailed archival research, considerably broadened the known repertoire of photographers.[4] While free of any theory of aesthetics or intellectual and cultural history, they provide invaluable reference texts for other scholars in the field. It was not until the late 1980s that scholars with art-history credentials, and armed with diverse and often conflicting theoretical perspectives, commenced the task of shifting the discourse from naive to more interestingly nuanced histories.[5] Known facts about the image and its maker started to be positioned in a broader cultural and sometimes critical framework.

And yet some persisting limitations of these art-historically informed Australian photographic histories can be seen when compared to those aligned with other branches of the humanities and social sciences, where images are valued less for their aesthetic innovations than for their evidential status. All too often, it seems, the potential for a rich cross-disciplinary analysis in photographic discourse is lost in favour of arbitrarily narrow, and in the end intellectually impoverished, categorisations. For example, we see in the photo histories generated by art curators and historians David Moore's compelling image of migrants arriving in Australia, but not Juno Gemes' equally compelling image of a young girl leading a land rights march in Sydney (Fig. 39).[6] The problem cannot be dismissed simply as art versus activism, as if activist-driven art lacks lyrical and aesthetic qualities. Why is Gemes' haunting image of the little girl leading the land rights march in 1982 ignored in our photo histories, while Picasso's etchings and aquatints of the young girl carrying a candle of hope, or a dove of peace in a world hardening to fascism, celebrated? Why is Elaine Pelot-Kitchener's (now Pelot-Syron) image of local kids in Eveleigh Street, Redfern, who so confidently mimic the Aboriginal and Islander Dance Troupe's performance at the opening of the Murawina women and children's centre, found in state libraries rather than state galleries, in the illustrated history books but not in the photo histories?[7] Is the absence of these kinds of images from the photo histories robbing the discipline of opportunities to tap into deeper cultural forces, leaving the discourse all the poorer for their erasure? To counter-argue by pointing to the embrace by art museums of Mervyn Bishop's emphatically documentary, indeed restaged documentary, image of Prime Minister Gough Whitlam pouring the red earth into the hands of Vincent Lingiari is simply to note an exception, rather than address the substantive issue of predictable collecting practices.

With some exceptions, it seemed that the apparently arbitrary inclusions and exclusions about who can be seen to be saying what about all kinds of issues, in the arts discourse in particular, needed to be re-examined. So it was in order to try to understand these issues that I returned to Bernard Smith's *Spectre of Truganini*, because his thinking in 1979–80 was clearly influenced by cultural transformations leading up to the Australian Bicentenary, including the regular spectacle of land rights marches, especially in Sydney (so ably represented by Gemes and Kitchener, at the behest of Indigenous leaders, at a time when Indigenous photographers were not on the scene).

It is more than thirty years since Smith wrote his Boyer Lectures and, in many ways, they can be seen as symptomatic of their time, for better and for worse. Delving into both the distant and very recent past, he drew upon the work of historians, artists and writers to argue for political and cultural change that would acknowledge continuing injustices towards Aboriginal people, and recognise a case for land rights. Just because since that time we have had the Mabo (1992) and Wik (1996) judgements, Keating's Redfern Park speech acknowledging atrocities in the past (1992) and Kevin Rudd's Apology to the Stolen Generations (2008)—cultural transformations that seemed but a dream in 1980—it doesn't follow that Smith's argument is now redundant. Nor do some of the errors of detail, such as the then-common assertion that with the death of Truganini in 1876 'the last of the original Tasmanian Aborigines died' (p. 9), substantially weaken the bigger argument informing the talks. In this chapter I want to reflect on a few insights made in the lectures that continue to challenge the reader, especially the contemporary art historian.

Smith's bookends to his argument are significant. He refers at the outset to W. E. H. Stanner's 1968 Boyer Lectures, *After the Dreaming*, where the anthropologist identifies 'a cult of forgetfulness practised on a national scale' (p. 25).[8] Just as Stanner had to transcend his discipline of anthropology in order to speak to a wide and general public on issues of structural racism in the form of social amnesia, so too Smith stepped outside his discipline of art history in order to look more broadly at 'our cultural history' and to understand both the 'mechanisms of forgetfulness' on the one hand, and the possibility of 'cultural convergence' on the other. In concluding his talks, Smith refers to Toynbee's idea that near-defeated people who nonetheless possess the 'beau role' are likely to win in the end. Thus, having affirmed that 'Aboriginal people possess the beau role', he concludes: 'And they will win. If they do not we of European descent, who continue to live in Australia, together with our children and grandchildren[,] will lose' (p. 52). The idea that we will all be the poorer, culturally poorer, if we fail to find some way to address past and current wrongs by 'adequate reparations', hinges, in Smith's text, on the idea that we need to forge some manner of 'cultural convergence', a phrase he takes from poet Les Murray. As Smith was later to elaborate in an essay on cultural convergence, Les Murray in 1977 had referred to this convergence as 'a fact, a subtle process, hard to discern often, and hard to produce evidence for '.[9] This, continues Murray, is because it is 'the slow moulding of all people within a continent or region towards the natural human form which that continent or region demands, that is a real process'.[10] By drawing attention to the Latin word *convergere*, meaning to meet together, Smith, and by extension Murray, seemed to be instinctively sympathetic to concepts of Aboriginality that were yet to be published by Marcia Langton. In her 1993 book *Well, I Heard It on the Radio and I Saw It on the Television*, Langton defined Aboriginality as 'a field of interdisciplinarity that is remade over and over again in a process of dialogue, of imagination, of representation and interpretation', emphasising the need for 'actual dialogue, where the individuals test and adapt imagined models of the other to find satisfactory forms of mutual comprehension'.[11]

These two big ideas—the desire to step outside his disciplinary comfort zone in order to draw attention to issues often overlooked in our cultural history, and the idea that any real change is likely to come about over time and through simple goals of meeting together and exchanging ideas—remain valid, it seems to me.

Smith's assumption as to how this convergence might happen, however, rests on a precondition that is confronting and difficult. He posits that 'A culture cannot live upon other people's universals. It requires moral values born of its own historical experience, values which are continuously tested against the successive challenges of its history' (p. 11).

Given that it is not always easy to detect 'moral values' born of settlers' own historical experiences, where those experiences are grounded on dispossession, Smith observed that we tend to suppress our collective experiences and so end up with a limited repertoire of aesthetic strategies. He says that 'in our arts and letters we have tended to cultivate the lyric and the satire, the comic and the pastoral ... but to avoid tragedy' (p. 16).

Of course, Smith was not looking for a quick fix that might, for instance, superimpose an environmentalist and ethnocidal reading on a pastoral landscape. But it is strange that more of us don't draw on our histories to tell stories that might engage with Marx's 'high moral drama' that so inspired Smith. A rare but well-documented example of such an approach is where some descendants of the 1838 Myall Creek murderers outed their history in 2000, resulting in cathartic transformations of the local rural culture (Fig. 40).[12] Equally, research on contested interpretations of the dispossession of sedentary Aboriginal groups from their land by a colonial squire in Victoria's Western District reminds us that the task does not need to be biographical, although the more we take on our own histories the more we clear the way for collaborative projects.[13] For many of us it is too late to ask our grandparents or even parents to reflect honestly on their memories of attitudinal values, let alone allude to Smith's 'damaged goods' (p. 14) in our genealogical cupboard. But there is nothing to stop us reflecting on the present!

A sense of history as high moral drama, understood on personal and community scales, is exactly what we find not only in Aboriginal art, but in the writings on it, especially since the Indigenisation of the art museum and tertiary sectors following the upheavals of 1988. Unmistakable is the degree to which a mindfulness of history, especially colonial history, is *ever* present in the work of urban practitioners, be they artists, curators or writers. For many urban practitioners it is rarely an option to put colonial history to one side, let alone out of mind. As artist Fiona Foley said in the 2012 *Artlink* Indigenous issue:

> Largely, the premise behind my public art is to write Aboriginal people, Aboriginal nations and Aboriginal history back into the Australian narrative. I do this because we have been written out too often.[14]

Even in such serious projects, there is often a sense of humour, albeit sometimes gallows humour. Occasionally this is furtive, as when Foley only revealed to authorities the hidden intent behind her major public art projects in Brisbane and Sydney (to name massacre sites and other atrocities) when the works were unveiled and impossible to remove. At other times humour is explicit in the work itself, as in Daniel Boyd's pastiches of prized colonial history paintings that provoke both laughter and insight. In his book on the art of the novel, Milan Kundera commends the use of jokes, not in the sense of deflecting attention to get us out of a tight moral corner, but because they serve as 'the best evidence that a sharp sense of the real and an imagination that ventures into the implausible can make a perfect pairing'.[15] The joke is something well understood and used by artists such as Destiny Deacon and Richard Bell, but it is hardly something the artist or writer who is not Indigenous can bring to settler critiques of dispossession, assimilation or unfair appropriation. How might one address Smith's 'high moral dramas' through more explicit strategies of convergence, or collaboration, especially through curated and written arguments?

An examination of current practices in Australian art history shows that a significant percentage of scholars now challenge Stanner's 45-year-old observation that we suffer chronic forgetfulness: many scholars, Indigenous and not, write on Aboriginal art and artists, and my suspicion is that this reflects a genuine desire to both know the 'other' and to better know ourselves. This paradigm shift is evidence, I think, of a kind of congruence. As McLean painstakingly documents in the opening chapter to his book *How Aborigines Invented the Idea of Contemporary Art*, the congruence process, which Langton calls the 'creolisation of Australian culture',[16] was spearheaded in the field of curatorial practice in a manner that was slow, erratic, but ultimately decisive.[17] Collectively, writings on Aboriginal art allow us to understand ourselves in new ways, because it is almost impossible to look at and think about Aboriginal art without reflecting on the many issues the artists direct at settler and international audiences. Langton puts it nicely: when settler

Australian audiences reflect on the different conceptions of the land embedded in Aboriginal art, they come to feel they 'belong to this place rather than another'.[18]

Given that many Australians are now mindful of Aboriginal art and issues, and given that so much of it is inspirational, it seems rather po-faced to return to Smith's suggestion that no genuine transformation is possible until we learn to deal with tragedy. What kinds of tragedies? Perhaps he refers to massacres, dispossession, stolen generations and the like. But also, surely, he refers to the tragedy of separation stemming from deep cultural divisions. So my question is: What options are open to art historians who want to bridge some of these divides and put into practice a richer sense of cultural convergence? Can it be done of one's own volition, with little or no cross-cultural dialogue? The rest of this chapter is a response to these questions; I'll briefly consider a few documented strategies of convergence, and then draw the discussion to a conclusion.

The first model of convergence entails what might be called polyphonic stories. A trailblazer in terms of multiple voices addressing a common subject was the 1984 publication *Reading the Country: Introduction to Nomadology*.[19] Here transcription of storylines by local custodian Paddy Roe, visual interpretations of the shared journey by Krim Benterrak (a painter of Moroccan origin), plus a reflexive critique of the whole process by cultural theorist Stephen Muecke, were combined into the one publication so that the reader would be constantly aware of the multiplicity of interpretations through texts and imaging. An innovative strategy at the time, it is one that has attracted few adherents to date in Australian art history.

A second model of convergence is typified by dialogic and reflexive texts. Here I am not referring to those extensive writings on contemporary Indigenous artists, because they follow a familiar pattern of extensive interviews between author and artist. Rather, there are interesting studies where dialogue with descendants of the represented subject opens a discussion about the legacies of past (colonial) images on present-day communities. Such studies question knowledge derived solely from the visual archives, by seeking out the oral histories and collective memories of the repercussions of the photographic encounters and representations on the photographed person's descendants.[20] Paul Ricoeur refers to three kinds of mnestic, or memory, traces: 'the written' (documentary, historiographical), the 'psychical' and the 'cerebral'.[21] All three trace-modalities enrich the analyses by scholars such as

Roslyn Poignant and Jane Lydon, neither of whom is an art historian, but each vitally interested in the image and its meanings in both their own academic communities as well as in relevant sections of the Indigenous communities. Their use of dialogue is quite distinct from the more self-absorbed reflexive writings (interesting though they may be) by cultural theorists such as Katrina Schlunke, whose accounts of nineteenth-century Aboriginal massacres do not exclude referencing her own sexuality and family history.[22] Like some of Roland Barthes' often personal and idiosyncratic writings on photographs, reflexive writings at least show an attempt to question the limits of the archive and to make abundantly clear the agency of the writer in constructing histories.

Reflexive writings of these sorts often sit awkwardly with art historians, with two exceptions. One is when art historians use their professional knowledge to inform their fiction—as we see in novels by Janine Burke and Candice Bruce.[23] The other, as already noted, is much of the writings on art by Indigenous authors where autobiography and relationship are intrinsic to their histories and criticisms.[24]

A third model of convergence is that of encounter. In her histories of the Pacific, historian Bronwen Douglas looks for 'encounters', or 'situated intersections of multiple personal agencies, both indigenous and foreign'.[25] So, when dealing with documents from the eighteenth century, she aims 'to identify traces of Aboriginal or Melanesian agency in voyagers' descriptions of encounters', in order to not over-identify with the voice of the writer. In art curating the idea of encounter in the field has been brought into exceptional focus through the work of Ace Bourke. Little did Bernard Smith realise the extent to which one individual could draw on his 'own historical experience' to engage with contemporary Indigenous issues. In his exhibitions *Flesh+Blood: A Sydney Story 1788–1998* (1998),[26] *Lines in the Sand* (2008)[27] and *Ace Bourke: A Collector's Journey* (2012),[28] Bourke thoroughly explored his own extraordinary family's history (descended as he is from governors Richard Bourke and Philip Gidley King), his ancestors' relationships with Aboriginal people, as well as his own (Fig. 41). Bourke claims he found the courage to 'fess up to his family history, with its share of 'damaged goods', because of the relationships he had built up with Aboriginal artists, especially Tracey Moffatt and Michael Riley.[29] This is not altogether surprising given that it was in Ace Bourke's first show, *NADOC '86 Exhibition of Aboriginal and Islander Photographers* at the Aboriginal Artists Gallery, that many people in Sydney, and I suspect Australia, first saw an exhibtion solely of urban Koori photography presented as art.[30] With the assistance of Tracey Moffatt, Bourke brought together key photographers, such as Moffatt, Riley, and Brenda Croft, some of whom carried a sustained critique of the colonial archive marked by creative resistance to colonial stereotypes. *NADOC '86* was also the exhibition that provided an *art* forum for showing key works by established photojournalist Mervyn Bishop. The 1986 exhibition post-dated the 1979 Biennale of Sydney and the 1981 *Perspecta*, which played a significant role in bringing Aboriginal art to a contemporary art milieu, but it brought together contemporary urban Indigenous photography, and so expanded the recognised repertoire of art practice from bark paintings and acrylics to include a range of new media. Compared to the 1982 exhibition *After the Tent Embassy*, which was both cross-culturally collaborative and unabashedly political in content, the 1986 exhibition was generally more allusive and shaped as much by the imperatives of the artists as by the cultural milieu in which they worked. To Sydney audiences, the critique of the colonial archive through imaginative and witty visual strategies was a manoeuvre that not only established the aesthetic and contemporary credentials of the artists, but masterfully revealed the political gravitas and authenticity of the long-neglected urban Kooris.

The examples above show the capacity of cognate disciplines to accept Smith's idea of cultural convergence. To return to the preamble about Australia's photo histories, publications by Gael Newton, Helen Ennis and especially Penny Taylor's *After 200 Years: Photographic Essays of Aboriginal and Islander Australia Today* (1988), show evidence of historians and curators searching for signs of cross-cultural agency in photographic practice.[31]

This chapter has examined the legacy of Bernard Smith's thinking in his *Truganini* Boyer Lectures, mainly as seen through the prism of Australian photo historiography. In general it would seem that while many areas of curatorship and cultural history have changed and now embrace intriguingly varied responses to ideas of cultural convergence, there is still plenty of room for development in photographic discourse in the art museum and the academy. Critically, Smith had to wear the hat of cultural, rather than art, historian in order to reflect on deeper cultural motivations. Perhaps a similarly encompassing view is needed when art historians and photo historians attempt to ask meaningful questions about an object.

CODA

Bernard Smith, in *The Spectre of Truganini*, urged us to consider our own histories. Smith, I presume, was referring to our collective histories, and yet much Aboriginal writing, as well as Ace Bourke's curatorial projects, tell stories that are at the one time both collective and personal. In the catalogue for his exhibition *Collector's Journey*, Bourke expresses the hope that it will 'encourage others to think about their own stories'.[32] His exhibition at Hazelhurst Regional Gallery finished late in September 2012 and so overlapped for several weeks with Djon Mundine's *Bungaree: The First Australian* at Mosman Art Gallery, before a national tour.[33] In a chance meeting at this time, Ace reiterated to me his aim that others of us should 'think about our own stories'. So here is one of mine, triggered by the Bungaree exhibition. Bungaree (1775–1830) was granted land at Georges Heights, in Middle Head, Mosman, the suburb where I grew up. About five years ago some girls from my kindergarten class organised a reunion, and they worked hard to contact the entire class of boys and girls. Just one boy was missing, Dennis Kitchener, but the other boys filled us in on who he was. There wasn't much interaction between the boys and girls at the time, so many of us girls hardly knew Dennis. But Tony and Michael not only knew that Dennis was Aboriginal, they also well remember being invited to his home in Clifton Gardens, a deluxe precinct in an affluent suburb. The difference was that Dennis, and his family, lived in a cave, and it was Dennis who taught Tony and Michael how to fish. They very happily remember the freedom experienced in afternoons spent with Dennis, scrambling down the hillside, past his home, to the beach. How, one wonders, did Dennis's parents manage to get their kids properly dressed for school? And had Dennis's family survived in the area from before Bungaree's time until the early 1960s, at which time a number of families in the north shore and lower northern beaches were resettled in western Sydney's Blacktown?[34]

In her *Quarterly Essay* on 'The history question', Inga Clendinnen argued that 'To embrace uncertainty and ambiguity is the historian's special duty'.[35] Ace Bourke's exploration of the concept of the personal as the political in curatorial practice enriches the national narrative, and in so doing shows but one of many possible strategies for thinking afresh about the *longue durée* of more than two hundred years of cross-cultural encounters. Such projects suggest the legacy of Bernard Smith's argument in the *Spectre of Trugannini*. There is plenty of room for more. Finally, recognising that personal stories can enrich the more general collective history by adding unexpected convergences, I wish that Dennis and his family, certainly, but also his friends Tony and Michael, could have contributed in a small way to the *Bungaree* exhibition, if only to show that there are probably more shared stories than we have yet grasped. And they are not all tragedies.

NOTES

1 Bernard Smith, *The Spectre of Truganini*, The 1980 Boyer Lectures, Australian Broadcasting Commission, Sydney, 1980. In the text of this chapter, all quotations followed by page references are from this book.

2 Jack Cato, *The Story of the Camera in Australia*, 2nd edn, Institute of Australian Photography, Melbourne, 1977.

3 Keast Burke, *Gold and Silver: Photographs of Australian Goldfields from the Holtermann Collection*, Penguin Books Australia, Melbourne, 1973.

4 Alan Davies and Peter Stanbury, with assistance from Con Tanre, *The Mechanical Eye in Australia: Photography 1841–1900*, Oxford University Press, Melbourne, 1985; Alan Davies, *An Eye for Photography: The Camera in Australia*, Miegunyah Press, Melbourne University Press, Melbourne, and State Library of New South Wales, Sydney, 2004.

5 Gael Newton, with essays by Helen Ennis and Chris Long, and assistance from Isobel Crombie and Kate Davidson, *Shades of Light: Photography and Australia 1839–1988*, Australian National Gallery and Collins Australia, with assistance from Kodak, Canberra, 1988; Anne-Marie Willis, *Picturing Australia: A History of Photography*, Angus & Robertson, Sydney, 1988; Catriona Moore, *Indecent Exposures: Twenty Years of Australian Feminist Photography*, Allen & Unwin in association with the Power Institute of Fine Arts, Sydney, 1994; Helen Ennis, *Photography and Australia*, Reaktion Books, London, 2007; Helen Ennis, *Reveries: Photography and Mortality*, Australian National Portrait Gallery, Canberra, 2007.

6 For Gemes' image, see Marcia Langton, *After the Tent Embassy: Images of Aboriginal History in Black and White Photographs*, Valadon Publishing, n.p., 1983, p. 104.

7 See Nigel Parbury, *Survival: A History of Aboriginal Life in New South Wales*, Ministry of Aboriginal Affairs New South Wales, Sydney, 1986, p. 141.

8 W. E. H. Stanner, *After the Dreaming: Black and White Australians—An Anthropologist's View*, The Boyer Lectures, 1968, Australian Broadcasting Commission, Sydney, 1969.

9 Bernard Smith, *The Death of the Artist as Hero: Essays in History and Culture*, Oxford University Press, Melbourne, 1988, p. 291. For a critical account of Smith's embrace of cultural convergence, see Colin Symes and Bob Lingard, 'From the Ethnographic to the Aesthetic: An Examination of the Relationship between Aboriginal and European Culture in Australian Art, 1788–1988', in Paul Foss (ed.), *Islands in the Stream: Myths of Place in Australian Culture*, Pluto Press, Sydney, 1988, pp. 188–215.

10 Les A. Murray, 'The Human-hair Thread', *Meanjin*, vol. 36, no. 4, December 1977, p. 596.

11 Marcia Langton, *'Well, I heard it on the radio and I saw it on the television': An Essay for the Australian Film Commission on the Politics and Aesthetics of Filmmaking by and about Aboriginal People and Things*, Australian Film Commission, Sydney, 1993, pp. 23 and 81 respectively.

12 For useful references to this story, see Catherine De Lorenzo and Vivien Chow, 'Contained Memories or Catalysts? Some Aboriginal Memorials in Australia', *Memory Connection Journal*, no. 1, 2011, www.memoryconnection.org.

13 Harriet Edquist, 'Remembering Murndal: Place and Displacement in a Western District Homestead', 'Contained Memory' Conference, Te Papa Tongarewa, Wellington, New Zealand, 2010; and 'Homesteads of the Western District', in Lisa Byrne, Harriet Edquist and Laurene Vaughan (eds), *Designing Place: An Archaeology of the Western District*, Melbourne Books, Melbourne, 2010, pp. 126–49.

14 Fiona Foley, 'The Elephant in the Room: Public Art in Brisbane', *Artlink*, vol. 32, no. 2, June 2012, p. 66.

15 Milan Kundera, *The Curtain: An Essay in Seven Parts*, Linda Asher (transl.), Faber and Faber, London, 2007, p. 75.

16 Ian McLean, 'How Aboriginal Art Conquered the Art World', in Ian McLean (ed.), *How Aborigines Invented the Idea of Contemporary Art*, Power Publications with the Institute of Modern Art (Brisbane), Sydney, 2011, pp. 17–75. The Langton reference is from p. 62, quoting Langton, *Terra Alterius: Land of Another*, exhibition catalogue, Ivan Dougherty Gallery, University of New South Wales, Sydney, 2004, n.p.

17 See also Brenda L. Croft's perceptive review: 'How *did* Aborigines Invent the Idea of Contemporary Art?' [book review], *Artlink*, vol. 32, no. 2, June 2012, pp. 113–15.

18 Langton, *Terra Alterius*, quoted in McLean, 'How Aboriginal Art Conquered the Art World', p. 63.

19 Krim Benterrak, Stephen Muecke and Paddy Roe, *Reading the Country: Introduction to Nomadology*, Fremantle Arts Centre Press, Fremantle, WA, 1984.

20 Roslyn Poignant, *Professional Savages: Captive Lives and Western Spectacle*, University of New South

Wales Press, Sydney, 2004; Jane Lydon, *Eye Contact: Photographing Indigenous Australians*, Duke University Press, Durham, NC, 2005.

21 Paul Ricoeur, *Memory, History, Forgetting*, Kathleen Blamey and David Pellauer (transl.), University of Chicago Press, Chicago, 2004, p. 415.

22 For example, Katrina Schlunke, 'In-between the Memorial, the Library and the Lesbian: Moments in Postcolonial Community', *Cultural Studies Review*, vol. 9, no. 1, May 2003, pp. 77–84; and Katrina Schlunke, *Bluff Rock: Autobiography of a Massacre*, Fremantle Press, Fremantle, WA, 2005.

23 Janine Burke, *Company of Images*, Greenhouse, Melbourne, 1989; Candice Bruce, *The Longing*, Vintage Books, Sydney, 2012.

24 For example, Hetti Perkins, *Art + Soul*, Miegunyah Press, Melbourne University Press, Melbourne, 2010. The vast literature of Indigenous writings on Indigenous art is beyond the scope of this chapter.

25 Bronwen Douglas, 'Voyages, Encounters, and Agency in Oceania: Captain Cook and Indigenous People', *History Compass*, vol. 6, no. 3, May 2008, pp. 712–37.

26 Ace Bourke, *Flesh+Blood: A Sydney Story 1788–1998*, exhibition catalogue, Historic Houses Trust of New South Wales, Sydney, 1998.

27 Ace Bourke, Djon Mundine and Keith Smith, *Lines in the Sand: Botany Bay Stories from 1770*, exhibition catalogue, Hazelhurst Regional Gallery and Arts Centre, Gymea, NSW, 2008.

28 Ace Bourke, *A Collector's Journey*, exhibition catalogue, Hazelhurst Regional Gallery and Arts Centre, Gymea, NSW, 2012.

29 *A Collector's Journey*, p. 24.

30 Tim Johnson and Vivien Johnson's *Koori Art '84* (Artspace, September 1984), and Suhanya Raffel and Chris Watson's *Urban Koories: Two Exhibitions of Urban Aboriginal Art* (Workshop Arts Centre, Willoughby, May–July 1986), both showed urban Aboriginal art, but only the '84 exhibition showed photography and photomedia—by Michael Riley, Ian Craigie and Fernanda Martins.

31 See especially Newton, *Shades of Light*; Ennis, *Photography and Australia*; and Penny Taylor (ed.), *After 200 Years: Photographic Essays of Aboriginal and Islander Australia Today*, Aboriginal Studies Press, Canberra, 1988.

32 Bourke, *Collector's Journey*, p. 10.

33 *Bungaree: The First Australian*, exhibition curated by Djon Mundine, Mosman Art Gallery (Sydney), 1 September to 25 November 2012, then touring nationally.

34 Efforts have been made to track the whereabouts of Dennis, without success.

35 Inga Clendinnen, 'The History Question: Who Owns the Past?', *Quarterly Essay*, no. 23, September 2006, p. 67.

Bernard Smith's blind spot: Aboriginal and Australian art

IAN McLEAN

> The insight exists only for the reader in the priveleged position of being able to observe the blindness as a phenomenon in its own right ... To write critically about critics thus becomes a way to reflect on the paradoxical effectiveness of a blinded vision that has to be rectified by means of insights that it unwittingly provides.
>
> *Paul de Man*[1]

Anyone who has had the pleasure of a good argument with Bernard will have experienced the breadth, depth and tenacity of his mind. If he had any blind spots, he kept them well covered. His worldview was grounded in a philosophy that he developed early in life from his reading of the Bible and Marx, and to a lesser extent Hegel, Spengler and Toynbee. From these cosmological thinkers he inherited a global view and a tendency to think in terms of the *longue durée*, as if a world spirit was at work that could account for everything. This Lordly yet cosmopolitan perspective served as a template for interpreting things at a more local and ephemeral scale, giving him a tight grip on whatever questions came his way. The masterpiece of this approach is *European Vision and the South Pacific*, which united the sciences and the arts, and the northern and southern hemispheres, into a thesis about the cross-cultural and world-encompassing legacy of the post-Enlightenment and early modern period. It framed his interpretation of twentieth-century art.

While the essential elements and sweep of Bernard's worldview are evident in his earliest writings, he kept abreast of the latest ideas and research until the last years of his long life, even when such approaches and conclusions conflicted with his. He even tried to come to grips with postmodernism, though with little success, as it was alien to his thinking. This failure perhaps points to various omissions in Bernard's approach. However, they are not blind spots. A blind spot is a knot or hole in the fabric of one's worldview. In Bernard's case the fabric was particularly close-knit. This is not to say that it didn't have any knots, but that they were difficult to untangle. Besides, Bernard had always been there before, shoring up his defences and laying a few booby-traps for the unwary intruder. However, towards the end of his life, Bernard did admit to a blind spot. Summing up his achievements in his eighty-fourth year, he wrote: 'During my professional career I had said virtually nothing about Aboriginal art'.[2]

Bernard was not one to remain silent, especially on something that played a central role in the ideological battles of his formative years, had great aesthetic appeal to many of his generation, and appeared in exhibitions of Australian art during this time (the 1940s and early 1950s). The problem for Bernard was not Aboriginal art *per se*, but the Western ideology of primitivism. No one, not even its most ardent enthusiasts, considered Aboriginal art to be modern art. Some—a coalition of anthropologists and modernists under the influence of French modernism—accepted it as fine art, but while Aboriginal art was exiled from the contemporary, Bernard could see no use for it in his history.

That Bernard remained relatively silent on Aboriginal art indicates neither an indifference to it, nor an unconscious repression of it. Bernard did not have a limited horizon over which he could conveniently push difficult issues. Rather, his silence suggests that the attitudes to Aboriginal art in his lifetime marked a triangle of uncertainty that he could not incorporate into his worldview. His silence signalled his caution, and thus his acknowledgement of both the significance of the issue and its potential to radically challenge his worldview and the way in which the West had more generally constructed its view of the world. Bernard waited until after his retirement before fully tackling the issue.

Nevertheless, during what Bernard called 'my professional career', he did broach the subject on occasions, particularly in his first book, *Place, Taste and Tradition*.

PLACE, TASTE AND TRADITION

Bernard self-consciously wrote *Place, Taste and Tradition* as the first Marxist history of a national art. Published when Bernard was in his late twenties, the book presents a worldview that was virtually fully formed. Tellingly, when the book was republished in 1979—when Bernard was sixty-three and retired—he found almost nothing to change. Its 'themes and issues', he said, 'have dogged me for most of my life'.[3] His case against Aboriginal art reflected his strategic approach to writing a history of Australian art in the ideologically charged atmospherics of the 1930s and early 1940s. Three interconnecting themes in *Place, Taste and Tradition* conspired to prevent Bernard from considering Aboriginal art as a serious subject of art history: nationalism, conservatism and modernism. This is because each purloined Aboriginal art to its own cause.

NATIONALISM

Bernard's professional life was devoted to understanding the idea of a national art, even though he resisted the very idea of it. The absence of Aboriginal art from Bernard's histories of Australian art goes to the heart of his struggle in *Place, Taste and Tradition* to write a history of Australian art from his cosmopolitan perspective. Thus he had little patience for the idea of a national art. For him it was the invention of ideologues, which it was his calling to counter. He said:

> [Our] local prophets who have championed and fought for a purely national art … ignore the general tendency of art during the last two centuries [which] has been toward an international fusion of many national styles … a *purely* national art can only be considered today as an archaistic movement running counter to the dominant historical movement.[4]

Lines and colours, he trumpeted, 'have no nationality', which in turn meant that there could be 'no such thing as an Australian *art-form*', except, he suggested, 'the art of the aborigines'.[5]

Why is Aboriginal art the exception? The lines and colours of Aboriginal art, he implied, have a 'racial' and therefore ethnic quality, like Celtic or Indian art, rather than following the formalist concerns of modernism, which for him was the period style of twentieth-century art and which he would at the end of the century name 'the Formalesque'.[6] 'In our time', he continued, 'when the formal qualities of art are being increasingly determined by factors that are international in scope and operation', there is little 'chance of such a *purely* national form arising in the future'.[7] Thus it was a 'hopeless endeavor to create an *art-form* peculiar to this continent—an aboriginal art'.[8]

Aboriginal and modern art, then, were completely different categories—the former a racial or ethnic manifestation and the latter a cosmopolitan one. Bernard held this view for the rest of his life, though he did, as we shall see, find a way to modify it to account for the advent of Aboriginal contemporary art.

CONSERVATISM

During Bernard's formative years, competing factions sought to define an ideology for the Australian nation-state as it struggled free from the discourse of empire. Shaped by an emerging modernism confronting an academic establishment, it consumed the Australian art world in the second quarter of the twentieth century. In his determination to strike his own course through this ideological minefield, Bernard reserved his greatest spleen for the conservatives. In *Place, Taste and Tradition* he admonished their 'chauvinism' and 'pseudo-nationalism', and in the *Communist Review* he judged them 'reactionary' and having a 'pre-fascist mentality'.[9] He considered *Place, Taste and Tradition* as his contribution to the larger struggle against fascism.[10]

A major argument of *Place, Taste and Tradition* is aimed against the critics who supported the national landscape school of painting that came to the fore after World War I, and which is most associated with the hated conservative critics. They applied a metaphysical interpretation of landscape, inherited from nineteenth-century romanticism, in order to ascribe existential meaning to local landscape. A tried and tested method for ideologues of the nation-state around the world, it was a raging success in Australia.

If Bernard had thus picked a difficult battleground, it gave him his most original contribution to the discipline, fully spelt out in *European Vision and the South Pacific* but first tested in *Place, Taste and Tradition*. Here he argued that the most progressive nineteenth-century landscape art was essentially part of the natural sciences. In this way he sought to dismiss romanticism as a philosophical disposition alien to the spirit of modernity, and at the same time to overcome the prevailing belief of the national landscape school: that Australian colonial art was un-Australian.

If this was good art history, it counted for little in the ideological cut and thrust of the day. The popular success of the national school of landscape painting rested on its answering what Ian Burn characterised as a collective 'psychological need' to represent the 'idea of Australia',[11] particularly since Australia 'was a nation with little concept of itself as a nation'.[12] The popularity of the school was epitomised in a generously illustrated book, *Australia: Land of Contrasts*, published in 1943, which promoted the national landscape school of painting with a lively text by Ernestine Hill on national identity. Her text is an Aboriginalist polemic. 'In Australia', she said on the first page, 'the Stone Age meets the Twentieth Century'.[13]

By this time Aboriginal culture, serving as a home-grown primitivism, had been co-opted into the conservative agenda. Its most obvious manifestation was the Adelaide-based Jindyworobak poets. This conservative predilection for Aboriginal art and culture appeared, to Bernard, to be a symptom of fascism. If the modernist Aboriginalists were similarly suspect, modernism's appeal to universal values and its internationalism countered the archaism of the conservatives. One of modernism's great achievements, he said, was 'its capacity to erode the narrow Eurocentrism which has dominated western art and its colonial appendages. Modernism revealed that an art could emerge which was in the best sense international'.[14]

This explains Bernard's soft spot for Margaret Preston. She at least framed her nationalism and Aboriginalism within the tenor of an international modernist style. Bernard had invited her to give the first in the series of lectures on art that he organised at the Teachers' Federation Art Society in 1941. In this Preston argued that Aboriginal art's aesthetic forms had the potential to 'produce a National Art like none other in the world'.[15] Preston seems an odd choice, until we realise that Bernard was particularly worried that the Jindyworobak poets were 'keen to convert her to their pro-fascist position'.[16]

Bernard's argument for Preston's work shows how wily he could be in bending his philosophy to the commitments of the day. Her art, he said, might become a 'valuable contributing factor … for a truly Australian art', but the reason was because it was part of an international modernism that drew on the formal aspects of Indigenous art, rather than because it was a purely national development. Citing American modernists who adapted 'Indian art-forms' to 'contemporary expression', and French artists doing likewise with the 'art work of the negroes of the French colonies', he believed that it 'is the one definite cultural contact that has been established with a race being exterminated by our "culture"'. Though, he added, 'it cannot be claimed reasonably [as Preston did] that an art based upon the decorative quality of aboriginal art will provide the bases for a truly Australian art'.[17]

MODERNISM

By 1945, when *Place, Taste and Tradition* was published, the conservatives were on the back foot. Bernard was well attuned to the tendencies of his time, which is why he took the modernists more seriously than he took the conservatives. His main argument in *Place, Taste and Tradition* was with modernism. His attack on the conservatives was a flanking action to outmanoeuvre the modernists. Bernard had an ambivalent attitude towards modernism. Not schooled in the continental forms of Western Marxism, such as the Frankfurt School, Bernard followed a more doctrinaire Soviet scepticism towards modernism. He attempted to develop a third position in the mainstream struggle between the modernists and the conservatives. In the process he became one of the first art historians to develop a theory of modernism as a period style.

In *Place, Taste and Tradition* it is possible to track Bernard working out a theory of modernism in Australian art. In the earlier chapters, written in 1942 and 1943 at the height of the war, by modernism he meant a specific style after impressionism that today is associated with aestheticism and symbolism, rather than a general period style. However, by the end of the book—the final chapter was written in February 1944 as the final victory against fascism in the long war was in sight—he was also using the term as a period style largely concerned with questions of formalism after the 'formlessness of impressionism' and, most importantly, as a period that was finished—no longer a vital part of contemporary art. The other thing that was finished with the defeat of fascism, he judged, was nationalism and the whole conservative agenda associated with it.

Smith believed that the chauvinism of the conservatives and the aestheticism of the modernists were inextricably linked. For him each came into being, and was defeated, at the same time, and each shared an ideological commitment to Aboriginalism. Both used it to advance, in his mind, a spurious nationalism. For him this association revealed a blind spot in modernism, particularly evident in its prohibition on politics in art: 'Its fundamental weakness was to borrow the forms and ignore the meanings'.[18] Thus modernist aesthetic engagements with Aboriginal art, he claimed, ignored the ethical minefield of colonialism and, ipso facto, of Aboriginal art. Bernard was not against cross-cultural developments. As an internationalist he believed that all cultures are cross-cultural: 'in the growth of the nation', he said, 'it can be extremely beneficial'. However, it required 'a two-way development, the mutual contribution of two living traditions that eventually intermingle as they continue their adaptation to a common environment'. But in Australia, he continued, 'the aboriginal culture will not affect Australian art unless the slow physical extermination of the aborigines by our own predatory culture is arrested'. We must, he insisted, begin

> to see the aboriginal, not as an idealised figure symbolic of the perfect cultural amity of man and environment, but as a contemporary of our own with very real problems who has never had even the semblance of a fair deal.[19]

Bernard returned to this theme in his 1980 Boyer Lectures and in one of his last publications, in 2006, at the age of ninety:

> What I was asserting in 1945 was that it would be time enough to talk about identifying our own white settler culture with Aboriginal culture after we had

> faced up to the moral issues presented by living in the same land with the Aboriginal people before we attempt to appropriate their culture as the source of our own.[20]

Thus *Place, Taste and Tradition* is not so much against Aboriginal art, as against the way it was being used by conservatives and modernists in the cause of nationalism. Aboriginal art was collateral damage in Bernard's larger project of writing a cosmopolitan history of Australian art. For all he has to say against the contemporary appeal of Aboriginal art, *Place, Taste and Tradition* never actually discusses the work of an Aboriginal artist.

AFTER *PLACE, TASTE AND TRADITION*

Bernard's attempts to develop a narrative for the art of the Australian nation-state framed his thinking on Aboriginal art. This is evident, as we have seen, in his criticism of those who appropriated it to the causes of nationalism and modernism, and also in his first rare discussion of the work of Aboriginal artists. The latter is particularly revealing. It occurred, albeit very briefly, in his 1962 classic, *Australian Painting*. The artists in question were Albert Namatjira and the Pareroultja brothers, Edwin and Otto. However, Bernard did not mention their Aboriginality, let alone the Aboriginality of their art. Rather, he said they belonged to 'Rex Battarbee's Central Australian group of painters founded on Hans Heysen's vision'[21]—thus aligning them with the hated 'proto-fascist' national landscape school of painters (though Bernard, now a lecturer at the venerable University of Melbourne, no longer used this sharp rhetoric of his twenties).

Bernard's alignment of the Hermannsburg painters with the European rather than Aboriginal tradition was a normal view at the time. In the 1940s several state art galleries purchased the watercolours of Namatjira and Edwin Pareroultja. However, it is misleading to claim that these were the first Aboriginal artworks to enter Australia's state art galleries, as they were collected as Australian, not Aboriginal, art. Aboriginal art was not even being collected then (in the 1940s), though natural history museums collected Aboriginal artifacts as anthropological documents of a dying race. The watercolours of Namatjira and the Pareroultja brothers were generally not considered Aboriginal art, but rather, as one anthropologist said in 1951, 'non-indigenous art of a local Aboriginal group'.[22] Bernard held this view until the end of his life.[23]

Bernard did not think much about Aboriginal art again until two years after he retired, when he had a sudden revelation. Twenty years later he clearly remembered the circumstances. *Place, Taste and Tradition* was being republished and he was in the middle of intense efforts to catalogue the drawings and paintings of Cook's voyages. Further, he had been invited to present the ABC Boyer Lectures the following year and 'was at a loss to know what to talk about'. Then, one Sunday evening in June 1979, he heard Dr H. C. 'Nugget' Coombs speaking on the ABC. Coombs was advocating a treaty with the Aboriginal people, and, as Bernard remembered it, reminding his audience of 'the shameful conditions that Aboriginal people suffered as they endured and survived in their own country'.[24] Bernard was clearly moved. The 1970s had been a decade of Aboriginal political action in the struggle for land rights. Bernard's condition, set down in *Place, Taste and Tradition*, had not been met but it was being addressed by militant Aboriginal action, from the Gurindji strike (in which notable communist writer Frank Hardy played a prominent role) to the Aboriginal Tent Embassy. Now, Bernard felt, was the time to confront the blind spot in his historiography. In 1980, his sixty-fourth year, inspired by what the anthropologist W. E. H. Stanner had called the 'great Australian silence', Bernard presented his Boyer Lectures. They addressed what he termed the 'mechanisms of forgetfulness' in Australian art and literature. His first lecture was delivered in these memorable biblical intonations:

> It would seem as if all the culture of old Europe were being brought to bear upon our writers and artists in order to blot from their memories the crimes perpetrated upon Australia's first inhabitants … How shall we redeem it from the guilty awareness that these acts of genocide … were being enacted most vigorously at that very time when our own white Australian culture was being conceived and born, and that its very growth presupposed the termination of a black culture?[25]

The Boyer Lectures are the closest that Bernard ever came to admitting his omissions. However, they were not a confession. That was not Bernard's style.

Indeed, his Boyer Lectures are themselves a good example of the 'mechanisms of forgetfulness'. In his most important treatise on Aboriginal art, Bernard, as usual, had very little to say about the subject. 'I had little to say about Indigenous visual art' in the Boyer Lectures, he later reflected, 'because I was not sure what to say'.[26] Bernard, who knew so much about everything, never hesitated to announce his ignorance about Aboriginal art and defer to the anthropologists. Indeed, he was relatively ignorant. There is no evidence in the Boyer Lectures that he knew of Papunya Tula or Geoffrey Bardon, whom he would soon come to admire.

Bernard also did not feel the need to change his history of Australian art. When his Boyer Lectures inspired a new generation of art historians and curators to rethink his narrative of Australian art, he vigorously defended it. However, it would be wrong to conclude that he did not at the same time address the blind spot. Bernard walked a fine line, as all good critics do. In the same paragraph he could support the 'scholarly revisionists of our art history' and their 'successive recognition and incorporation of Aboriginal art … within the Australian tradition during its Colonial, Impressionist and Contemporary manifestations', yet warn against 'the fatal temptation to anachronise history'—by which he meant to 'Aboriginalise' it—'in a futile attempt to redeem it'.[27] He reasoned that retrospectively revealing what had been repressed would create another blindness.

> To understand historical judgments it is wise to assess them against the social and ethical values current in the time in which they were made. Otherwise one is likely to fall down into the historical black hole of anachronism.[28]

Blindness and its overcoming are the stuff of history. We should not, Bernard argued, rewrite the past to erase its blind spots as if they never existed.

Yet Bernard was also convinced 'that profound historical changes are taking place' in Australian art.[29] In the early 1980s, shortly after he presented the Boyer Lectures, he formed the view that the emergence of the Papunya Tula movement in 1971 was the pivotal moment when Aboriginal art entered the story of Australian art. From this point, he believed, Aboriginal art becomes visible as fine and modern art and thus as a legitimate part of the narrative of Australian art. It was also the moment that Aboriginal people, following the 1967 referendum, were effectively incorporated into the Australian nation-state. The referendum was a victory for, and the culmination of, assimilation policy. It changed the game rules of what constituted an Australian citizen and, by implication, the narrative of Australian art to date. Conveniently for Bernard this was also the moment when his history of Australian painting had ended.

What then did he do?

At the practical level he sank his own resources, ironically from the sale of his Australian art collection, into promoting Aboriginal art through establishing the Kate Challis RAKA. This was his first move. However, while Bernard remained an active scholar for the next twenty-five years, he never undertook an investigation of Aboriginal art or revised his narrative of Australian art. His second move was to authorise two further updatings of his classic text, *Australian Painting*, by two younger art historians, Terry Smith in 1991, and Christopher Heathcote in 2001. While Bernard gave each free rein, he was part of the process and at times points were argued. The main addition to his existing narrative, besides a greater consideration of women artists, was the entry of Aboriginal art into the story in a significant way during the last three decades of the twentieth century. Each edition reproduces an Aboriginal painting on the back cover. Although these images were chosen by Terry Smith and Heathcote respectively, the two co-authors had no trouble convincing Bernard about reproducing Aboriginal art so prominently in each edition.

The sense of a 'profound historical change' in the course of Australian art is particularly evident in Terry Smith's treatment of the 1970s and 1980s. In this sense Terry Smith and Heathcote served as surrogates for Bernard. Terry felt this was particularly true for Aboriginal art.[30] However, although Bernard endorsed these new chapters, it would be wrong to assume that Terry and Heathcote spoke for him on matters of Aboriginal art. Each had a very different perspective. If their texts act as surrogates for Bernard's voice, it was in a symbolic rather than literal sense. Bernard was not interested in policing the details of their analysis but in maintaining a broader architecture—an architecture in which Aboriginal art only enters the story of Australian art after 1970.

Bernard's third move came in the last years of his life. After he finished his last great project, *Modernism's History*, in 1998, and especially after the publication of Gombrich's *The Preference for the Primitive* in 2002, Bernard devoted more time to fireproofing his history of Australian art from the advent of Aboriginal art. In 2006 he warned against a recent penchant in Australian art historiography:

> the tendency to attempt to … insert the art work of Aboriginal peoples chronologically in one continuous narrative [of the history of Australian art], seems to me to be a cultural hangover from the politics of assimilation, treating it as if it were all one story.[31]

To make his argument, Bernard invoked Socrates' distinction between art in the general and special senses—an argument he had rehearsed earlier.[32] This, essentially, was a distinction between the applied and fine arts, with the added presumption that art history is a history of fine art. 'In my view', wrote Bernard, 'all Indigenous art is, in its beginnings, art in the general sense'. Art in the special sense, he argued, emerged in Europe during the fifteenth century, at 'the beginnings of modern art', and arrived in Australia 'when the English convict settlement was established at Sydney Cove in 1788'.[33] Susan Lowish points out that in an exchange in 1987 with his nemesis, Donald Brook, Bernard argued against this classical distinction, accusing Brook of 'taking words too seriously' and criticising his 'reluctance to accept tribal artefacts as art'.[34]

Bernard was willing to run with the devil if it served his cause. However, in 2006 this hoary classical distinction between applied and fine art served his current needs. It provided something like a universal imperative with which to integrate Aboriginal art into a history of Australian art and at the same time defend his hard-won history of it. Thus, in his view, the question to be addressed was the transformation of Aboriginal art from art in the general to the special sense—what he called its 'modernisation'.[35] This process of 'convergence', as he also called it, was 'facilitated' by Europeans and the 'commoditisation of Aboriginal art' in the twentieth century.[36] Bernard identified Namatjira and his followers as the first school of Indigenous art in the special sense, but singled out developments at Papunya as the most significant and decisive moment in the transformation of Indigenous art from art in the general to the special sense, and, as he said, 'from the sacred to the secular'.[37]

Bernard's 2006 article was, in part, written as a response to Susan Lowish's accusation the previous year that he was 'blind to the possibilities of Aboriginal art',[38] which Bernard characteristically rejected.[39] In a literal sense Bernard was not wrong. In his formative years Aboriginal art was highly visible. Daniel Thomas made this point in his defence of Bernard. He suggested that the reason Bernard didn't include Aboriginal art in *Australian Painting* is because he knew that Ronald Berndt's book, *Australian Aboriginal Art*,[40] based on Tony Tuckson's 1960 exhibition, was being prepared for publication. We should, says Thomas, see this pair of books as a two-volume edition on Australian art.[41] And so we should. However, Thomas is indulging in sophistry if he thinks they add up to a fully rounded history of Australian art. Not only is *Australian Aboriginal Art* not an art-historical account, let alone one of Aboriginal art as part of Australian art history, but it bears no relationship to Bernard's project. There is no way of getting around the blind spot in Bernard's narrative of Australian art.

Lowish had a better plan for redeeming Bernard. Quoting Paul de Man's well-known claim 'on the paradoxical effectiveness of a blinded vision' and the 'insights that it unwittingly provides', she suggested that Bernard's 'great insight lies in recognising that aesthetic conventions shape perception', including his own.[42] Another important and related insight, I would suggest, is Bernard's pursuit of a rigour of thinking that resisted any easy redeeming of the blind spot. The blind spot, he knew, was not his invention. Rather it existed at the level of the universal. This meant that its logic could not simply be repealed. This yielded another important insight: that we are each of our own time. This is why he did not revise his story; that would be the duty of future generations. Instead, he undertook a revision of the larger history that, in its Eurocentrism, reflected at the deepest levels the assumptions of the blind spot. *Modernism's History*, often seen as the quixotic folly of an old man, is the greatest insight he got from his critique of the blind spot—a critique that first began to take shape one Sunday evening in June 1979 as he listened to Nugget Coombs on the ABC.

NOTES

1 Paul De Man, *Blindness and Insight: Essays in the Rhetoric of Contemporary Criticism*, Oxford University Press, New York, 1971, p. 106.

2 Bernard Smith, 'Introduction: A Bibliographical Memoir', in John Spencer and Peter Wright (eds), *The Writings of Bernard Smith: Bibliography 1938–1998*, Power Institute: Foundation for Art and Visual Culture, Power Publications, Sydney, 2000, p. 12.

3 Bernard Smith, *Place, Taste and Tradition: A Study of Australian Art Since 1788*, 2nd edn, Oxford University Press, Melbourne, 1979, p. 20. Smith lists eighteen amendments for this 260-page book. Nearly all are of minor errors that came to light after the first edition, and reflect his scholarly fetish for detail. Only two are of some substance, but even they had no effect on his argument. He no longer believed that industrialism produced a decline in taste, only a decline in the quality of painting and sculpture, and he acknowledged that he had misjudged Glover (although omitting the reason, which was that in the war years he could not travel to Hobart, where most of Glover's art could be seen).

4 ibid., p. 30.

5 ibid., pp. 78–9.

6 Bernard Smith, *Modernism's History: A Study of Twentieth-Century Art and Ideas*, University of New South Wales Press, Sydney, 1998; Bernard Smith, *The Formalesque: A Guide to Modern Art and Its History*, Macmillan, Melbourne, 2007.

7 Smith, *Place, Taste and Tradition*, p. 78–9.

8 ibid., p. 30.

9 Bernard Smith, 'The Fascist Mentality in Australian Art and Criticism', *Communist Review*, no. 58, June 1946, pp. 182–4 (part 1) and no. 59, July 1946, pp. 215–17 (part 2), under pseudonym 'Goya' (republished in 1989 in *The Critic as Advocate*).

10 Smith, *Place, Taste and Tradition*, p. 16.

11 Ian Burn, *National Life and Landscape: Australian Painting 1900–1940*, Bay Books, Sydney, 1990, p. 8.

12 ibid., p. 7.

13 Ernestine Hill, *Australia: Land of Contrasts*, Sydney Ure Smith (ed.), John Sands, Sydney, 1943.

14 Bernard Smith, *The Spectre of Truganini*, The 1980 Boyer Lectures, Australian Broadcasting Commission, Sydney, 1980, p. 51.

15 See Bernard Smith, *A Pavane for Another Time*, Macmillan, Melbourne, 2002, p. 81.

16 Bernard Smith, 'Creators and Catalysts: The Modernisation of Australian Indigenous Art', *Australian Cultural History*, vol. 26, 2006, p. 23.

17 Smith, *Place, Taste and Tradition*, p. 197–9.

18 Smith, *Spectre of Truganini*, p. 51.

19 Smith, *Place, Taste and Tradition*, p. 176.

20 Smith, 'Creators and Catalysts', p. 15.

21 Bernard Smith and Terry Smith, *Australian Painting, 1788–1990*, 3rd edn, Oxford University Press, Melbourne, 1991, p. 115.

22 Ronald M. Berndt, 'A Review of Modern Australian Aboriginal Art by Rex Battarbee', *Oceania*, vol. 22, no. 1, September 1951, pp. 77–80.

23 Smith, 'Creators and Catalysts', pp. 21–2.

24 Smith, 'Introduction: A Bibliographic Memoir', p. 12.

25 Smith, *Spectre of Truganini*, p. 10.

26 Smith, 'Creators and Catalysts', p. 16.

27 Smith, 'Introduction: A Bibliographic Memoir', p. 4.

28 Smith, 'Creators and Catalysts', p. 16.

29 Smith, 'Introduction: A Bibliographic Memoir', p. 4.

30 'You are', he wrote in an email to me, 'right about the surrogacy re Aboriginal art', (25 October 2012).

31 Smith, 'Creators and Catalysts', p. 13.

32 Smith, *Modernism's History*, pp. 17, 41; Smith, 'Introduction: A Bibliographic Memoir'.

33 Smith, 'Creators and Catalysts', pp. 12–14.

34 Susan Lowish, 'European Vision and Aboriginal Art: Blindness and Insight in the Work of Bernard Smith', *Thesis Eleven*, vol. 82, no. 1, 2005, p. 69. See Bernard Smith, 'Concerning Donald Brook's "New Theory of Art"', *Meanjin*, vol. 47, no. 1, Autumn 1988, pp. 5–10.

35 Smith, 'Creators and Catalysts', p. 14.

36 ibid., pp. 17–19.

37 ibid., p. 23.

38 Lowish, 'European Vision and Aboriginal Art', p. 70.

39 Smith, 'Creators and Catalysts', p. 16.

40 Ronald M. Berndt (ed.), *Australian Aboriginal Art*, Ure Smith, Sydney, 1964.

41 Daniel Thomas, 'Aboriginal Art: Who Was Interested?', *Journal of Art Historiography*, no. 4, June 2011, https://arthistoriography.files.wordpress.com/2011/ 05/daniel-thomas-document.pdf.

42 Lowish, 'European Vision and Aboriginal Art', p. 70.

I have always found it more
congenial to work
at the fringes of a discipline
where I cannot become over
confident about method,
than at the centre of one.

Bernard Smith

ACKNOWLEDGEMENTS

The editors would like to thank all those at the universities of Sydney and Melbourne and at the Art Gallery of New South Wales who contributed to the symposium 'The Multiple Legacies of Bernard Smith' that was organised by and hosted between these institutions in October and November 2012.

The symposium was supported by the Power Institute and by the Dean of the Faculty of Arts and Social Sciences at the University of Sydney at the time of the symposium, Professor Duncan Ivison. Among those who helped to organise and coordinate the symposium, we especially wish to thank Susan Thomas, Vicki Mallett, Emma White, and Amelia Kelly. We would also like to thank Bernard's daughter Elizabeth Heathcote and granddaughter Kate Challis for their involvement, as well as Max Solling and all those at the Glebe Society who helped us celebrate Bernard's achievements as an activist and community historian in Glebe.

We would like to thank the partners of the Australian Institute for Art History, who supported the Melbourne instalment of the symposium. Thanks in particular to Kerry Gardner and Andrew Myer of Andyinc, the Helen Macpherson Smith Trust, the Sidney Myer Fund, and the Australian Academy of the Humanities for their support, which enabled two keynote speakers to come to Australia, Professor Nicholas Thomas, Professor of Historical Anthropology and Director of the Museum of Archaeology and Anthropology, the University of Cambridge, and Professor Rüdiger Joppien from the University of Hamburg. Last, but certainly not least, we thank the Dean, Mark Considine, and the Faculty of Arts at the University of Melbourne for their ongoing contribution to our program and their sponsorship of this event.

Like the symposium, this collection of essays has been a coordinated effort between the Power Institute at the University of Sydney, the Australian Institute of Art History at the University of Melbourne, and the Art Gallery of New South Wales.

Special thanks are due to Marni Williams at Power Publications for all her work in shepherding the publication into print. The publishing team at the Art Gallery of New South Wales, particularly Publications Manager Julie Donaldson, Senior Designer Analiese Cairis and Production Manager Cara Hickman, have turned these pieces into a handsome volume, and we are thankful for the expert eyes of editor Belinda Nemec and proofreader Amber Cameron. We are most appreciative to the Art Gallery Society of New South Wales for its financial support, without which we would not have been able to mark the centenary of Bernard Smith's birth with such a broad celebration of his life and work.

CONTRIBUTORS

JAYNIE ANDERSON was foundation director of the Australian Institute of Art History at the University of Melbourne (2009–15) and Herald Chair of Fine Arts (1997–2014). She is a fellow of the Australian Academy of the Humanities and immediate past president of the International Committee of Art History. In 2015 she received, from the President of the Republic of Italy, the knighthood of Ufficiale dell'Ordine della Stella d'Italia. Educated at the University of Melbourne, Bryn Mawr College, and the University of Oxford, she has curated exhibitions in Australia, Europe and the United States, and published widely, particularly on Italian art of the Renaissance.

PETER BEILHARZ is Professor of Culture and Society in the School of Media, Culture and Creative Arts at Curtin University in Western Australia. Most recently he was a fellow of the Stellenbosch Institute of Advanced Study in South Africa. He published the first major study of Bernard Smith, *Imagining the Antipodes*, twenty years ago, and his essays on Smith are collected in *Thinking the Antipodes* (2015). He is now working (with Sian Supski) on the writing of Ivan Vladislavić, is collecting essays on Marx and Gramsci, and writing a study of 'The Rationalization of the World'. He is planning a major essay called 'After Bernard'.

JIM BERRYMAN works as a librarian at the University of Melbourne. He has a PhD in art history from the Australian National University. His interests include Australian art and cultural history, interdisciplinary studies, and Australian political history.

KATE CHALLIS is the granddaughter of Bernard and Kate Smith. She trained as an art historian and completed a PhD at the University of Melbourne on the subject of early Renaissance illuminated manuscripts. For a decade she lived with her grandfather, during which time they discussed and debated every aspect of Western (and other) civilisations, over cups of tea, good meals and the washing up. Bernard was one of the most influential people in Kate's life, shaping her critical thinking and endowing her with a curious mind. Today she oversees Bernard's literary estate. Now an interior designer, Kate's first loves—Bernard, art history and art—remain close to her heart.

JOHN CLARK is Emeritus Professor in Art History at the University of Sydney, author of five books and editor or co-editor of another five. His *Asian Modernities: Chinese and Thai Art of the 1980s and 1990s* (2010) won the Best Art Book Prize of the Art Association of Australia and New Zealand in 2011. His most recent book is *Modernities of Japanese Art* (2013), and he is currently working on a two-volume study: *The Asian Modern, 1850s–1990s*. His *Contemporary Asian Art at Biennials* is scheduled for publication by National University of Singapore Press in mid-2016.

KATHLEEN DAVIDSON is an independent scholar. In 2014 she was a visiting scholar at the Yale Center for British Art, and in 2012–13 was C. P. Snow Visiting Fellow at the University of Texas at Austin. Recent publications include 'Colonial Science and Photographic Portraits' in *The Photograph and Australia* (AGNSW, 2015) and 'Connecting the Senses: Natural History and the British Museum' in *Stereoscopic Magazine, 19: Interdisciplinary Studies in the Long Nineteenth Century* (2014). Her book *Photography, Natural History and the Nineteenth-Century Museum: Exchanging Views of Empire* is forthcoming. Previously, she was curator of international photography at the National Gallery of Australia.

CATHERINE DE LORENZO is Honorary Associate Professor at UNSW Art & Design, University of New South Wales, Sydney, and Adjunct Associate Professor at Monash Art Design and Architecture, Melbourne. She is a chief investigator on an Australian Research Council Linkage Project, 'Australian Art Exhibitions 1968–2009: A Generation of Cultural

Transformation', examining the influence of curatorial strategies on Australian art history. Her research also examines Australian art historiography, Australian and European photographic exchange, and contemporary public art. She is on the editorial boards of *History of Photography, Design and Art Australia Online*, and *Visual Studies*.

ROBERT W. GASTON took his BA (Hons) in history and MA (Hons) in art history at the University of Melbourne, and his PhD at the Warburg Institute, 1967–70. He taught at Bryn Mawr College, Boston University, La Trobe University and the University of Melbourne. He was a fellow and visiting professor at Harvard's Villa *I Tatti* in Florence, and Kress Senior Fellow at CASVA, Washington DC. He is currently Principal Fellow in Art History at the University of Melbourne. His latest book, *Pirro Ligorio, Libro dei Fiumi e dei Fonti antichi: Napoli. Biblioteca Nazionale, codice B.9* was published in 2015.

PAUL GILES is Challis Professor of English Literature at the University of Sydney. He was director of the Rothermere American Institute at Oxford University (2003–08) and president of the International American Studies Association (2005–07). Among his books are *Antipodean America: Australasia and the Constitution of U.S. Literature* (2014), *The Global Remapping of American Literature* (2011), *Atlantic Republic: The American Tradition in English Literature* (2006), *Virtual Americas: Transnational Fictions and the Transatlantic Imaginary* (2002), and *American Catholic Arts and Fictions: Culture, Ideology, Aesthetics* (1992).

RÜDIGER JOPPIEN was born in 1946 in Barkhausen, Germany. He studied art history, history of theatre and English literature, in Cologne and London. He worked on a research project on images of voyages and travels of the eighteenth and nineteenth centuries, before entering the Museum of Decorative Art in Cologne in 1977, and subsequently in 1987 the Museum of Art and Industry in Hamburg. He has published widely on art, design, craft and photography, and since retiring in 2011 has been teaching at Hamburg University.

MARK LEDBURY is Power Professor of Art History and Visual Culture at the University of Sydney, and Director of the Power Institute. A scholar of European art of the eighteenth and nineteenth centuries, he is the author of *Sedaine, Greuze and the Boundaries of Genre* (2000); *James Northcote, History Painting and the Fables* (2014) and his interests lie in the relations between theatre and visual art as well as histories and theories of pictorial genre. As Director of the Power Institute he oversees conferences, publications and research projects that deepen knowledge of visual art and its place in culture.

CHRISTOPHER R. MARSHALL is Senior Lecturer in Art History and Museum Studies at the University of Melbourne. His publications on museums and curatorship include *Sculpture and the Museum* (2011) and contributions to *Museum Making, Making Art History* and *Reshaping Museum Space* (2005, 2007 and 2012). His publications on Neapolitan Baroque art include *Baroque Naples and the Industry of Painting* (2016) and a chapter contribution to *The Economic Lives of Seventeenth-Century Italian Painters* (2010). His research distinctions include two years' support from the Australian Research Council, the Paul Mellon Visiting Senior Fellowship at the National Gallery of Art, Washington DC, a senior research fellowship at the Henry Moore Institute, a research fellowship at the Museo Poldi Pezzoli, and visiting senior lecturing fellowships at the Hubei Institute of Fine Arts and Duke University.

IAN McLEAN is Senior Research Professor of Contemporary Art at the University of Wollongong and an Adjunct Professor at the University of Western Australia. He has published extensively on Australian art and particularly Aboriginal art within a contemporary context. His books include *Double Desire: Transculturation and Indigenous Art, How Aborigines Invented the Idea of Contemporary Art, White Aborigines: Identity Politics in Australian Art*, and *The Art of Gordon Bennett* (with a chapter by Gordon Bennett). He is a former advisory board member of *Third Text*, and is currently on the advisory boards of *World Art* and *National Identities*.

JOANNA MENDELSSOHN is an Associate Professor in Art and Design at the University of New South Wales. She was in the first cohort of University of Sydney undergraduate students to be taught by Bernard Smith. After graduation she worked at the Art Gallery of New South Wales, Newcastle Region Art Gallery and the S. H. Ervin Gallery. After the publication of *Lionel Lindsay: An Artist and his Family*, she was appointed art critic for the *Bulletin*, and was awarded the Pascall Prize in 1991. In 2003 she initiated the digital project that became *Design and Art of Australia Online*. With Catherine De Lorenzo, Catherine Speck and Alison Inglis she is currently completing a major study of exhibitions of Australian art.

STEVEN MILLER is head of the National Art Archive and the Capon Research Library at the Art Gallery of New South Wales in Sydney. In 2015 he published, with Eileen Chanin, *Awakening: Four Lives in Art*. Their earlier co-authored publication, *Degenerates and Perverts: The 1939 Melbourne Herald Exhibition of French and British Contemporary Art* (2005), was awarded the NSW Premier's History Prize, as well as being shortlisted for the 2005 Vance and Nettie Palmer Prize for Non-Fiction. Steven is also the author of *Dogs in Australian Art* (2012).

SHERIDAN PALMER is an independent curator and art historian and an Honorary Fellow at the University of Melbourne. She has worked as an art practitioner and at the National Gallery of Australia and the Ballarat Art Gallery. Her book *Centre of the Periphery: Three European Art Historians in Melbourne* (2008) is a major study of the establishment of art history in Australia, and her biography *Hegel's Owl: The Life of Bernard Smith* has recently been published (2016).

SIMON PIERSE is a Senior Lecturer at Aberystwyth University and author of *Australian Art and Artists in London 1950–1965: An Antipodean Summer* (2012). He has written extensively on British postwar art and the Australian creative diaspora to London. He was a Sir Robert Menzies Bicentennial Fellow in 2000–01, based at La Trobe University. In 2014 he returned to Australia as visiting fellow at the Australian Institute of Art History, University of Melbourne. Other publications include contributions to *Figure and Ground: Keith Vaughan Drawings, Prints and Photographs 1935–1962* (2012), *Impact of the Modern: Vernacular Australian Modernities in Australia 1870s–1960s* (2008), *Melbourne Art Journal* and *Australian Dictionary of Biography*.

ANDREW SAYERS AM (1957–2015) was an artist, scholar, curator and museum director. After graduating with honours in art history from the University of Sydney, he became a curatorial assistant then registrar at the Art Gallery of New South Wales (1979–81). This was followed by roles as assistant director of Newcastle Region Art Gallery (1981–85), curator of Australian drawings then deputy director (collections) at the National Gallery of Australia (1985–1998), inaugural director of the National Portrait Gallery (1998–2010) and director of the National Museum of Australia (2010–13). He curated many substantial exhibitions, and his publications include seminal books on Australian art, including *Drawing in Australia* (1989), *Aboriginal Artists of the Nineteenth Century* (1994) and *Australian Art* (2001). In 2010 Andrew Sayers was awarded the Order of Australia in recognition of his services to arts administration and Australian portraiture.

TERRY SMITH is Andrew W. Mellon Professor of Contemporary Art History and Theory in the Department of the History of Art and Architecture at the University of Pittsburgh. In 2010 he was named Australia Council Visual Arts Laureate, and won the College Art Association (USA) Mather Award for art criticism. He has held fellowships at the Getty Research Institute, Los Angeles; National Humanities Research Centre, Raleigh-Durham; and Clark Institute, Williamstown. From 1994 to 2001 he was Power Professor of Contemporary Art and Director of the Power Institute at the University of Sydney. He has published widely, and contributed to the third and fourth editions of Bernard Smith's *Australian Painting, 1788–1960*.

MAX SOLLING is a historian, and author of *Grandeur and Grit: A History of Glebe*, which was shortlisted for the 2008 NSW Premier's History Awards. He was completing his MA thesis on nineteenth-century Glebe when he became involved with Bernard Smith in resident activism, especially the anti-expressway movement, and writing pamphlets. Max has been a practising solicitor since 1967, and a law lecturer.

CATHERINE SPECK is Professor of Art History at the University of Adelaide, and Coordinator of Postgraduate Programs in Art History and Curatorial and Museum Studies (co-taught with the Art Gallery of South Australia). Her publications include *Heysen to Heysen: Selected Letters of Hans Heysen and Nora Heysen* (2011), *Beyond the Battlefield: Women Artists of the Two World Wars* (2014) and *Australian Art Exhibitions: A New Story* (2016).

ANN STEPHEN is Senior Curator, University Art Gallery, University of Sydney. Her books include *On Looking at Looking: The Art and Politics of Ian Burn* (2006); and *Modernism & Australia* (2006) and *Modern Times* (2008), both co-edited with Andrew McNamara and Philip Goad. She curated the award-winning exhibition *1969: The Black Box of Conceptual Art* (2013), and co-curated with A. D. S. Donaldson *Abstraction-Création: J. W. Power in Europe* (2014–15). She is a fellow of the Australian Academy of the Humanities, a past president of the Art Association of Australia and New Zealand, and chair of *Art Monthly Australasia*.

NICHOLAS THOMAS first visited the Pacific in 1984 to research his PhD thesis on culture and history in the Marquesas Islands. He has since written widely on material culture, exploration, empire and art. His books include *Oceanic Art* (1995), *Discoveries: The Voyages of Captain Cook* (2003) and *Islanders: The Pacific in the Age of Empire* (2010), which was awarded the Wolfson History Prize. A collaborative work, *Art in Oceania: A New History* (2012) received the Authors' Society's Art Book Prize. Since 2006, he has been director of the Museum of Archaeology and Anthropology in Cambridge.

ANDREW YIP is an art historian, producer and researcher, whose interests range from the politics of Australian artists at war to digital approaches to preserving intangible cultural heritage. He holds a BA (Hons) and PhD in art history from the University of Sydney. In 2006 he was a visiting researcher at Bosphorus University, Istanbul, and is currently a Postdoctoral Research Fellow at the Laboratory for Innovation in Galleries, Libraries, Archives and Museums, University of New South Wales. He has worked at the Art Gallery of New South Wales since 2010 on numerous exhibitions and programs, including co-curating the gallery's World War I commemoration program and managing tertiary education.

INDEX

References in **bold** refer to illustrations.

B